# Film Adaptation and Its Discontents

# Film Adaptation and Its Discontents

From *Gone with the Wind* to
*The Passion of the Christ*

Thomas Leitch

The Johns Hopkins University Press
*Baltimore*

© 2007 The Johns Hopkins University Press
All rights reserved. Published 2007
Printed in the United States of America on acid-free paper

Johns Hopkins Paperback edition, 2009
9  8  7  6  5  4  3  2  1

The Johns Hopkins University Press
2715 North Charles Street
Baltimore, Maryland 21218-4363
www.press.jhu.edu

*The Library of Congress has catalogued the hardcover edition of this book as follows:*

Leitch, Thomas M.
    Film adaptation and its discontents : from Gone with the Wind
    to The Passion of the Christ / Thomas Leitch.
        p. cm.
    Includes bibliographical references and index.
    ISBN-13: 978-0-8018-8565-5 (hardcover : alk. paper)
    ISBN-10: 0-8018-8565-5 (hardcover : alk. paper)
    1. Film adaptations—History and criticism.  I. Title.
    PN1997.85.L35 2007
    791.43′6—dc22          2006037744

ISBN 13: 978-0-8018-9271-4
ISBN 10: 0-8018-9271-6

A catalog record for this book is available from the British Library.

*To Barbara T. Gates and James M. Welsh*
*mentors • colleagues • friends*

# Contents

# Acknowledgments

Like so many film teachers of my generation, I was trained in literary studies and drifted into film studies through a mixture of infatuation and happenstance. Given my background and interests, film adaptation would have seemed a logical focus for my work. But I was slow to come to the study of adaptation. I was convinced that George Bluestone had said everything necessary on the subject years before. I agreed with Dudley Andrew's implication that adaptation study as it was currently practiced wasn't especially interesting. And I didn't realize that anyone since Bluestone had added anything significant to the debate between medium-specific theorists who focused, as Seymour Chatman put it, on what novels could do that films couldn't (and vice versa) and reviewers for whom the book was always better.

I owe my interest in adaptation to Barbara Gates and Jim Welsh. In thanking Jim, the founding editor of *Literature/Film Quarterly* for over three decades, I echo the thanks of dozens of scholars he has encouraged to take a closer look at books and movies. Although the citations in this volume duly record some of my debts to the leading theorists of adaptation since Bluestone—Brian McFarlane, Deborah Cartmell, Imelda Whelehan, Robert Ray, Robert Stam, James Naremore, Sarah Cardwell, Kamilla Elliott—I remain convinced that Jim has worked harder than anyone else for a longer period to keep interest in adaptation studies alive, and I'm proud that, for nearly twenty years, my own work has had the benefit of his midwifery.

Five years ago, Barbara Gates encouraged me to join her in team-teaching a course in adaptations of Victorian novels, even though she knew that I had no appetite for either team-teaching or adaptation. Midway through the term, she urged me to apply with her to the Salzburg Seminar's Session 403, From Page to Screen, and then withdrew her own application so that it would not compete with mine. Her extraordinary generosity paid me rich dividends at

Salzburg, where I joined a group of sixty scholars and filmmakers taught by Steven Bach, Peter Lilienthal, Gerald Rafshoon, Richard Schickel, and David Thacker. I can never repay the debts I incurred at the session, but I'd like to record my obligation to the fellow students from whom I learned the most: Martina Anzinger, Mireia Aragay, Slawomir Bobowski, Derek Chase, Karen Diehl, Lindiwe Dovey, Scott Eyman, Lynn Higgins, Michael Kitson, Irina Makoveeva, Sohail Malik, Margaret McCarthy, Mohi-Ud-Din Mirza, Manjiri Prabhu, Tatiana Smorodinska, and Alexie Tcheuyap. On my return to America, Slawomir Bobowski, Mireia Aragay, and Lynn Higgins offered me the opportunity to try my hand at three essays—"The Word Made Film," *Studia Filmoznawcze* 25 (2004); "The Adapter as Auteur: Hitchcock, Kubrick, Disney," *Books in Motion: Adaptation, Intertextuality, Authorship* (Amsterdam: Rodopi, 2004); and "Post-Literary Adaptation," *PostScript* 23, no. 3 (summer 2004)—which, variously revised and expanded, became the bases of chapters 3, 10, and 11 of this book.

In the meantime Kathryn Osenlund had kindly invited me to give the keynote presentation at the Pennsylvania College Educators Association and introduced me to John Desmond and Peter Hawkes, whose passion for the subject spurred my own. In response I pressed many friends to help me during annual meetings of the Society for Cinema and Media Studies and the Literature/Film Association. I'm particularly obliged to Richard Allen, Lesley Brill, Linda Costanzo Cahir, David Kranz, Peter Lev, Nancy Mellerski, Walter Metz, Sarah Miles Watts, and Donald Whaley for helping me identify and analyze heretofore neglected problems in adaptation.

At the University of Delaware, students in my graduate course on adaptation offered me a laboratory for my ideas and provided a constant stream of intellectual challenges. And two of my PhD students, David DeMare Stivers and Kathleen Newell, helped me work out problems with my chapter on adaptation and auteurism. It was a special honor to work with Kate on her prize-winning dissertation, "What We Talk about When We Talk about Adaptation," at the same time that I was pondering many of the same questions on my own. The greater part of this book was drafted during a sabbatical leave I was awarded for 2004–5. Cheryl Kingan introduced me to the mysteries of Walt Disney World, and Allison Thibert-Bragg provided a timely and welcome bit of last-minute help.

Of the many people who helped bring the book to press, I am especially grateful to Michael Lonegro, my editor at the Johns Hopkins University Press, who supplied its title, and Joe Abbott, my manuscript editor, who added three footnotes and three thousand corrections.

Finally, I humbly thank Lisa Elliott for sitting through all those Sherlock Holmes movies with me and Gardner Campbell for suggesting, in response to a conference paper I gave on literacy ten years ago, that it needed a little something more to be complete. Well, Gardner, here it is.

# Film Adaptation and Its Discontents

# CHAPTER ONE

# Literature versus Literacy

Adaptation theory, the systematic study of films based on literary sources, is one of the oldest areas in film studies. Its fifty-year-old founding text, George Bluestone's *Novels into Film,* predates the rise of French-inspired poststructuralism and American academic study of film, and its prehistory goes back even further.[1] Yet adaptation studies have had little influence on either film studies generally, a discipline to which they have always been ancillary, or discussions of contemporary film adaptations by literary scholars, largely because of a rupture between the theory and the practice of adaptation studies. This rupture appears in ritual response to each new film adaptation of a canonical novel. On the release of Mira Nair's brisk, colorful 2004 adaptation of *Vanity Fair,* the director disputed an interviewer's remark that "Thackeray condemns Becky more than you do," arguing that the novel was serialized "in a tabloid and editors would respond to him constantly about his last episode. That's what I ascribe to the classic 'Hollywood interference mode': the inconsistencies of the character. . . . He was actually admonished: 'You're enjoying Becky too much. Make it clearer who's the virgin and who's the whore.'"[2]

Contributors to Indiana University's VICTORIA listserv responded with predictable outrage. Patrick Leary, disputing Nair's suggestion that "she has somehow rescued Thackeray's original, frustrated intention" as "pure fantasy," insisted that "the ever-compliant Bradbury & Evans never once in all their long association with Thackeray had anything in particular to say about the content of the fiction he published with them. Nor would Thackeray have paid them any attention if they had." Sheldon Goldfarb agreed that *Vanity Fair* was serialized not in a "tabloid" but in its monthly parts, adding, "The ending in the novel reflects the tension that builds up in its latter stages: a tension between the desire to get into high society (the social climbing impulse) and the fear of getting into it (the fear of then being set upon by all the high society ladies etc.). This is a very interesting tension in the novel (I think reflecting a tension in Thackeray himself), and it is much better expressed by the novel's ending than the film's." Micael Clarke, however, defended Nair's film as "follow[ing] the novel in important ways": its "surface sumptuousness," its critique of society, its sympathy for women. Sarah Brown added that "the Natasha Little version of a few years back [written by Andrew Davies and directed by Marc Munden (1998)] was conspicuously good—sophisticatedly alert to Thackeray's irony—and it had a real sense of narrative drive and momentum which I don't think is consistently true of the novel." Tamara S. Wagner added: "Talking about videos and dvds, I have just been given a catalogue by my university's AV department: a list of 'Highly Acclaimed Video Programs from Professor Elliot Engel (They're Light & Enlightening),' featuring such titles as 'The Brilliant and Bizarre Brontës' and 'A Dickens of a Christmas.' Has anyone ever seen (or used) any of those? (Otherwise, we'll rather go on and order movies like *Wild Wild West* or *Round the World in 80 Days* [*sic*] starring Jackie Chan—light and entertaining enough, I suppose, if one wanted to be entertaining of course.)"[3]

Despite their differences of opinion, all these statements, including Nair's, ignore fifty years of adaptation theory in their uncritical adoption of the author's intention as a criterion for the success of both the novel and any possible film adaptation. Only Brown suggests that the film might actually improve on the novel. Even she shares the habit, articulated most openly by Wagner, of ranking films that are based on canonical literary sources above merely "entertaining" films and incidentally in preferring evaluation to analysis in considering films in general and adaptations in particular. Although it is unlikely that these commentators or their colleagues would defend these positions as theoretical principles, they do not hesitate to adopt them in practice.

One reason that adaptation theory has had so little effect on studies of specific adaptations is that, until quite recently, adaptation study has stood apart from the main currents in film theory. The field traces its descent more directly from literary studies. Studies of Shakespeare on film, for example, use Shakespeare as a locus around which to organize their analysis of film adaptation. As the center around which individual adaptations orbit or the root from which the adaptations all grow, Shakespeare or Thackeray provides not only an organizing principle for the study of specific adaptations but an implicit standard of value for them all. Kamilla Elliott observes that "theories of the novel and of the film within their separate disciplines appear to have been significantly influenced by interdisciplinary rivalries."[4] More specifically, studies of adaptation tend to privilege literature over film in two ways. By organizing themselves around canonical authors, they establish a presumptive criterion for each new adaptation. And by arranging adaptations as spokes around the hub of such a strong authorial figure, they establish literature as a proximate cause of adaptation that makes fidelity to the source text central to the field.

Few empirical studies of adaptation accept these assumptions uncritically. In *Novels into Film*, widely regarded as the founding text in adaptation study, George Bluestone notes that "changes are *inevitable* the moment one abandons the linguistic for the visual medium," and he concludes: "It is as fruitless to say that film A is better or worse than novel B as it is to pronounce Wright's Johnson's Wax Building better or worse than Tchaikowsky's *Swan Lake*."[5] Both Sarah Cardwell's study of television adaptations of four classic English novels and most of the essays collected in Deborah Cartmell and Imelda Whelehan's recent anthology question the primacy of literature as a touchstone for cinema.[6] To the extent that adaptation study subordinates both specific adaptations to their canonical source texts and cinema as a medium to literature as a medium it serves either faithfully or not, however, adaptations are studied under the sign of literature, which provides an evaluative touchstone for films in general.

This approach has dominated a half century of adaptation studies for several reasons. Few of the first generation of scholars who led the charge to introduce film studies to the academy had received formal training in film studies themselves. Most of them came from English departments, where they had been absorbed in the pedagogical habits of close reading and the aesthetic values of literature—what James Naremore calls "the submerged common sense of the average English department . . . a mixture of Kantian aesthetics and Arnoldian ideas about society."[7]

Although Naremore traces these Arnoldian ideas to *Culture and Anarchy,* the program of comparative evaluation at the heart of Arnold's own aesthetics emerges even more clearly in "The Study of Poetry." Having offered poetry, in which "the idea is everything," as a substitute for a religious tradition undermined by such heterodox facts as the discovery of ancient fossils and the theory of evolution, Arnold urges:

> We should conceive of poetry worthily, and more highly than it has been the custom to conceive of it. We should conceive of it as capable of higher uses, and called to higher destinies, than those which in general men have assigned to it hitherto. More and more mankind will discover that we have to turn to poetry to interpret life for us, to console us, to sustain us. Without poetry, our science will appear incomplete; and most of what now passes with us for religion and philosophy will be replaced by poetry.[8]

If the burden Arnold places on poetry seems quaintly anachronistic, the passage may readily be freshened by replacing the term with *literature* or *novels* or, indeed, *cinema*—though not, clearly, with *popular culture,* from whose degrading influence Arnold assigns poetry, as successors like Tamara Wagner would presumably assign canonical cinema, the specific function of rescuing us.

The earliest films to come in for academic study under the Arnoldian dispensation that still ruled in American universities in 1960 fell into two categories: adaptations of canonical classics that served as adjuncts to the literary canon and classic works of cinema that could be studied as members of a supplementary quasi-literary cinematic canon. The first approach generated myriad courses in Shakespeare and film, the second courses in the masters of European art cinema from Dreyer to Bergman, Antonioni, and Godard and, still later, in quasi-canonical Hollywood masters like Chaplin, Welles, and Hitchcock. Under this dispensation many films were studied under the aegis of the literary works that gave them currency. Courses in Shakespeare and film were often courses in Shakespeare through film. Other courses were conducted under the sign of literature, analyzing and evaluating the films at hand as if they were literary works themselves, mining them for the ambiguity, complexity, penetration, and personal expressiveness traditionally associated with literature. Even in Robert Stam's recent *Literature through Film* (2005), specific literary works and literature in general continue to be stipulated as touchstones. Elliott has traced in trenchant detail the conflict between categorical approaches to adaptation, which follow Lessing's *Laocoön* in emphasizing the differences among such sister arts as literature, painting, and cinema that make them distinct modes with different expressive and representational possibilities, and analogical approaches, which follow Horace's "Ars Poetica" in emphasizing similarities among the arts that make it reasonable to imagine translations from one medium to another. What she does not emphasize in opposing these two approaches is their shared assumption that adaptation study is and should be essentially aesthetic. Both categorical studies of adaptation and studies that emphasize analogies among the arts take as their central line of inquiry the question of what makes works of art successful—or what, in the more old-fashioned language adopted by both Horace and Lessing, makes them beautiful.

This inquiry is remote from the central inquiry of academic film studies, which from its beginnings had staked its insurgent disciplinary claims by rejecting the aesthetic appreciation of literature and developing a competing methodology of cultural critique rooted in the revolutionary intellectual ferment in France during the 1960s and 1970s. Films and film were valuable not because they formed a canon of fully achieved works of art according to traditional aesthetic criteria but because they raised illuminating questions, offered insight into overdetermined historical moments or the contemporary scene, exploded shibboleths that stifled critical discussion, or otherwise promoted a more thoughtful analysis of what Michel Foucault called the human sciences. The rift between the aesthetic approach of literary studies and the analytical approach of cinema studies marked adaptation studies in two ways. It isolated adaptation studies from film studies, aligning it more closely with the programs in literary studies from which so many of its early practitioners had come. The further film studies drifted toward the left, mining film after film for political critique, the more firmly adaptation scholars dug in their heels on the right, championing the old-guard values of universalist humanism. At the same time, the rift widened between the theory and the practice of adaptation studies, which continued to take literary aesthetics as its touchstone and canonical works and authors as its organizing principle. It could hardly have been otherwise, since even potential methodological inversions of Shakespeare on Film—Hitchcock's Literary Sources, for example—would have enshrined Hitchcock the auteur, film studies' version of the literary classic, in place of Shakespeare as the locus of meaning and value.

The persistence of humanist values in adaptation studies is not so much a triumph of Arnold as a triumph of an evaluative impulse to insist that originals are always touchstones of value for their adaptations, unless of course the adaptations are better. Even the staunchest partisans of textual fidelity, after all, urge their students to revise their papers. Fidelity makes sense as a criterion of value only when we can be certain that the model is more valuable than the copy. In the absence of this certainty, teachers license Hitchcock's free adaptations and urge students to revise, not because they make no assumptions about different versions' relative value but because they make the reverse assumptions. Students may be starting with some promising material, but it stands to reason that they can make it better by reworking it, because final drafts are more likely than first drafts to offer exemplary models. Hitchcock, too, may be adapting literary originals, but he is making them into Hitchcock films, to which film scholars come to ascribe an even higher prestige value, though that value escaped Hitchcock's first American producer, David O. Selznick.[9] The only Hitchcock adaptation that has continued to attract anything like the harsh criticism Selznick leveled at *Rebecca* is *Sabotage* (1937) because its literary source, Joseph Conrad's novel *The Secret Agent*, still has a higher prestige value than Hitchcock's film.[10]

In sum, the notion of fidelity as a criterion of value is based on a marketplace of competing models. Producers like Selznick insist on fidelity to literary models; filmmakers like Hitchcock get a special dispensation from following those models because they provide a brand name with even greater commercial and critical cachet; and production companies like Merchant Ivory or the BBC revive the Selznick legacy by providing what might be called a negative cachet, a guarantee that they will protect the audience from the shock of experiencing any new thoughts or feelings that would not have been provoked by their source texts. This surprising diversity of practice in the filmmaking industry and the corresponding diversity in beliefs about fidelity among different camps of film scholars raises an inescapable question. In the twenty years since Dudley Andrew complained that "the most frequent and most tiresome discussion of adaptation . . . concerns fidelity and transformation,"[11] why has the field continued to organize itself so largely around a single one of these positions, the proposition that novels are texts, movies are intertexts, and in any competition between the two, the book is better?

One reason is that beneath the sharp disagreement between Hitchcock and Selznick is a deeper level of agreement that most teachers of adaptation share as well. Although Selznick traces the success of a movie to its source text ("We bought *Rebecca,* and we intend to make *Rebecca*")[12] and Hitchcock to its direction ("What I do is to read a story only once, and if I like the basic idea, I just forget all about the book and start to create cinema"),[13] their shared view of a movie as the product of a single imagination is based on a classical view of art, grounded in both cases by a healthy respect for the marketplace. Though neither of them ever puts it this way, they share a view of art as a series of expressive works, whether literary or cinematic, whose value inheres in their finished, achieved qualities, their success in *being themselves,* which, for Selznick, forbids any tampering with a proven literary product and, for Hitchcock, justifies all possible uses of raw material in the service of a new work. This constellation of aesthetic appreciation assigns a doubly subordinate place to adaptation study. As the analysis of precisely those cinematic works that have failed to achieve the auteur status that would consecrate them as quasi literature, it falls into the gap between the study of literature as literature and the study of cinema as literature. Standing outside the mainstream of both literary studies and film studies, its place is marginal and liable to shrink still further with the ebb of Arnold's idea of literature as a substitute for religion. This ebb is reflected by the passing of the belletristic ideal of appreciation in literary studies, in the waning influence of elitist cultural institutions like symphony orchestras and the Broadway theater, and in the decline of auteurism as the leading tendency in film studies.

An equally dim future for adaptation studies is implicit in the more pragmatic rationale for national literacy that E. D. Hirsch advocates in *Cultural Literacy.* Unconsciously echoing the etymology of *literacy,* which did not appear in the language until two hundred years after *illiteracy* as its antonym, Hirsch traces a breakdown in "effective nationwide communications" to problems in acquiring the kinds of common ideas and referents that foster communication by stipulating the sorts of shared knowledge and assumptions that allow development and discriminations within that common area.[14] The crux of Hirsch's argument is that contemporary students communicate less effectively because their knowledge, though often considerable, is more parochial and ephemeral than that of their forebears. Hence they are less conversant with the shared cultural markers that would allow them to grasp the meaning of what they read more precisely and effortlessly and to write with a surer sense of what their readers already know and believe. A knowledge of *Hamlet* is more useful than a knowledge of *I Love Lucy* because more past writers have used *Hamlet* as an analogy or point of departure in formulating their arguments and sharpening their examples, and referring to Hamlet provides contemporary readers access to a wider and more enduring audience than referring to Lucy and Ricky. Hirsch proposes to reverse the modern pedagogical tendency from Rousseau to Dewey toward fostering critical thinking by subordinating rote learning to intensive study of a smaller number of texts and problems. Instead, he emphasizes an older educational ideal, the acquisition of specific information that will fit students to assume the unexpectedly onerous mantle of the common reader. In "What Literate Americans Know," the appendix of five thousand names, phrases, dates, and concepts Hirsch prescribes as essential to cultural literacy, Arnold's touchstones are pressed into a new function in this post-Arnoldian ideal. Instead of serving as a suitably inspiring substitute for religious beliefs discredited by inconvenient facts, they are intended as a national lingua franca without which communication would be limited to the most obvious and primitive ideas. In principle they help speakers and writers to develop, and readers to grasp, more complex ideas by allowing them to build on a sure foundation of common ground with their audiences—a program Hirsch develops in his *Dictionary of Cultural Literacy* and a series of books titled *What Your Kindergartner* [through eighth grader] *Needs to Know.*

The culture wars that have followed Hirsch's ambitious proposal to remake American education have made the implications for film adaptations dismayingly clear. It is valuable to watch a screen adaptation of *Hamlet* because it gives viewers access to something like Shakespeare's world and people and issues. And because, as Hirsch acknowledges, "the information essential to literacy is rarely detailed or precise," something like that world is close enough to allow them to play along with other citizens more or less familiar with *Hamlet* as they all join in the national conversation.[15]

Adaptation is at the heart of Hirsch's program for cultural literacy in a more general but equally limited sense as well. His emphasis on widely shared but superficially understood cultural touchstones presents every instance of a particular touchstone (for example, Annie Oakley, NATO, "April showers bring May flowers") as in effect an adaptation of a single original that does not exist apart from its adaptations. Hirsch is not interested in ranking different appearances of a single touchstone; evaluation enters his program only in the selection of touchstones. Just as a Google search ranks Web sites by their links to other Web sites, Hirsch's program ranks literary or cinematic works and their consumers in terms of the number of touchstones they share.

Although the metaphor of adaptation might well be used to describe

Hirsch's network of touchstones and their users, however, it relegates adaptation study itself to an even more marginal position than Arnold's aesthetic study of literature. In Hirsch's post-Arnoldian program for literacy, adaptations have value only to the extent that they allow access to the world of the great originals that establish their credentials. Even when cultural literacy is defined in terms of effective citizenship rather than aesthetic sustenance, adaptations are still to be consumed under the sign of literature. By valuing film adaptations to the extent that they make prescriptive cultural touchstones widely accessible, Hirsch's program is even more likely than Arnold's to treat Shakespearean adaptation as the spoonful of sugar that helps the Bard's medicine go down.

Under either Arnold or Hirsch, adaptation study seems condemned to a bleak and servile future. Yet a closer consideration of Hirsch's principles indicates an alternative future that is far more exciting, a future that subordinates the process of reading adaptations to the process of writing them. A striking feature of Hirsch's program is the extent to which it neglects writing in favor of reading—not necessarily the reading of literature but reading under the sign of literature, reading assuming the subordinate position of a receptive reader whose basic aim is to consume an informative text whose cultural authority is greater than the reader's own. Throughout his discussion Hirsch assumes that if students learn to read, writing will take care of itself. Hirsch praises the conservative linguistic, orthographic, and cultural presuppositions in the radical newspaper the *Black Panther:* "To be conservative in the *means* of communication is the road to effectiveness in modern life, in whatever direction one wishes to be effective."[16] Although he lauds their mastery of consensual norms of communication, Hirsch never explains how the Black Panthers acquired the ability to develop and advocate their revolutionary social and political principles, overlooking the fact that a mastery of the touchstones of cultural literacy would have given them only a shared vocabulary, not the means to formulate an original viewpoint. In fact, although Hirsch insists that "cultural literacy is represented not by a *prescriptive* list of books but rather by a *descriptive* list of the information actually possessed by literate Americans,"[17] his list of markers must be framed by one of two unappealing alternatives. Either it introduces a prescriptive bias in its choice between designating "literate Americans" as the standard-bearers for public discourse, or it abandons all bias in the manner of the television quiz show *Family Feud,* in which contestants can win prizes by identifying Germany and Japan as modern countries with large armies, not because these answers are correct but because they are among the most popular answers in a survey the show has conducted. Like *Family Feud* Hirsch's cultural schemata neither reward original analytical thinking nor explain how it could ever come to pass within such a rising tide of mediocrity.

Although he often pauses to pay lip service to critical and analytical writing, Hirsch clearly regards such writing as a simple extension of literacy instead of its crucial instance. In treating writing and critical thinking as skills that inevitably follow the acquisition of cultural literacy, Hirsch promulgates a strikingly passive ideal of literacy. Like the documentation for computer software, Hirsch's program acculturates its novitiates by reducing them to consumers of a prepackaged culture they are taught specifically to absorb but not to analyze, question, change, or otherwise rewrite.

Hirsch offers the example of the *Black Panther* specifically to counter the objection that his program for cultural literacy is intrinsically conservative. But American citizens are likely less passive than he assumes, even when they are reading less obviously charged material. Do readers perusing the letters to the editor of a daily newspaper really ask what the writers mean, decide that they understand the meaning, and then either debate the meaning or turn the page in satisfaction? Such a hermeneutical model of understanding is at the heart of Hirsch's program. But readers left asking questions like, "Is there compelling evidence for life on Mars?" or "Should poker become an Olympic sport?" or "Has the Electoral College outgrown its usefulness?" are having a reading experience other, and more, than hermeneutical, an experience that involves an active, critical analysis of what they read. Literary scholars have long accepted this view of professional discourse, but it seems even more true of such nonprofessional statements as "For tomorrow, a 30 percent chance of afternoon showers."

According to Hirsch this analytical process is discrete from reading, as he had argued twenty years earlier in *Validity in Interpretation* by distinguishing between *meaning,* "that which is represented by a text," and *significance,* "a relationship between that meaning and a person, or a conception, or a situation, or indeed anything imaginable."[18] Hirsch's assertion that "significance always implies a relationship, and one constant, unchanging pole of that relationship is what the text means" has often come under attack. But he maintains it under the sign of Herbert Spencer in his analysis of writing in *The Philosophy of Composition,* which advocates a normative, maximally "readable" prose based on Spencer's analogous distinction between "the decipherment of meaning" and "framing the thought expressed."[19] The best writing, Hirsch implies, is that which is most easily consumed on the terms the author stipulates. Hirsch never considers the possibility that literacy might be in decline precisely because of the triumph of passive acculturation through repeated exposure—through television, through advertising, through political discourse—to utterances whose goal, like that of Hirsch's normative prose, is "readability"[20]—that is, discourse aimed at minimizing the likelihood of active analysis by indoctrinating readers rather than by engaging them.

Consider the analogy between Hirsch's program for cultural literacy and what might be called music literacy or literacy in the visual arts, but what is more commonly and revealingly called music and art appreciation. This sort of literacy involves the recognition of certain pivotal formal conventions, historical trends, and particular masterpieces in order to foster one's enjoyment at opera houses or concert halls or museums but not in order to be able to create new works by painting or sculpting or composing, or to be able to reinterpret preexisting works in performance by mastering the steps of ballet or the fingerings of the violin. As the guardians of culture at the Book-of-the-Month Club used to remind us, this sort of literacy is useful mainly as a way of protecting one's reputation for cultural attainments. It is nothing more than an education in enlightened consumerism.

Such passive acculturation is the hallmark of the current orthodoxy of literacy that takes reading rather than writing as the central activity of the literate citizen. Hirsch anticipates the objection that "the very existence of such a list [as his five thousand touchstones of cultural literacy] will cause students merely to memorize the bare items which it contains and learn nothing significant at all. Students will trivialize cultural information without really possessing it" by acknowledging that "such misuse of the list is not only a danger but a near certainty" when "whole sections of our bookstores are already devoted to paring down complex information into short, easily digested summaries— crib sheets for every school subject."[21] The years since the publication of *Cultural Literacy* have seen this dangerous tendency broaden to an extent that would be comical if it were not so perilous. Hirsch's own guides to what gradeschoolers must know have joined the proud ranks of primers on nonacademic subjects from *The Complete Idiot's Guide to Personal Finance in Your 20s and 30s* to *Sex for Dummies*. In the meantime the No Child Left Behind Act, educational reform legislation whose formula for pedagogical accountability is based on students' performance in standardized tests, has spurred a national frenzy

as teachers rush to teach to the tests in order to prevent their schools from being cited and themselves from being dismissed. The result has been an ever-
widening gap between literature and literacy—that is, between reading under
the sign of literature, whose goal is the consumption of information from authoritative sources, and the more active literacy Hirsch optimistically assumed
would follow, a literacy whose goal is engagement, analysis, and reasoned debate. What the nation needs is a program for fostering active literacy as
provocative and useful as Hirsch's program for consumerist literacy, as well as
a powerful and persuasive model for connecting the two.

In principle we have long had a theoretical program for a more active literacy. More than twenty years before Hirsch wrote, Roland Barthes had distinguished the "work," on whose behalf defenders of established cultural norms
from Arnold to Hirsch had fought, from the "text," which Barthes wished to
liberate from the work. Unlike the work, "an object that can be computed,"
Barthes' text is irreducibly "plural," *"experienced only in an activity of production";* instead of being designed for passive consumption, it "asks of the reader
a practical collaboration."[22] Works are designed to be read, texts to be
written—a distinction Barthes makes in somewhat different terms at the out-
set of *S/Z,* when he distinguishes "the readerly"—"a classic text" designed to
be consumed by readers limited to "the poor freedom either to accept or reject
the text"—from "the writerly"—"a perpetual present" that amounts simply to
*"ourselves writing,"* producing the texts we read.[23] Barthes' analysis is echoed
and amplified by Mikhail Bakhtin's distinction between the *authoritative discourse* of fathers, law, and Scripture, which "binds us, quite independent of any
power it might have to persuade us internally," and *internally persuasive discourse,* "a contemporary word" or "a word that has been reclaimed for con-
temporaneity," whose "semantic structure . . . is *not finite,* [but] it is *open;* in
each of the new contexts that dialogize it, this discourse is able to reveal ever
newer *ways to mean."* Bakhtin finds internally persuasive discourse, "half-ours
and half-someone else's," to be "of decisive significance in the evolution of an
individual consciousness."[24]

For half a century and more adaptation study has drastically limited its hori-
zons by its insistence on treating source texts as canonical authoritative discourse or readerly works rather than internally persuasive discourse or writerly
texts, refusing in consequence to learn what one might have expected to be the
primary lesson of film adaptation: that texts remain alive only to the extent that
they can be rewritten and that to experience a text in all its power requires each

reader to rewrite it. The whole process of film adaptation offers an obvious practical demonstration of the necessity of rewriting that many commentators have ignored because of their devotion to literature. Any Thackeray novel must be better than the additions, subtractions, or transformations of any film version simply because it is literature. When theorists reverse this procedure and allow Hitchcock to adapt Daphne du Maurier more freely than she or Selznick might approve, they are actually confirming the same principle—except that this time, they assume that Hitchcock, a more canonical filmmaker than du Maurier is an author, has a greater claim to be producing the kinds of works typically associated with literature and so deserves all the rights and privileges pertaining thereto. And the first of all those rights and privileges is the demand to be read instead of rewritten.

Although Barthes' distinctions amount to an uncanny prophecy of the composition theory that would spring up twenty years later, they have had lamentably little impact on teaching on the broader terrain of English departments generally. Most teachers continue to think of writing as the gradable symptom of critical thinking. As Barthes' distinction implies, however, it is more than that; it *is* critical thinking, even when the writer is not actually sitting at the word processor but preparing to do so by sifting, scrutinizing, actively engaging each given text. Writers are like the old lady in E. M. Forster's anecdote who asks, "How can I tell what I think till I see what I say?"[25] The distinction may seem like a quibble—is writing postreading, the visible sign of reading, or is reading prewriting, a necessary preliminary to writing?—but the overwhelming support for the first model over the second has produced a pedagogical orthodoxy of literacy that persists throughout the educational establishment, defining a literature of the readerly in a way that guarantees that adaptation study will remain as trivial as the adaptations it prescribes.

The real cost of our institutional attachment to literature, however, runs much deeper. Barthes complains that "what the (secondary) School prides itself on is teaching to *read* (well) and no longer to *write*."[26] That situation has changed remarkably little over the past forty years. Except for required courses in composition and electives in creative writing or preprofessional courses in journalism, college English courses are overwhelmingly devoted to reading rather than writing. They are named after what gets read in them and arranged according to these readings, and it is discussions of the reading that occupies most of class time. Even though students are typically graded almost exclusively on their writing, most English teachers spend little time teaching it, preferring instead to assume it is an adjunct to the reading we do teach. We end up teaching our students *books* instead of teaching them *how to do things with books* because our college English curriculum is organized around literature at the expense of the active, writerly engagement, the sense of performance and play, the unquenchable sense of agency even in the presence of canonical works, that we call literacy.

The privilege the educational establishment accords reading over writing continues to promote the evaluative tendency that shapes both Arnold's aestheticism and Hirsch's pragmatism in a widely deplored institutional snobbery about writing.[27] Professors of English have long decreed that intensive work in writing ought to come before college and that if students cannot write, it is the fault of their high-school teachers. Although college students are routinely asked to do writing assignments on which their grades depend, directed instruction in writing is commonly limited to elementary composition courses and preprofessional courses in business and technical writing.

Hence the college English curriculum is free to promote reading as a pedagogical goal to the virtual exclusion of writing. The few courses specifically designated as courses in writing are introductory, remedial, or preprofessional—as if only slow learners, freshmen, journalists, and authors of computer documentation need instruction in writing—and teachers mark their own professional advancement by their growing success in avoiding the task of teaching these courses. Except for the writing specialists hired specifically to teach them, new colleagues are hired by a process that specifies areas of expertise in reading, not achievement in teaching writing. And despite the continuing debate about the wisdom of common texts and authors for core courses for the major (should it be possible for students to graduate without reading Shakespeare?), there is rarely any central oversight for the kinds of writing colleges assign and the ways they assess it.

Although these priorities are not always shared by English departments in nongraduate or emerging or two-year colleges, the sense of academic class-consciousness is. English departments that emphasize writing are schooled to look up at those that emphasize reading as a universally desirable norm for English studies. The profession does everything possible to underscore the message to students, junior and part-time colleagues, and fellow colleges that the teaching of writing is at worst something beneath the notice and abilities of higher education, at best something that does not deserve its top professional priority. Peter Elbow has summarized the resulting inequity: "When writing programs are housed in English departments, as they so often are, teachers of writing are usually paid less to teach more under poorer working conditions—in order to help support literature professors to be paid more to teach less under better working conditions."[28]

The educational establishment could do greater justice to both its texts and its students if it paid greater attention to a vital countercurrent in English studies that goes back at least as far as Arnold. In "The Function of Criticism at the Present Time" Arnold presses the aesthetic study of poetry into the service of *"a disinterested endeavour to learn and propagate the best that is known and thought in the world"* in order "to create a current of true and fresh ideas."[29] The paradoxical goal Arnold sets criticism is to change the world by renouncing any direct practical interest in it—not to read one's culture more accurately but to rewrite it more compellingly. Hirsch himself acknowledges this countercurrent when he moderates his dissent from generations of skills-centered educators by concluding that "the polarization of educationists into facts-people versus skills-people has no basis in reason. Facts and skills are inseparable."[30] Although the foundation of Hirsch's argument about language acquisition and the corresponding acquisition of cultural literacy is that active inferences greatly increase the ability to recall the particulars of a given abstract schema, surely students ought to be trained to be more active readers than Hirsch acknowledges, reading not only to understand but to consider, to compare, to criticize, to debate. These skills are not superadded to training in rhetoric or literacy; they are the very essence of that training.

This is particularly true, of course, in college English courses, which are precisely forums for helping students get beyond a passive receptivity to texts toward an active engagement with them as literary studies' distinctive contribution to liberal education's goal of getting students to think better for themselves. In effect, college English teachers are not teaching their students how to read but rather how to read against simple understanding, how to see further into a poem or play or novel than a literal reader, armed only with a general knowledge of cultural touchstones, could see. College courses commonly test the cogency and depth and power of those counterreadings by asking students to talk, and especially to write, about them, and that kind of testing seems uniquely appropriate, not only because English courses teach writing along with reading but also because the kind of active reading they teach is already tantamount to a rewriting of the text. Hirsch might well prefer to describe this project of reading-against as *counterliteracy,* since it aims at active interpretation and creation rather than neutrally receptive understanding. If we called Hirsch's cultural literacy a program for *preliteracy,* however, and reserved *literacy* as a label for the kind of active textual engagement that focuses more directly on writing than reading, we could hardly find a more effective focus for programs in literacy than cinematic adaptation.

The kind of adaptation study central to this discipline contrasts sharply with adaptation study under the sign of literature. Taking off from Frank Zingrone's anti-Hirschian remark that the "one-medium user is the new illiterate,"[31] this alternative approach to adaptation study does not approach adaptations as either transcriptions of canonical classics or attempts to create new classics but rather as illustrations of the incessant process of rewriting as critical reading. It is informed by the conflict Bakhtin discerns between heteroglossia, whose protean, internally persuasive meanings are irreproducibly dependent on the contexts generated by particular readers and reading situations, and canonization, which seeks to standardize authoritative meanings for all readers.[32] Just as Bakhtin celebrates, however prematurely, the novel's resistance to canonization, this approach to adaptation study treats both adaptations and their originals as heteroglot texts rather than as canonical works, emphasizing the fact that every text offers itself as an invitation to be rewritten.

Emphasizing literacy over literature does not assume that all adaptations are equally valuable or that they are just as good as their originals. It simply declines to place the question of evaluation at the center of the discipline. After all, no matter how clever or audacious an adaptation is, the book will always be better than any adaptation because it is always *better at being itself.*

But this reductio ad absurdum, which is true by definition, indicates just how trivial a claim we make when we argue that the book is better. Of course it's better at being itself; so is the movie better at being itself; so is everything in the universe. Fidelity as a touchstone of adaptations will always give their source texts, which are always faithful to themselves, an advantage so enormous and unfair that it renders the comparison meaningless. To evaluate adaptations fairly, we need to evaluate their source texts as well—an activity traditional adaptation study, which takes the literary text as an unquestioned touchstone of value for any adaptation, has traditionally avoided. To revitalize adaptation study, we need to reframe the assumption that even the most cursory consideration of the problem forces on us—source texts cannot be rewritten—as a new assumption: source texts must be rewritten; we cannot help rewriting them.

Whenever we teach a film adaptation—whenever we watch an adaptation as an adaptation—we treat it as an intertext designed to be looked through, like a window on the source text. Although it is certainly true that adaptations are intertexts that depend in a special way on their source texts, thinking of them exclusively in these terms inevitably impoverishes them because it reduces them to the single function of replicating (or, worse, failing to replicate) the details of that single source text. In practice, to extend Bakhtin's argument, every text, from *Ulysses* (1922) to *Jay and Silent Bob Strike Back* (2001), is an intertext that incorporates, refracts, refutes, and alludes to many other texts, whether literary, cinematic, or more broadly cultural. Taking fidelity as the decisive criterion of an adaptation's value is tantamount to insisting that it do the same job as its source text without going outside the lines that text has established, even though adaptations normally carry heavier burdens and labor under tighter restrictions than we would ever impose on any novel.

As sadly as such rules and regulations impoverish adaptations, they do even greater damage to their source texts. By elevating Thackeray's *Vanity Fair* above its film adaptations as a literary classic, we ignore its own status as an intertext designed, just as surely as any of its adaptations, to be looked *into* and *through* as well as *at*. To the extent that we praise a TV miniseries for its fidelity to a Thackeray novel because it does not omit telling passages or import irrelevant biases, we ignore the fact that every novel comes with programmatic omissions and biases of its own, telltale traces of other novels it could have been. When we focus on fidelity as the central problem of film adaptation, we overlook the problematic nature of source texts that makes them worth studying in the first place by choosing to emphasize their privileged status as literature over their capacity to engage and extend our literacy.

It is ironic that literature and literacy, intimately related notions stemming from the Latin *littera* (letter), should have become so blankly opposed as centers for contemporary English studies. Elbow has noted that "the word *literacy* really means power over letters, i.e., reading and writing. But as *literacy* is used casually and even in government policy and legislation, it tends to mean *reading*, not writing."[33] As commentators from Arnold to Hirsch have acknowledged, however, reading and writing depend on each other, even if literature for more than a century has claimed such precedence over literacy that it has often sought to repress or marginalize it. The need to incorporate both activities into what might be called the discipline of textual studies—the study of how texts are produced, consumed, canonized, transformed, resisted, and denied—offers a unique opportunity to adaptation studies, which can serve not as an avatar of literacy over literature but as a sorely needed bridge between the two.

In her monograph on *The Awakening,* Marilyn Hoder-Salmon offers a practical illustration of how new directions in adaptation study can combine the study of literature with the development of a more active literacy. Hoder-Salmon uses the form of her annotated screenplay of Kate Chopin's novel to raise questions about "the omission from the Hollywood cinema of classics of women's literature and the counterpart phenomenon of reductive treatment when such classics are adapted."[34] Her use of screenwriting as a medium of criticism is readily adapted to the classroom by getting students to write their own adaptations of specific scenes in the novel, turning them from readers looking up to Chopin into writers meeting her on their own ground and on her own level. This approach does not neglect the traditional activity of interpretation; it simply changes the medium through which the novel must be interpreted from the critical essay into the screenplay, which selects what the screenwriter takes to be most important about the novel and rewrites it. Such courses are balanced between their loyalties to literature (its choice of a canonical text like Chopin's and its insistence on paying that text, or whatever text is chosen in its place, the compliment of intense and extended scrutiny) and literacy (its encouragement to students to become active producers of the text they might otherwise be content simply to read).

Teachers unwilling to reconfigure their literature courses as screenwriting courses could profit by encouraging their students to think of adaptation itself in different terms. Over the years adaptations have been studied as translations and transformations, as selections and specifications, as reimaginings and imitations of literature. It would help redress the balance between literature and literacy to think of each adaptation not in terms of what it faithfully reproduces—what it selects, emphasizes, and transforms—but of what it leaves out. Instead of acting as if the power of a story lay in what it explicitly portrayed, we might explore further the "gaps" Wolfgang Iser calls "a kind of pivot on which the whole text-reader relationship revolves," because "whenever the reader bridges the gaps, communication begins."[35] The very process of supplying omitted material draws each reader closer to the story, its world, and the process of world making.

Lindiwe Dovey offers a model that links Iser's theoretical analysis to Hoder-Salmon's impulse to rewrite classic texts as screenplays or films in her reflections on *Perfect Darkness* (2000), Dovey's own film adaptation of Olive Schreiner's *Story of an African Farm* (1939). She quotes Schreiner's observation that "[t]he whole of the story is not written here, but it is suggested. And the attribute of all true art, the highest and the lowest, is this—that it says more than it says, and takes you away from itself."[36] Responding to Schreiner's invitation, Dovey distinguishes between an "appropriational" mode of adaptation that "involves simply borrowing plot and characters" and her own "pro-creative" approach, "an interpretive mode" that analyzes rather than borrowing plot and character and also "foregrounds the way in which the film constructs a self for and expresses the desire of the adapter. . . . The pro-creational adaptation claims a kind of freedom for itself, but does not assume dominance over the text. It thus works in an antithetical way not only to conventional critical discourse but also to appropriational adaptation" by incessantly raising rather than settling questions of motive, agency, and interpretation.[37] Dovey's procreational adaptations are exactly those whose gaps and questions and doubts about themselves—whose problems—seek to foster their audiences' active literacy.

No story, of course, is the whole story, and no film adaptation of *Vanity Fair* can include every detail Thackeray does. But thinking about the elements a given adaptation strategically omits in order to engage its audience's literacy— the details of family background, the thoughts we are allowed to infer, the authorial commentary so essential to our sense of Thackeray—can lead us back to the equally strategic omissions that make Thackeray's novel a performance text itself. Emphasizing the ways in which readers and viewers always complete the stories they think they are merely consuming can replace the pedagogical goal of inculcating a dutiful love and respect for literature with the goal of empowering students to think more critically about the ways they read, the ways writers write, and the surprisingly intimate connections between the two.

Whatever strategy theorists and teachers of adaptation pursue, it is unlikely to resolve a series of knotty questions about the relation between literature and literacy. Why should we study literature? If the goal of literary study is enlightened appreciation, how material is that goal to the more general goals of liberal education—effective national and global citizenship—and how is it connected to those other goals? If knowledge is power, is it more important to have a knowledge of what is in the canonical works of literature and cinema or a knowledge of how they can be used? Who ought to be empowered by literature and literacy, and empowered to do what? Adaptation study has unique potential as the keystone of a new discipline of textual studies less ideologically driven, and therefore more powerful, than either contemporary literary or cultural studies not because it resolves these questions but because it keeps them front and center—beginning with whether we want to organize textual studies around the question "What should we be reading?" or the question "What should we be reading for?"

This book differs from other studies of cinematic adaptation in fundamental ways. It is a study not so much of specific adaptations as of specific problems adaptations raise. Its opening chapters consider how early silent short films sought to borrow the weight of seriousness from literature whether or not they were based on specific literary sources; what particular kinds of demands audiences bring to scriptural adaptations like *The Passion of the Christ* (2004); what it means for a film to pose as an introduction to rather than a replacement for a beloved classic; and whether it is possible to distinguish between adaptation and allusion, or to construct a systematic grammar of intermediate modes between these two kinds of intertextual reference. Although each of these investigations involves forays into close analysis of particular films, this is not a collection of paired readings of films and novels, and it spends less time on close reading, and especially on comparing each given film to its putative source, than most books on the subject.

Nor does it focus on the question earlier adaptation theorists routinely pursue as soon as they have disavowed it: what it means for a movie to be faithful to its literary source. The subject of fidelity will often arise in my discussions of adaptations of the Gospels or Jane Austen's novels or the adventures of Sherlock Holmes. But I treat fidelity as a problem variously conceived and defined by the filmmakers at hand, not as an unquestioned desideratum of all adaptations. In my two central chapters I consider scrupulous fidelity first as an aberration (in *Gone with the Wind* and *Lord of the Rings*), then as the founding move in a genre (the Tradition of Quality, an umbrella term for adaptations as different as those of David O. Selznick, Merchant Ivory, and the BBC). Because filmmakers occasionally, and adaptation theorists more frequently, have made fidelity central to their enterprise, their work provides highly suggestive material for study, and I prefer to study it rather than attacking or defending it.

Twenty years ago, Harris Ross, noting the widespread tendency toward evaluation in studies of literature and film, suggested that "rather than arguing the proper mix of images and words or the proper type of dialogue for film, a systematic analysis of how dialogue actually functions in film and literature is needed."[38] Although I share this sentiment deeply, readers of this book will have no trouble finding that I have many value judgments of my own. I have tried, however, to avoid three kinds of licentious evaluation. First and most obviously, I follow many other recent theorists of adaptation in my skepticism of fidelity to a given precursor text as an unquestioned criterion of value. Second, in emphasizing the specific reasons I value a particular adaptation or interpretation or theory of adaptation, I mean to link evaluation and analysis instead of allowing the first to substitute for the second. Finally, I often waive evaluations of particular adaptations, giving as much weight to Barry Levinson's *Young Sherlock Holmes* (1985) as to Merchant Ivory's *The Golden Bowl* (2000), partly because I wish to focus more closely on the problems these films raise than on their aesthetic value, partly because I wish to dethrone evaluation as the unmarked or central activity of adaptation study. If these films are valuable to me because of the theoretical problems they raise, that criterion of value seems less arbitrary for adaptation studies than for any other.

The topics in the second half of this book take me ever further from the normative model of adaptation studies: one-on-one comparisons between film adaptations and their canonical literary sources. Chapters 8 and 9 consider adaptations based on visual texts and on a popular franchise rather than a specific published text. Chapter 10 traces the emergence of three prominent cinematic adapters to auteur status in order to consider why some adaptations seem to transcend their sources while others do not. My final two chapters consider films based on nonliterary sources—board games, video games, amusement-park concessions—and finally on sources they identify only as "a true story." My goal in these chapters is to widen the range of adaptation studies by considering more broadly what we mean by a source text and how texts get promoted from intertexts to full textual status.

Despite the forbiddingly broad range of topics I investigate, I hope my focus is consistent: the status of adaptations as examples of rewriting that can inspire storytellers and analysts alike to their own productive and inevitable rewriting of everything they need not and cannot simply read. The text is dead; long live the text.

# CHAPTER TWO

# One-Reel Epics

Although it may come as news to modern viewers who consider early film primitive at least partly because of its innocence of literary inspiration, cinematic adaptation is as old as cinema itself. John Tibbetts, surveying Kemp R. Niver's catalogue *Motion Pictures from the Library of Congress Paper Print Collection, 1894–1912*, reports that "of the thousands of titles listed and described, over one-third contain references that demonstrate that they were either derived from stage plays or that they at least in some way simulated the illusion of a theatrical presentation."[1] Audiences were eager for whatever adaptations the available technology could supply. Less than a year after the first commercial screening of short films, Thomas A. Edison's one-shot subject *The May Irwin Kiss*, presenting the climax of John J. McNally's musical comedy *The Widow Jones*, became the studio's most popular film of 1896. It was soon followed by George Méliès's *Faust et Marguerite* (France, 1897) and *Guillaume tell et le clown* (France, 1898) and George Albert Smith's *The Corsican Brothers* (UK, 1898).

Tibbetts's second criterion for adaptations—"they at least in some way simulated the illusion of a theatrical presentation"—might seem treacherously loose. But it places the emphasis exactly where it should be, for the earliest film adaptations are less likely to take as their standard fidelity to any particular text than the success with which they create a simulacrum of the institutional text of literature, most often of theater. In particular, *The Kiss*, in which John C. Rice, as Billie Bikes, kisses May Irwin, as the Widow Jones, might seem both more and less than a true adaptation—more, because it is a literal reenactment of a theatrical piece whose actors are simply playing this particular performance for the camera; less, because it captures only a moment of its nominal source, lasting less than a minute. But to reason along these lines is to accept as definitive a narrow conception of adaptation—a given adaptation refers to a single complete literary text—that has little relevance to these early films. It is more helpful, and more likely to expand current ideas of adaptation, to begin by entertaining the idea that *The Kiss* is indeed an adaptation and considering the ways it differs from more recent adaptations.

The *Kiss* shares at least four distinctive qualities with most early film adaptations. It is parasitic, depending on a well-known theatrical source of which it expects its audience to have some knowledge. It is highly selective in drawing on that source, making no attempt to reproduce all of what Roland Barthes calls the cardinal functions or nuclei that constitute the armature of its narrative.[2] It is not, strictly speaking, a narrative itself (although it is based on a narrative source and represents a temporal sequence of movements) since these movements constitute only a single gesture rather than an Aristotelian action with a beginning, middle, and end. Finally, it attempts both to memorialize its subject, in the manner of André Bazin's death mask,[3] and to bring it to the widest popular audience—even though it is much more likely that viewers in 1896 could have seen the play staged in a local theater more easily than they could have seen the film, which could be presented only in a venue equipped to display the infant medium. Early performers, recognizing the power of cinema to preserve their work over the passage of time, joined Sarah Bernhardt in seeing the new medium as their best hope of immortality.[4] In fact, *The Kiss* was so successful in bringing theater to the masses that it was the first American film to provoke widespread demands for censorship.

Viewers looking back on *The Kiss* from the perspective of Merchant Ivory or the epic *Lord of the Rings* franchise may find it hard to categorize a film that is nothing more than a cinematic record of a kiss between two people who could have been anyone in any romantic situation as an adaptation. But turn-of-the-century viewers would have had no trouble placing the film in an older context of adaptations that accepted parasitism and selectivity—the assumption that knowledge of the original would supply a narrative continuity from which the adapted excerpt was absolved—as the price of the new experience. Film historians have long identified lantern slides as a precursor so exact that "many if not most of the first moving picture showmen were lanternists, who regarded this new accessory as an unusually complicated mechanical lantern slide—which in a sense it was."[5] Tom Gunning has added magic theater and trompe l'oeil painting as two more modes of visual exhibition that had a decisive impact on early cinema.[6] To this list can be added several other modes of exhibition common throughout the nineteenth century. Tableaux vivants, melding the conventions of historical painting and classical ballet, condensed pivotal moments from large-scale historical or theatrical actions into a relatively small number of highly charged scenes.[7] Grand opera conventionally divided its music into readily reproducible arias that, like song-and-dance numbers in Broadway musicals a century later, marked moments of heightened lyricism and emotional intensity and recitative passages designed, like musicals' more severely functional continuity, to move the story along. The song cycles of Schubert, Schumann, and Hugo Wolf, whose career was ending just as movies were coming to birth, similarly look forward in their lyrical intensity and narrative discontinuity to Alfred Hitchcock's definition of drama as "life with the dull bits cut out."[8] Most American audiences' experience of Shakespearean performance was limited to programs of excerpts and digests of great speeches and set pieces lampooned by Mark Twain in the farragoes cobbled together by the Duke and Dauphin in *The Adventures of Huckleberry Finn.*

Transmedia adaptations like these form a natural matrix not only for *The Kiss* but for the more ambitious *Rip Van Winkle,* also released in 1896 by Edison's former camera operator William Kennedy Laurie Dickson in the form of eight one-shot scenes from Joseph Jefferson's five-act dramatic adaptation of Washington Irving's 1819 story. Although the scenes contain no dialogue or intertitles—intertitles would not be introduced to cinema until Edison's *Uncle Tom's Cabin* (filmed by Edwin S. Porter, Arthur White, and others [1903]), and spoken dialogue would not be heard until *The Jazz Singer* (1927)—all but the first, "Rip's Toast," are relatively continuous in action. Their story would have been easily intelligible to an audience reading the accompanying lantern slides or the labels attached to the series of eight mutoscopes on which each shot was originally designed to appear. More important, as Scott Simmon observes, "The new makers of motion pictures . . . could expect viewers to know the performance, at least by reputation." Noting the unusual twenty-year sweep and four-minute length of the narrative comprising the eight films, not all of which were routinely projected together, Simmon notes that "for 1896, it is an epic."[9]

As its reissue as a single continuous eight-shot film in 1903 confirmed, *Rip Van Winkle* is indeed an epic, though one of a special kind. Instead of telling a story, it follows song cycles, tableaux vivants, and programs of excerpts from plays or operas in presenting theatrical highlights from a well-known story, emphasizing performance, scope, and spectacle rather than continuity. The static, distant placement of the camera and two-dimensional blocking of the action, which make the film seem staid to many modern viewers, faithfully imitate the experience of sitting in the tenth row of a theater to watch America's most famous actor in his best-known role. Even fidelity to the experience of attending a theater, however, is subordinated to the added thrill of outdoor settings more realistic than anything a theater could produce and discontinuous editing that presents Rip's life with the dull bits cut out.

Mutoscope films like *Rip Van Winkle* were standardized at a single shot running less than a minute. Even when the industry decisively accepted projection over peep shows, the one-thousand-foot standard reels with which most projectors were equipped limited films to some twelve minutes during the rise of fictional narrative film around 1908. Producers adopted remarkably similar strategies for compressing their most ambitious subjects into the compass of a single reel. They chose well-known stories, like Edison's *Jack in the Beanstalk* (directed by Edwin S. Porter and George S. Fleming, 1902), that would not require exposition to audiences familiar with them and reduced these stories to a series of skeletal outlines of obligatory scenes. Scenes like the awakening of Frankenstein's monster and Dr. Jekyll's first experimental transformation into Mr. Hyde were obligatory not in the sense that they were required either by the original source or by narrative continuity but in the sense that viewers would have come specifically to see them. Filmmakers consistently treat these scenes as set pieces or spectacles, stellar examples of Gunning's "cinema of attractions," which "addresses the audience directly," soliciting "a highly conscious awareness of the film image engaging the viewer's curiosity" instead of inviting the audience to "get lost in a fictional world and its drama."[10] Like the more recent examples of musicals, action films, and pornography, early adaptations like *The Wonderful Wizard of Oz* (1910) are organized around a series of spectacular individual scenes rather than a rising narrative curve to which those scenes are subordinated. Hence they are free to elide narrative continuity or relegate it to slides, intertitles, or narrators.[11] The goal of these adaptations is not to provide a faithful transcription of their original sources but to use those sources as inspiration or pretext for a digest, reminiscence, hybrid, or inflation—at any rate, for something new and different.

Between 1903, when the first theater dedicated exclusively to movie projection opened and the first intertitles appeared as part of a film whose producer could standardize and control them, and 1907, when fictional narrative began to emerge as the leading model for all cinema, the cinema of attractions set the agenda for adaptations. The boldly free-flowing, capitalized intertitles that introduce each separate shot of *Uncle Tom's Cabin* make no concession to a hypothetical audience's need for background information or narrative continuity (the first two titles are "ELIZA PLEADS WITH TOM TO RUN AWAY" and "PHINEAS OUTWITS THE SLAVE TRADERS," and Simon Legree is never identified). The film's staging of Harriet Beecher Stowe's novel as a revue, a series of variously spectacular one-shot tableaux, complete with a steamboat race and explosion, an escape across mechanically moving ice floes, two dance ensembles, and angels hovering over the deaths of both Eva and Tom, strongly suggests that cinema's epic pretensions precede its interest in developing coherent, self-contained narrative.

Some contemporaneous adaptations were reduced or essentialized into a single defining theatrical moment, like the death of Sir Herbert Beerbohm Tree's monarch in *King John* (1899) or Biograph's aptly titled *Duel Scene from Macbeth* (1905).[12] Sometimes fictional narratives alternated the location shooting typical of Edison's *actualités*—nonnarrative films designed to show staged train crashes or airplane launches or to transport viewers to such exotic locales as the Wild West or New York's Lower East Side—with more obviously stylized interior sets for the main action. John Tibbetts remarks, for example, that Edwin S. Porter's *The Kleptomaniac* (1905) alternates naturalistic exterior shots rooted in actualités with stylized two-dimensional interior shots before ending with "a written title card with the word 'tableau' printed on it, followed by a shot of curtains parting to reveal a posed, draped woman against a black backdrop" holding the scales of justice, one side "weighted down with a bag of money."[13] For four years filmmakers wrestled with the problems of making fictional films that would also showcase the exhibitionistic appeal of the new medium as entrepreneurs rushed to open nickelodeons in every town across America.

Film historians have identified the economic fulcrum of this turbulent period as 1907 to 1908, when the saturation of America with movie theaters became effectively complete. Charles Musser maintains that "by mid 1908, cinema had become a form of mass communication" whose increasingly standardized norms of production, distribution, and exhibition, coupled with a dramatically growing need for new product that could no longer be met by recycling new versions of familiar stories, meant that "reliance on the spectator's prior familiarity with a story was becoming rapidly outmoded."[14] When the 1908 formation of the Motion Picture Patents Company was followed by a round of censorship attacks in 1908 and 1909, producers became convinced that "material taken from decorous literary works would provide critics with little excuse for further attacks."[15] Literary sources could provide more than the refuge of respectability. Observing that nickelodeons aimed to provide cheap entertainment for the masses, Adolph Zukor, head of Famous Players in Famous Plays, calculated that filmmakers could extend their reach to the lucrative middle-class market if they could "produce longer and more expensive films modeled after familiar middle-class forms of entertainment."[16] Under this model familiarity with the general conventions of a product line replaces familiarity with the source of a given film as an entrance requirement.[17]

Once filmmakers looked to literary works as a model for their films, a new problem arose that was crucial to the path film adaptation was to follow. How could a one-reel film running only twelve minutes convey something of the weight or gravitas, something like the epic sense, of a story that might run to many years, dozens of characters, and hundreds of pages? The best-known early narrative films, like Porter's misleadingly titled *Life of an American Fireman* (1903), *The Great Train Robbery* (1903), and *The Dream of a Rarebit Fiend* (1906), had largely taken the form of self-contained anecdotes. How could films scarcely longer than these suggest the sweep and scale of their literary sources?

Crucial as it was to emerging fashions in adaptation, this problem may not have seemed as overwhelming to early filmmakers as it would today, even after they ventured away from universally familiar subjects that could be presented discontinuously. Although novels have long been considered movies' most frequent source of literary inspiration, few early film adaptations are based directly on novels. Early filmmakers more often chose to adapt material that required less drastic compression: short stories like "Rip Van Winkle" and "William Wilson," fairy tales like "Jack and the Beanstalk" and "Goldilocks and the Three Bears," poems like "Pippa Passes" and "The Raven," and plays ranging from *The Widow Jones* to Shakespeare, most of whose works had been filmed by 1912. Patrick G. Loughney has gone so far as to assert that "the 'theatrical writing' forms of the *playscript* and *scenario* . . . evolved as *the* organizational elements essential to the production of all performing media decades before the advent of motion pictures."[18] Even when novels were adapted, films like *Uncle Tom's Cabin* (1896) and *Dr. Jekyll and Mr. Hyde* (1912) were typically based on intermediary stage adaptations that had broken down the novelists' often sprawling narrative to a manageably limited series of dramatic scenes—a pattern that continued through *The Great Gatsby* (1926) to the formative decade of Hollywood feature adaptation extending from *Dracula* (1931) and *Frankenstein* (1931) to *The Adventures of Sherlock Holmes* (1939) and *Pride and Prejudice* (1940).

In adapting shorter texts like "The Bells" (filmed twice in 1913, both films based on dramatic adaptations of Poe's poem), early filmmakers still found it necessary to condense their material to fit a given length. But this necessity may have seemed no more daunting than the need to compress a novel as complex as Michael Cunningham's *The Hours* to two hours for screenwriter David Hare's 2002 adaptation because there is no more reason to assume that early filmmakers considered one-reel films to be "short" than that twenty-first-century filmgoers consider two-hour films short. Since virtually "all films in 1907 were one reel or less in length,"[19] the prevailing length, like the greater length of sync-sound narratives, became standardized as feature length, the mold into which all material would be poured as one element of an entertainment package that included at first live vaudeville acts and later, once the movies had moved out of nickelodeons, a program of other one-reelers. Because no short film was ever intended as an entertainment complete in itself, the emerging challenge was not to make shorts seem longer—certainly not as long as an unimaginable two-hour feature, for example—but to make them seem bigger, broader, deeper, and more highbrow.

Several strategies soon came to the fore. On the one hand, filmmakers inclined to familiar stories that "assured the intellectual level of the works to be seen by an upward-striving middle-class audience" could choose as their sources canonical literary works like Shakespeare's plays, nineteen of which were filmed, some of them several times over, between 1907 and 1912.[20] Shakespeare's plays provided ideal source material because they were familiar, sanctified by age and expert judges, well constructed, replete with exciting scenes, and endlessly quotable. What these early adaptations mainly quoted from the Bard, however, was not speeches but tableaux. None of Shakespeare's verse survives in intertitles, which by convention gave expository information rather than dialogue. J. Stuart Blackton's 1910 adaptation of *Twelfth Night* for Vita-graph, for example, begins with a mouth-filling intertitle that forgoes Shake-speare's language: "Viola, separated from her twin brother Sebastian by a ship-wreck, finds herself in the realm of the Duke Orsino. She dresses herself from her brother's trunk, cast up by the sea, and finds her way to the Duke's palace where she is believed to be a young man and meets with strange adventures." Unwary viewers watching the following one-shot scene, in which Viola stands on the shore taking items of masculine attire from the providential trunk, might have been disconcerted to realize that this initial title summarized not only this opening scene but a good deal of the story to follow. But there were presumably few unwary viewers for the film, whose swift exposition, confined entirely to the intertitle, would be nearly unintelligible for an audience unfa-miliar with the play to follow. Instead of providing information, the film's sub-sequent intertitles have more the air of reminders, right down to the one that precedes the final tableau: "Sebastian is mistaken for Viola by Olivia. The twins are reunited. The Duke finds a sweetheart, and Olivia, discovering that she has been in love with a girl, finds consolation in the arms of Sebastian."

This selective quotation of Shakespearean tableaux, interspersed with inter-titles summarizing intervening plot developments and glossing the upcoming scene, is less like contemporary adaptation than like illustration—not the il-lustration of multimodal words-and-pictures volumes of Thackeray or Dr. Seuss but the illustration of books written long ago by someone else. In both cases strategically chosen images are created to embellish an existing text rather than replace it. The goal is to highlight obligatory scenes and render them more vivid, present, and contemporary (even in period costume, a silent Viola is more contemporary than a Viola speaking Shakespeare's English) while pass-ing over the rest of the verbal text as quickly as possible. It is a natural out-growth of "performance priorities of the late nineteenth and early twentieth century stage" which did not always "privilege language over spectacle."[21] As an almost casual means to this end, one-reel adaptations invariably regularize Shakespeare's chronology, dispensing with any backstory they cannot drama-tize in its temporally appropriate place. Percy Stow's 1908 British adaptation of *The Tempest* is so conscientious about dramatizing the events leading up to Fer-dinand's shipwreck on Prospero's isle—Prospero's arrival there, his discovery of Caliban, his freeing of Ariel from a tree, Ariel's protection ten years later of budding Miranda from Caliban—that more than half its twelve-minute length has been passed by the time it gets to the storm in Shakespeare's opening scene.

Paradoxically, the resulting chronological regularization wrecks the Aristotelian unity of the play, but since it is Shakespeare's only play to observe the unities of time, place, and action, the loss would probably have gone unnoticed and certainly unmourned by even the most ardent Shakespeareans.

This chronologically normalized, simplified, illustrative approach is typical of other Shakespearean one-reelers. The 1909 Vitagraph adaptation of *A Midsummer Night's Dream*, directed by Blackton and Charles Kent, introduces its opening shot with an intertitle that summarizes the long first scene of the play: "The Duke of Athens, soon to be married to Hippolyta, decrees that his subject, Hermia, shall give up her lover, Lysander, and shall marry Demetrius who her father has chosen. The lovers decide to elope. They are followed by Demetrius and by Helena in love with Demetrius." Although the title, like the opening intertitle in *Twelfth Night*, seems unduly far-reaching to modern analysts, it perfectly suits the shot it introduces, whose piecemeal exodus also summarizes Shakespeare's entire first scene. The film follows the formulaic pattern of expository intertitle then illustrative tableau (there are only two straight cuts without titles) until the end. Yet *A Midsummer Night's Dream*, like *The Tempest*, offers ideal material for this Cliff's Notes approach. Its action is already farcically swift in Shakespeare; its characters, except for Nick Bottom, have no psychology to speak of (indeed their lack of individuality is a running joke behind the transpositions of the four bewitched lovers' affections); and it is filled with magical transformations well suited to the technology available in 1909. Although the film cuts Shakespeare's final act, including the mechanicals' staging of the tedious brief scene of Pyramus and Thisby, it magically introduces Penelope (the friend of Titania who mysteriously stands in for the quarrelsome Oberon) and Puck through the miracle of stop-motion photography, shows Puck circling an unrealistically cylindrical but readily recognizable globe, instantaneously endows Bottom with an ass's head onscreen, and incidentally has no trouble dramatizing Helen and Hermia's fight over Demetrius, even though neither contestant is given any words. The result forgoes Shakespeare's language to create a mood as thoroughly Shakespearean as Arthur Rackham's contemporaneous illustrations.

Although few Shakespearean adaptations used sets that suggested either the period in which they were set or Shakespeare's own period, preferring instead outdoor settings whose period could not be pinned down, most of them favored period costumes that further emphasized the respectability of their historical lineage. *A Midsummer Night's Dream* sets its opening scene among some marble columns, suggesting ancient Athens, before moving to the timeless world of the surrounding woods for the rest of the story. Shakespeare remained a popular source for one-reelers throughout the period, even though most of the adaptations necessarily dispensed with the poetry that had won him so many readers.[22] This habit of adapting literary sources notable for a verbal brilliance that silent film could not replicate reached a climax in Ernst Lubitsch's celebrated feature-length adaptation of *Lady Windermere's Fan* (1925), whose polished acting and direction made it a brilliant film despite Lubitsch's decision to cut every one of Oscar Wilde's signature epigrams.

Adapting a literary source did not prevent filmmakers from introducing contemporary social problems. Alice Guy Blaché's *Falling Leaves* (Solax, 1912) mitigated its pathetic central situation, borrowed from O. Henry's 1907 story "The Last Leaf," with a hopeful portrayal of an impending cure for tuberculosis. Biograph, which had produced *The Widow and the Only Man* (1904) only three weeks after its source, Henry's story "Transients in Arcadia," appeared in the *New York Sunday World*, borrowed the "title and some plot elements" for *A Kentucky Feud* (1905) from "a popular melodrama" that capitalized on widespread knowledge of the feud between the Hatfields and the McCoys. The following year Edison mixed the currency of contemporary crime with literary weight in *Kathleen Mavourneen*, whose heroine, kidnapped in period attire, "helped lead to the adaptation of theatrical material that became common in later years."[23] Biograph managed to combine classic and contemporary appeal in *Resurrection* (1909), a "Free Adaptation of Leo Tolstoy's Powerful [1899] Novel."[24]

In general, however, it was less difficult for one-reel adaptations, freely borrowing the conventions of actualités, to portray the problems of modern life than to suggest the heft and respectability of their literary sources. Many of them rose to this challenge by selecting sources that offered the opportunity for spectacular attractions, in Gunning's sense of the term, large-scale set pieces, or iconic apparitions. The first consistently popular source for culturally upscale adaptation, dating back to 1897, was the Passion Play, the dramatic account of Christ's passion and death in a series of episodes that offered the advantages of a familiar story, an instantly recognizable iconography, roots in a long-standing tradition of lantern slide presentations, and a dispensation from narrative continuity, since the source itself was so discontinuous. More than a decade later, adaptations like *Frankenstein* (1910) and *The Wonderful Wizard of Oz* (1910) continue to forgo narrative continuity and psychological development in favor of spectacular iconic tableaux. In doing so, they claim a theatrical rather than a narrative pedigree, implying that the ability to tell a story without parasitic reliance on an established literary source is less important than the ability to stage larger-than-life spectacles more resoundingly than any theatrical adaptation. This focus on epic scale subordinates fidelity to any specific narrative source to a generalized attempt to harness the scale and respectability of literature as an institutional project, a generic cultural text more powerful than any particular text could be. Throughout this period fidelity to a single source takes a backseat to the dual imperatives of implying the cultural scale and weight of literature as such and the need to fill a container of a given thousand-foot length.

The restriction on length could be evaded, of course, by making a film in several parts, as D. W. Griffith did with *His Trust* (1910) and *His Trust Fulfilled* (1910) or the two one-reel segments of *Enoch Arden* (1911). This tendency would become more widespread with the rise of multichapter serial adventures in 1914. Although serials were designed specifically as counterparts to the new feature-length films they introduced, the particular strategies they adopted for suggesting epic weight and breadth are highly suggestive. In confronting a virginal but enterprising heroine with a series of adventures, they bring into conflict the worlds of familiar domestic experience and exotic melodrama. Breaking their story of nonstop threats and dangers into chapters of equal length that replicate the same essential structure, they suggest both one-reel and larger-scale structures, a suggestion made explicit in the Lubin Film Manufacturing Company's advertisement for *The Beloved Adventurer* (1914) as "a series of 15 single reel dramatic pictures, which might be run singly, as released or used on threes and fives as special features."[25] *The Beloved Adventurer,* whose title neatly encapsulates its attempt to link small-scale intimacy with large-scale impressiveness, was, like most serials, based on a literary source—in this case, a series of stories by Emmett Campbell Hall—but one released in book form at the same time as the films, in an early example of a marketing synergy that would become as enduring an intertextual model as fidelity.

Extended serials like *The Adventures of Kathlyn* (1913–14), *The Perils of Pauline* (1914), and *The Exploits of Elaine* (1914) were, in fact, antiepics, each an indefinitely prolonged series of thrilling but reassuringly predictable adventures marketed, like newsreels and the short comedies of Mack Sennett and Charlie Chaplin, as counterweights to the epic features they introduced. By the turn of the decade, comic short subjects from *The Breath of a Nation* (1919) to *The Original Movie* (1922) could adopt an unmistakably satiric or parodic attitude toward the epics against which they were set. *The Frozen North* (1922) takes no longer than its opening title and the shot that follows ("Last stop on the subway," which introduces Buster Keaton emerging from an underground station to a snowy wasteland) to establish its mock-epic credentials.

Films like *The Frozen North* demonstrate that epic scale has little to do with length; it can be established in a single shot, as Chaplin demonstrated three years later in the Chilkroot Pass sequence in *The Gold Rush*. The earliest actualités seek to establish some such largeness of scale by consciously expanding the experience available to their audience. The Lumière brothers' pioneering *Arrival of a Train* (1895), selecting an oblique angle in order to fit its entire subject into the train, placed viewers in the path of a train moving toward them. Hale's Tours, the series of travelogues shot from a moving train and projected in theaters fitted out as railroad cars, simulated the visual appeal of railroad trips for audiences who would never take them. Even such a homely film as the two-minute Edison actualité *New York City "Ghetto" Fish Market* (1903) derives its appeal from a bird's-eye view of an exotic setting most viewers would never experience for themselves.

The allure of the foreign, unusual, or exotic is emphasized by action that is not reducible to motion, as in Edison's *Annie Oakley* and *Bucking Broncho* (both 1894), which feature them in signature exhibitions of skill, demonstrating their marksmanship or fighting to stay on a bucking horse, instead of simply posing for the camera. But the industrial film *Panoramic View, Aisle B,* from the *Westinghouse Works* series (Edison, 1904), creates an epic sense of its quarter-mile manufacturing site not by focusing on individual people, or even groups of people, and their work but through its dramatization of the immense space itself through a single forward crane shot quite as majestic in its way as the corresponding shot in the Babylonian sequence in *Intolerance* (1916).

Instead of expanding an audience's world by recording an exotic locale or activity, short subjects can borrow the cachet of respectability by filming duly sanctified subjects. Zukor's four-reel *Queen Elizabeth* (1912) was successful and influential not only because it was long but because it introduced so many viewers to historical pageantry and Sarah Bernhardt. Cinema could achieve a similar sense of cultural enlargement on a briefer scale by presenting some famous person—Thomas Edison at work in his laboratory, President Coolidge or George Bernard Shaw talking to the camera—or an opera like Griffith's one-reel condensation of *Rigoletto* as *A Fool's Revenge* (Biograph, 1909) or a ballet like Martha Graham's *The Flute of Krishna* (Kodak, 1926).

Within the emerging framework of melodramatic narrative the surest way to imply a larger scale was through contrast. In addition to the dramatic contrast indispensable for melodrama, additional contrasts could be visual (including both interior and exterior shots in order to present a more comprehensive world than one set exclusively indoors or outdoors), scalar (setting the intimate world of private experience against the larger-scale world of public history by using a combination of close-ups and long shots), thematic (creating parallels or crosscutting in order to configure opposing characters as representatives of larger forces), or all three at once. Such parallels could be as simple yet effective as those of Edison's dramatically hand-colored *Three American Beauties* (Edison, 1906), which dissolves from a shot of a rose to a second shot of a young woman to a third and final shot of an American flag.

More extreme examples of conflict or parallelism involve crossing generic, diegetic, or metatextual lines to mix modes. Such mixed modes appear as early as *The "Teddy" Bears* (Edison, 1907), which greatly expands the range of its story of Goldilocks and the three bears by adding two sequences. In the first, Goldilocks looks through a knothole in the bears' wall and sees a row of six stuffed bears animated in stop-action; in the second, at the end of the film, she encounters a hunter who rescues her from the pursuing bears by shooting Papa Bear and Mama Bear but sparing Baby Bear's life in the manner of President Roosevelt. The result is a fairy tale so complicated by elements of surrealistic whimsy and political satire that it refuses closure, since, "thrust into the 'real' world, the term 'bears' abruptly changes its meaning: the droll neighbors revert to mere beasts, cadavers in the snow."[26] Comically mixed modes are the specialty of Winsor McCay and Dave Fleischer, whose films combine live action and animation to suggest a world larger than either one, larger even than the cartoon universe of Fleischer's *Out of the Inkwell* and *Inklings* series (1920–25), which subordinate narrative logic to nonstop visual transformations. The self-reflexivity of Fleischer's cartoons, with their blithe disregard of the conventions of time and space, is echoed in the eighteen live-action two-reel comedies Charley Bowers produced, wrote, and starred in between 1926 and 1928. Bowers's *There It Is* (1928), if it does not exactly suggest epic sweep, still manages to cram a world of surreal threats and outrageous transformations into twenty minutes by eliminating exposition, causality, establishing shots, and logical explanation from its tale of how a Scotland Yard detective and his sidekick, MacGregor, an animated doodlebug who sleeps in a matchbox, investigate strange doings at a haunted house.

A less frivolous example of mixed modes shows just how effective combining genres can be in enlarging the world of the one-reel film. *The Land beyond the Sunset* (Edison, 1912) begins with a shot of Joe (Martin Fuller), a young newshawk, against a blank background, attempting, it seems, to sell papers directly to the audience. A dissolve locates Joe in more orthodox fashion on a busy city street, where the passersby ignore him until a girl gives him a ticket to a charity outing to the beach. The slatternly grandmother with whom Joe lives forbids him to go, but he sneaks off anyway and joins the crowd of children against whom his ragged clothing still makes him an outsider. As the children gather around, one of the adult chaperones reads them the story of the land beyond the sunset, which the film illustrates with a costumed fantasy sequence featuring a menacing witch, a protective fairy, and a dashing hero. After the story the chaperone leads the other children back to their ride home, but Joe lingers behind, wandering along the beach until he finds a rowboat. Pushing off from the shore, he climbs into it and drifts along without rowing until he has left the shore behind. A long, slow dissolve on the boat drifting in the sunset brings the film to its ambiguous end. Although it is never clear whether Joe merely imagines this happy ending, whether he has chosen to escape his harsh world through suicide, or whether he really has broken through the boundaries of his story's conventions, it is clear that the film's haunting effect is incomparably enriched by the three sequences that depart from its general conventions of social realism—the plaintive opening address to the audience, the fantasy sequence illustrating the story, and the poetic final shot—to suggest a world outside those conventions, a land beyond the sunset.

The filmmaker most accomplished in exploring the different kinds of contrasts that enlarged the scope of one-reelers was D. W. Griffith. Griffith is remembered best as a technical innovator and the American director who led the charge from short subjects to features that could independently provide what Richard Koszarski has called an evening's entertainment. Yet it would be more precise and revealing to characterize him as the filmmaker who succeeded most consistently in broadening and deepening the dramatic range of the one-reel films that contained from early on the seeds of Griffith's later features. Beginning with *The Adventures of Dollie* (1908), whose structure of three perilous episodes would have justified the title *Dollie's Busy Day,* Griffith worked to find a middle ground between melodramatic thrillers like *The Lonely Villa* (1909) and morality plays like *The Usurer* (1910). The most strikingly successful of his successes was *A Corner in Wheat* (1909).

*A Corner in Wheat,* announcing itself as "suggested by Frank Norris' 'The Pit,'" is an epic built on an epic. *The Pit* (1902), the second novel in a projected trilogy, *The Epic of the Wheat,* left unfinished by Norris's early death, was a sequel to *The Octopus* (1901), which traced the battle between the monopoly of the railroad company that owned the land on which wheat was raised and the California farmers fighting to control the crops they raised.[27] *The Pit* moved to Chicago and dropped all the characters of *The Octopus* except "the Wheat" to tell the story of Curtis Jadwin, a speculator whose obsession with cornering the global wheat market destroys him and many others. The connections among the two novels and their unwritten sequel, *The Wolf,* thus involve a high degree of abstraction already indicated in Griffith by his film's complicated lineage. It borrows the central contrast between the conspicuous consumption of the rich and the starvation of the masses they impoverish from *The Pit* and its short-story predecessor, "A Deal in Wheat" (published posthumously in 1903). But it piles epic on epic in borrowing its crosscutting between an opulent dinner and the starving masses from book 2, chapter 8 of *The Octopus,* where Norris moves back and forth between a dinner given by the magnate Gerard and the last hours of Mrs. Hooven, dispossessed of her farm by Gerard's railroad, and its climactic sequence of the Wheat King's horrific death in a grain elevator from the following chapter of *The Octopus,* in which the victim is the railroad representative S. Behrman.[28]

Griffith's film, in effect, completes Norris's unfinished trilogy by juxtaposing three groups of people: the producers of wheat from *The Octopus,* the distributors of the wheat from *The Pit,* and the consumers of the wheat from *The Wolf.* It intercuts the story of the Wheat King, killed just after he triumphantly corners the wheat market by being buried beneath the commodity he has vainly sought to control, with vignettes from the lives of wheat farmers and bread buyers equally impoverished by the Wheat King's manipulation of the market. As Tom Gunning has shown, the absence of any characters or settings that continue from any one of these three threads to another, or even any clear sense of their spatial or temporal relations, produces "cutting patterns . . . more radical and . . . relations between shots more abstract. . . . We see a series of disparate scenes of American life, brought together only by their economic relation."[29] The result, as a reviewer in the *New York Dramatic Mirror* recognized on the film's first release, is "not a picture drama" but "an argument, an editorial, an essay on a subject of deep interest to all."[30]

Gunning is surely correct in concluding that "parallel editing becomes in this film a form of economic analysis, linking elements in an economic chain dispersed in time and space."[31] Yet much of the work of rhetorical analysis and generalization is done by intertitles that render individual scenes intelligible ("The Wheat King/Engineering the Great Corner" for the film's third shot, showing a businessman arising from a telephone to bark orders to a group of underlings in suits), establish ironic contrasts between successive scenes ("The Gold of the Wheat," introducing the Wheat King's banquet, is followed by "The Chaff of the Wheat," introducing a bakery whose doubled costs for bread price poor customers out of the market), and point ironies ("In the Wheat Pit/The Final Threshing," a process that involves not literal threshing but the Wheat King's mad scramble on the floor of the stock exchange for control of wheat futures). All these rhetorical devices underline the central irony of the film's visuals: the contrast between the lively movement of excited crowds in the Wheat King's world and the extremely slow movement in the worlds he has impoverished, reaching such an extreme in the shot of an unmoving breadline at the baker's that many viewers mistake this shot for a freeze-frame. The figures who move the most are doing the least; the ones whose movement is most important scarcely move at all.

The climax of this contrast, and the one that best establishes the film's epic credentials, is between the death of the Wheat King, buried by the senseless and irresistible movement of the wheat, and the film's final shot, which echoes its second shot, with important differences. The film had begun with a sequence showing a small group of wheat farmers sowing grain by hand in a broad field. In the final shot two of the farmers and a horse-drawn harrow have disappeared without explanation; only one man remains to walk slowly toward the camera in an obvious allusion to Millet's painting *The Sower*, hesitate in the foreground as if uncertain whether to go on, and then turn and continue as a long fadeout "eternalizes the image, fixing it as an emblem for the film."[32]

*A Corner in Wheat* succeeds as a one-reel epic by borrowing images and actions selectively from an ambitious trilogy; reducing the central premise of that trilogy, already highly abstract in its view of human relations, to its bare essentials; organizing its images, intertitles, and leading action around a series of thematic contrasts; and being even more willing than Norris to subordinate narrative causality and narrative tropes to rhetorical argument and figuration. Except for the Wheat King, the film includes not one figure who could truly be called a character, and the narrative links in its main story—the Wheat King celebrates his triumph by taking his friends on a visit to a grain elevator, where he slips and falls to his death—are nearly as casual as in the two thematically contrasting stories.

Several less obvious one-reel epics borrow techniques Griffith had developed for *A Corner in Wheat* to convey their own sense of epic scale. In a series of Civil War shorts in 1910 and 1911, for example, Griffith not only laid the groundwork for *The Birth of a Nation* (1915) but developed a formula that endowed melodrama with deeper thematic significance. These films provide textbook examples of how to use the cachet of history rather than literature to imply epic scale within twelve minutes. The choice of the war as the background for so many of Griffith's Biograph melodramas provides films like *Swords and Hearts* and *The Battle* (both 1911) not only with historical gravitas but with an established background conflict and the material for all the moral complexity viewers could wish. These films consistently explore a series of conflicts that begins with spatial contrast. *In the Border States, The House with Closed Shutters,* and *The Fugitive* (all 1910) begin with departure scenes that move from intimate interior settings, in which the newly enlisted soldiers bid farewell to their families and sweethearts, to bustling exterior spectacles just outside, in which the soldiers join a parade marching past their house and are filmed in long shot before a picturesque natural tableau that remains after the last remnants of the parade have passed.[33] These spatial contrasts lay the groundwork for thematic contrasts to come. Griffith sets the Union against the Confederacy, of course, but also systematically opposes women's domestic sphere to the public battlefield and proceeds to climaxes that encourage the heroes to transcend their partisan loyalties in the interests of a universalist humanism seeking a common ground between the two sides. *In the Border States* repays a young Union girl who hides a wounded Confederate soldier from pursuit by Union troops by showing his refusal later on to seize her father's sensitive papers, leading her to offer him the handshake she had refused when he was a fugitive. The more exuberant opening sequence of *The House with Closed Shutters,* which substitutes a toast and an enthusiastically unfurled flag for the family prayer of *In the Bor-*

*der States,* is the prelude to its hero's contrasting cowardice when he flees the battlefield to hide in his mother's house. After his sister takes the field and is killed in his uniform, his mother protects the family honor by pretending that he has died and his sister is ill, hiding him from all eyes and keeping the sister's faithful suitor at bay until all the principals are old and gray. Most programmatic of all in its universalism is *The Fugitive,* which begins with a pair of contrasting departure scenes for Confederate and Union soldiers both named John and then shows the wounded Union John killing the Confederate John and taking refuge with his victim's mother. When she learns the identity of the fugitive, the mother is tempted to betray him to the rebel army, but, as an intertitle announces, "She thinks of another mother awaiting a son's return" and keeps her visitor safe until he departs. In a final transcendent gesture she places the sprig of flowers he has given her on the uniform of the son he killed.

   *The Country Doctor* (1909) shows Griffith's ability to create this sense of spacious universality in a modern setting that does not depend on the War between the States. Like Griffith's Civil War one-reelers, the film's narrative premise is no more than an anecdote. Dr. Harcourt's daughter, Edith, falls seriously ill, presumably of diphtheria, just as a poor neighboring girl is stricken. Reluctant to leave his ailing daughter, the doctor eventually accedes to the pleas of the other girl's mother, goes to her bedside, and performs an emergency procedure that saves her life. When he returns home, however, he discovers that Edith has died in her mother's arms. What makes the film affecting beyond its pathetic story is Griffith's staging of the action. The film is long for a one-reeler, and Griffith parcels out the fourteen minutes of its running time in unusual ways. The film begins with two intertitles. The first—"A story of the temporal deeds that reap spiritual reward"—pointedly advances a thematic generalization about the action to come, and the second—"The peaceful valley of Stillwater"—suggests through its metaphorical choice of place name and adjective, both unnecessary to clarify or advance the story, a further figurative frame. The shot that immediately follows is an extraordinary pan lasting nearly a minute from a vista across an untroubled lake along a stone wall through a grove of trees to the front door of Dr. Harcourt's house, from which the doctor (Frank Powell), his wife (Florence Lawrence), and Edith (Gladys Egan) have just emerged hand in hand. Their palpable sense of joy and contentment is deepened by the following two shots. First Griffith presents a field of wheat through which viewers can gradually glimpse the family playfully appearing; then he shows them strolling through a field of flowers, from which Edith plucks one for her father and another for her mother. This three-shot prologue to the story runs so long—nearly three and a half minutes, a quarter of the entire film—that viewers given no significant action to watch are left with only tableaux of the family itself. The result is to leave viewers with a thematic sense of the loving family values the Harcourts incarnate and a strong rooting interest in their well-being.

When disaster strikes in the form of Edith's illness, Griffith shows Dr. Harcourt, entering to Edith's sickbed, jovially pooh-poohing his wife's concern until he realizes how ill his daughter is. Everything about the shot—the bars that form Edith's bed rails, the blank window behind it, the flat blocking—emphasizes a severe two-dimensionality contrasting with the dramatic depth and movement of the natural world outdoors. Griffith blocks the other girl's sickbed almost identically. Her bed is slightly farther to the right, and a shade is partly drawn over the paneled window, but bed, window, door, and human figures are assigned almost identical places in the frame. As Griffith begins to emphasize the conflict raging within the doctor—shall he stay with his beloved daughter or attend the other girl? shall he stay with his new patient or respond to the frantic pleas his maid makes on behalf of his wife?—he uses thematically insistent title cards ("Duty beckons him on," "His duty fulfilled") and cuts back and forth in accelerated rhythm between the two interiors, just as he does in melodramatic chase films like *The Lonely Villa*. Now, however, the lack of visual contrast between the two scenes and the even more emphatic lack of movement in either one subordinate their differences to their similarities and emphasize the doctor's moral dilemma rather than any physical action. In effect, Griffith spends most of the film showing the doctor divided almost to the point of paralysis and the characters doing nothing but celebrating life or fearing its departure. In the longest shot in the film the doctor returns to his home, discovers that his daughter has died, sinks into grief and despair, then turns to embrace his grieving wife. But this seventy-two-second shot, containing so little physical action but so much pathos and psychological intensity, is little longer than the film's opening pan, which is echoed in a pan left from the now-closed door of the house back past the trees and wall and lake to the original framing. This final shot, which "has the effect of generality, of quite literal distance, from which the drama is extracted as a particular,"[34] is introduced by a final title: "And the valley of Stillwater is shrouded in darkness." This unusually deliberate thematic frame insists that Harcourt is not just an unfortunate doctor, by turns unselfish and condescending,[35] but that he is Everyman whose loss of Every-family the film encapsulates both through this final repetition and through the pointed omission of any reference to the film's second and third shots, which showed the Harcourts at play in a natural paradise to which they can never return.

Griffith's sensitivity and skill in teasing larger significance from intimate anecdotes of action or suffering made him an eminently logical adapter of literary texts in the name of an aesthetic he virtually paraphrased from Joseph Conrad: "The task I'm trying to achieve is above all to make you see."[36] But two complications arise here. Griffith, unlike Conrad, was not trying to make viewers see. The visual medium, which supplied the images novelists like Conrad had to work so hard to evoke, made seeing all too easy. Instead, Griffith was trying to create images that would make his viewers think and feel. Moreover, several of the techniques that made his Biograph shorts seem elemental, novelistic, or thematically powerful were ironically unavailable to him as an adapter. He could not simultaneously follow a literary source and exploit spatial, thematic, or generic contrasts unless those contrasts appeared in the source itself. Certainly metafictional experiments like those of Dave Fleischer and Charley Bowers were well beyond the scope of any Griffith adaptation, even had the director been inclined in that direction.[37]

In *The Sealed Room* (1909) the possibilities of visual contrast are drastically limited by the nature of the story, which, as an opening credit announces, is "Inspired by the Haunting Works of Edgar Allan Poe and Honoré de Balzac." The haunting works in question are presumably "The Cask of Amontillado" and "La Grande Brêteche," both of which involve characters walling their enemies alive in closed rooms that become their tombs. But Griffith's story concerns neither a man who chains his old enemy in the catacombs beneath his house nor a husband who walls his wife's lover in her closet over her screaming protests but rather a king who entombs both his queen and her lover in a dovecote he has built for her. An equally plausible inspiration might have been *Aida,* more recent than the stories of Poe and Balzac, which also ends with a heartrending tableau of entombed lovers suffocating together. Clearly Griffith's goal is not fidelity to a particular source but the assumption to a literary mantle of prestige for his simple story for the same reason he gives his story greater weight by setting it in an unspecified historical period.[38]

The story is unusually simple in its visuals because its twenty shots involve only three camera setups, two interiors outside the dovecote and one inside. The lack of visual contrast appropriate to such a claustrophobic narrative poses the challenge of bringing contrast to the story. Griffith rises to this challenge through his blocking and his direction of the performers. At first the queen and the musician exchange flirtatious glances from opposite sides of a screen crowded with courtiers and ladies in waiting, moving to embrace each other only after a general exodus. Later, as the lovers adjourn unsuspectingly to the dovecote, Griffith cuts back and forth between shots of them reclining in the lower half of the frame, the only door on screen right, and shots of the king standing above them outside, with the door on screen left. Only a silent film could get away with the premise that the besotted lovers do not hear the king's return, even in the shot in which he looks in on them; his orders to the workers just outside the curtain; or especially the sounds of the stone wall being built as they wait for the sand to run through an offscreen hourglass and warn them of the king's expected return. As in *The Country Doctor*, Griffith minimizes physical action while the wall is being built, concealing its construction from the lovers by the curtain and from the audience by the workers' bodies, even though it is the sole physical action of any consequence in the film. Instead, he emphasizes the psychological tension of the king's first suspicion of the lovers, as he intercepts their glance halfway through a shot running nearly three minutes that ends just halfway through the film. This movement away from physical motion toward psychological drama is developed by understating the contrast between the workers under the king's direction hardly seeming to move as they methodically add stones to the imprisoning wall and the lovers inside playing with a garland of flowers while hardly moving their own bodies. When the lovers finally discover their peril, their acting, like the king's own, becomes considerably more histrionic. As he exults outside the wall, they rush around the confining room, throwing themselves against the wall, tearing down the curtains, pointing accusations at each other, and eventually collapsing in a heap, where the musician, in his dying breath, uses his lute to fan the queen.

These tactics work to generalize the film's anecdote of transgression and punishment within a strict economy of visual contrast. The historically remote but indeterminate setting, balanced by the small number of camera setups, removes the film from the realm of the present and emphasizes the story's elemental nature. The lack of scenic interest, accentuated by the remorseless cutting back and forth between two visually similar spaces representing life and death, intensifies this elemental sense. To an unusual extent the film is about space: the space between the lovers on either side of a frame filled with potentially deadly witnesses, the ironically contiguous but unbridgeable spaces of the dovecote and the public chamber outside, the contrast between the closed space the lovers take to be their safe refuge and the barely glimpsed action that is swiftly making that space into their tomb, the offscreen spaces indicated in every shot of the film's second half by the doorway from one room to the next and even by the offscreen hourglass that counts down the lovers' last minutes. All of these spatial metaphors revolve around the film's central contrast between the open space of public action and the closed space of sin and death. The film aims for thematic generalization not by inflating its anecdote but by insistently reducing it to its most essential terms.

Repetition rather than contrast is even more essential to the effect of *The Unchanging Sea* (1910), the third of Griffith's four treatments of a story best remembered from Tennyson's poem "Enoch Arden" (1864): a woman whose husband, presumed lost at sea, returns many years later.[39] The film, as its opening intertitle acknowledges, is based more immediately on another source: "Suggested by Charles Kingsley's poem 'The Three Fishers.'" "Suggested" is a judicious choice of words, for the twenty-one-line poem contains only hints of narrative, which the film freely develops and extends. Griffith directly quotes four passages constituting some two-thirds of the poem in the intertitles punctuating its first half. The last of these, in which the final three lines of the poem appear between two shots of the foreign strand on which the hero is cast, suggests the flavor and function of them all:

> For men must work and women must weep,
> And the sooner it's over the sooner to sleep,
> And good-bye to the bar and its moaning.

Despite its conscientiousness in quoting from Kingsley, the film departs from the poem in focusing on a particular husband and wife rather than a group of three couples, in cutting back and forth repeatedly between the separated couple, and in providing its leads with an unlikely reunion never hinted in Kingsley. Its interest, like that of most short silent adaptations, is less in reproducing its nominal original's narrative than in invoking the sense of spaciousness, scope, and seriousness associated with literature.

*The Unchanging Sea* tells its story of long separation and unlikely reunion through thirty shots and fourteen titles, using only six camera setups, all exteriors. Griffith suggests the passage of time almost entirely through the ways he repeats three of these setups: the opening shot outside a row of houses from which the fisherman hero and his wife emerge; the second shot, in which the two play on the shore (a seaside analogy to the second and third shots of *The Country Doctor*); and the sixth shot, a closer shot of the shore that shows the fishers casting off. Not surprisingly, he uses repetitions of the second and sixth shots to emphasize the pathos of the hero's departure, his wife waving forlornly long after his boat casts off; her obsessive return to the place to ask a lookout if there has been any sign of him; her rejection years later of a proposal from another fisher as her young daughter runs lightheartedly in the background; her daughter's more successful wooing by a neighboring boy; and the amnesiac hero's landing in his initially unrecognized homeland many years later. In each case the sea provides a reminder of the hero's absence, establishes an ever-changing yet never-changing background to different foreground actions, and roots all these actions in the timeless rhythms of nature.

Surprisingly, Griffith returns to the opening setup even more frequently. At first the row of houses functions merely as background for the couple's entrance and return from their playful walk. After the intertitle "Out to Sea," however, its immediate repetition, almost as if the title had interrupted a continuously running shot, suggests that the title itself marks a passage of time in contrast to the unchanged background. The visual stability of the mise-en-scène becomes increasingly ironic and pathetic when the wife stands in front of the houses holding a baby (shot 14), who reappears in shot 17, following the title "Years roll by," as a child, and then, after the title "Their child grown," as a young woman (shot 20). Most affecting of all is a pair of scenes in which a young man who has bumped into the couple on the beach follows them home, waits outside (shot 22), and is rewarded in shot 26, when he and the daughter, in bridal clothing, bid farewell to the lonely heroine. If the shots set against the sea evoke a context of natural rhythms, these shots before the long-separated couple's home root their separation in a context of continuing life-cycle events against which that separation is delicately measured.

Griffith's distinctive approach to adaptation in his one-reel films is best indicated by comparing *The Unchanging Sea* to *Enoch Arden* (1911). Although Griffith directed the latter film only two years later, its attitude toward its original is vastly different. Because a two-reeler like *Enoch Arden* did not have to imply epic scope by programmatic spatial contrasts or repetitions, Griffith could be more forthright in his epic aspirations in this tale of Annie Lee, torn between loyalty to Enoch Arden, the husband she mistakenly thinks dead, and his longtime rival Philip Ray, her former suitor. Like the earlier film, *Enoch Arden* quotes its source in intertitles, but now the quotations function less like static set pieces that stabilize and moralize the action of the film and more like illustrative allusions to specific telling lines: "Philip looked, and in their eyes and faces read his doom"; "He slipt aside, and like a wounded life crept down into the hollows of the wood"; "Ev'n to the last dip of the vanishing sail, she watches it, and departed weeping for him." The past tense, faithfully copied from Tennyson, contrasts jarringly with the present tense of new intertitles like "Verging on despair, Enoch embraces an opportunity to recoup his fortunes," an inconsistency reproduced in the third of the quoted passages from Tennyson, which changes the tense of one of Tennyson's verbs ("watches") but not the other ("departed").

Its treatment of its nominal source (an opening intertitle describes the film as "From the Poem by Alfred Lord Tennyson") as supplying material for the film's narrative and imagery rather than a necessary magnifying or moralizing force is not the only way *Enoch Arden* departs from Griffith's one-reel adaptations and looks forward to more familiar trends in adaptation. Griffith's decision to present his story in many more shots, and many more unrepeated shots, than *The Unchanging Sea* means that the film depends less on motivic contrast and repetition. When the supposedly widowed Annie accepts Philip's marriage proposal on the very same rocky shore where he had earlier wooed her unsuccessfully, the visual repetition of background and blocking is doubly powerful for its rarity.

*Enoch Arden* retains improbable remnants of Griffith's earlier interest in the race against time. Crosscutting between the shipwrecked Enoch and the frantic Annie, he shows Enoch failing to attract the attention of a passing ship just before Philip presses his long-rejected suit and intercuts a shot of Annie fully accepting her new husband's love as Enoch is boarding the ship that will finally bring him home. On the whole, however, the film is less interested in either the suspenseful chases of Griffith's melodramas or the typological patterning of the unnamed principals in *The Sealed Room* and *The Unchanging Sea* than in psychological development of more particularized characters. If *The Unchanging Sea* is a study in constancy maintained against the vicissitudes of time and space, *Enoch Arden* features no less than four episodes in which characters change their minds in crucial ways. First Annie, who has been shown in close conversation with Philip—a scene with no precedent in Tennyson—accepts Enoch as her suitor. Then Enoch, who, unlike Tennyson's hero, is not clearly bred to sea, decides to accept a berth to retrieve his fortunes and must break the news to his unhappy wife. Years after Enoch vanishes, Philip, following Tennyson, persuades Annie to accept his help for her children and, eventually, his hand in marriage. In a distinct final change on her part, Annie accepts her new husband as a worthy successor to the absent figure who has continued to shadow her life (cf. Tennyson, lines 509–22). These changes, which actually extend Tennyson's interest in the characters' development, are complemented by a final change from *The Unchanging Sea:* the restoration of the poet's original ending, in which Enoch returns after many years to find the wife who spent so long awaiting his return finally and happily settled with a new husband and a new baby to complete the family of his now grown children by replacing his own baby, who died soon after birth. As in Tennyson, Griffith's Enoch slips away from the domestic scene he has glimpsed through the window, returns to the gossipy neighbor who has told him of his wife's remarriage, takes to his bed, and dies in an act of final renunciation.

Griffith's one-reel epics work through quite different means. Instead of seeking to follow the narrative curve of their literary originals, they reduce those originals to their thematic essence or create a thematic nexus that implies something of the scale or prestige of a literary original. Beneath their constant moralizing is the more general aesthetic moral that small can be beautiful. Limericks may have less cultural prestige than novels, but that is not simply because they are shorter; haikus manage to be shorter still without any loss of prestige because their very brevity implies a radical figurative compression rather than the limerick's naughty wit. Nor does the sense of epic scale necessarily depend on a literary source, since cinema can create an epic sense of space and scale or invoke in general terms the aesthetics, the conventions, and the prestige of literary culture without adapting any particular literary source. Griffith one-reelers like *A Corner in Wheat, The Country Doctor,* and *The Unchanging Sea* bypass the nineteenth-century novelistic tradition of exhaustively catalogued social and psychological realism. When they cannot achieve the scope of epic poetry, they create their own brand of cinematic haiku.

# CHAPTER THREE

# The Word Made Film

Long before its release on Ash Wednesday 2004, *The Passion of the Christ*, Mel Gibson's story of the final days of Jesus Christ, had already generated the kind of publicity most filmmakers can only dream about. "Inadvertently," Gibson told Peter J. Boyer in the *New Yorker*, "all the problems and the conflicts and stuff—this is some of the best marketing and publicity I have ever seen."[1] At the heart of all the problems and the conflicts and stuff were widespread accusations that viewing the film could fuel anti-Semitism, especially because of its implication of Jewish leaders and a Jewish mob in the crucifixion of Jesus on the orders of the Roman procurator Pontius Pilate. Controversy particularly swirled around Gibson's use of a speech by the high priest Caiaphas after Pilate condemns Jesus to death but then washes his hands, publicly disclaiming any responsibility for his execution: "His blood be upon us, and upon our children"—a transparent device for fixing the guilt for Jesus's death on the Jewish community that Gibson shot in Aramaic for his rough cut, removed from a later cut, then restored to release prints without providing an English subtitle translating it.

Speaking to Boyer six months before the film's release, Gibson defended the speech and regretted removing it from the film under pressure from Abraham Foxman, head of the Anti-Defamation League, and others. "I wanted it in. My brother said I was wimping out if I didn't include it. It happened; it was said. But, man, if I included that in there, they'd be coming after me in my house, they'd come kill me."[2] The warrant for Gibson's assurance that it happened is the Gospel according to St. Matthew, which alone of the four Gospels includes the line, though ascribing it not to Caiaphas but, in the Authorized Version, to "all the people" (Mt 27:25). This literal fidelity to Matthew has led commentators like Steven Waldman to conclude that if Gibson's film is anti-Semitic, that is only because Matthew's record itself is. "Jews should admit that some of their forefathers probably helped get Jesus killed," Waldman, writing for *Slate*, admonishes, adding, however, that "there is a strong possibility that the Bible itself, in effect, distorted the history of the 'Jewish' role. . . . The New Testament either gave Jews a bum rap or, at minimum, was written in a way that left it highly susceptible to misuse."[3]

Does following Matthew, even if he tones his source down by transferring the offending speech from "all the people" to a single high priest, provide adequate cover for Gibson? Or is it true, as a group of ecumenical Catholic scholars have argued, that "one cannot assume that by simply conforming to the New Testament, that antisemitism will not be promoted"?[4] Invited to comment on the doctrinal controversy, film scholar Jeanine Basinger agreed with this group that religious films as different as Martin Scorsese's *The Last Temptation of Christ* (1988) and Kevin Smith's *Dogma* (1999) have often aroused controversy, but she offered another perspective, subordinating religious doctrine to entertainment: "People have an entertainment experience, not a religious experience, at the movies. People who go to this movie will be going to a Mel Gibson movie."[5]

The controversy surrounding Gibson's film raises three general questions about filmed lives of Jesus that it brings into unusually sharp focus: What is the relation between inspiration ("a religious experience") and mass entertainment? How does Scripture focus problems of fidelity more urgently than any other precursor text filmmakers could possibly choose to adapt? And what does it mean to make a film that is faithful to the Gospels? Reviewing the ways earlier movies based on the life of Christ deal with these questions provides a firmer basis for assessing the claims Gibson and his critics have made about *The Passion of the Christ.*

Since most commentators would probably agree with Basinger that entertainment and inspiration rarely coincide as goals for filmmakers, it might seem especially challenging for an entertainment text, in this case a movie designed to entertain enough people to recoup its investment and return a profit, to be faithful to a text designed originally to win people to the way of Christ. The simplest strategy for encompassing both these goals is to emphasize exactly those elements in the original that are most likely to attract a contemporary audience, whatever that audience may want, from the reverentially static tableaux of Sidney Olcott's *From the Manger to the Cross* (1912) to the exoticism of Cecil B. DeMille's *The King of Kings* (1927) to the widescreen spectacle of Nicholas Ray's *King of Kings* (1961) and George Stevens's aptly named *The Greatest Story Ever Told* (1965) to the harsh neorealism of Pier Paolo Pasolini's *The Gospel according to St. Matthew* (1964) to something like the unrelenting violence of Gibson's *Braveheart* (1995) in *The Passion*.[6] Apart from Franco Zeffirelli's six-hour *Jesus of Nazareth* (1977), most filmed versions of the Gospels spend little time on Jesus the preacher and storyteller—the Sermon on the Mount from Matthew 5 through 7 is typically compressed to a few choice aphorisms—and not much more on Jesus the healer and worker of miracles. Every filmed life of Christ includes a selection of obligatory scenes. But those scenes, surprisingly, do not include Jesus's miraculous multiplication of the loaves and fishes (Mt 14:13–21; Mk 6:34–44; Lk 9:12–17; Jn 6:1–15), the Transfiguration (Mk 9:1–8; Lk 9:28–36), the parables of the Good Samaritan (Lk 10:25–37) or the Prodigal Son (Lk 15:11–32), the meeting with the Samaritan woman (Jn 4:1–42), the debate over his healing of the blind man (Jn 9:1–41), or even necessarily the resurrection. The scenes most likely to be chosen—the Nativity, the adoration of the Magi, the baptism, the temptation in the desert, the calling of the apostles, the beheading of John the Baptist, the raising of Lazarus from the dead, the prophecies of Jesus's suffering and death, the triumphal entry into Jerusalem, the cleansing of the Temple, the Last Supper, the denial of Peter, the Crucifixion—are those that are most dramatic, most readily compressed, most easily visualized, least preachy, and least likely to bore or offend contemporary audiences.

It is rarely enough, however, simply to select judiciously from the Gospels; any movie with a hope of attracting a large audience must improve them. Virtually all filmed lives of Christ, for example, assign much more prominent roles to Mary Magdalene and Judas Iscariot than the Gospels do. Norman Jewison's *Jesus Christ Superstar* (1973) and Scorsese's *The Last Temptation of Christ*, preparing the ground for Jesus's controversial postcrucifixion marriage to

Mary Magdalene in Dan Brown's best-selling novel *The Da Vinci Code* (2003), envision an intimate relationship between Jesus and Mary Magdalene; and Andrew Lloyd Webber's Judas gets nearly as many songs, nearly as much screen time, and nearly as much opportunity for high drama as the superstar against whom he struggles. *The Greatest Story Ever Told* inflates the raising of Lazarus, already a clear harbinger of Jesus's resurrection in John's Gospel, into a spectacular set piece, complete with Handel's "Hallelujah Chorus," that sets the stage for the intermission. And virtually all Hollywood tellings of the life of Christ revel in all-star casts, from the muscular Baptists of Robert Ryan in *King of Kings* and Charlton Heston in *The Greatest Story Ever Told* to the awe-inspiring cast of *Jesus of Nazareth:* Rod Steiger, Anne Bancroft, James Earl Jones, James Mason, Anthony Quinn, Peter Ustinov, Laurence Olivier, Christopher Plummer, Donald Pleasance, Ian McShane, Ernest Borgnine, Valentina Cortese, Stacy Keach—right down to the fatally overinspired casting of John Wayne, chosen to deliver exactly one line as the Centurion in *The Greatest Story Ever Told:* "Truly this man was the Son of God."

More generally, none of the Gospels excels as narrative. Matthew and Mark are especially episodic and halting in their forward movement. Film adaptations, rejecting the way biblical hermeneutics roots the unity of the texts in "the spirit of the author" or "the consciousness of Jesus,"[7] approach this problem in one of two opposing ways. *From the Manger to the Cross,* the Nazarene sections of D. W. Griffith's *Intolerance* (1916), and Pasolini's *Gospel according to St. Matthew* are organized as illustrations rather than retellings of the Gospel story, which they count on to provide a narrative armature for their versions. For much of its running time, *From the Manger to the Cross* alternates explicitly marked scriptural intertitles ("She brought forth her firstborn son," "Fear not, for I bring you tidings of great joy," etc.), with single shots illustrating them. As in *Uncle Tom's Cabin* (1903), every shot is a tableau; there are no background shots or merely expository shots, and few sequences that establish narrative relations among successive shots. The effect is like watching a slide show with moving pictures instead of frozen slides; it is only the audience's knowledge of the story, not the images or the intertitles, that supplies the narrative continuity. The same is true for the Nazarene section of *Intolerance,* which alone of the four sections of Griffith's monumental epic alludes to a story rather than recounting it, relying once more on the audience's knowledge to supply the continuity between episodes in Jesus's Passion and death that would otherwise be incomprehensible. Most curious of all is Pasolini's film, made long after the rules of continuity editing had become standardized but still persistently relying on viewers to supply expository information it withholds, as in the audacious opening, in which Pasolini cuts from paired medium close-ups of a grave woman and man looking almost directly into the camera (and apparently at each other) to a midshot revealing that the woman is pregnant before a full shot shows the man walking abruptly away, identifying the couple as Mary and Joseph. Pasolini's handling of the slaughter of the innocents, Herodias's preparation of Salome for her dance before Herod Antipas, and even the Crucifixion is equally elliptical, depending on the audience's familiarity with episodes for which the film declines to supply any explanation.

Most Hollywood adaptations, however, take the opposite tack by heightening narrative elements in the Gospels and pruning nonnarrative material. *Jesus Christ Superstar* achieves impressive dramatic compression by jettisoning Jesus's entire life before his final entry into Jerusalem. But even adaptations that strive for greater fidelity emphasize this final week of Jesus's life, so rich in narrative connections and reversals, over his earlier years, even the three years of preaching and healing the Gospels document relatively thoroughly. Such adaptations do everything they can to root the events of this final week in his earlier life. *King of Kings* not only provides an elaborate backstory for Barabbas, the insurrectionist and murderer Pilate releases to the crowd instead of Jesus, that makes him and his henchman Judas into Jesus's militaristic/revolutionary doubles, but also invents the character of Lucius Catanus, a Roman centurion who tracks Jesus's life from his boyhood to his death, when he accepts him as savior at the foot of the cross.

Additions, selections, rearrangements, and transformations like these, which clearly foster entertainment values at the cost of fidelity to the sacred source texts, seem to illustrate the dichotomy Basinger constructs between religious experience and entertainment experience. And the gap between entertainment and inspiration is evidently widened still further by the uniquely uncompromising nature of the scriptural demand for fidelity raised by my second question. As Erich Auerbach has put it in contrasting the severe, uncompromising style of Genesis 22, filled with lacunae and shrouded in mystery, with the beguiling, discursive style of Homer, filled with endless explanations and descriptive details:

> The Bible's claim to truth is not only more urgent than Homer's, it is tyrannical—it excludes all other claims. The world of the Scripture stories is not satis-

fied with claiming to be a historically true reality—it insists that it is the only real world, is destined for autocracy. All other scenes, issues, and ordinances have no right to exist independently of it, and it is promised that all of them, the history of all mankind, will be given their due place within its frame, will be subordinated to it. The Scripture stories do not, like Homer's, court our favor, they do not flatter us that they may please and enchant us—they seek to subject us, and if we refuse to be subjected we are rebels.[8]

Mikhail Bakhtin has given an even more central place in his theory of the novel to the parallel distinction between "authoritative discourse," which, like Scripture, "demands that we acknowledge it" and "binds us, quite independent of any power it might have to persuade us internally," and "internally persuasive discourse" like that of novels—protean, marked by echoes and parodies of multiple voices, inviting playfulness rather than unquestioning loyalty, and "affirmed through assimilation, tightly interwoven with 'one's own word.'"[9] In these formulations Homer and Dostoevsky play Hollywood to Scripture's demand for fidelity, a demand that extends far beyond the literal fidelity a secular writer like Jane Austen could ask of her adapters. The worst that can happen to a screenwriter who is unfaithful to *Pride and Prejudice* is to be associated with a flop and to get flamed by the Austen listserv; the worst that can happen to an unfaithful adapter of Scripture is accusations of heresy or blasphemy (though these are still a healthy step up from getting tortured by the Inquisition).

For Auerbach and Bakhtin scriptural texts are the model for all texts seeking to exercise unquestioned authority rather than an invitation to playfully creative adaptation or an assimilation to new language or new media. They therefore pose unique problems to anyone with the temerity to adapt them to film, however reverent and non-entertaining the adaptation might seek to be. The Gospels compound this problem further by presenting four narratives of Jesus's ministry, each of which presents itself as the unvarnished truth. Although the Gospels agree on many subjects and incidents, they diverge on many others, leaving adapters the problem of wrestling with the resulting inconsistencies. What were Jesus's last words on the cross? In Matthew and Mark he quotes Psalm 22—"My God, my God, why hast thou forsaken me?" and then cries out again "with a loud voice" (Mt 27:46, 50; Mk 15:34, 37). In Luke he says, "Into your hands I commend my spirit" (Lk 23:46). In John, having bidden his mother, Mary, and his disciple John to become mother and son to each other, he says, "I thirst," and then, after receiving a sponge soaked in vinegar, adds, "It is finished" ( Jn 19:28, 30). Most adaptations allow him to deliver all these speeches, usually saving Luke for last. In *Jesus Christ Superstar* he delivers them in such rapid succession that he sounds disconcertingly chatty.

Clearly, this sort of blanket or additive fidelity could never be sustained for an entire film. The alternative is to pick and choose, as Gibson does in deciding that since Matthew reported the speech, "His blood be upon us, and upon our children," it must be true. Pasolini, practically alone among filmmakers approaching the subject, sticks entirely to a single Gospel; other filmmakers usually emphasize elements common to all four narratives but pause to include scenes like the Nativity, which occurs only in Luke, or the raising of Lazarus, which occurs only in John. In effect, the films hedge their bets by using the different Gospels as checks on each other's authenticity. The same strategy is behind the frequent choice of Middle Eastern locations for the filming ("filmed on the actual locations" is a common publicity claim of scriptural adaptations), implying that whatever its fidelity to the story of Jesus's life, the film at hand will at least have the benefit of a faithful mise-en-scène.

But picking and choosing among competing Gospels or filming on location is far from the most important way filmed lives of Christ hedge their bets. Franco Zeffirelli indicates a more serious problem when he recalls television producer Lew Grade's insistence that each segment of *Jesus of Nazareth* had to "satisfy an international audience with very different conceptions of their 'Lord.' Lew Grade was emphatic that the films should be acceptable to all denominations."[10] As the basis for a narrative that would be coherent and playable, even to unbelievers, without giving offense to any religious group, Zeffirelli shunned modern biblical locations as too much changed, preferring instead to film in the relatively unspoiled landscapes of northern Africa, and used as his basis a screenplay by Anthony Burgess that "had obviously drawn on a wealth of sources, Biblical and Rabbinical, to weld the sometimes patchy history that the apostles have left us into a homogeneous story."[11] The broad implication of this summary is that for all their sacred authority, the four Gospels and the Holy Land were not an adequate basis for a filmed narrative that had to be fuller, more coherent, more dramatic, and less potentially offensive. Other texts, from Josephus to Morocco to Rabbinic commentaries, had to be brought in as supplements and buttresses or checks on their authority. More pointedly, Zeffirelli follows practically all other Jesus films in casting in the title role an actor (Robert Powell) who does not look Jewish. As Adele Reinhartz has observed of the rarity of head coverings and fringed garments among movie Jesuses, "even films that attempt in some way to convey Jesus' Jewishness visually distinguish Jesus from his Jewish opponents by means of their clothing."[12]

This problem, common to all biblical movies, is most amply documented in the case of Cecil B. DeMille, who developed elaborate bibliographic summaries of research for all his biblical epics, distributed several of them to a limited number of scholars and libraries, and arranged for the most extensive of them to be published. Henry S. Noerdlinger's *Moses and Egypt: The Documentation to the Motion Picture "The Ten Commandments"* is an illuminating compendium of facts, beliefs, and textual histories concerning state-of-the-art scholarship on Moses, the Jews, and the world of Egypt at the time DeMille was filming. Even as he does his best to amass citations that will provide further authority for the design of buildings, chariots, costumes, jewelry, and political history, however, DeMille is clear from the beginning that "the producer will sometimes overrule the research consultant, deliberately and without apology, for reasons of legitimate dramatic license."[13] How old is Moses at the time of the Exodus? Eighty, according to Exodus 7:7. But Charlton Heston's Moses is clearly much younger, acknowledges Noerdlinger, justifying this decision not by appealing to any text that explicitly gives his age as younger but by appealing to a textual tradition urging that "the ages given in the early books of the Bible are not to be taken literally,"[14] even though the reason for making Moses younger presumably has less to do with historical accuracy than with box-office appeal. More often, however, DeMille departs from the scriptural text not so much to conform to the imperatives of the box office as to tell a compelling story for believers and nonbelievers alike. Melanie J. Wright notes that "*The Ten Commandments'* audience for the most part knew what would happen; De-Mille created a fascinating film because he shifted attention to *how* things happen—to questions of narrative theme and character relation." She concludes, "Yet DeMille's need to create a film in which compelling characters form believable societies and undergo intelligible life experiences results in his including much that appears to be sheer fabrication."[15]

Nowhere is this process of invention in the service of narrative clearer than in the arresting opening of *The King of Kings*, whose inspiration DeMille has described in unusually candid terms:

> I knew that there would be in the audience religious people fearful of how a subject dear and sacred to them would be treated, and people who were skeptics and

had come to scoff, and people who were cynics and had come to witness deMille's [*sic*] disaster. I decided to jolt them all out of their preconceptions with an opening scene that none of them would be expecting: a lavish party at the luxurious home of a woman of Magdala, and that beautiful courtesan surrounded by the leering, sensual faces of her admirers who taunt her because one of their number, young Judas, has evidently found the company of some wandering carpenter more interesting than hers. When Mary Magdalene, goaded to jealous fury, calls for her chariot to take her to the Nazarene carpenter who has bewitched her favorite suitor, the people in the audience have forgotten their preconceptions: they want to see what happens when Mary, Judas, and the Carpenter meet.[16]

DeMille can be forgiven for not pointing out that once she falls under Jesus's divine power in the scene that ends this opening sequence, Mary Magdalene swiftly recedes in importance or that little is made later of Judas' onetime infatuation with her. The business of the scene, to hook the audience by presenting a familiar story in an unexpected and thoroughly dramatic new way, owes less to the Bible than to the bible of show business.

In the same way, when DeMille defends the film against the charge of anti-Semitism, he does so not by citing any texts that directly contradict or supplement the Gospel accounts but by arguing, like Mel Gibson's critics, against including anything in the film that might be construed as fixing the responsibility for Jesus's death on the Jewish people. His Caiaphas, urging Jesus's crucifixion, revises Matthew 27:25 by announcing, "If thou, imperial Pilate, wouldst wash thy hands of this man's death, let it be upon me—and me alone!" Although this might seem to be a correction with no textual authority of its own, DeMille cites two texts in its support. One is in the film: Caiaphas, delivering this speech from just offscreen left, is plainly posed behind Pilate's right shoulder, in the same pose as the Tempter whom Jesus confronted earlier, shifting responsibility from the Jewish people to a single rogue priest possessed by the Devil. The other is in his autobiography, where DeMille cites Brooklyn rabbi Alexander Lyons's claim that *The King of Kings* "should make the Jew more nobly and proudly Jewish, the Christian more emulous of the character of Jesus."[17] Remarkable as it seems, DeMille is consistently determined to offer some sort of textual support even for inventions that seem clearly inspired by box-office formulas or the desire not to offend audiences.

At the heart of this battle of dueling texts is a paradox of authority. Because DeMille is seeking textual support to bolster the Gospels' claims of authority, he is acknowledging that authority as worth supporting. Yet his search for other texts that can substantiate the Gospels implies that they are in need of corroboration from historical or religious resources somehow more reliable than they are. The problem would not be a problem for most texts in need of support, since most texts implicitly present themselves as intertexts indebted to a broad range of other texts. But Scripture is not just another text; it is a series of texts that, as Auerbach and Bakhtin point out, claim a literally transcendental authority that should brook no appeal to what can only be lesser texts. The harder DeMille works to bolster Scripture's authority, therefore, the more insidiously he undermines it.

The most remarkable of all these tortuous manipulations of textual authority is one rarely noticed: DeMille's habit of using scriptural intertitles to provide moral or rhetorical authority for incidents he and his screenwriters have transformed beyond recognition or created out of whole cloth. When Caiaphas, worried that Jesus may escape death, instructs his underlings, "Bribe rogues to cry his death!" one of them replies in a line invented for the film, "Nay, do not our scriptures teach us that no man shall take a bribe against the innocent?"—to which the intertitle adds the helpful reference "Ps. 15:5." The high priests still warn, "This man is not of God" (Jn 9:16), but now the admonition is menacingly addressed to the young boy Mark, the future evangelist whose blindness Jesus has just cured in a wholly fictional incident. When DeMille's Jesus says, "Get thee behind me, Satan!" (Lk 4:8) he is rebuking not Peter but the Tempter himself, and his teaching, "Blessed are the pure of heart—for they shall see God!" (Mt 5:8) is excerpted from the Sermon on the Mount and addressed to Mary Magdalene after Jesus has cleansed her of the seven deadly sins, which emerge in a series of ghostly double exposures. Such transplanting of scriptural tags suggests that DeMille is treating the Gospel narrative as a multiple text not because it exists in more than one telling but because it is divisible into microtexts, any one of which is available to authenticate any other, or indeed any invented incident like the curing of Mark that might be added to the story.

Such a free handling of the Gospel text might seem remote from the idea of fidelity. But it returns to the larger question of what it means to make a film that is faithful to the Gospels precisely because it reveals divergences among at least three different ideals of fidelity, all of them relevant to movies about the life of Christ. The first is fidelity to the lexical particulars of the text—its literal words (Gibson's initial decision to film in Greek and Aramaic without subtitles), its pivotal incidents, its narrative sequence. Despite Gibson's claim that the Jews' assumption of responsibility for the Crucifixion "happened; it was said," no existing film of the life of Christ, not even *The Gospel according to St. Matthew* or *Jesus of Nazareth*, sticks closely enough to the particulars of any one Gospel, or all four Gospels together, to be able to advance this claim to fidelity without support from other claims to other sorts of fidelity.

The second ideal is based on the hermeneutical idea of "ostensiveness," the assumption that there is "a sequence in the spatiotemporal world to which the narratives supposedly refer."[18] In practice this claim of fidelity to the historical truth implied by the Gospel narratives most often takes the form of DeMille's claim to the historically accurate background of epics like *The Ten Commandments* (1956) or the claim of authenticity implied by the act of filming in the Holy Land, even though the Sphinx before which DeMille's Mary and Joseph rest in their sojourn in Egypt lacks the nose that most archaeologists agree it still had hundreds of years later. It does not matter whether the details of costume and topography are any more germane to the Gospels than the details of period architecture and period music are to Jane Austen's novels; the ideal is to recreate a biblical world as authentic in its details as the world to which Austen was presumably, however elliptically, referring. Another approach to this kind of authenticity, however—the attempt to recreate as closely as possible the sense of the reality of Jesus's human experience, as Gibson implied when he defended his film's graphic violence by saying, "I wanted to bring you there, and I wanted to be true to the Gospels. That has never been done"—already approaches a third ideal of fidelity.[19]

This third ideal, moral and spiritual rather than historical or circumstantial, addresses the question of what Jesus's ministry, Passion, and death mean for movie audiences today. Nicholas Ray hinted at the problems behind this ideal when he said that *King of Kings* should present its events "as though they were happening before us for the first time."[20] If viewers really felt they were seeing Jesus's ministry for the first time, they would not see him as the Messiah but as an itinerant preacher from a vanished world whose teachings might or might not appeal to them. Most filmed lives of Christ, however, temper Ray's quest for immediacy with a pietism that acknowledges and encourages viewers' previous attitudes toward the subject. Since Jesus is likely to be perceived very differently by unbelievers and believers, or indeed by believers of different sorts, films for which this ideal of fidelity is important tend to take two different, though by no means mutually exclusive, tacks. Either Jesus is a white-bread

Messiah like saintly H. B. Warner in *The King of Kings* or strenuously under-stated Max Von Sydow in *The Greatest Story Ever Told*, whose word could not possibly offend any right-thinking viewers; or Jesus is an all-too-human figure like Ted Neeley in *Jesus Christ Superstar* or Willem Dafoe in *The Last Temptation of Christ*, who serves as a lightning rod for viewers' least-common-denominator fears and beliefs about moral and spiritual struggle regardless of their religious affiliation. It is in avoiding these two types, in fact, that the principal originality of Gibson's intensely physical yet unmistakably divine Jesus consists. Just as the Hebrew Bible has inspired generations of rabbinic commentary over the years, much of it now endowed with its own authority as Midrashic and Talmudic texts that seek to guide interpretation by correcting each other on any number of crucial points, the Gospels have been used to raise innumerable moral problems over the years, for the most ardent searchers of Scripture are likely to find exactly what they are looking for. So this third brand of fidelity is always problematic.

But it is no more problematic than the other two. Every film adaptation that seeks to adapt the Gospels inevitably depends on countless other texts as well in order to authenticate its background, soften its potentially partisan challenges, provide an entertaining narrative, and reassure its target audience, who already know and believe the familiar story of Jesus's acceptance of his divine mission, that their piety is not misplaced. Hence every film makes the contradictory claim of fidelity to multiple sources, whether they are invoked as supplement, authority, or corrective to the Gospel narrative.

The demand of remaining faithful to multiple sources is clearly impossible. Yet it is eminently appropriate to the subject of Jesus's life, ministry, Passion, and death. For what are the Gospels themselves but multiple attempts to order a life shaped by a series of insurmountable contradictions, the life of a humble carpenter and itinerant rabbi whose fame continued to expand long after his death until it embraced the whole world, a preacher who claimed to be both human and divine, both priest and sacrifice, both uniquely intimate with God and tragically estranged from Him? Quite apart from the healthy dose of Hollywood entertainment enshrined in the Gospels themselves—the miracles, the parables, the reversals, the dramatic death and resurrection—Jesus, the Word made Flesh, is the ultimate problem text, a text that literally incarnates the Word of God. Unless, of course, you're one of those viewers who find the New Testament such an unsatisfactory sequel to the Hebrew Scriptures that you conclude he isn't—exactly the sort of fundamental debate that remains at the heart of any intertext, from *The Passion of the Christ* to Matthew's Gospel.

The controversy at the very heart of Jesus's incarnation might seem to defuse the controversy Gibson's movie provoked. But there are several reasons why *The Passion of the Christ* was more controversial than any earlier filmed life of Christ. The most obvious was Gibson's refusal to accept the safety net Basinger had offered in the form of a sharp distinction between inspiration and entertainment. In a pair of television interviews with Diane Sawyer, the first broadcast on *Primetime Live* on February 16, 2004, the second on *60 Minutes* on February 22, 2004, he offered blankly contradictory accounts of the film. Glossing his earlier statement that "the Holy Ghost was working through me," Gibson told Sawyer that "God ordains everything," but "it really is *my* vision. . . . I'm not taking myself out of the equation here, I'm a proud bugger, I did this. But I did it with God's help. I mean, this is my version of what happened according to the Gospels."[21] Yet his acknowledgment that the film represents his own interpretation of the story was countered by several assertions that his depiction of Jesus's Passion corresponds to the literal truth. Paula Fredriksen has summarized Gibson's contradictory rationales:

> When promoting *The Passion,* he proclaimed its historical veracity: the script, he said, was based on the "rock-solid" eyewitness reporting of the evangelists themselves. Presented with the long list of the film's goofs, at odds with both Scripture and history—the spoken Latin [instead of Greek]; the outsized, impossible cross that James Caviezel's Jesus lugs along the way to Gibson's Golgotha; the improbably softened character of Pontius Pilate; the destruction by earthquake of the Temple—he's shrugged, "It's a movie, not a documentary." His only obligation, he claims, was to make the best movie he could, exercising his right to artistic freedom of expression. Asked if so much gore was really necessary, he responds, "That's just what's in the Gospel. I know how it went down." When pressed on his potentially harmful depiction of Jews, he blocks with a counter-punch: "People like this don't have a problem with me, they really have a problem with the Gospels."[22]

The passage is quoted from Fredriksen's contribution to *Perspectives on "The Passion of the Christ,"* an invaluable volume on which the rest of this chapter will draw heavily. Gibson's inconsistency about whether his film is to be regarded as literally true, as historically true, or as his personal interpretation of the Gospels' spiritual truth may at first seem simply evasive. Taken together with earlier biblical films' attempts to succeed as mass entertainment, however, it reveals problems in any categorical distinction between inspiration and entertainment. Commentators have widely noted the film's indebtedness to medieval representations of the Passion, from the fourteen tableaux in the Stations of the Cross to the Oberammergau Passion Play, the *Pietà* of Michelangelo, a 1555 altarpiece by Lucas Cranach the Younger, and "the gruesome and gangrenous *Crucifixion* of the Northern Renaissance painter Matthias Grünewald (1515)."[23] Such representations, blurring the line between devotion and aestheticization, have led Lawrence E. Frizzell to conclude that "Gibson has indeed given us an extremely accurate historical representation of Jesus's passion, *as viewed from the high Middle Ages.*"[24]

This line is blurred still further by the film's widely noted resemblances to a much more recent body of work: Gibson's own films, which typically cast him as a charismatic action hero capable of absorbing intense physical torments only to bounce back triumphantly. The seeds of this role, planted in Gibson's performance as Sgt. Martin Riggs in the four *Lethal Weapon* films (1987–98), flower in his portrayal of the Scottish nationalist hero William Wallace in *Braveheart* (1995), a film that won Oscars for Best Picture and Best Director (Gibson). These films, establishing Gibson's body as a site of physical suffering, paved the way for a life of Jesus in which only a series of brief flashbacks to Jesus's life, ministry, and teachings—all motivated by their relevance to the immediate context of his Passion and death—provide any rationale for his atrocious physical suffering. Hence evangelical activist Jim Wallis argues that Gibson's "Christology turns the thirty-three years of the life of Christ into a period of almost wasted time—just getting Jesus ready to be the blood sacrifice"—and Leon Wieseltier observes sardonically that "Jim Caviezel, who plays Jesus, does not act, strictly speaking; he merely rolls his eyes heavenward and accepts more makeup."[25] Even more temperate critics agree that the film, which apportions "fifteen minutes for the scourging, but only one minute for the resurrection," follows its medieval models in proposing that "Christ saved humanity not so much through his death and resurrection (which would be closer to the New Testament's understanding) as through his endless, unspeakable, unbearable suffering."[26]

Susan Thistlethwaite traces this emphasis on corporeal suffering to what she takes to be Gibson's chosen genre: the war movie. Like Rocky and Rambo, Gibson's Jesus not only "endured more pain than any other human being ever could" but then rose miraculously from the grave in a "martial resurrection" especially reminiscent of Sylvester Stallone's rise in *Rambo: First Blood* (1982).[27] Along the road to this quietly angry coda, Thistlethwaite contends, Gibson supplies all the leading elements of the war film: the moral absolutism that separates heroes from villains who are repeatedly aligned visually with the Devil, the exaggerated facial expressions and physical acting of the villains, the marginalizing of women through the specious (though hardly original) identification of the heroine Magdalene as "the beautiful redeemed prostitute."[28] Stephen Prothero noted the film's indebtedness to "the macho brutality of the action-adventure movie (blood, gore, repeat) and the supernatural horror of the Gothic tradition of Edgar Allan Poe and Stephen King"; Leon Wieseltier called it "the greatest story ever told as Dario Argento might have told it" and "a sacred snuff film."[29]

Even before *The Passion of the Christ* was released, a group of biblical scholars convened by the Secretariat for Ecumenical and Interreligious Affairs of the U.S. Conference of Catholic Bishops and the Anti-Defamation League had supplied Gibson with a confidential report on the film's script that expressed concern about the film's "theology of pain," under whose aegis "the motives of the principal characters—Caiaphas, Annas, Pilate, and even Jesus—are unexplained. . . . The drama and pathos seems almost entirely driven by violence."[30]

Jim Wallis, observing that "the death of Jesus on the cross and the new life of Jesus in the resurrection are the ultimate repudiation of revenge and triumph over violence," concludes that several nonhistorical details in Gibson's muscularly entertaining vision of Christianity invert this repudiation by suggesting that "unjust violence leads, ultimately, to 'just' payback."[31] This theology of just revenge, like Christian evangelical teaching, extends beyond the life of Christ as Gibson represents it. Mary C. Boys, one of the theologians who contributed to the original report on Gibson's script, reflects on the e-mail messages she received when her views became public:

> A common note sounded in these numerous e-mails condemning the scholars' report, or my own comments in subsequent interviews, is outrage. Outrage at what their authors perceive to be assaults against a Christianity under siege from a "godless" culture. Who are the "godless" who mount such attacks? Not simply persons who reject religion; not only those who are themselves Christian. Rather, the outraged relegated those of us with public, explicit religious commitments to the lowest circle of hell reserved for the godless: To point out the problems in

Gibson's project was to "attack" it—an act that, in their eyes, was tantamount to attacking the Gospels, and even Christianity itself. For Gibson's furious fans, criticism of the film made one a heretic.[32]

In other words the film's value as entertainment exceeded whatever pleasures viewers may have felt as they watched it; its most important manifestation was justification for the vindictive moral outrage with which its newly empowered audience could condemn a hostile culture. As Susan Thistlethwaite observes, "The film labors to *convict* the viewer."[33] Viewers' paradoxically resulting sense of entitlement is accurately reflected by a contradiction in Gibson's remarks to Diane Sawyer. Invited to describe the focus of his film, he replied, "He was beaten for our iniquities, he was wounded for our transgressions and, by his wounds, we are healed. That's the point of the film. It's not about pointing the finger, it's not about playing the blame game. It's about faith, hope, love and forgiveness." Yet he immediately goes on to play the blame game in identifying "a big dark force [that] didn't want us to make this film": "I'm a believer . . . so if you believe, you believe that there are big realms of good and evil and they're slugging it out."[34] Gibson's Manichean vision of faith, hope, love, and forgiveness requires an opposing dark force with whom there can be no quarter.

Commentators on the film largely agree that its moral dualism, its relentless emphasis on corporeal suffering, and its theology of revenge draw less on the Gospels than on Gibson's other acknowledged source: *The Dolorous Passion of Our Lord Jesus Christ,* a transcription by the poet Clemens Brentano of the visions of nineteenth-century Augustinian nun Anne Catherine Emmerich. This source not only supplies Gibson's emphasis on a theology of suffering rather than ministry and resurrection but bolsters his action-movie Manicheism by "imagin[ing] Judaism as the eternal opposite of Christianity, and Jews as the eternal enemies of Christ."[35] To the common question of how to be faithful to multiple and sometimes conflicting Gospel accounts must therefore be added a question peculiar to Gibson's film: to what extent does its fidelity to Emmerich's visions supersede its fidelity to the Gospels? Most commentators would agree with Philip A. Cunningham that "*The Passion of the Christ* is less a movie based on the Gospels than it is a filmed version of Emmerich's imaginative interpretation of them. The movie's credits should have stated 'Based on a story by Anne Catherine Emmerich.'"[36]

Among the ideas Gibson's film draws from Emmerich are Jesus's arrest by the Jewish Temple police (rather than Roman centurions) and a crowd that marches him from Gethsemane to the high priest Caiaphas's house and then pushes him off a bridge, where his body dangles before the terrified Judas; the representation of Pontius Pilate, the procurator who condemned Jesus to death by crucifixion, as acting out of fear of Caiaphas; the spectral child carried by the Devil; the presence of demons disguised as children who taunt Judas into hanging himself; the oversized T-shaped cross Jesus carries to Golgotha, unlike the crosspieces the two condemned thieves carry to be affixed to standing supports; the gift from Pilate's wife of the linens Jesus's mother and Mary Magdalene use to mop up the blood he has left along his way to Golgotha; and the crow that pecks out the eyes of the unrepentant thief.[37] The cumulative effect of these revisions and supplements to the Gospels is to emphasize the unique intensity of Jesus's suffering over his ministry and resurrection, to "make the Jews look worse and Pilate look better,"[38] and to imply that a betrayal of the Son of God surely deserves avenging.

Gibson has repeatedly denied, however, that Emmerich is his primary source. In his *Primetime Live* interview he told Diane Sawyer, "I didn't do a book on Anne Catherine Emmerich's Passion. . . . I did a book [*sic*] according to the Gospels."[39] His authority, he avers, comes from the Gospel accounts. Mary C. Boys, discussing Gibson's assumption that biblical texts make "plain sense" in which human history coincides with theological truth, quotes an interview in which Gibson told the audience of the Eternal Word Television Network that "the Gospels are eyewitness accounts. (Here he even goes beyond church tradition, which holds Mark as a secondhand account, and Luke as a third-hand account; Peter supposedly confided his memories to Mark; Paul—not among the original twelve—to Luke.) With his frequent references to the Holy Ghost as the movie's real director, Gibson offers a 'blessed assurance' that his film is the most authentic presentation ever of the way the Passion and death of Jesus actually happened."[40]

Philip Cunningham, however, argues that literal fidelity to the facts of the Passion, even were it possible, would be inadequate as a criterion for Gospel adaptations, because the four Gospels "are not simply reporters' notes from eyewitnesses. They are narratives composed so that readers 'may come to believe that Jesus is the Christ, the Son of God' ( John 20:31)."[41] Gibson's film looks completely different if it is judged in terms of its intended future effects rather than in terms of its representation of past events. Like Brentano's published version of Emmerich's mystical vision and the Gospels themselves, it is a testament of faith intended to spread that faith through all the world. In one sense,

Gibson's success exceeded all expectations, since a largely evangelical audience, many urged by pastors who used their pulpits to promote the film or bought out whole screenings for their flocks, made its $370 million box-office gross the highest ever for an R-rated film. In another sense it is questionable how successful the film has been if its goal is to change hearts and minds, for its principal observable effect among viewers of every persuasion is the one Rabbi Lyons commended to C. B. DeMille: to strengthen them in the beliefs they already had.

If Gibson's primary goal in making *The Passion of the Christ* was to confirm Christians in their faith, the film follows a long tradition of Passion narratives presenting the evidence most likely to make Jesus's final hours powerfully compelling. As Adele Reinhartz points out, "Gibson's movie falls squarely within the norms and conventions of the Jesus film genre in that it takes the outline and some details primarily from the Gospels, and adds elements from later Christian tradition, individual imagination, and popular culture."[42] Gibson's method here is no more exceptionable than Scorsese's, Zeffirelli's, or DeMille's combination of fidelity and free invention. The only thing that makes Gibson's case unusual is his intermittent insistence that his film is "'historically accurate,' 'like traveling back in time and watching the events unfold exactly as it [*sic*] occurred'"[43]—that is, that his version does indeed present a literal truth to which it has a unique access denied every other filmed life of Jesus—and his more consistent defense of his film's controversial aspects as required by its fidelity to the Gospels. In this respect he demonizes those who attack his film as heretical even as he disregards the 1988 *Criteria for the Evaluation of Dramatizations of the Passion* issued by the Bishops' Committee for Ecumenical and Interreligious Affairs: "A clear and precise hermeneutic and a guiding artistic vision sensitive to historical fact and to the best Biblical scholarship are obviously necessary. Just as obviously, it is not sufficient for the producers of Passion dramatizations to respond to responsible criticism simply by appealing to the notion that 'it's in the Bible.' One must account for one's selections."[44] (As Wieseltier observes more tartly, "Gibson created this movie; it was not revealed to him.")[45] This document, like others cited in an appendix to the Ad Hoc Scholars Report submitted to Gibson before his film was released, took its cue from *Nostra Aetate*, the 1965 document of the Second Vatican Council, which ruled, "The Jews should not be represented as repudiated or cursed by God, as if such views followed from the holy Scriptures."[46] Although he has repeatedly defended his film against charges of anti-Semitism, Gibson has made no secret of his quarrel with the teachings of Vatican II, which have represented official Roman Catholic doctrine for forty years. Just as the Gospels themselves may be construed, in the terms of biblical historian Geza Vermes, as "a family quarrel within Judaism,"[47] it is possible to see Gibson's film as marking a family quarrel within Catholicism and Gibson as "the patron saint of disaffected Catholics."[48] Once more, there is ample historical precedent for such a situation, though not the sort of precedent that would give the film the authority Gibson has claimed for it.

Perhaps the strangest turn yet in the strange career of *The Passion*'s reception is the appearance within months of the film's release of the collection *Perspectives on "The Passion of the Christ."* Instant anthologies on contemporary cultural phenomena from *The Simpsons* to *The Sopranos* are increasingly commonplace, and Gibson was more than willing to cover the risk of his own investment in the film, which he estimated at $30 million, by licensing products from T-shirts to "Passion Nail pendants."[49] What is most remarkable about *Perspectives on "The Passion of the Christ,"* published by Hyperion's Miramax imprint, is what it says about the film. Despite Miramax editor Jonathan Burnham's assurance that "no single perspective on the movie dominates this collection,"[50] every one of the eighteen essays collected in the volume is highly critical of Gibson's film. (The broadly critical strain extends even to the concluding satirical piece by the comedian Steve Martin, which takes the form of a studio memo: "Love the Jesus character. So likable. He can't seem to catch a break!")[51] Not one of them demurs from Paula Fredriksen's conclusion that whether or not the film is anti-Semitic, it certainly is "inflammatory, and . . . its depiction of Jewish villainy—exaggerated well beyond what is in the Gospels and violating what historical knowledge we have of first-century Judea— will give aid and comfort to anti-Semites everywhere."[52] And several go beyond criticizing Gibson to citing Catholic guidelines that would have prevented any possible incitement of anti-Semitism[53] or sketching out alternative scenarios that would have been equally faithful to either the historical record, as illuminated by recent biblical scholarship, or "a Christian faith experience."[54]

It would be easy to regard this uniquely disapproving tie-in volume as cynical and perverse, an attempt by Miramax to distance itself from another studio's controversial film by criticizing it mercilessly while cashing in on the controversies the film had stirred up. But surely its publication is no more cynical than the nearly simultaneous appearance of *The Bible, the Jews, and the Death of Jesus,* a collection of earlier Catholic pastoral instructions gathered into book form by the U.S. Conference of Catholic Bishops, who had hoped that the controversy surrounding *The Passion of the Christ* would make their teachings more timely, or than the release of Gibson's movie itself. Each document is presented out of strong inner conviction, amounting in some cases to moral certitude, in the full knowledge that it is fighting for attention with competing convictions and the hope that it provides "a teachable moment."[55] With this best will in the world, each new incarnation of Jesus's teaching is guaranteed to bring not peace but a sword.

Ella Shohat has recently asked what is at stake in an adaptation that is "not of a book but rather of *The Book*, and one that virtually decrees that it *not* be adapted."[56] The ban on graven images she finds so central to theologies of adaptation that stem from Judaism and Islam is countered in cinematic lives of Christ by an inveterate impulse to incarnation that makes Jesus both a unique figure in the history of the world and the ideal model for all the world, from his terrified followers to Mel Gibson's target audience. We do well to remember, after all, that for the four evangelists, the life and teachings of Jesus were not a primary text but an intertext through which the Hebrew scriptures were fulfilled. Indeed, many of the discrepancies among the accounts of Matthew, Mark, Luke, and John stem from the very different ways they sought to present his works and speeches as referring to earlier scriptural texts. Jesus is not only a stellar example of the prototext that turns out to be an intertext but also the exemplary text that must be shattered before it can be used. Prophesying both his own death and the demand to conversion, Jesus told his fearful disciples, "Except a corn of wheat fall into the ground and die, it abideth alone; but if it die, it bringeth forth much fruit" (Jn 12:24). Whatever its limitations, Gibson's film seizes on a central truth of Christianity: the body of Christ, the Word made flesh, is a text most valuable when it is broken. The conflicts that follow in the wake of each new incarnation, from the Gospels to Gibson and beyond, are as Catholic, and as catholic, as the Council of Nicea, the Second Vatican Council, or the Crusades.

# CHAPTER FOUR

# Entry-Level Dickens

Whether or not it deserves the distinction of having been "adapted by the mass media more than any other work in the history of English literature," Charles Dickens's 1843 tale *A Christmas Carol* has been adapted so often that many of its wilder or lamer incarnations are more likely to provoke apology than analysis.[1] When Dickens's classic tale has been reimagined as an antiwar allegory (*Carol for Another Christmas* [1964]), two westerns (*The Trail to Christmas* [1957]; and *Ebenezer* [1998]), a rock musical (*Scrooge's Rock 'n' Roll Christmas* [1984]), a country and western musical (*Skinflint* [1979]), a parable about the need for quality control in business (*The Quality Carol* [1984]), and a vehicle for such varied stars as Robert Guillaume (*John Grin's Christmas* [1986]), Tim Curry (the animated 1997 *A Christmas Carol*), Brer Rabbit (*Brer Rabbit's Christmas Carol* [1992]), Gumby (*Scrooge Loose* [1957]), Alvin and the Chipmunks (*Alvin's Christmas Carol* [1983]), and Beavis and Butt-Head (the 1995 MTV television segment *Huh-Huh-Humbug*), surely some blanket formula of apology is in order.

Fred Guida, in his monumental study and catalogue of film and television adaptations of *A Christmas Carol,* has come up with a particularly suggestive formula of apology. After he pronounces the 1982 Australian animated film version voiced by Ron Haddrick and Phillip Hinton "dull," he acknowledges that "one has to applaud anything that exposes young viewers to Dickens, particularly in a feature-length format." Dismissing Disney Productions' twenty-five-minute *Mickey's Christmas Carol* (1983) as "too heavily truncated," he concedes that it "will introduce many youngsters to both Dickens and the *Carol*, and for that we should indeed be truly grateful." He tempers his disappointment with *The Muppet Christmas Carol* (1992) with a concession: "It is likely, though, that this film will introduce many young children to both Dickens and the *Carol*, and, given the rampant illiteracy and electronic barbarism that children are inundated with these days, that is no small accomplishment." Noting the modest budget of the 1985 Canadian television segment *Buckaneezer Scrooge*, he concludes that "in this day and age—in any day and age—an opportunity to introduce children to Dickens and his 'Ghostly little book' is most welcome indeed." And he summarizes a 1988 segment of the Inuit Broadcasting Corporation's television program *Takuginai*, which presents the story in three minutes by combining still drawings with voice-over narration, by observing that "children are given an entertaining introduction to the *Carol* and older viewers are reminded of the universality of its message."[2]

Guida's sentiment echoes André Bazin's defense of Christian Jacque's film adaptation of *The Charterhouse of Parma* (*La chartreuse de Parme* [1948]) despite its "betrayal" of Stendhal's novel: "All things considered, it provides an enchanting introduction to Stendhal's work and has certainly increased the number of its readers."[3] This chapter will consider just what it means for film and television adaptations of *A Christmas Carol* to pose as introductions to a literary classic for children or others. Although I will often pass judgment on particular adaptations, my goal is not to grade them up or down but to examine the ways they exemplify the problems involved in the charge of providing an introduction to a literary classic and the contradictions built into that charge.

The desirability of providing such an introduction is rooted in a developmental notion of cultural literacy. Instead of being asked to read *David Copperfield* or *A Tale of Two Cities* at an unwisely early age—how many young people have been put off Dickens for life by premature exposure to the literary pyrotechnics that often cloak his most broadly comic or pathetic conceits?— children who are not yet equal to the task of reading Dickens are instead offered Dickens for the Young, which will provide a wholesome, albeit diluted, dose of a classic author while serving to whet the appetite for stronger meat and drink when the time is ripe. Guida's final remark puts the point of this early exposure neatly. Children who watch adaptations of *A Christmas Carol* are being taught something they need to know ("an entertaining introduction to the *Carol*"), whereas adults are being reminded of something they already know ("the universality of its message").

Apart from the universal message about compassion and conversion, children who watch these adaptations are presumably learning about at least three other things. First, they are learning something about *A Christmas Carol* itself, the kind of information about its iconic hero and his dreamlike adventures that will equip them to navigate not only Dickens's story but also its more advanced or obscure adaptations like the pantomime *Marcel Marceau Presents a Christmas Carol* (1973); the 1971 animated *Christmas Carol* that Richard Williams and Chuck Jones produced for British television, which Guida observes "seems to require a pretty solid familiarity with the original text in order to be fully appreciated"; and the 1993 BBC *A Christmas Carol*, featuring the Northern Ballet Company, which would be "rather tough going for anyone unfamiliar with the story."[4] The note of reluctant discontent that qualifies Guida's enthusiasm for these two versions reveals a paradox beneath the project of introducing new audiences to a familiar story: introductory adaptations derive their value in large measure because they are parasitic on an established classic, but they assume a thorough knowledge of that classic at their peril. The ideal audience for such introductory adaptations evidently takes it on faith that the underlying story is a literary classic without having inquired too closely into its particulars. In other words, the best audience for an introduction to *A Christmas Carol* is an audience that has already been introduced to it—or at least to the proposition that it is a literary classic worth serious attention.

In addition to introducing children to *A Christmas Carol*, these adaptations are also, as Guida points out, introducing them to Dickens. Hence the need for each adaptation to convey not only the particulars of the story but something recognizably Dickensian in their tone, their attitude toward Christmas, or the moral lessons they inculcate. In fact, the developmental model might be expanded by observing that as a children's adaptation is an entry-level *Christmas Carol*, so *A Christmas Carol* is entry-level Dickens, one of the smallest principalities in a vast continent likely to remain largely unexplored by many viewers. This problem is greatly alleviated by the fact that *A Christmas Carol*, unlike *Barnaby Rudge* or *American Notes* or *A Child's History of England*, constitutes something like zero-degree Dickens in the popular imagination, the work that more than any other defines its author for a mass audience. Even so, the conclusion is inescapable that for many viewers, film adaptations of A *Christmas Carol* are likely to substitute for Dickens, to become Dickens, rather than serving as merely the lowest rung on the Dickens ladder.

Such a possibility becomes especially troubling in the case of the third text to which adaptations of A *Christmas Carol* are introducing children: the text of high culture, of adult culture, of culture as such. This text is far trickier to turn to developmental purposes than either A *Christmas Carol* or Dickens the literary classic because it is precisely what is most likely to be lost in any retelling aimed at an audience outside full membership in the culture. Although no adaptation of the story that indicated the full range and weight of its cultural import would be likely to appeal to children, no adaptation that failed to register that import would provide a worthwhile cultural introduction—unless, as Guida suggests of the Northern Ballet version, the target audience had been introduced to the story already.

Entry-level adaptations of literary classics assume that the elements that make a book a classic can be made available to viewers who have limited interest or ability to enjoy the book itself. These elements cannot be Dickens's densely playful language or even the exact selection and arrangement of incidents, for these are the most likely things to be changed in any adaptation. They must be more universal elements: Dickens's warmly sentimental attitude toward Christmas, his ready outrage over social injustice, the irrepressible humor that emerges when Scrooge is confronted by the ghost of his late partner, the pietistic faith that even the most misanthropic citizens can be converted to charity and goodwill by a Christmas miracle. But of course these elements cannot be truly universal, or their target audience would already know them. They must be just out of reach, inaccessible to readers disinclined to pick up Dickens but subject to proper education and acculturation within the compass of the movie or television segment.

Viewers who watch entry-level adaptations of A *Christmas Carol* with profit have not just acquired the universal lessons the story teaches; they have acquired the story itself, along with something of Dickens and something of the literary classic's quite distinct units of cultural capital. These adaptations do not merely teach Dickens's lessons; they teach Dickens himself. Just as television programming developed for children teaches children how to become adult consumers of television programming, entry-level classics teach them the value of literary classics, even if what it teaches them is remote from whatever Dickens, or the cultural custodians of Dickens's reputation, may have in mind. The problem of bundling the text, its author, and the institution of classic literature together with the injunction to have more care for the downtrodden is a small-scale version of the essential problem of cultural transmission and education. If Dickens's call to charity and social engagement is indeed universal, why does it need to be taught at all, and what is the effect of combining its injunction with a call to deeper cultural literacy? More generally, how should children and other cultural outsiders be educated in an adult culture that is their own but at least initially feels foreign? Considering these questions in the detail they demand would swiftly take this discussion far outside the scope of this chapter and this book. Fortunately, *A Christmas Carol* itself offers more specific terms in which to cast these problems, for it tackles them head-on in the figure of Scrooge, a nominal adult whose blindness to the culture around him is as complete as a child's. How can the three spirits of Christmas teach Scrooge lessons that are universal even though he has somehow remained ignorant of them? How can this superannuated infant, who for all his worldly shrewdness retains an infant's blinkered self-absorption, be taught the ways of a culture that is already his own?

This is not to say that Scrooge's cultural myopia is the same as a child's. Not only has he spent years armoring himself against demands on his wealth and love, but it is as ill-advised to generalize about his motives as about those of his myriad viewers because his backstory and his strategies for defending himself vary subtly from one adaptation to the next. Seymour Hicks makes him mean, George C. Scott willfully blind, Patrick Stewart calmly sardonic. Not all these differences, however, nor all the additional differences between any Scrooge and any young viewer, preclude the hope that children will identify with Scrooge's conversion from detachment to immersion in his culture. Just as the three spirits repeatedly blur the line between reminding Scrooge of harsh or sentimental realities he already knows and informing him about sufferings of which he has been ignorant, introductory adaptations of *A Christmas Carol* dispense cultural wisdom to their target audience in the course of reminding the fictional hero about them. As Audrey Jaffe has argued, "it projects images of, has come to stand for, and constitutes an exemplary narrative of enculturation into the dominant values of its time."[5]

It was not always so. Paul Davis has demonstrated that since "the dominant point of view in the *Carol* . . . is that of an adult," the story's status as "a children's classic" must be a later development, one Davis traces to the beginning of the twentieth century.[6] Many adaptations ostensibly directed at children, like Zoran Janjic's 1969 animated version, continue to imply an adult audience, as Janjic's Fred does when he follows Dickens (9) in describing his uncle as "dismal" and "morose" and turns Dickens's paean to Christmas as valuable however unprofitable (10) into a six-line aria to which Scrooge responds with four sung lines of his own.[7] And of course adaptations continue to appear every Christmas—the most recent, as of this writing, starring Kelsey Grammer as Scrooge, broadcast over NBC television during the Christmas season of 2004—that are not aimed primarily at children. Because Dickens was writing not only about conversion but about acculturation, however, there is an important sense in which every version of the story, including Dickens's own, is a parable for children. Entry-level adaptations of *A Christmas Carol* are not bastardizations of Dickens; they are in important ways the most Dickensian adaptations of all.

It is true, of course, that children's adaptations of the story are pressed to serve diverse and often incompatible functions for their viewers, but that is nothing unusual, for adaptations of *A Christmas Carol* for adults are just as diverse in their goals and methods, even if their stated goal is fidelity to Dickens's story. Most of them mitigate this fidelity by melding it to the norms of very un-Dickensian generic modes. Even the ones that announce themselves as most resolutely Dickensian have to deal with the contradictions of remaining faithful to a classic while insisting on its classic status—an insistence Dickens never registers and one that separates their text ever more completely from his the more stridently they register it. All of them, finally, must submit to the incompatibilities in the story's nerve center, Scrooge himself, the most blankly contradictory character Dickens ever created.

In every version of *A Christmas Carol*, Scrooge undergoes a dramatic change on Christmas Eve and awakens Christmas morning a new man.[8] Clearly a lesson is being taught about the openness to change and redemption. What Scrooge is like, and what he is being redeemed from, however, have been subject to broad variation. Scrooge's most commonly diagnosed fault is a greed so consuming that it denies the possibility of love. But different adaptations take sharply differing views of just what it is that Scrooge ought to be loving. In the 1938 MGM *A Christmas Carol* Reginald Owen's Scrooge wants to remain an invisible guest at his nephew Fred's party, but the Spirit of Christmas Present tells him, "Don't be a fool, man! You don't like Christmas!" Scrooge replies, "But I do! I do love Christmas!"—Christmas, not his fellow beings. Albert Finney, in the 1970 *Scrooge*, is even more ecumenical. Having announced soon after awaking that "I think I'm going to *like* children," he confides in a toy seller who asks what has happened to him: "I've discovered that I like life." In *A Flintstones Christmas Carol* (1993), Fred Flintstone's affliction is self-absorbed vanity, not greed, and the sign of his conversion is his willingness to invite his wife's mother for Christmas. *Christmas Carol: The Movie* (2001) is so intent on diagnosing Scrooge's leading problem as his rejection of romantic love that it allows him to save the physician with whom his long-ago fiancée, Belle, works from financial ruin and hints at the possibility of a final romantic union.

Such widely differing diagnoses of Scrooge's malady depend on sharply differing views of his past. Dickens offers only a few hints about the forces in Scrooge's early life that made him what he was. His father sent him away to school and left him there over the holidays. His apprenticeship to Mr. Fezziwig was marked by his employer's generosity in arranging a memorable Christmas party for his friends and employees. His loving sister, Fan, died young, leaving behind her son, Fred, from whom Scrooge remains estranged. Belle released him from their engagement when it became clear that he had grown to care more for money than for her. He assumed full responsibility for the firm of Scrooge and Marley on the death of Jacob Marley on Christmas Eve seven years ago.

The vignettes revealed to Scrooge by the Spirit of Christmas Past show scenes from his early life without providing a rationale for his development. But they certainly encourage speculation about what made Scrooge the man he is, and many adaptations are eager to fill in these speculative gaps, even when their theories are manifestly inconsistent with Dickens. *The Gospel according to Scrooge* (1983) and Arthur Allan Seidelman's 2004 television *Christmas Carol*, the Kelsey Grammer vehicle, both borrow freely from Dickens's own life in consigning Scrooge's father to debtor's prison, providing an instant explanation for Scrooge's lifelong obsession with moneymaking. *An American Christmas Carol* (1979) creates a more elaborate history for its hero, Benedict Slade (Henry Winkler). He begins as an apprentice to New Hampshire furniture maker Mr. Brewster (Chris Wiggins), goes to work for a rival manufacturer who shuns Brewster's insistence on handmade craft in favor of assembly-line efficiency, and unwittingly ruins his beloved old employer's family, including his beloved Helen Brewster (Susan Hogan), when his midnight visit to their woodworking shop plays a crucial role in starting a catastrophic Christmas Eve fire. Even

Brian Desmond-Hurst's highly regarded 1951 *Scrooge* shows no compunction about fleshing out Scrooge's past. New scenes show the young Scrooge blaming his newborn nephew for Fan's death in childbirth and walking out on her deathbed pleas to take care of the boy. Afterward, Scrooge goes to work for Fezziwig's rival Mr. Jorkin (Jack Warner) and joins forces with Marley (Michael Hordern) to rescue their embezzling employer in return for a controlling interest in his firm.

F. Dubrez Fawcett's reaction to this last set of additions "allowing us to see how and why Scrooge became such a misanthrope" is instructive: "Even to those who are not Dickens purists, the grafting of new material, and of unauthorized dialogue, on a Dickens story is anathema. But Alastair Sim was great, the finest Scrooge possible to imagine, and the exuberance of his joy when he discovered he was still alive, and able to make atonement, had everybody laughing in sympathy, the kind of laughter that is a relief from tears, for there had been moments in the film which had set the audience sniffing and throat-clearing."[9] Fawcett criticizes Noel Langley's screenplay for being un-Dickensian on the grounds that any explanation of Scrooge's character that exceeds Dickens's own words is a betrayal. But he does not praise Alastair Sim's performance for being Dickensian; he praises it for being an effective piece of acting, capable of arousing by turns tears and laughter, even though much of the business Sim uses in his Christmas morning scene to provoke laughter, from his comically demented determination to stand on his head to his protracted byplay with his maid, Mrs. Dilber (Kathleen Harrison), are equally new additions to Dickens.

If he were pressed, Fawcett might well claim that what Sim was doing was simply giving expression to Scrooge's joy by inventing new external behavior and that his interpretation of the character, which is of course written into Langley's screenplay as well, is Dickensian in its illumination of the continuity between Scrooge's zestful selfishness and his equally zestful incredulity at his miraculous conversion and escape from death (a particular theme of Desmond-Hurst's adaptation that is by no means universally observed in other adaptations). This justification would be tantamount to an admission that Scrooge was a contradictory figure in need of explaining, even though any specific explanation would inevitably exceed the hints Dickens offered.

Additions to Scrooge's character may be un-Dickensian, but they are necessary to any screen version. Any actor playing the role has to devise particular behavior—ways of talking, walking, looking (or not looking) at interlocutors, picking up objects, snorting, nodding, and shaking his head—that is optional and discontinuous for a writer like Dickens. Apart from the additions that any continuous performance requires, Scrooge is a character who must either be explained or pointedly not explained because he is, as Edmund Wilson noted more than sixty years ago, two discontinuous characters. In his pioneering essay "Dickens: The Two Scrooges," Wilson, who is clearly skeptical of the efficacy of Scrooge's conversion, argues that his irreducible dualism is central to Dickens's personality and career: "Shall we ask what Scrooge would actually be like if we were to follow him beyond the frame of the story? Unquestionably he would relapse when the merriment was over—if not while it was still going on—into moroseness, vindictiveness, suspicion. He would, that is to say, reveal himself as the victim of a manic-depressive cycle, and a very uncomfortable person."[10]

To the extent that adaptations of *A Christmas Carol* provide Scrooge with a coherent backstory that explains his initial misanthropy—usually as a fall from childhood grace and innocence that can be corrected by a timely conversion—they are investing in that conversion, trying to make it as powerful and credible as possible for a contemporary audience likely to include skeptics like Wilson. Though the means of this effort may be un-Dickensian, the ultimate goal is eminently Dickensian. Indeed, it is Wilson himself whose interpretation of Scrooge is un-Dickensian. Instead of seeking the author's sanction for his interpretation, as Fawcett implies adapters ought to do, it seeks to explain Dickens along with his character and therefore assumes a stance outside and above the author. In his emphasis on the unconscious motives behind Dickens's most characteristic fictional patterns, Wilson may well be more penetrating about Scrooge than Dickens himself, but that penetration makes him by definition less, not more, Dickensian.

In fact, despite the enormous influence of Wilson's essay, it is clear that there are not two Scrooges but three: the greedy and misanthropic Scrooge of Dickens's First Stave, the ecstatic reformed sinner of the Fifth Stave, and the increasingly penitential figure of the middle three, who begins with grumbling protests and ends by weeping for himself and Tiny Tim. Wilson overlooks this middle Scrooge, even though he occupies by far the greatest space in *A Christmas Carol* (and gets most of the screen time in most of its adaptations) and marks the greatest advance over Dickens's earlier fiction, because taking note of him would undermine Wilson's argument about the paramount importance of unresolved dualities in Dickens. Pace Wilson, Scrooge is not an unresolved duality. Along with Mr. Dombey, Mr. Gradgrind, and Pip, he represents Dickens's most sustained attempt to resolve this duality by adding a third term, the possibility of conversion from the bad Scrooge to the good.

Contemporary Dickens scholarship has largely followed Wilson in emphasizing Scrooge's duality, and several adaptations of *A Christmas Carol* insist on it as well. Mr. Spacely, the Scrooge figure in *The Jetsons' Christmas Carol* (1985), expressing bored impatience with every vision of his employees' past, present, and future, retains his meanness until the moment he sees the Jetson family ensconced in the palatial house they have purchased after suing George's boss for the defective sprocket that killed their dog Astro. His rush to bring his own veterinarian on a Christmas house call to remove the sprocket from Astro's stomach suggests that Spacely has learned not so much charity as the kind of alertly defensive behavior that wards off liability suits. Carface Carruthers, the gang-leading dog in *An All Dogs Christmas Carol* (1998), turns against the even more evil Belladonna, who plans to ruin Christmas, after Charlie Barkin and Itchy Itchiford stage a series of scenes featuring ghosts Carface never believes in, but Carface immediately warns Charlie and Itchy that his change of heart is superficial: "Don't expect it to last long. I've still got a business to run."

Such one-dimensional conversions are especially appropriate to cartoon characters posing as Scrooge. Other performers, however, balance the three Scrooges differently. If Alastair Sim is the most emphatically giddy reformed Scrooge and Seymour Hicks the sternest preconversion Scrooge, many adaptations place primary emphasis on the second Scrooge, the figure undergoing a gradual conversion as he is given a wider view of the world around him and sees the error of his ways. In the 1954 television adaptation for CBS, Fredric March portrays Scrooge as a stiff, unyielding man who gradually softens and abates his angularity during the three visitations. In the 1999 Hallmark film made for TNT, Patrick Stewart offers broad hints of Scrooge's clipped humor, especially in the dryly Dickensian reception he accords Marley's Ghost, that presage his conversion from the beginning. And in the 1984 *A Christmas Carol* George C. Scott portrays perhaps the subtlest Scrooge of all, marking his conversion not as a single dramatic reversal when he is confronted by his tombstone but as a series of carefully calibrated stages. Scott's Scrooge is defensive, abrupt, imperious, and demanding. Yet the humility that will mark his Christmas awakening is never far from the surface, masked only by the blindness this adaptation takes as its keynote.

The choice of three possible Scrooges to emphasize means that even an adaptation that took fidelity to Scrooge as its chief aim would face an insuperable problem, for the three Scrooges are so different from one another. Just as the desire to be faithful to Dickens and the institution of the literary classic generate demands at odds with the demand to be faithful to *A Christmas Carol,* Scrooge is only the most obvious of many microtexts within and behind the text of Dickens's story. No single adaptation can possibly be faithful to all these microtexts, even those of the three Scrooges.

A good introduction to the inescapable importance of these microtexts is the 1910 Edison *Christmas Carol,* which compresses the story into ten minutes by staging it as a series of discontinuous sketches alternating with explanatory intertitles. This approach may seem reductive, but it is eminently Dickensian, for Dickens's story itself is constructed as a series of discontinuous theatrical spectacles readily subject to abridgment, expansion, or elaboration.[11] The Edison film breaks the story into a series of fifteen vignettes, most of them unfolding in single camera shots introduced by the following title cards:

[1] The day before Christmas. Scrooge, a hard-fisted miser, receives an appeal from the Charity Relief Committee.

[2] His nephew calls to wish him a Merry Christmas.

[3] The ghostly face of his former partner, Marley.

[4] The ghost of Marley, who was like unto Scrooge, warns him of his punishment hereafter unless he becomes a different man.

[5] The Spirit of Christmas recalls incidents of his youth and early manhood.

[6] Visions of the present. What the miser's wealth could do.

[7] The Christmas dinner of Bob Cratchit, his clerk. A toast to all the world— even Scrooge.

[8] He sees his nephew rejected for the want of money.

[9] Want and Misery.

[10] Visions of the future. A miser's death.

[11] Christmas morning. Awakened by a Christmas Carol to a new life.

[12] "Peace on Earth, Good Will Toward Men."

[13] The Spirit of Christmas at work.

[14] [close-up of handwritten note] "As my business partner you, my nephew, will be able to marry the girl of your choice. E. Scrooge."

[15] The Cratchit's [*sic*] Christmas dinner.

Although this early version departs from Dickens by staging practically all its action inside Scrooge's bedchamber, where the visions of past, present, and future are displayed as insets almost like magic-lantern shows, it makes a determined attempt to be faithful to a number of Dickensian microtexts. Apart from the most obvious narrative elements—an elderly miser named Scrooge, ghostly visitations from his late partner Marley and three spirits, an awakening Christmas morning to a dramatic change of heart—the Edison adaptation marks several notable features as obligatory. Scrooge is visited in his office not only by his nephew but by three gentlemen collecting for charity whom he turns away. He is taken aback by a vision of Marley's face superimposed on the knocker to the door of his home. He sees past visions of Fan, Fezziwig's Christmas party, and Belle. The present vision focuses on a Christmas celebration and the future vision on Scrooge's glimpse of his own tombstone. His conversion is marked by his generosity toward the charity collectors he had spurned and by his acceptance of his nephew's romantic partner. Finally, he joins Bob Cratchit for a climactic scene of celebration.

The Edison adaptation makes a particular effort to stand alone as a story that can be understood without previous knowledge of Dickens. Scrooge is identified as "a hard-fisted miser" and Marley as having been "like unto Scrooge" for the benefit of viewers who do not already know them. Bob Cratchit, unnamed in the opening scene at Scrooge's office, is identified by a later title as "his clerk." It is true that certain details drawn from Dickens, like the allegorical figures of Want and Misery, are introduced with little explanation, but the intertitles are equally laconic about the film's departures from Dickens, like his nephew's imperiled courtship of the sweetheart who has not yet become his wife. The adaptation thus comes across less as an introduction than as a substitute for Dickens's story, though one determined to remain faithful to certain distinct elements of that story.

Of all the possible microtexts the Edison adaptation dismisses as unimportant, the most striking is the omission of Tiny Tim. The Cratchits, to be sure, have several children, but none of them stands out from the others; none uses a crutch; and none seconds Cratchit's toast, at the time he makes it or later, by saying, "God bless us, every one!"—an omission less surprising in an adaptation whose title cards, following contemporaneous industry practice, dispense with dialogue altogether. Apart from the apparition of Marley's face on Scrooge's door knocker, a relatively minor scene that is retained in almost every adaptation, the most surprising microtext the Edison film identifies as essential is the tableau of Scrooge wearing a pointed white nightcap seated at screen right below the eye level of Marley and all three Christmas spirits. This costuming and blocking is drawn not from Dickens but from John Leech, who illustrated the 1843 edition of *A Christmas Carol*. Leech's eight illustrations have been variously influential on film adapters—Richard Williams's 1971 animated adaptation takes its visual inspiration directly from them—but one of them, the apparition of the gigantic, benevolent, green-gowned Spirit of Christmas Present appearing to a shrunken, white-capped, timidly smiling Scrooge perched gamely in profile in the lower right-hand corner of the image, provides blocking and costuming cues for virtually all adapters of this scene. For the purposes of this one scene only, fidelity to the story seems to demand fidelity to the 1843 edition of the story illustrated by Leech.

More surprisingly, the Edison adaptation is faithful to several obligatory microtexts that appear nowhere in Dickens. The most obvious of these is what Edmund Wilson has described as the image of "Scrooge bursting in on the Cratchits" at their Christmas dinner, which Wilson takes as crucial evidence of the manic-depression Scrooge shares with his creator, even though the scene does not appear in Dickens.[12] The temptation to unite Scrooge with his clerk's family on Christmas Day must have been irresistible to both adapters and unwary commentators, especially once later adaptations had restored Tiny Tim and promoted him to an ever-more central symbolic role. More often than not in these later adaptations, Scrooge carries him on his shoulder in the final scene—an image drawn from an iconographic tradition showing Bob Cratchit carrying his son that did not get underway, as Paul Davis observes, until 1867[13]—and Tim gets to reprise his most famous (and indeed his only) speech, a reprise Dickens gives to his narrator.

An even more remarkable microtext that the Edison film establishes in clear defiance of Dickens is the weather. Guida quotes Richard Burton as saying that "there were not many white Christmases in our part of Wales in my childhood—perhaps only one or two—but Christmas cards and Dickens and Dylan Thomas and wishful memory have turned them all into white."[14] Unlike those of Thomas and Hallmark, however, Dickens's Christmas is by and large not white. It is not snowing outside Scrooge's house, or Fred's, or the Cratchits', or even when the Spirit of Christmas Present takes Scrooge far afield to observe the festivities of the miners or the sailors at sea. The only place where Dickens specifies "snow upon the ground" (26) is on the road outside Scrooge's old school, where he watches his merry schoolmates returning home for the holidays and leaving him behind.

The weather outside Scrooge's office, by contrast, is "cold, bleak, biting weather: foggy withal,"[15] but the only hints of snow concern Scrooge himself ("a frosty rime was on his head, and on his eyebrows, and his wiry chin"), an implacable natural force who evidently carries his own weather with him: "External heat and cold had little influence on Scrooge. No warmth could warm, nor wintry weather chill him. No wind that blew was bitterer than he, no falling snow was more intent upon its purpose, no pelting rain less open to entreaty. Foul weather didn't know where to have him. The heaviest rain, and snow, and hail, and sleet, could boast of the advantage of him in only one respect. They often 'came down' handsomely, and Scrooge never did" (8). But it always snows, or has at least very recently snowed, in film and television adaptations of *A Christmas Carol*.[16] The result is not the foul weather this passage implies as the logical exterior projection of Scrooge's misanthropy but a trackless and pristine coating suggested first in the flakes that cling to the window of Scrooge's bedchamber, then shown on Christmas morning on the street outside his nephew's house and as a feathery frosting on his cape and the coats of the ministers of charity.

This snow, far from blustery, inconveniences no one but merely sets a picturesque scene, blanketing the city's ugliness and creating a pastoral sense of preindustrial innocence most notable in the 1938 MGM adaptation, which opens with a scene in which sliding on the ice is a festive urban avocation that brings Fred together with Tiny Tim. It might be the Snow of Christmas Past, little known to Dickens's own London but an indispensable invocation of Dickens as the past now represented by any retelling of *A Christmas Carol*.

Telegraphic as it is, the Edison adaptation sets a pattern for many adaptations that follow. Their departures from its model are for the most part highly predictable. As their running times lengthen and their budgets grow, they take Scrooge outside his bedchamber for visits to the scenes of Christmas past, present, and future, often using elaborate visual effects to show the spirits flitting about outside his building or Scrooge himself flying through the air with the Spirit of Christmas Past. They give the Cratchits a Christmas tree and the Christmas Scrooge a bundle of presents, shifting the emphasis from a Dickensian holiday feast to a twentieth-century gift exchange. They introduce scenes showing the reformed Scrooge shopping for toys to bring to the Cratchit children or playing Santa Claus. And they organize themselves increasingly as vehicles for their stars.

This last non-Dickensian microtext, fidelity to what Richard Dyer has called star discourse, does not affect the Edison film because cast members did not begin to be identified until 1912. But movie stars arose soon afterward, and their personas became quite as influential in shaping films as the films' nominal literary sources.[17] Scrooge offers an especially choice role, for he is not only the hero of his story and the only character who changes but the only important character at all. Marley, Fred, Belle, Bob Cratchit, Tiny Tim, Mrs. Dilber—all of them, whatever symbolic importance may be attached to them, are little more than walk-ons, most of them restricted to a single scene or two. Only the three spirits appear onscreen for any substantial length of time. They function more as impresarios, though, than as characters. Indeed, most adaptations follow Dickens in making Christmas Yet to Come a nonspeaking role.

Scrooge is not always played by a great actor, or even a good actor, but he is always played by a star, or at least the starriest performer available to and consistent with a given production.[18] Seymour Hicks, who adapted and starred in the 1913 Zenith adaptation, based the film adaptation on the J. C. Buckstone play, in which he had already appeared some two thousand times,[19] and by the time he returned to the role in the 1935 adaptation, he must have been the most experienced Scrooge in the world. Both Bransby Williams, who starred in two television versions for the BBC in 1950 and 1953, and Patrick Stewart, who starred in the 1999 Hallmark production first seen on Turner Network Television, had toured for many years in one-man theatrical versions of the story. Other adaptations have been tailored to the distinctive talents of John Carradine (the 1947 DuMont Television production), Ralph Richardson (the 1951 NBC Television production), Basil Rathbone *(The Stingiest Man in Town* [1956]; and again in the *Christmas Carol* segment of Harry Alan Towers's 1959 British television series *Tales from Dickens)*, Sterling Hayden *(Carol for Another Christmas)*, Michael Hordern (the 1977 BBC television production), Rich Little *(Rich Little's Christmas Carol* [1978]), Henry Winkler *(An American Christmas Carol)*, Susan Lucci *(Ebbie* [1995]), Cicely Tyson *(Ms. Scrooge* [1997]), Vanessa Williams *(A Diva's Christmas Carol* [2000]), and Kelsey Grammer (2004). Each of these adaptations is calculated to display the performance style of its Scrooge, from Richardson's clipped understatement to Little's florid impressions of the celebrities ostensibly playing different roles in his one-man production.

In addition, each of them revolves around the casting, as well as the performance, of its lead. It is not as simple as selecting a star whose persona will be consistent with a turn as Scrooge. Henry Winkler, who essayed the role halfway through his long run as Arthur Fonzarelli on *Happy Days* (1974–84) to show that he was capable of playing roles besides the Fonz, must put aside his white wig and whiskers to satisfy his core audience with a Fonzie-like bit as the younger romantic Scrooge; Vanessa Williams must be allowed to sing at least one show-stopping number with a backup girl group; the performers surrounding the relatively lightweight Kelsey Grammer must be carefully chosen to avoid upstaging him. Since many more viewers are fans of the stars most likely to play Scrooge than of Charles Dickens, great care must be taken to avoid disappointing them, even if, for example, George C. Scott chooses to play the role with an American accent at Dickens's expense. Even though adaptation theorists consider each of these productions an adaptation of Dickens's story, the major precursor text for a very large number of viewers is the star rather than the author or the author's story.

The point of all this is not to pillory adaptations for fetishizing non-Dickensian, or selectively Dickensian, microtexts while marginalizing or ignoring others but to suggest that fidelity to *A Christmas Carol* involves numberless choices concerning which elements of Dickens's story and its incrustations to be faithful to. As in biblical adaptations, the goal of fidelity itself assumes a particular resonance here, for the inescapable microtext in *A Christmas Carol*, without which the story would fall apart, is the ideal of faith itself, the faith that Scrooge can plausibly be rescued from his selfish greed so that all three Scrooges may be one. Fidelity to this ideal of faith is a special challenge in a secular age that often embraces the story as a literary classic while rejecting its pietistic theology.

The most obvious kind of faith in Dickens's story is the Christian faith incarnated in the newborn Christ and exemplified by his teachings and his sacrificial death and resurrection. Bob Cratchit strikes this note most explicitly when he describes Tiny Tim as having hoped "the people saw him in the church, because he was a cripple, and it might be pleasant to them to remember upon Christmas Day, who made lame beggars walk, and blind men see" (45). The emphasis is not on Christ crucified or risen but on Christ the teacher, with Tiny Tim standing in for the infant whose birth the festival celebrates. Significantly, most adaptations cut this Christlike speech, even though virtually all of them retain Scrooge's sudden concern lest Tiny Tim die (47). And all adaptations follow Dickens in omitting any indication, in Scrooge's joyful awakening (71), that thanks are due to Jesus or God for his second chance.

In place of religious faith, film and television adaptations are more likely to emphasize another kind of Dickensian faith: faith in Christmas as such, in Christmas as a feast that brightens the darkest season by bringing families together in feasting and forgiveness. Although commentators generally agree that in works like *Pickwick Papers* and the five Christmas books, Dickens essentially invented Christmas as a family celebration, it is easy to forget what a radical step it was to characterize the holiday not as a religious observance—Cratchit's ecclesiastical devotions, though undeniably sincere, take place offstage and are accompanied by only one of his children—but as a family gathering already more secularized in its piety. Quoting turn-of-the-century Dickens commentator Edwin Whipple to the effect that Dickens "christianizes eating and drinking. . . . The glutton idolizes meat and drink; Dickens idealizes them," Davis contends that "Dickens sought to express spiritual truth in the humanized language of the self-mirroring secular city."[20] In particular, most adaptations mirror Dickens's faith in the sort of charitable benevolence that can be awakened by childhood memories and the spectacle of innocent suffering.

Rare is the adaptation, however, that does not combine this faith in sentimental Christmas benevolence with other kinds of faith that have their own quite different requirements. A great many adaptations in recent years have implicitly and formally placed their faith in the power of a specific kind of spectacle: the musical number that expresses heightened emotional poignancy ("What If?" from *Christmas Carol: The Movie*) or communal celebration ("Thank You Very Much," from *Scrooge* [1970]). Faith in musical numbers looms especially large in the increasing number of adaptations that have been structured as musicals, from the 1954 to the 2004 television adaptations, since the song-and-dance numbers they display develop a momentum of their own that can give them preeminence over Dickensian homiletics.[21]

Whether or not they are musicals, many adaptations of *A Christmas Carol* employ a device long associated with musicals: inflating pivotal moments through emotional intensification. When Scrooge first beholds the vision of his old school friends shouting happily to each other as they return home for Christmas, the Spirit of Christmas Past tells him, "These are but shadows of the things that have been. . . . They have no consciousness of us" (27). In any number of adaptations, however, this observation is lost on Scrooge, for he makes increasingly strenuous attempts to interact with the apparitions he is seeing. Reginald Owen marks his distance from his own past by vainly attempting to hail his young schoolmates in the 1938 *Christmas Carol,* and when Ebony Scrooge, in *A Diva's Christmas Carol,* asks in frustration of the cognate scene, "Why can't anybody hear me?" she is told, "Because these aren't real people. It's like Los Angeles." George C. Scott impotently prompts the participants in the word games at Fred's Christmas party: "Quick as a *wink.* Idiot." When Belle absolves Scrooge from their engagement in the most pathetic scene from his own past, the older Scrooge shouts, "Say something, you young fool!" in *The Stingiest Man in Town* (1978) and "Say something, damn you!" in *Christmas Carol: The Movie.*

A counterweight to this Hollywood faith in music, musical numbers, and privileged moments of emotional intensity is often provided by a faith in Dickens—not Dickens's original text but Dickens the author figure, imported directly into a surprising number of adaptations to bolster their credentials as entry-level classics. Dickens makes his initial *Christmas Carol* appearance as early as *Scrooge* (1913), looking, as Guida points out, too old to be writing the story and sitting in the library at Gad's Hill, which he did not purchase until thirteen years after writing the story.[22] He returns, played by Alan Napier, in the NBC Television adaptation of 1951; by Marshall Borden in the 1982 filming of the Guthrie Theater's dramatic production; by Gonzo the Great in *The Muppet Christmas Carol;* and by Simon Callow, who also voices Scrooge, in the live-action frame story to *Christmas Carol: The Movie* (a segment cut from the film's MGM Kids release). None of these apparitions make the story more faithful, of course, since they all add a frame absent from Dickens's own story. Except for the unusual performance of Gonzo, they seek instead to shore up the adaptation's classic status by rooting its story more securely in the past or to emphasize its contemporary relevance by showing Dickens as a professional writer working against a deadline or, in *Christmas Carol: The Movie,* altering a public reading of his story in America to incorporate a mouse that has appeared in the lecture hall. The result is that Dickens sometimes confers authority and at other times receives it through a strategic updating.

Many adaptations have sought to guarantee the relevance of Dickens's apparently timeless story by changing its setting to a later period in order ultimately to reaffirm their faith in values from the historical past. *An American Christmas Carol,* set in New England in the early twentieth century, opposes handcraftsmanship to assembly-line furniture construction. The first spirit in *A Diva's Christmas Carol* takes the form of a room-service waitress in New York's Plaza Hotel, where Ebony Scrooge is staying while she performs in a concert ostensibly designed to raise funds for charity but actually intended to publicize her new album. Most notoriously, *Scrooged* (1988) turns its hero into soulless television executive Frank Cross (Bill Murray), whose proposed Christmas lineup includes the Lee Majors action vehicle *The Night the Reindeer Died, Bob*

*Goulet's Old-Fashioned Cajun Christmas,* and a production of *A Christmas Carol* that casts Buddy Hackett as Scrooge and gymnast Mary Lou Retton as a Tiny Tim whose miraculous recovery allows him to do backflips in the street. Each of these Scrooge figures is redeemed by memories and associations tied not only to their earlier lives but to a presumably more innocent period in cultural history to which the hero secretly longs to return as well.

If *Christmas Carol: The Movie* places its ultimate faith in the redemptive power of romantic love, these updates place their faith in a Christmas defined by sharp cultural conflict. They often defuse the potential problem of their audience's disbelief in the spirit world by building it into their characters. In *An American Christmas Carol* Benedict Slade skeptically asks if each of his ghostly visitors is the Spirit of Christmas Past, Present, or Future, and each of them smilingly evades a direct answer ("You do have an interesting way of putting things," the second Spirit tells him). *A Diva's Christmas Carol* turns these meetings into jokes. When she guesses that her room-service waitress is the Ghost of Christmas Past, the waitress, resplendent in bouffant lavender, asks, "Was it the dress?" and Ebony rejoins, "I hope you know you're not getting a tip." In Toshiyuki Hiruma Takashi's 1994 *Christmas Carol* for GoodTimes Entertainment, Scrooge begins to ask the third apparition, "Are you the Spirit of Christmas Who Is to Come?" and then interrupts himself: "I know, stupid question." Moments like these simultaneously express viewers' skepticism about the story's supernatural apparatus and prepare them to accept it and its ultimate moral implications.

Dickens's Scrooge famously rejects Christmas out of hand as "humbug" and "a poor excuse for picking a man's pocket" (11, 14) by requiring him to give his clerk a holiday. The tendency in recent adaptations, however, is to replace the conflict between Christmas and non-Christmas with a conflict between the good Christmas and the bad Christmas from which it must be rescued. The bad Christmas is marked by the commercialism behind Ebony Scrooge's self-promoting holiday concert ("Christmas exists for one reason only," she avers: "to sell crap to the masses"), Fred Flintstone's sacrifice of his family responsibilities to his immersion in his role as Scrooge and his eleventh-hour determination to buy them presents at the local mall, and Frank Cross's rejection in *Scrooged* of a television lead-in that shows "America's favorite old fart reading a *book* in front of a *fireplace*" in favor of a montage of epic disasters over the line: "Acid rain. Drug addiction. International terrorism. Freeway killers. Now more than ever, it is important to remember the true meaning of Christmas."

The film consistently links Frank to this cynical exploitation of Christmas on behalf of allegedly traditional values. "I want to see her nipples!" he says of a scantily clad dancer in the ensemble, and when the censor reminds him, "But this is a Christmas show!" he retorts, "Well, Charles Dickens would have wanted to see her nipples then." So completely does Frank embody this spirit of bad Christmas that his climactic reunion with his lost love, Claire Phillips (Karen Allen), is as unconvincing as the bromides he hurls at the camera in the film's closing scene: "You do have to get involved. There are people that are having trouble making their miracle happen. . . . There are people that don't have enough to eat. . . . If you give, then it can happen. Then the miracle can happen to you."[23]

Given its barrage of references to and excerpts from earlier adaptations of the story, *Scrooged*, like *A Diva's Christmas Carol*, is more clearly successful as both a satire and an example of the misdirected excess of the bad Christmas than as an exhortation to keep the good Christmas in which both updates eventually holler their faith. By establishing their worldly, ironic skepticism about pervasive heresies of Christmas—mercantilism, commercialism, self-absorption, a determination to follow the prescriptions of popular entertainment—so much more powerfully than their call to conversion, these films faithfully register the faithlessness of the modern world, or at least its resistance to traditional expressions of faith. The adaptations that most successfully issue a call to faith link this faith to belief in an existing entertainment franchise whose members can be drafted into some version of *A Christmas Carol* less real than they are.

Such versions have become ubiquitous for several reasons. The holiday entertainment market associated in *Scrooged*, *A Flintstones Christmas Carol*, and *A Diva's Christmas Carol* with the bad Christmas continues in the real world to demand seasonal holiday programming. Community-theater productions of *A Christmas Carol* can be as essential to the theater's financial health as seasonal productions of *The Nutcracker* are to ballet companies. Christmas episodes allow television sitcoms from *Family Ties* to *The Jetsons* to confirm their intimacy with an audience celebrating the same holiday offscreen while virtually giving writers a week off, since "the regular characters in a successful situation comedy series can be fitted with very little difficulty into the various roles in [*A Christmas Carol*], and when that has been done, the parody has virtually written itself."[24]

The most widely praised of these franchise adaptations, *Mr. Magoo's Christ-*

*mas Carol* (1962), provides a model for the strategies all the others use to adapt Dickens's story to the requirements of the franchise. In Magoo's case the conflicts between the two are modest because Quincy Magoo, the UPA cartoon character voiced since 1949 by Jim Backus, has few leading characteristics other than a near-sightedness so aggressive that it serves as an apt metaphor for Scrooge's moral myopia. Since Magoo is always well-meaning and vaguely benevolent, however, he requires a makeover to play Scrooge. Hence adapter Barbara Chain frames Dickens's story as a theatrical production in which Magoo is starring, allowing him to frame the story by singing "It's Great to Be Back on Broadway" and mistakenly walking into a nearby restaurant and the ladies' dressing room. Once the curtain rises, Magoo loses his single signature trait— the only joking evidence of his nearsightedness comes in the final sequence, when he introduces himself to the poulterer by shaking his turkey's drumstick—in a role that is clearly and reassuringly marked as only a role. Viewers of the cartoon get to see the crowd inside the theater watching the production and watch the falling curtain divide the story into three acts with commercial intermissions before Magoo's curtain call. Only then does he return to Magooesque form, bowing the wrong way, catching his foot in a rope, and bringing down all the theatrical flats in a climactic series of crashes that make him say, "Listen to that applause! Ah, Magoo, you've done it again! I've brought down the house!"

A *Flintstones Christmas Carol* uses the same model, casting Fred Flintstone as Scrooge in the Bedrock Community Players' production of *A Christmas Carol*, with the complication that his absorption in the role is making his self-evaluation—"There's more to acting than memorization. I *am* Scrooge"—all too accurate. Fred never sounds very much like a Dickens character, but that is not a problem for the many adaptations whose Dickensian pleasures are rooted less in the promise of fidelity than in the surprising emergence of discrete Dickensian echoes and analogies in unexpected contexts.[25] The film uses regular cast members as Scrooge's clerk Cragit (Barney Rubble) or Tiny Tim (Barney's son Bamm-Bamm) but intertwines Scrooge's need for conversion more closely with Fred's by having Fred's aggrieved wife, Wilma, substitute for several key cast members unable to go on, so that the play increasingly imitates the Flintstones' domestic problems. Although the cast members are presented as more real than the Dickensian roles they assume, A *Flintstones Christmas Carol* waives the obvious problem raised by the conflation of Fred's character and his role as Scrooge. Even after his alleged conversion, Fred, unlike Scrooge, will still be an overbearing, loudmouthed boor—a problem Edmund Wilson would have appreciated.

If *Mr. Magoo's Christmas Carol* works to adapt the Dickens and Magoo franchises to each other, and incidentally to the structure of cartoon musicals, *A Flintstones Christmas Carol* subordinates Dickens to the requirements of a cartoon franchise whose target demographic is economically more powerful. The apotheosis of this pattern of subordination is *Mickey's Christmas Carol*, designed as Mickey Mouse's comeback in 1983, thirty years after his last cartoon appearance. Although it begins with credits in an old-style font against a background that looks like antique parchment, this credit sequence is used as the basis for a strategic transition to a familiar cartoon world already illustrated during the credits by a new song, "Oh, What a Merry Christmas Day," and a series of black-and-white line drawings of familiar Disney characters in the Dickensian roles they will assume. In addition to Scrooge McDuck, a natural choice for Scrooge, and Mr. Toad, from *The Wind in the Willows* (1949), as Fezziwig, the studio reaches deep into its vaults for highly appropriate figures to play the three ghosts: Jiminy Cricket, Willie the Giant from *Mickey and the Beanstalk* (1947), and Mickey's old antagonist Black Pete. Mickey himself is cast as Bob Cratchit, with Minnie as his wife and Morty (or is it Ferdy?) as Tiny Tim.

Other cast choices are more problematic. Goofy is the right physical type for Marley's Ghost, but since his hallmark is amiable physical ineptitude, the role has to be extensively reworked for him. The result is a Marley that ingeniously combines slapstick humor with hints of the supernatural but ends up more clumsy and good-natured than foreboding. ("You'll be visited by three spirits," he tells his former partner, emphasizing his point by holding up two fingers.) Donald Duck, normally impatient and splenetic, is utterly miscast as Scrooge's sanguine nephew. And the obvious casting of Daisy Duck as "lovely Isabel," with whom Scrooge breaks off his romance by foreclosing on their honeymoon cottage, means that the nephew's home life cannot be shown, since Daisy, Donald's customary romantic partner, is already spoken for. Even Mickey himself, whose game good nature suits Bob Cratchit very well, throws the adaptation off-kilter, for although Paul Davis observes that "for the Victorians the Cratchits were the center of the story,"[26] the family gets little screen time or thematic emphasis here. It is not Mickey's Christmas Carol but Scrooge's—or it would be if its primary task were not to resurrect Disney's signature hero by introducing his backlist to the videotape audience.

This process of "Disneyfication"—the term by which Richard Schickel influentially summarized the cultural imperialism that led the studio to reduce each of its many literary properties "to the limited terms Disney and his people could understand"[27]—is even more pronounced in "The Making of *Mickey's Christmas Carol*," which Disney released simultaneously with its companion film. The two films are better described as a pair than a feature and its appended featurette, since they are equally long (twenty-five minutes each) and have been bundled together on their release on VHS videotape and DVD. More surprisingly, they are equally fictional, since "The Making of *Mickey's Christmas Carol*" intersperses its interviews of the film's creators with the live-action/animated story of how Jiminy Cricket is called on to produce it, from the injunction to "have a good show, but watch the budget" to a scene in which he calls Donald from the golf course back to the studio.

Even the alternate account, in which live technicians rather than the studio's animated heroes produce the film, substitutes Walt Disney, who had died in 1967, for Dickens as the presiding genius. The voice-over narrator makes only two references to "Charles Dickens's classic Christmas tale." The first concerns the challenges of matching Disney regulars to Dickens's characters. The second is immediately followed by an announcement celebrating "the return to the screen of the world's most popular mouse. The resulting film is a classic addition to the fabled Disney heritage."

An important function of "The Making of *Mickey's Christmas Carol*" is to shift the subject of "classic" from Dickens to Disney by invoking a background history that belongs exclusively to the Disney franchise. "Past Disney masters" are shown consulting archives in the Animation Research Library "dating back to the studio's earliest cartoons" as the camera tracks in over a formidable array of drawings and endless shelves of files.[28] Both animators and vocalists refer to cartoon characters like Mickey and Scrooge as "performers," and one of them, Mark Henn, says that "people think of [Mickey] as a friend, and they're just happy to see him back again." In short, the featurette would be more accurately titled "Rooting Dickens in Disney Prehistory" than "The Making of *Mickey's Christmas Carol*."

*An All Dogs Christmas Carol* adopts an approach very different from Disney's uncompromising cultural imperialism. Although the credit line "Based upon Goldcrest's original motion picture *All Dogs Go to Heaven*" (which substitutes for obligatory "Based on the story by Charles Dickens") would seem to align it with *Mickey's Christmas Carol* and *A Flintstones Christmas Carol*, its attitude toward the Dickens story is considerably more ambivalent and its loyalties correspondingly divided. An early scene shows Charlie Barkin taking the part of a reindeer in a charity production intended to raise money for Timmy, a puppy with a bandaged paw. But subsequent performances are far less clear-cut in their framing. Itchy Itchiford's description of Carface Carruthers as "a total Scrooge" (a cliché that is still assumed to retain its power to move Carface to conversion) gives Charlie the idea of scaring Carface into giving up his part in Belladonna's scheme to "ruin Christmas" by presenting a fake television broadcast giving a Dickensian view of Christmas past, present, and future. Although Carface is never fooled by this broadcast, he is moved to pity and protectiveness of Timmy, and he finally defies Belladonna with a ringing cry, "This is for Timmy!" even though he makes it clear that his conversion ("Ain't I a little Dickens?") is only temporary. The film wants to express grade-school skepticism about the sentimental supernaturalism of *A Christmas Carol* (and the film *It's a Wonderful Life*) even as it assumes that their continuing mythopoetic power is available to its own franchise.

The difficulty of reconciling joking skepticism about Christmas faith with an unvarnished desire to trade on it is ultimately not resolved within *An All Dogs Christmas Carol* but implicitly referred to its predecessor, *All Dogs Go to Heaven* (1989), whose premise is Charlie's miraculous return to Earth after he has been executed by Carface's thugs. Like the earlier film, *An All Dogs Christmas Carol* wants to be both scary and funny, threatening and uplifting, skeptical and accepting toward supernatural claims. But so, of course, does Dickens's story, whose hero first greets his late partner as the likely side effect of indigestion ("You may be an undigested bit of beef, a blot of mustard, a crumb of cheese, a fragment of an underdone potato" [18]) and ends by "ha[ving] no further intercourse with Spirits, but liv[ing] upon the Total Abstinence Principle" (76). The reason that *An All Dogs Christmas Carol*'s tone seems so uncertain is not because it fails to take Dickens's story consistently seriously but because it never reconciles its intermittent irony toward *A Christmas Carol* with its earnest acceptance of its own franchise's premise that supernatural and virtually omnipotent animals can meddle freely in the moral problems of animals on Earth. If *Mickey's Christmas Carol* illustrates a powerful franchise's ability to vanquish other contending progenitor texts like Dickens through faith in itself, *An All Dogs Christmas Carol* shows the problems when that faith is not justified by a sufficiently powerful franchise.

It might seem that the authors of entry-level Dickens adaptations have a limited number of unappealing choices. They can market their adaptation in developmental terms like the 1910 Edison short, offering due obeisance to *A Christmas Carol* as a classic story their audience may not know well enough to treasure. They can invite their audience to laugh at Dickens's sentimentality through irony or parody, as in *Scrooged,* even though their jokes will disrupt the continuity of the story. They can translate Dickens's sentimental fable into more contemporary terms, like *An American Christmas Carol* or *A Diva's Christmas Carol,* compromising their faith in the story's universality with a competing faith in its updating. Or they can seek to displace Dickens's authority with that of their own franchise. One last possibility remains: They can graft the Dickens franchise onto another commercial franchise and make a running joke of the whole project of adaptation. This is the method of *The Muppet Christmas Carol.*

The film is launched by Gonzo the Great, who announces, "Welcome to *A Muppet Christmas Carol.* I am Charles Dickens—" at which point he is interrupted by Rizzo the Rat: "No, you're not. . . . Charles Dickens was a nineteenth-century novelist. A genius." The note of playful self-reflexivity continues throughout the repeated appearances of Gonzo's Dickens and Rizzo. "Wow, that was scary stuff," Rizzo says of the two Marley Ghosts, Robert and Jacob (played by Statler and Waldorf). "Should we be worried about the kids in the audience?" "Nah, that's all right," replies Gonzo. "This is culture." When the Spirit of Christmas Yet to Come appears, Rizzo recoils: "This is too scary. I don't want to see any more." Gonzo agrees: "You're on your own, folks. We'll meet you at the finale." Here the story's alleged author, who has been watching his creation unfold just beyond his line of vision, is suddenly too frightened to watch further.

Nor is this note of joking self-reflexivity restricted to the conceit of the frame. Telling Rizzo that "this really is a dirty city," Gonzo uses a small nameless Muppet to wipe the window to Scrooge's office, and the Muppet speaks up: "Thank you for making me part of this." Scrooge's schoolmaster (Sam the Eagle) tells him, "You will love business. It is the American way." After Gonzo whispers into his ear, he corrects himself: "It is the British way." Young Scrooge's first job is at a rubber-chicken factory run by Fozziwig (Fozzie Bear). When Scrooge asks the Spirit of Christmas Present, "Aren't you a little absent-minded, Spirit?" he replies, "I'm a *large* absent-minded Spirit."

This byplay can continue uninterrupted save for the obligatory musical numbers without undermining the film's faith in conversion, Christmas, Dickens, or the Muppet franchise because self-reflexive parody is a hallmark of the

Muppets—at least the Muppets who appear on *The Muppet Show*.[29] Of course it is absurd for Muppets Kermit the Frog (Bob Cratchit) and Miss Piggy (Emily Cratchit) to interact with Michael Caine's Scrooge or for Fozziwig's guests to include both Muppets and humans, but it is no more absurd than the analogous interactions each week on *The Muppet Show*, ostensibly a musical variety show constantly interrupted by misfits between the regulars and the guest stars, problems with the cast and technicians, and heckling from audience members Statler and Waldorf. When Scrooge, in one of the film's few direct borrowings of Dickens's dialogue, tells the Marley brothers that there's more of gravy than of grave about them, Robert responds, "'More of gravy than of grave?' What a terrible pun!" and Jacob adds, "Where do you get those jokes?" Here the adaptation is Dickensian not because it uses Dickens's language but because it plays with it.

Indeed, the keynote of *The Muppet Christmas Carol* is not so much faith in Dickens or in the Muppet franchise as faith in the possibilities of play already implicit in both franchises. By refracting its realistic Scrooge through the unlikely lens of Muppet neighbors, victims, and author figures, it invites its viewers to play with him and through him quite as closely, though in somewhat different terms, as Alastair Sim's playfully malevolent, and finally playful, Scrooge, who constantly looks as if he had just eaten a piece of bad meat. Instead of running its credits over a bookshelf of Dickens titles or introducing Charles Dickens as author or character to bolster the company's own authority, *The Muppet Christmas Carol* ends with a gesture that really does offer a bridge from the Muppet version to Dickens's. "Nice story, Mr. Dickens," Rizzo tells Gonzo, who replies, "Oh, thanks. If you liked this, you should read the book."

# CHAPTER FIVE

# Between Adaptation and Allusion

Not all adaptations are created equal. Geoffrey Wagner, writing in 1975, found it useful to distinguish three types of "transition of fiction into film": *transposition,* "in which a novel is given directly on the screen, with a minimum of apparent interference"; *commentary* (alternatively "re-emphasis or restructure"), "in which an original is taken and either purposely or inadvertently altered in some respect"; and *analogy,* "a fairly considerable departure for the sake of making *another* work of art."[1] A decade later Dudley Andrew, limiting himself "to those cases where the adaptation process is foregrounded, that is, where the original is held up as a worthy source or goal," defined three modes of adaptation: borrowing, in which "the artist employs, more or less extensively, the material, idea, or form of an earlier, generally successful text"; intersecting, in which "the uniqueness of the original text is preserved to such an extent that it is deliberately left unassimilated in adaptation"; and transforming, whose quest for fidelity of one kind or another inevitably "raises questions about the specificity of these two signifying systems" of literature and cinema.[2] More recently, Kamilla Elliott has posited six critical approaches to theorizing adaptation based on different ways of conceiving the relations between narrative form and content: the psychic concept, the ventriloquist concept, the genetic concept, the de(re)composing concept, the incarnational concept, and the trumping concept.[3] And Gérard Genette, in the second volume of his monumental trilogy on transtextuality—the term Genette uses to encompass "all that sets a text in a relationship, whether obvious or concealed, with other texts"—defines five modes of possible relations between one text and another. First is *intertextuality*, "the actual presence of one text within another" via quotation, plagiarism, or allusion. Second is *paratextuality*, which concerns elements that place the text "within the totality of the literary work": "a title, a subtitle, intertitles; prefaces, postfaces, notices, forewords, etc.; marginal, infrapaginal, terminal notes; epigraphs; illustrations; blurbs, book covers, dust jackets; and many other kinds of secondary signals, whether allographic or autographic." Third is *metatextuality*, a commentative mode like that of literary criticism in which one text refers to another "without necessarily citing it (without summoning it), in fact sometimes without even naming it." Fourth is *hypertextuality*, "any relationship uniting a text B (which I shall call the *hypertext*) to an earlier text A (I shall of course call it the *hypotext*), upon which it is grafted in a manner that is not that of commentary." Fifth, finally, is *architextuality*, the "completely silent" directing of readers' expectations via generic cues or conventions "of a purely taxonomic nature."[4] Genette's classifications thus have the considerable merit of subsuming film adaptations, a phenomenon that he never discusses but that clearly fits into the category of hypertexts, into a larger matrix of intertextual (or, as Genette would say, transtextual) relations.

The problem with Genette's painstaking taxonomy, like that of other distinctions among modes or types of adaptation, is that it does not adequately demarcate the frontiers of adaptation, the places where it shades off into allusion. Everyone can agree that Walt Disney's animated musical cartoon *Cinderella* (1950) and Ralph Nelson's *Cinderella* (1957), in which Julie Andrews and others sing a Rodgers and Hammerstein score, are both adaptations of Charles Perrault's fairy tale that draw freely on other elements as well. And most commentators would probably agree that Frank Tashlin's *Cinderfella* (1960), with Jerry Lewis in the title role, is a rather freer adaptation. In that case, is *Pretty Woman* (1990), in which wealthy Richard Gere rescues Julia Roberts from a life of prostitution and in which she rescues him from an endless round of humdrum business dealings, a Cinderella story? What about Depression-era comedies like *Easy Living* (1937) and the role-reversing *My Man Godfrey* (1936)? For that matter, what of the innumerable television magazine accounts that labeled the 1979 marriage of Prince Charles and Lady Diana Spencer a modern-day Cinderella story, even though the bride was herself wealthy and aristocratic?

Most categorical discussions of adaptation ignore these problems entirely by privileging a small number of intertextual relations as exemplary of all adaptation and passing over the others in silence. As Wagner's reference to "*another work of art*" indicates, the main purpose of his three categories, as indeed of most of his discussion of individual adaptations, is evaluative. Other things being equal, commentary is for Wagner a more valuable activity than transposition, and analogy is more valuable still. Andrew's categories are scarcely less evaluative, with the booby prize this time reserved not only for servile adaptations "trying to measure up to a literary work" but also for the "tiresome discussion" of "fidelity and transformation."[5] But even Elliott and Genette, whose interest is more analytical than evaluative, offer little more help. Elliott observes that she offers her six concepts, all illustrated by different adaptations of *Wuthering Heights*, as "operative in practice" but not necessarily defensible in principle: "They overlap as frequently as they conflict and are by no means presented here as ideal, prescriptive, or even empirically 'true.'"[6] Her six competing ways of thinking about adaptation are a series of multiple centers sometimes forming logical pairs but with no firm boundaries and hence no frontiers. Even Genette's taxonomy, which addresses this question by drawing a categorical distinction between intertextual relations like quotation and allusion and hypertextual relations like adaptation, overlooks the slippery slope between adaptation and allusion and offers no place to draw a line between them.

It would seem worthwhile, then, to develop a more detailed grammar that would either break down adaptation into nonevaluative modes like Elliott's or at least provide a stronger rationale for the difference between intertextual and hypertextual relations. This chapter will propound a grammar of hypertextual relations as they shade off to the intertextual. Unlike Elliott's tour de force, I do not seek to ground my categories in adaptations of a single work but in a series of logical relations that refer to a wide range of adaptations in an attempt to be as comprehensive as possible. In the interest of anchoring the discussion by providing some common points of reference, however, I shall return repeatedly to adaptations of three sources: Shakespeare's plays, Jane Austen's novels, and monster stories.

· 1 ·

The obvious kind of adaptations to begin with are the *celebrations* that correspond roughly to Wagner's transposition and Elliott's trumping concept, which addresses "which medium represents better. Although it can take either side, the majority of adaptation criticism favors the novel over the film."[7] Adaptations that impute to their literary sources powers beyond their own fall into several categories. *Curatorial adaptations* subordinate whatever specific resources they find in cinema to the attempt to preserve their original texts as faithfully as possible. One well-known example is Kenneth Branagh's *Hamlet* (1996), whose four-hour length bespeaks its determination to avoid the usual cuts in the play. The most extensive sets of examples are the BBC adaptations of Austen's novels (1971–86, 1995–96) and of Shakespeare's plays, a series under the revealing collective title *The Complete Dramatic Works of William Shakespeare* (1978–85). Using stage-trained performers in both series, the BBC seeks to preserve in the case of Austen relatively faithful (though still abridged) transcriptions of each of her six completed novels and in the case of Shakespeare forthrightly stage-bound performances of each of his thirty-seven plays. Applying the even stricter measure of *replication* of every possible element of the original text—structure, action, character, setting, dialogue, theme, tone, and so on—Erich von Stroheim produced *Greed* (1924), an obsessive and exhaustive twenty-three-hour adaptation of Frank Norris's novel *McTeague* (1899) that MGM promptly cut down to two hours for commercial release. A third variety of adaptation whose leading impulse is to celebrate the power of its original is the *homage,* which most often takes the form of a readaptation that pays tribute to an earlier film adaptation as definitive. Gus Van Sant's *Psycho* (1998) follows Alfred Hitchcock's 1960 film scene by scene, often word by word, at times shot by shot, but adds color and a new cast to speak screenwriter Joseph Stefano's dialogue once more. Werner Herzog's *Nosferatu: Phantom der Nacht* (1979), less slavish in its devotion to the textual details of F. W. Murnau's 1922 *Nosferatu,* makes no secret of its admiration for Murnau's seminal film. Enlarging the text under adaptation from a single specific authored text to an authorless historical or cultural text produces the *heritage adaptation,* whose "'museum aesthetic,'" as Ginette Vincendeau calls it, is devoted to "celebrating rather than investigating" an idealized past typically marked by attractive people moving through attractive places, all suffused with nostalgia for bygone times and the values they are taken to represent.[8] Since Vincendeau groups such diverse projects as *Chariots of Fire* (1981), *The Jewel in the Crown* (1984), *Babette's Feast* (1987), *1492: Conquest of Paradise* (1992), *Shakespeare in Love* (1998), and *Elizabeth* (1998) in this group, it seems fair to add American films like *The Great Gatsby* (1974), which is at least as interested in recreating the Jazz Age ambience of the characters' world as in telling the story of F. Scott Fitzgerald's 1925 novel.

Since celebrations, as Elliott points out, overwhelmingly favor novels over films, it is not surprising to find so many adaptations of canonical authors like Shakespeare and Austen in this category. Celebrations of films over their novelistic sources tend to focus on films based on distinctly less respectable sources, like monster movies. Thirty years ago Leo Braudy pointed out that although Robert Louis Stevenson's story "The Strange Case of Dr. Jekyll and Mr. Hyde" (1886) indicated only a subtle and well-nigh indescribable deformation in the monstrous Edward Hyde, "all the great Jekyll and Hyde films make him undergo a physical transformation, exercising makeup and camera artistry."[9] Rouben Mamoulian's 1931 adaptation of the story uses a series of gelatin filters to showcase Fredric March's initial transformation in a scene that can still impress even viewers jaded by special-effects technology. The scene, like Mamoulian's film as a whole, is a textbook example of *pictorial realization,* a celebration of cinema's power to show things words can present only indirectly. In the same way, every feature film based on *Frankenstein; or, The Modern Prometheus* (1818) takes as pivotal a scene Mary Shelley sketches out in the most hasty and perfunctory terms: the moment when Victor Frankenstein succeeds in animating the creature he has stitched together from human tissue. Both the unforgettable visuals of James Whale's 1931 film version—the set design of Frankenstein's laboratory, the impressive look of his scientific paraphernalia, the costuming and makeup of Boris Karloff as the monster—and its trademark line of dialogue, Frankenstein's exultant "It's alive!" became trademarks of a film franchise that endure to this day. Every film version of Anthony Hope's 1894 novel *The Prisoner of Zenda* (1922, 1937, 1952, 1979, etc.) takes advantage of technical resources specific to cinema to show two Lewis Stones, Ronald Colmans, Stewart Grangers, or Peter Sellerses interacting with one another. So, too, Whale's *The Invisible Man* (1933) revels in its ability to create arresting visual effects (Jack Griffin's invisibility under his muffling layers of clothing, the footprints he is seen leaving in the snow) that H. G. Wells's novel can indicate as impossible without the power of showing the impossible.[10] Brian De Palma's thrillers *Carrie* (1976) and *The Fury* (1978) stage elaborate displays of the protagonists' telekinetic powers that the source novels by Stephen King and John Farris can only describe.

Adaptations of Shakespeare and Austen rarely take the form of pictorial realizations because canonical authors are generally assumed to be making other and higher claims on readers' attention. From time to time, however, a film adaptation can pose as a *liberation* of material the original text had to suppress or repress. Just as Bob Rafelson's 1981 remake of James M. Cain's censor-baiting novel *The Postman Always Rings Twice* (1934) restores the sexual interludes and the pun on attorney Arthur Katz's name missing from Tay Garnett's 1946 adaptation, Roman Polanski's *Macbeth* (1974) and Julie Taymor's *Titus* (1999) both present horrifically violent events Shakespeare only describes. The implicit rationale for these changes is that they present the stories liberated from the restrictions forced on Shakespeare by the conventions of his culture and his dramaturgy. Observers questioning this rationale should remember that however faithfully stage and screen directors seek to stage *Twelfth Night* and *Antony and Cleopatra,* they almost invariably cast female performers as Viola and Cleopatra on exactly the same grounds: that the plays are better served that way than by the Elizabethan proscription on actresses.

This line of reasoning might suggest that such adaptations, which celebrate not so much cinema's essentially visual properties as its contemporary freedom from earlier norms of censorship and decorum, be called *literalizations* if that term did not reintroduce the ideal of *litteras* (letters) as the norm for all representations. A more precise term is supplied by Elliott herself in her discussion of adaptation as incarnation, "wherein the word is only a partial expression of a more total representation that requires incarnation as its fulfillment."[11] In this view movies provide what novels can only hint at: words made flesh.

· 2 ·

By far the most common approach to adaptation is *adjustment,* whereby a promising earlier text is rendered more suitable for filming by one or more of a wide variety of strategies. This is the first of several approaches that correspond to different kinds of what Andrew calls borrowing. A closer analogy is to Elliott's genetic concept, which posits "an underlying 'deep' narrative structure akin to genetic structure" between the literary and cinematic versions of a given story.[12] Narratologists like Seymour Chatman and Brian McFarlane commonly distinguish between the story (or the *syuzhet* or *histoire* or *l'énoncé*) and its discursive manifestation in a given *fabula* or *discours* or *l'énonciation*.[13] The changes they recognize as inevitable at the discursive level include the following:

*Compression.* Three-hundred-page novels cannot be adapted to feature-length films without a great deal of systematic elision and omission. Neither can *Hamlet* or *Antony and Cleopatra.* An important subsidiary theme of McFarlane's detailed study of David Lean's film adaptation of *Great Expectations* (1946) is Lean's strategies for compressing Charles Dickens's five-hundred-page novel to a film of two hours.[14] Many early sound adaptations of celebrated monster stories—*Dracula* (1931), *Frankenstein* (1931), *Dr. Jekyll and Mr. Hyde* (1931)—were, like *Pride and Prejudice* (1940) and *The Heiress* (1949), based not directly on their source novels but on stage plays that had already done the hard work of whittling the material down to the right size for an evening's entertainment.

*Expansion.* The opposite tendency, though less often remarked, is equally important because a surprising number of films have been fashioned from short stories. Despite writing habits that made Ernest Hemingway's novels seem cinematic to many readers, the most successful Hemingway adaptation, *The Killers* (1946), is an expansion of his 1927 short story that treats the Swede's death as a mystery to be solved and then contravenes Hemingway by providing a detective, a detailed backstory, and a solution. *Bringing Up Baby* (1938), *Stagecoach* (1939), *Meet John Doe* (1941), *All about Eve* (1950), *Rear Window* (1954), *The Swimmer* (1968), *Field of Dreams* (1989), and *In the Bedroom* (2001)—to stick to films whose sources Stephanie Harrison has collected in a recent anthology—are all based on short stories.[15] So are such foreign classics as *Rashomon* (1950), *The Lady with the Dog* (1959), and *Blow-Up* (1966). Even Tod Browning's monstrous circus film *Freaks* (1932) is based on a monstrous short story. Stories based on songs offer still more extreme examples. *Tommy* (1975) is a staging of a closet rock opera, and *A Hard Day's Night* (1964) and *Yellow Submarine* (1968) are revue films with just enough plot to motivate the songs from the Beatles albums. But *Alice's Restaurant* (1969) and *Love Potion No. 9* (1992) are full-blown expansions of narrative hints that are especially thin in the most famous and successful of this subgenre, *Singin' in the Rain* (1952).

*Correction.* Just as most Shakespeare adaptations correct Elizabethan stagings of the Bard by allowing women to play the female characters, many films correct what they take to be the flaws of their originals. *Pygmalion* (1938) and *My Fair Lady* (1964) both brought Eliza Doolittle back to Henry Higgins instead of pairing her with Freddy Eynsford-Hill, the first time with the explicit blessing of George Bernard Shaw, who is credited as its principal screenwriter. Although *Pygmalion* had to improve Shaw by soft-pedaling the indiscreet exclamation ("bloody—") that nearly unmasks Eliza at the Ascot racetrack, *My Fair Lady* found it necessary to raise the stakes ("Move your bloomin' arse") for more jaded audiences. Countless Hollywood adaptations have improved their sources by providing improbably happy endings (for example, the American ending of *Love* [1927], in which Greta Garbo as Anna Karenina decides not to kill herself), toning down their language or juicing it up.

*Updating.* A far more frequent strategy is to transpose the setting of a canonical classic to the present in order to show its universality while guaranteeing its relevance to the more immediate concerns of the target audience. A particularly interesting example is Richard Lester's *The Three Musketeers* (1973) and *The Four Musketeers* (1974), in which the characters, moving in careful period dress through historically appropriate settings, display a distinctly modernist sensibility. Shakespearean examples mixing period and contemporary markers abound, following the frequent practice of updating Shakespeare onstage: *10 Things I Hate about You* (1999); *O* (2001); the Michael Almereyda *Hamlet* (2000), starring Ethan Hawke; and *She's the Man* (2006). Even Tony Richardson's period *Hamlet* (1970), starring Nicol Williamson, was marked as an update by its breakneck pace, its casting of pop singer Marianne Faithfull as Ophelia, and the publicity line "This above all, to thine own thing be true"—a modish phrase that instantly and predictably became the most dated feature of the film's release.

*Superimposition.* Even Shakespeare, who wrote for an often interactive audience, produced at least one play, *The Merry Wives of Windsor,* at the express request of Queen Elizabeth. So it is hardly surprising that cinema, a medium legendary for its multiple authors and its susceptibility to outside influence, should often superimpose more or less explicitly identified coauthors on the material it borrows from literary sources. An obvious example is Hollywood star discourse, which gives movie stars considerable power over the authorship of films even if they never set pen to paper. *Cleopatra* (1963), based on Carlo Mario Franzero's book, was conceived as a vehicle for Elizabeth Taylor rather than as a Shakespearean adaptation. *Sense and Sensibility* (1995) was undertaken because producer Lindsay Doran wanted her fellow Austen fan Emma Thompson to write it, even though Thompson had never before written a screenplay,[16] and Gwyneth Paltrow was cast in the title role of *Emma* (1996) because she made starring in it a condition of her appearance in the allegedly more commercial project *The Pallbearer* (1996).

Apart from stars who have the power to decree which properties get adapted, how big their own roles are, and how appealing those roles are likely to be, other unacknowledged coauthors in the act of adaptation have included the censors of the Hays Office (and indeed their preemptive counterparts within each studio). Between 1934 and 1956, at the height of its power, the Hays Office decreed that Rebecca de Winter's murder in Daphne du Maurier's *Rebecca* (1938) had to become an accident in the 1940 film because her husband could not be allowed to get away with murdering her and demanded that the final scene in Raymond Chandler's 1939 novel *The Big Sleep* be changed (and, ironically, made a good deal more violent) so that the audience for the 1946 film could leave the theater assured that Eddie Mars would be punished for his gang's criminal activities. Industry censors on the watch for sexual innuendo, racial slurs, and unpunished infractions of the law had a decisive impact on the shape of such diverse adaptations as *Scarface* (1932), *Gone with the Wind* (1939), and *Mildred Pierce* (1945).

A more general influence is a house style whose requirements can range from the subtlest to the most obvious. In one important sense the 1940 *Pride and Prejudice* is not a Jane Austen film at all, for apart from a 1938 British television adaptation of the novel, there had been no previous adaptations that could create a Jane Austen genre. Instead it makes more sense to speak of it as a Greer Garson film, a Laurence Olivier film, an Aldous Huxley film, a Jane Murfin film, even a Robert Z. Leonard film, and especially an MGM film. The MGM house style dictates beautiful actresses, lavish but not necessarily historically accurate costumes and sets, expressive music, bright and even lighting, clear enunciation, and a tendency toward declamation observed by even such minor characters as Caroline Bingley (Frieda Inescort) and Lady Lucas (Marjorie Wood). These studio conventions play an equally important role in MGM's *Romeo and Juliet* (1936). The quite different house style of producer Ismail Merchant and director James Ivory, fostered by their preference for working repeatedly with the same screenwriters, cinematographers, composers, and performers, gives their films a different but equally distinctive look and tone. So does the house style of the Hammer monster cycle, beginning with *The*

*Curse of Frankenstein* (1957) and *Horror of Dracula* (1958). Whatever the source, the Hammer style prescribes period settings, brilliant color that sets strategic shots of blood and gore against more sober backgrounds, provocative female characters, outbursts of sex and violence that made the films notorious in their day, and leading roles for a stable of character actors headed by Peter Cushing and Christopher Lee. Hence the Hammer *Hound of the Baskervilles* (1959) changed Beryl Stapleton from her husband's unwilling accomplice and victim to the lead villain, and *Frankenstein Must Be Destroyed* (1969) found time amid the carnage for Baron Frankenstein (Cushing) to rape his landlady Anna Spengler (Veronica Carlson).

A related requirement often noted by reviewers but often overlooked by film theorists is budgetary constraints, which might be said to constitute an anti-house style. Tight purse strings left their mark on all of Orson Welles's Shakespearean adaptations. *Macbeth* (1948), made for the Poverty Row studio Republic, bears indelible traces of its abbreviated shooting schedule. Iago's attack on Cassio in *The Tragedy of Othello: The Moor of Venice* (1952) was set in a steam bath because the costumes had been stolen from an unlocked trailer. Even *Chimes at Midnight* (1965), Welles's acknowledged masterpiece in the genre of Shakespearean adaptation, feels more like a magnificent torso than a finished product, and not just because its screenplay cobbles together bits of *1 Henry IV*, *2 Henry IV*, *The Merry Wives of Windsor*, and *Henry V*. Sometimes the crucial force behind an adaptation is the accountant.

More general still are the requirements of the popular genres into which so many adaptations have been shoehorned. This superimposition of generic conventions is especially notable in adaptations that have arrived in Hollywood after first being staged as Broadway musicals, from *Carousel* (1956) to *My Fair Lady*. But such conventions can operate far less obtrusively, as in Franco Zeffirelli's *Romeo and Juliet* (1968), the first Shakespearean adaptation, and one of the first films, to be marketed specifically to a niche audience of young viewers. The casting of Olivia Hussey and Leonard Whiting, young enough to be the children of the stars (Norma Shearer and Leslie Howard) who had played the lovers in 1936, was specifically intended to lure teenagers into the theater and helped establish a genre—the teenpic, the movie designed to appeal to teens—that has become the single dominant genre in Hollywood, spawning in the process such teen-friendly Austen adaptations as the 1996 *Emma* with Gwyneth Paltrow and the 2005 *Pride and Prejudice* with Keira Knightley. Such adaptations might well be described as repackaging canonical literary works for their target audiences.

· 3 ·

There have been so many different ways for the film industry to adjust its literary sources to the requirements of different audiences, institutions, and conventions in hopes of increasing its profits that adjustment might seem not only the dominant but the sole model for adaptation. One model that sounds similar but is quite different is based on Elliott's "de(re)composing concept," in which "film and novel decompose, merge, and form a new composition at 'underground' levels of reading. The adaptation is a composite of textual and filmic signs merging an audience consciousness together with other cultural narratives and often leads to confusion as to which is novel and which is film."[17] The leading example in English-language cinema is the Sherlock Holmes franchise, whose every new addition adds and deforms material in the hope that it will become an indistinguishable part of the canonical franchise.

The Holmes phenomenon will be treated at length in chapter 9, but its mention here serves as a fitting introduction to another more pervasive model that may be called *neoclassic imitation.* Unlike *10 Things I Hate about You* and *She's the Man,* which assume that Shakespeare is endlessly available for updating because his people and stories are universal, Richard Loncraine's *Richard III* (1995) relocates Shakespeare's story to a time and place that are both historically specific and contrary to fact: a 1930s fascist England. The film uses this fictional setting to illuminate Shakespeare's tangled story of scheming and betrayal even as it uses Ian McKellan's murderous, charismatic Richard to illuminate Hitler's rise to power. The mixture of Third Reich grandeur in the production design and English references in the language not only evokes Oswald Mosley's British Union of Fascists but creates a fictional zone that, like Shakespeare's Wars of the Roses, works through historical specificity to generality. Robert Wise and Jerome Robbins adopt a similar procedure in *West Side Story* (1961), whose transposition of *Romeo and Juliet* to contemporary New York is meant both to point out Shakespeare's relevance and to humanize the youth gangs most contemporaneous viewers would have known only as rumors or threats.

Neoclassic imitations take their cue from John Dryden, Alexander Pope, and their fellow satirists of the seventeenth and eighteenth centuries who overtly took the poets of Greece and Rome as their models. Dryden spent years translating Persius, Juvenal, Ovid, and Virgil; Pope was the lead collaborator on a celebrated translation of Homer's *Iliad* and *Odyssey*. Over the course of their careers both poets found reason to revisit their original assumption, in Pope's words, that "*Nature* and *Homer* were . . . the *same.*"[18] Increasingly, their imitations take their cue from the conviction that history is cyclic, not linear, and that they were close to Homer and Virgil not because the epic poets were universal but because their classical eras uniquely portended the neoclassical era of Dryden and Pope. Virtually all Pope's major poems, from his youthful pastorals to *The Dunciad*, explicitly adapt classical models. In both Dryden and Pope, however, the impulse to borrow from the past is increasingly directed toward a satiric vision that uses the past to judge the present. Dryden's "MacFlecknoe" and "Absalom and Achitophel" use biblical and classical models to satirize contemporary politicians and poets. The effect of simultaneously exalting and deflating his targets through association with their fabled originals is devastating. Pope uses the mock epic in *The Rape of the Lock* to make light of a practical joke on his Belinda by pretending to take it as seriously as she does. In his imitations of Horace he goes after bigger game, excoriating his culture for its materialism, its corruption, and its hypocrisy. In "The First Epistle of the Second Book of Horace Imitated: To Augustus" Pope uses the epistle that Horace addressed to Caesar Augustus (*Epistles* 2.1), often translating passages directly from Latin to English, ostensibly as a panegyric to King George II, whose middle name was Augustus, but actually to excoriate him by contrast for his licentiousness, his lack of expertise in foreign affairs, and his ludicrously accented English.

Of all recent adaptations that take the form of neoclassic imitations, the one that most acutely combines Dryden and Pope's satiric bent with their reverence for the past is Amy Heckerling's *Clueless* (1995).[19] *Reverence* may seem like exactly the wrong word to use of this Beverly Hills spin on *Emma*. But although Heckerling follows Austen in satirizing her spoiled, appealing heroine, now a student at Bronson Alcott High School named Cher Horowitz (Alicia Silverstone), for her willful ignorance of (young) men and her repeated attempts to meddle in romantic relationships she does not understand, Heckerling never satirizes Austen's novel. Indeed *Emma*, as early reviewers frequently noted, was a model nowhere acknowledged in the film's credits that probably passed unobserved among many viewers. Because it never explicitly identifies itself as a

Jane Austen knockoff, the film departs from *O* and *10 Things I Hate about You* in offering viewers the pleasure of surprised recognition for each similarity it establishes between Cher's round of classes, shopping, makeovers, and telephone intrigue and Emma's apparently more circumscribed world of visits, dances, and outings. This surprise and delight in the resemblance between two disparate cultures, a perspective that illuminates them both, is the defining pleasure of the neoclassic imitation.[20] John Mosier observes that although Austen's novel and Heckerling's film may seem to have little in common, "there is clearly a point in this film when anyone who knows the novel does a comic double take as the realization sinks in that the relationship must exist. In fact, this is the best of all possible relationships, and it is conveyed by the title: it is the cluelessness of Heckerling's heroine that makes her such a stand-in for Emma Woodhouse."[21] Cher is clueless about men, about herself, and about her relation to a fictional forebear whose comic limitations cast considerable light on her own. Indeed, her cluelessness "provides a sort of touchstone for an understanding of other Austen characters as well."[22] Cher's lack of self-knowledge, as in Austen, cues the audience's sympathetic self-satisfaction as they measure her lack of insight against their own, which is especially likely to be sharpened if they know *Emma*. Yet Heckerling's final joke is equally on both fans of Hollywood romantic comedies and Janeites who expect the film to follow the novel. At a garden wedding that turns out to be that of her teachers Miss Geist (Twink Caplan) and Mr. Hall (Wallace Shawn), Cher dismisses in voice-over the possibility that this might, as in Austen, have been her own: "You can guess what happened next. As if! I mean, I'm only sixteen! And this is California, not Kentucky."[23]

The mode of neoclassical imitation does not correspond to any of Elliott's six concepts of adaptation. Instead, it finds a close parallel in James Griffith's account of adaptation as imitation, in which a novel or film is "an aesthetic problem solved—or at least attempted—and communicated" through myriad "factual artistic choices that are purposeful rather than matters of abstract definition that are necessary" as restrictions of a given medium.[24] To the extent that it overlaps with any of Elliott's categories, imitation is most like incarnation. The link between these two apparently remote concepts is provided by Virgil's Fourth Eclogue, long cherished by neoclassic writers because it seemed to foretell the birth of Christ. Dryden revered Virgil as a classic not because he was universal but because he was prophetic in a way that required a completion Virgil himself could not consciously imagine. Although they might seek to subordinate themselves to their originals, imitations like the 1995 *Richard III* and *Clueless* have a similar capacity to complete them for viewers uniquely equipped by historical recursus to hear what they have to say.

It is hard to find monster movies that take the form of neoclassical imitations. Such films must forgo the luxury of claiming neoclassical status because they rarely treat their progenitors as classics, though the Hammer authorized remakes of Universal films, beginning with *The Mummy* (1959), make every effort to exploit their roots in classics of both horror fiction and horror cinema. When films like these emphasize their roots in earlier monster lore, they leave little opportunity for the delighted surprise viewers have in recognizing echoes of earlier novels or films. In one sense, however, monster films display Elliott's incarnational concept more fully than any other films: Practically all of them take incarnation as their subject. The relation between body and spirit is at the heart of monster films from *I Was a Teenage Werewolf* (1957) to *The Tomb of Ligeia* (1965). All the great Hollywood monster franchises—stories about Frankenstein's monster, Dracula, Dr. Jekyll and Mr. Hyde, the Mummy, the Invisible Man, and the Wolf Man—use nightmare scenarios of reincarnation (monsters like Dracula and the Mummy, who can never die) or misincarnation (incarnation in a monstrous body like Frankenstein's creature, monstrous transformation of one's own body like the Invisible Man's or the Wolf Man's, entrapment in the wrong body like Dr. Brandt [George Pravda] in *Frankenstein Must Be Destroyed*) to explore the mystery of human identity.[25] No wonder that films that insist so strongly that they are about incarnation should be reluctant to cast themselves in that role.

• 4 •

When adaptations frankly seek, in Andrew's terms, to transform their sources in ways that go beyond adjustment, the results are *revisions*. These differ from updates to the extent that they seek to rewrite the original, not simply improve its ending or point out its contemporary relevance. They differ from neoclassical imitations in their attitude toward the past that both kinds of adaptations invoke. In imitations the past is the measure of the present, even when it comes in for reassessment itself. Revisions make this reassessment primary. They bear some resemblance to Elliott's psychic conception of adaptation, in which "the spirit of the text . . . maintains a life beyond form that is neither constrained by nor dependent on form."[26] Unlike adaptations that aim to be faithful to the spirit rather than the letter of the text, however, revisions seek to alter the spirit as well.

The simplest Shakespearean example is Kenneth Branagh's *Henry V* (1989), which takes Laurence Olivier's celebrated 1944 film version as its antitext. Olivier's film had begun with self-reflexive artifice, an opening scene of pageantry that emphasized its theatrical nature, its status as canned theater, before opening up to a sweeping, heroic account of Henry's glorious victory at Agincourt. The mood of Olivier's wartime film echoes that of Shakespeare's play, first performed in 1595 in the first flush of England's new status as a world power. Branagh turns Shakespeare's pageant into a gritty antiwar tract that emphasizes the chaos and costs of battle and presents a Henry thoroughly chastened by the price of victory over France.

The most notorious recent revision of a literary classic is Patricia Rozema's 1999 adaptation of *Mansfield Park,* which Claudia L. Johnson called in an early review a "stunning revisionist reading . . . more of an intervention than an adaptation."[27] The decorous period production is disrupted by three decidedly noncanonical additions. Taking her cue from the suggestion that Austen's novels may be mined for autobiographical cues, Rozema merges her heroine, Fanny Price (Frances O'Connor), with the author who created her. Fanny's copious writing borrows liberally from Austen's own letters, journals, and juvenilia, and she frequently addresses the camera as if she were the author of her own story. In addressing the question that got her started on the project— "Who's paying for the party?"[28]—Rozema emphasizes Sir Thomas's economic dependence on the slave trade, which Austen had mentioned only once. The drawings Sir Thomas Bartram's son Tom (James Purefoy) brings back from Antigua show his father (Harold Pinter) beating and coupling with female slaves. The result is the first-ever Austen adaptation "rated PG-13 for brief violent images, sexual content and drug use."[29]

Rozema's insistence on showing the underside of life at Mansfield Park sharply divided reviewers and critics of her film.[30] If her emphasis of her abolitionist views was new to adaptation, however, her strategy was not. Rozema revises Austen's story by recontextualizing it, making its historical matrix an explicit part of the story. Her telescoping of Fanny Price and Jane Austen is only one aspect of this strategy. A broader strategy is importing historical events of 1805–6, the period during which the story is set,[31] into the film rather than eliding them, as Austen largely does. The result is an adaptation that also announces itself as a study of Austen and her times. It is a result fully in accord with the goal Rozema has prescribed for all adaptations of literary classics: "To examine stories that bear re-examination."[32]

The status Rozema claims for her film is one indicated more or less explicitly by the titles *Bram Stoker's "Dracula"* (1992) and *Mary Shelley's "Frankenstein"* (1994). These titles, which might be taken to imply unusual fidelity to the novels at hand, announce instead that the author and the author's world have become part of the subject along with the events of the novel. In *Mary Shelley's "Frankenstein"* Kenneth Branagh takes great care to date the events of the film in the early years of the nineteenth century, even though Shelley dated the events of her novel at the end of the eighteenth century, in order to motivate connections between romanticism and the rise of science. In addition to inventing a fifteenth-century prologue that makes its vampire hero more tragic, *Bram Stoker's "Dracula"* adds references to the early history and prehistory of the cinema contemporary with the novel's 1897 publication when Dracula (Gary Oldman) and Mina (Winona Ryder) visit a cinematograph, as well as visual references to two of the most famous of all vampire films, *Nosferatu* and *Vampyr* (1932). Indeed, Coppola's crosscutting between Mina's wedding to Jonathan Harker (Keanu Reeves) and Dracula's murderous consummation with her friend Lucy Westenra (Sadie Frost) recall nothing so much as the bloody climaxes of Coppola's three *Godfather* films (1972, 1974, 1990). Coppola and his screenwriter, James V. Hart, insisted that their film was "closer to Stoker's novel than anything done before. . . . We were scrupulously true to the book."[33] But this scrupulous fidelity, as Margaret Montalbano has pointed out, did not prevent the publication of a novelization of Hart's screenplay, whose first page announced that "what follows here is not Bram Stoker's 1897 novel . . . but Fred Saberhagen's retelling of the motion picture called *Bram Stoker's 'Dracula'* . . . based on [James V. Hart's] screen adaptation of that classic story."[34]

Revisionist adaptations of classic texts seen through recontextualizations of the periods in which they were written go back at least as far as the 1931 and 1941 versions of *Dr. Jekyll and Mr. Hyde*. Both films mount an explicit critique of Victorian mores. Mamoulian's 1931 film ascribes the fatal inability of Henry Jekyll (Fredric March) to govern the passions that will destroy him to the prudish refusal of General Carew (Halliwell Hobbes) to consent to shortening Jekyll's engagement to Carew's daughter, Muriel (Rose Hobart). Victor Fleming's 1941 adaptation presents Jekyll (Spencer Tracy) as a product of psychosexual contradictions, represented by galloping Freudian imagery, that range throughout Victorian culture, from the worshipper (Barton MacLane) who unaccountably goes mad in church during the film's opening scene to the pathetic barmaid, Ivy Pearson (Ingrid Bergman). Although few adaptations go as far as *The Innocents* (1961) and its unofficial prequel *The Nightcomers* (1972) in explicitly interpreting ambiguous literary forebears like Henry James's "The Turn of the Screw" (1898), it is hard to imagine an adaptation devoid of comment, deliberate or inadvertent, on any of its progenitor's historical or cultural contexts.

## • 5 •

A still freer approach to adaptation is *colonization*. The process closely resembles Elliott's ventriloquist concept, in which the adaptation "blatantly empties out the novel's signs and fills them with new filmic spirits" so that the adaptation is "a composite of novel and film, rather than pure film."[35] Colonizing adaptations, like ventriloquists, see progenitor texts as vessels to be filled with new meanings. Any new content is fair game, whether it develops meanings implicit in the earlier text, amounts to an ideological critique of that text, or goes off in another direction entirely. Many commentators were predictably affronted by Mira Nair's postcolonial adaptation of *Vanity Fair* (2004), which not only softened Thackeray's satirical portrait of Becky Sharp (Reese Witherspoon) but introduced many Indian motifs and incorporated three Bollywood-influenced dance numbers. Such reviewers presumably would have preferred a more deracinated adaptation, like the 1995 *Sense and Sensibility*, even though Emma Thompson's diary of her production records a traumatic cultural clash between the opinionated actors and director Ang Lee, who "ha[d] never had any actor question anything before" because "in Taiwan the director holds complete sway."[36]

Gurinder Chadha's *Bride and Prejudice* (2004), a Bollywood adaptation of *Pride and Prejudice*, received far more enthusiastic notices, perhaps because its outrageously stylized production was perceived as less a threat to an Austen establishment already sated by curatorial BBC adaptations. The success of Chadha's film even sparked a significant American audience's interest in *I Have Found It* (*Kandukondain Kandukondain* [2000]), Rajiv Menon's considerably more freewheeling Bollywood version of *Sense and Sensibility*. Interestingly, although American reviewers generally found *Bride and Prejudice* both charming and exhilarating, Indian reviewers worried that the film, a considerably shorter Indian Austen that stuck much more closely to the events of its source novel, might mark an unhealthy step toward the American colonization of Bollywood.

*Colonization* is a term that is difficult to empty of its pejorative charge, a charge that is usually leveled when a filmmaker from one country tackles a classic text from another. For every cineaste who admired Akira Kurosawa's *Ran* (1985), a purist insisted that Kurosawa's take on *King Lear* was hardly Shakespeare. But Kurosawa was surely entitled to colonize Shakespeare, for his own films *The Seven Samurai* (*Shichinin no samurai* [1954]) and *Yojimbo* (1961) had already been colonized as the westerns *The Magnificent Seven* (1960) and *A Fistful of Dollars* (*Per un pugno di dollari* [1964]), and *The Hidden Fortress* (*Kakushi toride no san akunin* [1958]) had provided a good deal of material for *Star Wars* (1977). Hollywood filmings of foreign material, from the reedited and partially reshot *Godzilla, King of the Monsters* (1956) to *Godzilla* (1998), are equally reviled in their countries of origin. Grigori Kozintsev's *Hamlet* (*Gamlet* [1964]) and *King Lear* (*Korol Lir* [1969]), using Shakespearean texts translated by Boris Pasternak, are among the few adaptations widely honored in both their own country and their poet's homeland.

But adaptations need not reach across national boundaries to display a colonizing interest. Following the Hammer studio's lead in linking sex and gore, films like Hammer's own *Dr. Jekyll and Sister Hyde*, directed by Roy Ward Baker (1971), and Frank Henenlotter's *Frankenhooker* (1990) had used their monster franchises to license even more sexually explicit material. The limiting case is the enormous number of pornographic films whose titles indicate their indebtedness to earlier novels or films. *Alice's Adventures in Wonderland: The World's Favorite Bedtime Story* (1976), *8 to 4* ("for those who like to get in early" [1981]), *Fleshdance* (1983), *Flash Pants* (1983), and *Meet the Fuckers* (two separate features [both 2005]) all empty their stories of their original meaning in order to use them as a narrative framework for the sex scenes that are their raison d'être.

Yet something of the hybrid nature of textuality that Elliott's ventriloquist concept prescribes survives even in these films. Midway through Stanley Kurlan's porn feature *Eruption* (1977), in which insurance salesman Peter Winston (John Holmes) and Hawaiian housewife Sandra Bevin (Leslie Bovee) conspire to kill Sandra's husband in a boating accident in between sexual interludes, the husband is shown with a broken leg. The reason for his broken leg is never satisfactorily explained, and it has no impact on his murder, which proceeds as planned. The broken leg is merely a holdover from James M. Cain's novella *Double Indemnity* (1936) and Billy Wilder's film adaptation (1944), from which *Eruption* borrows its perfunctory plot and little else—except for that leg, which continues to speak the earlier text like an eerily possessed ventriloquist's dummy.

### · 6 ·

From this point on the categories of Wagner, Andrew, and Elliott are less and less useful in the drift from adaptation to allusion. But Wagner's notion of reimagining and Andrew's of intersecting both help illuminate the more specific category of *(meta)commentary or deconstruction.* The most characteristic films of this sort are not so much adaptations as films about adaptation, films whose subject is the problems involved in producing texts. The obvious case in point is *Adaptation,* Spike Jonze's puckish 2002 film about the struggles of screenwriter Charlie Kaufman (Nicolas Cage) to bring Susan Orlean's nonfiction book *The Orchid Thief* (1998) to the screen. Whether they loved or hated the film's heady mixture of Hollywood in-jokes, existential dread, and self-reflexivity, audiences reacted to the film as if it were something wholly new. In fact there is ample precedent for its approach to its subject in Shakespeareana (Al Pacino's *Looking for Richard* [1996]), Austeniana (Merchant Ivory's *Jane Austen in Manhattan* [1980]), and monsteriana (E. Elias Merhige's *Shadow of the Vampire* [2000]).

*Adaptation* seemed fresh and original not because it inaugurated a new category of deconstructive commentary but because it pushed the conventions of the existing category to their limit. *Looking for Richard, Jane Austen in Manhattan,* and *Shadow of the Vampire* all fictionalize the problems of staging or adapting (all three films paper over the differences between the two processes) specific works for specific presentations. *Shadow of the Vampire* speculates on the relationship between vampirish actor Max Schreck (Willem Dafoe) and the Svengali of *Nosferatu,* director F. W. Murnau. The relationship, along with revelations of Schreck's uniquely Method approach to playing Count Dracula, are, one hopes, fictitious, but the film is real enough. *Looking for Richard* chronicles Pacino's attempt to come to terms with *Richard III* by staging his play. The film features real actors playing themselves playing leading roles in a stage production starring Pacino. Like Keith Fulton and Louis Pepe's *Lost in La Mancha* (2002), the film documents the problems in mounting a production it never

shows. *Jane Austen in Manhattan,* taking off from the real-life competition between collectors at an auction of Austen's juvenilia, is even more frankly fictional in its exploration of the conflicts between two directors representing utterly different approaches to their task: the fidelity of Lillian Zorska (Anne
Baxter) to the letter versus the devotion of her ex-lover Pierre (Robert Powell)
to what he takes to be its spirit. Despite their many differences, all these films
deconstruct the mimetic illusion by examining the problems of arranging or
staging preexisting material for the theater or the cinema.

Jonze's film pushes further (much further) into fictional territory by chronicling the fictional attempt to write a screen adaptation that was never really
undertaken. *Adaptation* satirizes both the misbegotten quest to bring Orlean's
decidedly uncinematic story to the screen and the debates about fidelity that
Ismail Merchant and James Ivory present with high seriousness by hypostasiz-
ing and internalizing the debate at the heart of *Jane Austen in Manhattan.* The
question for Charlie Kaufman is not which way of adapting Orlean is the most
faithful but whether he can complete the task on a looming deadline, and the
leading person with whom he is debating this question is his identical twin,
Donald, also played by Nicolas Cage. The fact that the film's screenwriter, Charlie Kaufman, gives the main character his own name, forces a hero with writer's
block to confront the commercial success of his unprincipled twin, and fills his
story with real-life people played by Meryl Streep, Chris Cooper, and Brian
Cox blurs the line between life and art, illusion and reality, a line Charlie's increasingly fevered imagination blurs still further. After supplying a wildly unfaithful but eminently Hollywood ending to Orlean's story of John Laroche
(Cooper) as an itinerant thief of tropical orchids, *Adaptation* ends with Charlie still unable to adapt his refractory source. The real-life Charlie Kaufman
succeeds by chronicling and comically anatomizing his fictional counterpart's
failure. Like Wes Craven's horror film *Scream* (1996) and its even more self-
reflexive sequel *Scream 2* (1997), the film interleaves a fictional story in a well-
worn genre with a running commentary on the rules of the genre. But unlike
*Scream* and *Scream 2,* which end by reaffirming their allegiance to the genre
they have been deconstructing, *Adaptation* achieves its comic effect by showing that anything like a faithful adaptation of Orlean's book, and by extension
of any literary text, is a contradiction in terms. The problems it explores con-
nect it to a long line of literary forebears that deconstruct the whole project of
telling their stories: Laurence Sterne's *Tristram Shandy* (1760–67), Denis Dide-
rot's *Jacques le fataliste et son maître* (1796), André Gide's *Les faux-monnayeurs*

(1925), Jean-Paul Sartre's *La nausée* (1938), Alain Robbe-Grillet's *Le Voyeur* (1957), and John Barth's "Lost in the Funhouse" (1967). Indeed Robert Stam, following Robert Alter in tracing this tradition of "partial magic" back to *Don Quixote*, calls it "'the other great tradition'" that complements novelistic realism, whose members "systematically flaunt their own condition of artifice, reflexively engaging their own procedures and techniques."[37] The best-known film adaptation of such a novel is Karel Reisz's *The French Lieutenant's Woman* (1981), which offers its own more narrowly focused deconstruction of the problems of knowledge, desire, and memory raised by John Fowles's 1969 novel; the most recent is *A Cock and Bull Story* (2005), Michael Winterbottom's fantasia on the impossibility of adapting *Tristram Shandy*.

· 7 ·

Still more tenuous in the connection it establishes with an earlier text is the *analogue*. In Helen Fielding's novel *Bridget Jones's Diary* (1998), the heroine, who is closer to her father than to her mother, has to choose between two suitors, her plausible boss Daniel Cleaver and barrister Mark Darcy. At first drifting into an affair with Daniel, she discovers his perfidy and ends up with Mark. All these are points of analogy with Elizabeth Bennet. Yet *Bridget Jones's Diary* is not an adaptation of Austen's novel, not even when it is filmed. Bridget, a neurotic loner who styles herself a career woman and whose closest friends are even odder than she, is remote from Lizzy in her trademark fixations: her weight, her sex life, her parents' and relatives' expectations of her (consistently more important to Bridget than Lizzy even though she lives on her own). The diary to which Bridget confides her story reveals her as savvy yet unperceptive about herself, witty, often acerbic, yet easily hooked by passing trends. She is less like Lizzy Bennet than like Emma Woodhouse or, for that matter, Cher Horowitz. If Bridget's need to choose between romantic partners who represent opposite ideals makes *Bridget Jones's Diary* an adaptation of *Pride and Prejudice*, then virtually the entire genre of female-oriented romance, especially the recent chick-lit explosion, has just as good a claim. Even Sharon Maguire's 2001 film—in which Fielding, as screenwriter, softened Bridget by making her less witty and more helpless, and Colin Firth's casting as Mark Darcy sharpened the evocation of the Mr. Darcy he had played in the 1995 television *Pride and Prejudice*—is an adaptation of Fielding's novel rather than Austen's. That does not mean that Fielding's novel and Maguire's film do not invoke Austen. But like

Whit Stillman's *Metropolitan* (1990), which repeatedly and often explicitly invokes *Mansfield Park* without ever crossing the line to adaptation, both Fielding's novel and Maguire's film invoke Austen's characters, along with their world and their story, in such discontinuous, even episodic, terms that they are more properly considered analogues than adaptations.

Hollywood's appetite for properties based on some formula of proven commercial appeal has made it home to many analogues. Bo Welch's *The Cat in the Hat* (2003) is an adaptation of Dr. Seuss's 1957 children's book, but a much closer model is Ron Howard's film *How the Grinch Stole Christmas* (2000), whose success in selling tickets to families over the holiday season of 2000 the later film, another special-effects extravaganza built around an equally manic star and timed for Christmas release, clearly hoped to emulate. A pair of more venerable examples are *The Mummy* (1932) and *The Wolf Man* (1941), which unlike *Dracula* and *Frankenstein* and *The Invisible Man* were inspired not by literary originals but by earlier entries in the Universal monster franchise. The former cast Boris Karloff, who had shot abruptly to fame the year before as Frankenstein's monster, in the title role. The latter starred Lon Chaney Jr., who was clearly being groomed to follow in the sinister footsteps of his famous father (*A Blind Bargain* [1922]; *The Hunchback of Notre Dame* [1923]; *The Phantom of the Opera* [1925]; *Laugh, Clown, Laugh* [1928]; et al.) and who went on to play both Dracula and Frankenstein's monster, as well as repeatedly reprising the role of Larry Talbot, the Wolf Man. One might indeed describe the formulas of all popular Hollywood genres—the western, the romantic comedy, the musical comedy, the gangster film, the war film, the science-fiction film, the sword-and-sandals epic—as analogues writ large.

Analogues can vary in force as well as specificity. *My Own Private Idaho* (1991), whose screenplay is credited to director Gus Van Sant, "with additional dialogue by William Shakespeare," combines several scenes that clearly echo Shakespeare's plays about King Henry IV with a story whose language, mood, and direction are so different that David Bevington, Anne Marie Welsh, and Michael L. Greenwald call it "a spin-off" that "bear[s] only the slightest relationship to Shakespeare's original."[38] The story of the slumming street hustler Scott Favor (Keanu Reeves), who is in perpetual flight from his domineering father, the mayor of Portland, is set against the story of Scott's friend Mike Waters (River Phoenix), a narcoleptic hustler who dreams of finding the mother he lost years ago. The structure of the film emphasizes two contrasts. One is between the Shakespeare-updated diction and action in the scenes between Scott

and Falstaff figure Bob Pigeon (William Richert) and the slower, more naturalistic, acting and dialogue in the scenes focusing on Mike and Scott. The other
is between Mike's hopeless search for his mother and Scott's ultimately doomed
flight from his father.[39] Van Sant's interest in Shakespeare focuses on the pain
of loss and the confusion of family relations. Scott calls Bob, his former lover,
"my true father," and the man Mike knows as older brother appears to be his
father instead, or as well. The film emphasizes not only Mike's failure to find
his mother in a search that extends as far as Rome but also the difficulty Scott
has in maintaining relationships with his father (with whom he is shown quar-
reling but never reconciling, although they have clearly reconciled by the end
of the film), his surrogate father (whom he constantly ridicules and ultimately
denies, though his rejection is "less clearly motivated and more stridently
heartless" than Prince Hal's denial of Falstaff),[40] and ultimately Mike, whose
love for him does not prevent Scott from falling for Carmella (Chiara Caselli),
a young Italian woman he meets in the search for Mike's mother. Scott eventually abandons Mike to an endless series of narcoleptic blackouts; hence, both
the search for a family and what might seem to be its negative analogy, the flight
from a family, become suffused with confusion, failure, and loss. In fact, the
film's thematic analogies to Shakespeare are subordinated to such a "passionate homage to Welles' *Chimes at Midnight*" that Van Sant often follows Welles
shot by shot.[41]

Not all analogues are intentional; commentators can make a case for them
years after the fact. A single example will serve to close out this category. No
writer could seem less like Jane Austen than Sholem Aleichem, often called the
Jewish Mark Twain. Yet Aleichem's best-known work, the cycle of stories
posthumously collected as *Tevye's Daughters* (1949), has distinct analogues
with *Pride and Prejudice.* In Tevye the Milkman's family another ineffectual father and another strong-willed but weak-minded mother repeatedly duel over
the future of their unmarried daughters. The young women all seem determined to make unsuitable matches, and not one of them marries a husband of
whom Tevye can fully approve. In the course of watching his daughters' court-
ships and reluctantly conferring his blessings, Tevye endures many other misfortunes, from worsening political oppression to the death of his wife, Golde.
Yet Aleichem's generosity and his hero's indomitable spirit, so different from
Austen's archly amusing satire, makes his father's-eye view of *Pride and Prejudice* equally comic in its way. Whatever similarities may exist between the two
stories are not allusions. There is no evidence that Aleichem ever read Austen,

let alone felt moved to incorporate his response to her into his work. Yet the analogues remain, and they were strengthened when *Tevye's Daughters* was transformed into the musical *Fiddler on the Roof* (1964, filmed 1971), which makes Tevye less unfortunate and his wife more ridiculous while reducing the number of daughters he needs to marry off from five to three, giving him in the end the same number of sons-in-law Mr. Bennet enjoys.

· 8 ·

Another category that is especially hard to locate on the continuum from adaptation to allusion is that of *parody and pastiche,* a heading still further complicated by its double nature. Perhaps the two modes of reference, the first designed to satirize its models, the second not, ought to get separate categories, but that would involve defining *pastiche* more satisfactorily than any scholar has yet done.[42] Even Fredric Jameson's influential account of pastiche as a distinctively postmodern practice defines it purely in contradistinction to parody: "Pastiche is, like parody, the imitation of a peculiar mask, speech in a dead language: but it is a neutral practice of such mimicry, without any of parody's ulterior motives, amputated of the satiric impulse, devoid of laughter and of any conviction that alongside the abnormal tongue you have momentarily borrowed, some healthy linguistic normality still exists. Pastiche is thus blank parody, a statue with blind eyeballs."[43]

Parody is more frequent, more easily recognized, and more easily defined than its more serious sibling. Jerry Lewis's *The Nutty Professor* (1963) and Tom Shadyac's *The Nutty Professor* (1996), starring Eddie Murphy, are not parodies but comic inversions of "The Strange Case of Dr. Jekyll and Mr. Hyde" similar to *Abbott and Costello Meet Frankenstein* (1948) in mining the comic potential of their originals (which in Abbott and Costello's case include the Universal monster franchises of Dracula and the Wolf Man as well) without ever making fun of Shelley's novel or Whale's film. Mel Brooks's *Young Frankenstein* (1974), by contrast, is a parody of *Frankenstein* (1931) that occasionally broadens its targets to parody scenes from *The Bride of Frankenstein* (1935) and *Son of Frankenstein* (1939). Brooks, a former television writer who built a second career as Hollywood's leading writer and director of film parody, has ranged in his targets from westerns (*Blazing Saddles* [1974]) to Hitchcock thrillers (*High Anxiety* [1977]), *Star Wars* (*Spaceballs* [1987]), Robin Hood (*Robin Hood: Men in Tights* [1993]), and Dracula (*Dracula: Dead and Loving It* [1995]). But he has never turned to Jane Austen and only briefly (and not as writer or director) to Shakespeare.

Brooks's Shakespearean flirtation is instructive, for it appears as a brief but crucially motivating episode in his appearance as Dr. Frederick Bronski in Alan Johnson's remake of *To Be or Not to Be* (1983). As in Ernst Lubitsch's 1942 film, the plot, involving a Polish acting troupe's attempt to outwit the Nazis during World War II, is set in motion by the extramarital liaisons of the hero's wife and leading lady (Anne Bancroft [or Carole Lombard before her]), who arranges her backstage rendezvous to coincide with the scenes in which her husband, playing Hamlet, will be occupied onstage. So every time Brooks (or Jack Benny before him) enters and says, "To be or not to be," an attractive young man in a front row creates a small commotion by squeezing past the neighboring patrons to leave the theater in what the abandoned actor playing Hamlet takes as a slur on his acting. The Shakespearean reference is not simply an allusion but an embedded parody, made humorous by two incongruities: the contrast between the actor's self-seriousness as Hamlet and his wife's deception, and the absurdity of casting either Jack Benny or Mel Brooks as Hamlet. *The Last Action Hero* (1993) turns the same Shakespearean line to similar parodistic purposes by casting Arnold Schwarzenegger, who plays Hollywood action hero Jack Slater, as an equally unlikely Hamlet in the fantasies of young Danny Madigan (Austin O'Brien). This time the punch line is less subtle: Jack concludes the speech in a manner more Schwarzenegger than Shakespeare by abruptly deciding, "Not to be," and spraying the area around him with automatic rifle fire.

A more extended Shakespearean parody is Billy Morrissette's *Scotland, Pa.* (2001), which translates *Macbeth* into black comedy. Duncan (James Rebhorn), until recently the owner of a chain of doughnut shops presumably bearing his name, is branching out into fast-food hamburgers. His dim employee Joe McBeth (James LeGros) is first shown answering an invitation to "get a look at your wife's beautiful cones"—she has been learning how to use the soft-serve machine—and enters to tell Pat McBeth (Maura Tierney) earnestly, "I love your cones, baby," before the first of many lip-locking sequences that constitute a running joke. The three witches become drugged hippies, one of whom predicts Mac's future with the help of a Magic 8 Ball. Mac, unsure what to make of the prophecy but determined to prevent Duncan from stealing his idea for an intercom that will make curbside service even faster, doubts that he can murder him but, after rifling his safe, accidentally kills him by knocking him into a deep-fat fryer, leading to still another round of necking and attempted sex a few feet from the corpse. When Duncan's son Malcolm (Thomas Guiry) sells the diner to the McBeths for a nominal amount, Mac assures him, "The most important thing is that we carry on his legacy. You know, keep his name alive." The next shot shows Mac and Pat knocking down the big "Duncan's" sign over the diner's façade, which is soon relabeled "McBeth's," the design of the logo broadly suggesting a similarly named burger chain. Lt. Ernie McDuff (Christopher Walken), called in to investigate, turns out to be a vegetarian who gets trapped into hugging each witness he interviews and drives along listening to a motivational tape that assures him: "Tomorrow is tomorrow. Tomorrow is not today. Today is who I am." When McDuff seems to be getting too close to the truth, one of the prophetic hippies (Timothy Speed Levitch) suggests a way out that closely echoes Shakespeare's tragedy: "I've got it! Mac should kill McDuff's entire family!" This suggestion prompts a withering reply from another hippie (Andy Dick): "Oh, that'll work! Maybe a thousand years ago. You can't go around killing everybody." After McDuff successfully battles a witless local deputy and the murderous Mac, who at the height of their struggle tries to jam a hamburger into his mouth, the final sequence shows him taking over the diner and renaming it McDuff's, "home of the garden burger."

These changes are different from the changes Amy Heckerling makes in transforming *Emma* into *Clueless* because they do not create a coherent new world for Shakespeare's story of ambition, murder, and revenge. Their comic force is negative. They are all unexpectedly humorous departures from Shakespeare rather than reasonable additions to Morrissette's new story, and most of them make sense only within the intertextual field available to the audience, not within the world of the characters. Despite a few transformations that pose exceptions to this rule (for example, the burning grease Pat thinks has made an indelible mark on her hand), the primary force of Morrissette's 1975 update of *Macbeth* is to make fun of Shakespeare's play, and it is hard to imagine anyone who did not know the play finding much to laugh at in the nonstop parody of *Scotland, Pa.*

The fact that parody need not be nonstop—witness the frequency of embedded parodies in films as different as *Shakespeare in Love, Wayne's World* (1992), and *Not Another Teen Movie* (2001)—demonstrates that parody can be successfully deployed and recognized even in small doses within larger texts. Pastiche, by contrast, seems to require the space of an entire text, even if that text itself is brief. Many Sherlock Holmes stories written by other hands than Conan Doyle's—Vincent Starrett's "The Unique Hamlet"; the dozens of Solar

Pons short stories by August Derleth; the proliferation of recent tales starring Holmes's wife, his nemesis Irene Adler, his police colleague Inspector Lestrade, or his landlady—announce themselves as pastiches. But few film adaptations do, even though the designation seems to fit Herbert Ross's film adaptation of *The Seven-Per-Cent Solution* (1976), for example, just as well as its source, the Nicholas Meyer novel universally identified as a pastiche. Is an adaptation of a pastiche still a pastiche? If not, why not?

This question complicates any attempt to classify movies like Stephen Frears's *Mary Reilly* (1996) or Neil LaBute's *Possession* (2002), both based on novels that are clearly pastiches themselves. In retelling "The Strange Case of Dr. Jekyll and Mr. Hyde" from the viewpoint of one of Jekyll's servants, Valerie Martin's 1990 novel, *Mary Reilly*, focuses on material Stevenson had repressed: the enabling role of women in propping up the rigidly stratified Victorian culture Stevenson took for granted and the monstrous power even the most marginal men in that culture, from Jekyll's butler, Poole, to Mary's impoverished father, had to abuse women still more powerless than themselves. A. S. Byatt's novel *Possession* (1990) examines Victorian culture through a different lens, as a pair of modern-day literary sleuths unearth a secret romance between two Victorian poets and embark on a parallel relation themselves. Unlike Martin's novel, Byatt's is a broad pastiche of several Victorian novels, at least one real-life romance (between Elizabeth Barrett and Robert Browning), Victorian culture, and Victorian studies. Neil LaBute's film faithfully picks up this web of intertextual references, though it focuses on the double love story instead of exploring the interrelations among different notions of the Victorian past in anything like Byatt's detail.

Even deciding that LaBute's film is a pastiche does not answer the question of what it is a pastiche of or what its attitude toward the subject of its pastiche is. Despite the misleading evidence of titles like *Snide and Prejudice* (1997) and *Jane Austen's Mafia!* (1998), Austen's novels are rarely parodied because comic novels are not obvious targets for parody, although they have been the subject of many pastiches. If the modern gothic romance is descended from *Wuthering Heights* (1847) by way of *Rebecca,* the equally ubiquitous Regency romance owes its conventions of plotting, characterization, diction, and decorum to Austen.[44] At this point the notion of pastiche expands to include whole genres of paperback originals that haunt used bookstores.

· 9 ·

The difficulties in defining and rationalizing pastiche prepare for an even more troublesome category: *secondary, tertiary, or quaternary imitations.* Such films, like the copy of a copy of himself that Doug Kinney (Michael Keaton) makes in Harold Ramis's *Multiplicity* (1996), often assume blurred outlines that make their precise status hard to determine. It seems clear that filmed versions of operas like *Otello* (1973, 1986), *Verdi's Falstaff* (1976), *Giuseppe Verdi: Falstaff* (1982), and *The Merry Wives of Windsor* (*Die lustigen Weiber von Windsor* [1965]), like the better-known film versions of *The Magic Flute* (*Trollflöjten* [1975]) and *Don Giovanni* (1979), are adaptations of adaptations. Perhaps they are better described, however, as filmed recordings of adaptations. Is a film version of an adaptation in another medium a second-order adaptation, a transcription of an adaptation, or something else?

Films like *The Bride of Frankenstein* and *Dracula's Daughter* (1936), which are sequels to adaptations, might be defined as adaptations not of an earlier story but of an earlier character, setting, or concept. *The Bride of Frankenstein* has an especially intimate relation to Mary Shelley's novel because it is inspired by an important episode from Shelley left untreated by the earlier Universal film, the monster's demand that Frankenstein create a mate for him; but its status as adaptation would be the same even if it were not. All Frankenstein films, in asking what would happen if the scientist had a son who carried on his work, or if he killed a colleague to supply himself with new material for his experiments, or if the subject of those experiments were a teenage boy (*I Was a Teenage Frankenstein* [1957]) or a prostitute *(Frankenhooker)* or even a dog *(Frankenweenie)*, focus more closely on a few central characters and situations from Shelley than on her plot. Adaptation theory tends to assume that adaptation focuses on the plot of the progenitor text, but arguments about fidelity to the earlier text's spirit should be equally open to adaptations based on a character like Sherlock Holmes or Frankenstein's monster with the ability to generate continuing adventures, especially if those adventures follow the same narrative formulas over and over again.

*Bridget Jones: The Edge of Reason* (2004) stands in the unusual position of being both a sequel to an adaptation and an adaptation of a sequel. As such, it explicitly invites an investigation of a wider range of intertextual links than sequels to adaptations that are not also adaptations of sequels (for example, *Son of Frankenstein*) and adaptations of sequels that are not also sequels to adaptations (for example, *The Hound of the Baskervilles* [1939]). It is not surprising that *Bridget Jones: The Edge of Reason* follows one of its models, Helen Fielding's sequel to her earlier novel, much more closely than the other, the film to which it is a sequel. But there are exceptions to this unexceptionable rule, most notably the much greater prominence the film accords Bridget's former boss, Daniel Cleaver (Hugh Grant), than the novel does. Daniel's popularity in the original film and his availability as a structuring device as the bad counterpart to the good suitor Mark Darcy (Colin Firth) made Bridget's new adventure not only a sequel but a virtual remake of the earlier film.

The web of intertextual reference is still further complicated by intersections of distinct franchises. Universal faced no great formal challenges in making *Frankenstein Meets the Wolf Man* (1943) because the formulas for the two franchises were so similar: a monster tormented by his own monstrosity was persecuted by an unfeeling mob, with fatal consequences. Even the hybrid *Abbott and Costello Meet Frankenstein* and its sequels did not represent much of a stretch because the contrast between Lou Costello's infantile cowardice and Bud Abbott's brusque impatience, already established in films like *Hold That Ghost* (1941), made the team a perfect comic foil for Universal's stable of monsters. But *Frankenstein Meets the Spacemonster* (1965) and *Jesse James Meets Frankenstein's Daughter* (originally released on a double bill with *Billy the Kid versus Dracula* [1966]) would have been even harder to craft if the Spacemonster and Jesse James had had full-fledged franchises of their own. Such hybrids shade away from adaptation toward the final category in this survey.

· 10 ·

Every film contains many examples of *allusion*. It is impossible to imagine a movie devoid of quotations from or references to any earlier text. The theoretical problems of these references, generally microtexts embedded in a film's larger structure, have been analyzed by many theorists, most influentially by Mikhail Bakhtin.[45] But their continuities with other modes of intertextual reference raise special problems for adaptation theory. James Griffith has noted that although *Superman* (1978) is nominally an adaptation of the comic-book franchise, its portrayal of the hero is complicated by other allusions as well, beginning with his departure from the doomed world of Krypton: "The capsule's rising to the ceiling and breaking through the skylight recalls the birth of

Frankenstein [*sic*]. His early life with foster parents, his summons to a wasteland to build a fortress of solitude, the asking of questions and seeking of answers with his father—all correspond to some details of the life of Moses or Jesus. But when we first see him fly, this Superman, part monster and part prophet, flies to the funny-page world of Metropolis to become all cartoon."[46]

Griffith is confident that he can distinguish local allusions from foundational generic conventions, and in this case he is surely correct. Few viewers persist in seeing Superman as a latter-day Moses, Jesus, or Frankenstein's monster. This distinction is less clear-cut, however, in other examples. Adrian Lyne's *Fatal Attraction* (1987) repeatedly alludes to Puccini's opera *Madama Butterfly* (1904) as a prototype for its lovelorn heroine Alex Forrest (Glenn Close). The model of Cio-Cio-San as an explanation for the way Alex sees herself is ironic, since Alex turns her death-dealing energies murderously outward, not inward, at least in the theatrically released version of the film.[47] More generally, Depression-era gangster movies cast themselves in a Horatio Alger mode that allows their self-made heroes to reap the rewards of their hard work, at least for a time. The Cook's Tours billboard that inspires Tony Camonte (Paul Muni) in *Scarface* (1932)—"The world is yours"—is ironically set against his inevitable violent end. Yet it has straightforward thematic force as well, for it acknowledges that given Tony's Italian ethnic background and limited education, a life of crime really is his best hope for getting ahead. Such allusions seem central to these stories.

Even passing allusions may establish a directorial signature, as Billy Wilder's constant in-jokes do. The closing scenes of *Some Like It Hot*, released in 1959 but set thirty years earlier, leaven the threat of the fictional gangster Spats Colombo (George Raft) by having Spats growl, "Where did you learn that cheap trick?" to a rival hoodlum idly flipping a coin (presumably he learned it from Raft's character in *Scarface*) and by costuming Jerry (Tony Curtis) exactly like the aged hero of *Citizen Kane* (1941) for his attempt to escape the gangster convention in a wheelchair. The mordant pathos of *Sunset Boulevard* (1950) is enriched for viewers who recognize the silent film that Norma Desmond (Gloria Swanson) screens for Joe Gillis (William Holden) as *Queen Kelly* (1928), Swanson's own last silent; Erich von Stroheim, who plays Norma's butler, Max, as her director in *Queen Kelly*; the "waxworks" played by H. B. Warner, Anna Q. Nilsson, and Buster Keaton as real-life silent stars; and Cecil B. DeMille as himself. Although each individual allusion may be limited in scope, the tone of both films depends on the dense pattern of references they create.

Allusion in turn shades off into the grammar of film and its collective unconscious. Whenever a reviewer compares a character to Frankenstein or Cinderella, a case is implied for a particular allusion, yet such comparisons are usually so offhand that they imply universal cultural currency, not acquaintance with any one textual manifestation. Brian De Palma's trademark 360-degree tracking/panning shots are widely held to allude to the pivotal shot in Hitchcock's *Vertigo* (1958), when Scottie Ferguson (James Stewart) finally succeeds in making over Judy Barton (Kim Novak) into his lost love Madeleine Elster (Novak). Do technically similar shots in more recent films like *Original Sin* (2001) constitute similar allusions? If so, do they refer to Hitchcock or De Palma? At what point does a stylistic device like Orson Welles's systematic use of deep focus or Max Ophüls's intricate tracking shots pass from a signature directorial flourish into the common syntax available to all filmmakers? Film grammar itself may be nothing more than intertextual borrowings regularized into prescriptive formulas.

Although these ten strategies might seem to form a logical progression from faithful adaptation to allusion, they are embarrassingly fluid. Their real problem, however, is the one Elliott hints at with her own sixfold classification. Although they certainly represent different intertextual strategies and attitudes, they are not adequate to categorize a very large number of films. Baz Luhrmann's film *William Shakespeare's Romeo + Juliet* (1996), for example, makes liberal use of all ten strategies:

1. Its extreme reluctance to change Shakespeare's exact words, despite heavy cuts throughout, indicates a fidelity fetish implied by its title to mark it as a *celebration* of Shakespeare's tragedy.

2. It makes many *adjustments* to its source. In addition to *compressing* by cutting many lines and speeches and even a few virtually complete scenes (e.g., 4.5). In addition, it *expands* Shakespeare's death scene and seeks to *correct* it by having Juliet awaken just in time to see Romeo poison himself, giving the doomed lovers time for one last living embrace. The generally breakneck pace and MTV editing are only the most obvious tokens of Luhrmann's *updates* and *superimpositions of his house style*.

3. Luhrmann's motivic creation of a visual track and a sound track pointedly at odds with Shakespeare's poetry (as when the Montagues and Capulets fight at the service station where they are gassing up

their pimpmobiles or on the beach where the Montagues are relaxing) separates the dialogue from the rest of the film, which assumes the status of a *neoclassical imitation,* not of Shakespeare's play but of Shakespeare's language.

4. Despite his modern-day production, Luhrmann seeks to translate the spirit of Shakespeare's play for a modern audience through *revision.* Taking great pains to avoid the period style of the MGM *Romeo and Juliet,* he provides the Capulets with a faux-Italian villa with marble columns and a convenient balcony and frequently uses masses of electric or neon lights to substitute for candles at the Capulets' ball and Juliet's funeral.

5. Luhrmann is notorious for his *colonization* of his sources. Perhaps his most distinctive stylistic device is the rapid superimposition of multiple layers of reference that evacuate the force of the situation they seem to be embellishing. An especially telling example is two quick shots of the "L'Amour" sign that appears in all Luhrmann's films, this time as a billboard borrowing the design of the Coca-Cola logo for the phrase "Wherefore L'Amour."

6. *Romeo + Juliet* constantly *deconstructs* itself through its *(meta)commentary.* After showing a television newscaster speaking the play's prologue, Luhrmann repeats the first four lines aloud again as voiceover, then intercuts them, one printed line at a time, in rapid alternation with an opening montage of images of a Verona Beach that is clearly not Shakespeare's Verona. The dissonance between the film and its ostensible story is frequently heightened by the extreme theatricality of both Montagues and Capulets, especially Mercutio (Harold Perrineau) and Tybalt (John Leguizamo), and by the uncertain Italian accents of the elder Capulets (Paul Sorvino and Diane Venora).

7. Of many examples of *analogy* in the film—for example, the expressive outfits Romeo, Juliet, Tybalt, and Dave Paris (Paul Rudd) wear to the Capulets' ball—by far the most important is the incessant emphasis on crosses and religious icons that turn up in the most inappropriate places (e.g., the clock-face Jesus that counts down the twenty-four hours Romeo has to get out of town, the tube of poison the apothecary takes from beneath a statue of the Blessed Virgin), all of them motivated by the "R + J" design on the ring Juliet gives Romeo, with

the plus sign, echoed in the film's title, spiritualizing their love by linking it to Christ's martyrdom on the cross.

8. The film is filled with examples of both *parody and pastiche*. Moments
    before Romeo accosts Juliet at her balcony, he gets their scene off to a
    slapstick start by tripping over the swimming-pool gear. Later, he falls
    on two separate occasions into the pool, once taking Juliet with him.
    The pool itself, however, is faithfully copied from the 1936 MGM
    *Romeo and Juliet*.

9. Luhrmann is fond of *secondary, tertiary, and quaternary imitation*. His
    beach is flanked by billboards advertising not only "L'Amour" but
    "Prospero Scotch Whiskey" ("such stuff as dreams are made on") and
    "Thunder Bullets" ("shoot forth thunder"). Even the image of Jesus
    that introduces this montage is labeled "The Merchant of Verona
    Beach."

10. Luhrmann's films depend more than most on a dense network of *al-
    lusion* running from images to songs. Even as Romeo and Juliet are
    dying, Luhrmann takes time for one new auditory allusion (the Lie-
    bestod from Wagner's *Tristan und Isolde* [1859]) and one new visual
    allusion (the Rosebud snow globe from *Citizen Kane* [1941]).

The result of this heavily overdetermined intertextual bricolage ought to be
chaos or reductive irony. But many viewers report a paradoxical effect associated with the grand opera that provides Luhrmann's truest generic model: the
very artifice of the conventions recognized and discounted as conventions
deepens these viewers' emotional response. One reason for this response is
surely that audiences are not so easily confused by logically incompatible
modes of intertextuality. Nor should they be, for it would be hard to find a film
that did not freely mix different strategies. Movies like *Bewitched* (2005) that
are based on television series rely on both compression (they have only two
hours, not thirteen or thirty-nine, to develop their central relationships) and
expansion (they add a teleology and a definitive endpoint that would spell
death for most series). John Ford maintained that *Stagecoach* (1939), an adaptation of Ernest Haycox's story "Stage to Lordsburg" (1937), was actually a free
adaptation of Guy de Maupassant's "Boule de suif" (1880). Hugh H. Davis
speaks for many commentators when he argues that *My Own Private Idaho* is
not an analogical treatment of *1 Henry IV* but "a remake of Orson Welles's
*Chimes at Midnight*."[48] *Mary Reilly* invokes not only Stevenson's story and Va-

lerie Martin's novel but Stephen Frears's earlier costume drama *Dangerous Liaisons* (1988), whose success it clearly hoped to invoke and repeat, through the participation of screenwriter Christopher Hampton, composer George Fenton, cinematographer Philippe Rousselot, production designer Stuart Craig, and performers John Malkovich and Glenn Close. Despite its director/star Jerry Lewis's disclaimers, *The Nutty Professor* is widely assumed to draw freely on his former partnership with Dean Martin in creating the character of Buddy Love. Sidney Gottlieb finds visual echoes of *The Magnificent Ambersons* (1942), *Rules of the Game* (*La règle du jeu* [1939]), and *Letter from an Unknown Woman* (1948) in Roger Michell's adaptation of *Persuasion* (1995).[49] Ellen Belton claims that even a curatorial adaptation like the 1995 *Pride and Prejudice*, "although encouraging the spectator to envision herself as participating in an imaginative repossession of the original, is equally preoccupied with a postfeminist rewriting of the novel's central romantic relationship."[50] Laura Carroll, suggesting that "*Metropolitan* manages to borrow from *and* intersect with *Mansfield Park*," concludes that "a major difficulty [with categories like Andrew's] arises from the lack of any sense that some films might exist as hybrids of two or more adaptational modes, and what the critic ought to do with such a film."[51]

It seems clear that the categories I have proposed in this chapter for bridging the gap between adaptation and allusion, however useful they may be in distinguishing particular strategies, are unable to separate particular adaptations into categories because even apparently straightforward adaptations typically make use of many different intertextual strategies. The slippery slope between adaptation and allusion cannot be divided into discrete stages because it really is slippery. The moral to draw from this chapter's failed exercise in demarcation is that intertextuality takes myriad forms that resist reduction to even so comprehensive a grammar as Bakhtin's or Genette's. Like Elliott, however, Genette grasps a truth that eludes many students of adaptation: There is no normative model for adaptation. Both adaptation and allusion are clearly intelligible only within a broader study of intertextuality that will not begin until students of adaptation abandon their fondness for huddling on the near end of the slippery slope between adaptation and allusion, where categorical distinctions still seem seductively plausible.

# CHAPTER SIX

# Exceptional Fidelity

Despite innumerable exceptions to the rule, adaptation theorists have persisted in treating fidelity to the source material as a norm from which unfaithful adaptations depart at their peril. Yet it should be clear by now that fidelity itself, even as a goal, is the exception to the norm of variously unfaithful adaptations. Instead of constantly seeking answers to the question, "Why are so many adaptations unfaithful to perfectly good sources?" adaptation studies would be better advised to ask the question, "Why does this particular adaptation aim to be faithful?"

One benefit of exchanging the first question for the second is that it properly treats fidelity as a special case rather than a rule more often honored in the breach than in the observance. Another is that it pointedly implies that the main reason adaptations rarely achieve anything like fidelity is because they rarely attempt it. A third, perhaps the most important, is that it acknowledges that every case of attempted fidelity is exceptional not only because faithful adaptations are in the minority but because they are so likely to be different from one another. Renouncing the unsupported assumption that all adaptations are, or ought to be, faithful reveals more clearly that the motives for undertaking a particular faithful adaptation are likely to be as distinctive as the results.

This is true even though the primary motive for fidelity in the most widely known adaptations is financial, not aesthetic. Because a well-known literary property has considerable power to presell spin-offs like adaptations and sequels even to viewers who have never read the property,[1] economic propriety long forbade adapters from tampering with speeches and characters and scenes these viewers were presumably expecting to see onscreen. In a letter to Sidney Howard, the principal screenwriter responsible for the adaptation of Margaret Mitchell's best-selling 1936 novel *Gone with the Wind,* David O. Selznick, the independent producer who had purchased the adaptation rights to the novel, noted that "people simply seem to be passionate about the details of the book. . . . I don't think any of us have ever tackled anything that is really comparable in the love people have for it," and added that "the ideal script, as far as I am concerned, would be one that did not contain a single word of original dialogue, and that was one hundred percent Margaret Mitchell, however much we juxtaposed it."[2] He commanded costume designer Walter Plunkett: "Do not vary anything from the book. The book is law; the book is the Bible."[3] The author herself, repeatedly prodded by Selznick to participate in the adaptation, declined on the grounds that "if news got out that I was in even the slightest way responsible for any deviations from the book, then my life wouldn't be worth living."[4]

When Peter Jackson approached the adaptation of J. R. R. Tolkien's epic fantasy *The Lord of the Rings*—originally published in three volumes, *The Fellowship of the Ring* (1954), *The Two Towers* (1954), and *The Return of the King* (1955)—his motives were profoundly different. As his supernatural thriller *The Frighteners* neared completion in 1996, Jackson realized that Weta Limited, the visual effects facility he had founded with Richard Taylor and Jamie Selkirk to provide digitized effects for Jackson's *Heavenly Creatures* (1994), would have no more work to do, "and we were wondering what would come next. I began thinking that I'd love to do a Ray Harryhausen–type fantasy, with fantastic creatures and extraordinary worlds—a '*Lord of the Rings* type of film' is how I envisioned it. It was then that we began looking into the rights for *The Lord of the Rings.*"[5] Although the project was special effects driven literally from the moment of its inception, Jackson was as determined as Selznick to remain faithful to his well-loved source. Executive producer Mark Ordesky has recalled that "virtually everyone in a significant position on the movie knew the books inside out—had been obsessed with them for years."[6] This obsession translated into a passionate desire to recreate Tolkien's world as fully and faithfully as possible.

Yet Selznick's project and Jackson's, both rooted in the desire to produce an adaptation that would justify its prodigious costs by returning a substantial profit by appealing to the enormous audience that the source text had created, are different in several important ways that illustrate just how idiosyncratic quests for fidelity in adaptation are likely to be. These differences include the very different nature of their source novels; the different approaches of the screenplays to the problems of adaptation; differences in the process of filming; differences in publicizing the films' initial release; and different strategies for marketing the film in the reincarnations following that first release. Although no two cases of faithful adaptation can exhaust the catalogue of motives for attempting faithful adaptation and the divergent results of these attempts, *Gone with the Wind* and *The Lord of the Rings* go a long way toward indicating the range of the problems involved in making and analyzing adaptations expressly premised on fidelity.

These problems begin with two that are common to both cases. *Gone with the Wind* and *The Lord of the Rings* are both impossible cases for faithful adaptation, thousand-page novels for which standard tactics of adaptation—selecting some obligatory speeches, characters, scenes, and plotlines and dropping others; compressing or combining several characters or scenes into one; streamlining the narrative by eliminating digressive episodes; reworking dialogue so that it is either more epigrammatic or more severely functional—are clearly inadequate. *Gone with the Wind* rose to this challenge by becoming the longest feature film yet released by Hollywood, *The Lord of the Rings* the longest trilogy. Moreover, each adaptation, no matter how conscientiously it tries to remain faithful to its nominal source, is haunted by the traces of many other texts. Some of these ghost texts are subsidiary sources the adaptation more or less consciously imitates, others antitexts it is equally determined to avoid.

*Gone with the Wind* is an adaptation of Mitchell's novel, of course, but it is also informed in complex ways by *The Birth of a Nation* (1915), D. W. Griffith's race-baiting epic of the Civil War and Reconstruction whose structure and Southern Agonistes viewpoint strongly inflect Mitchell's novel.[7] Faced with the question of whether to follow Mitchell in introducing the Ku Klux Klan as the avengers of the attempted attack on Scarlett O'Hara, Selznick advises retaining the episode but eliminating references to the Klan or its white-robed trappings as potentially incendiary and recalls that "a year or so ago I refused to consider remaking *The Birth of a Nation*, largely for this reason."[8] Initially reluctant to spend the $50,000 to purchase film rights to *Gone with the Wind*, Selznick cabled story editor Katherine Brown that he would be more interested if Mitchell's novel sold as well as Hervey Allen's *Anthony Adverse* (1933), whose prestigious and profitable 1936 film adaptation had just been released by Warner Bros. At the same time, he was wary about the fate of Stark Young's Civil War romance *So Red the Rose* (1934), "which also threatened to have tremendous sale and which in some particulars was in the same category and which failed miserably as a picture" when Paramount filmed it in 1935.[9] Selznick's reaction to Sidney Howard's draft screenplay makes it clear that he saw his own film adaptation of *David Copperfield* (1935) as another model for *Gone with the Wind*, which was also originally slated to be directed by George Cukor, because of its success in cutting another long novel down to feature length by the wholesale elimination of characters like Dr. Strong, Tommy Traddles, Rosa Dartle, and Steerforth's mother and of scenes like David's school days and Steerforth's wooing of Emily rather than by snipping a line here or there from every scene.[10]

Jackson's *Lord of the Rings* trilogy is similarly shaped not only by its attempt to remain faithful to Tolkien's epic but also by its determination to avoid duplicating the reception of Ralph Bakshi's 1978 animated adaptation. The surprising but logical attempt to translate Tolkien's unfilmable novel into an epic cartoon had earned respectful but unenthusiastic reviews but won little loyalty from fans of the novel and enjoyed no great financial success, partly no doubt because of Bakshi's dubious background as the auteur of the X-rated cartoon feature *Fritz the Cat* (1972). Jackson's trilogy has a more complicated relationship to two other fantasy trilogies, *Star Wars* (1977) and its first two sequels, *The Empire Strikes Back* (1980) and *Return of the Jedi* (1983); and *The Matrix* (1999) and its two sequels, *The Matrix Reloaded* (2003) and *The Matrix Revolutions* (2003). George Lucas's initial *Star Wars* cycle, drawing liberally on sources as diverse as Akira Kurosawa's *The Hidden Fortress* (1958) and Joseph Campbell's *The Hero with a Thousand Faces* (1949), had virtually created the genre of the big-budget, high-tech fantasy film with mythopoetic pretensions. The combination of eschatological aspirations, nonstop action, and dazzling visual effects had reached an apex in Larry and Andy Wachowski's *The Matrix*, whose success prompted two sequels and prepared the way for Jackson's own success. Yet both franchises presented not only models to be emulated but also dangers to avoid. Jackson's tireless insistence in interviews on the unity of his project, its status as a single three-part film rather than a trilogy, was meant to distance it from both *Star Wars* and *The Matrix* at the same time that it aligned Jackson's project more closely with Tolkien's.[11] *Star Wars* had been augmented for video shortly before Jackson's film went into production, and *The Matrix* had spawned two sequels unplanned at the time of the first film and widely perceived as aimless except for their desire to outdo its firepower and its computer-generated effects.

But within the context of these similarities—the attempt to bring unfilmable epics faithfully to the screen, the unavoidable invocation of other precursor texts as models or antitypes—Selznick and Jackson follow diverging paths. Their differences are in part forced on them by the very different nature of the novels they are adapting. At the time Selznick purchased the film rights to Mitchell's novel, *Gone with the Wind* was a contemporary best seller using a naturalistic mode to tell its story of war and reconstruction. Following the defining convention of the historical novel, Mitchell focused a story of tumultuous social and political upheaval on a small number of characters whose internal and external conflicts focused the contradictory forces of their milieu. Mitchell's hero, Rhett Butler, embodied the questionable but plausible charm of the new South; his foil, Ashley Wilkes, the combination of idealism and fatalism that doomed his class; and Mitchell's heroine, Scarlett O'Hara, the steely determination to survive amid the wreckage whatever the cost to herself and others. The romantic triangle among these three characters dramatized the defeat of the antebellum South and the rise of the new South in terms of heroic individual agents whose actions had the power to make or transcend history— a motif faithfully echoed in publicity posters for the film, which were dominated by an image of Rhett heroically carrying Scarlett in his arms as Atlanta burns in the background. The novel was aimed at an adult audience, sold rapidly even before publication—its publication date had to be pushed back from April 21 to May 5 to May 31, 1936, "when the publishers realized the book was a potential moneymaker of unusual extent,"[12] and then to June 30 when it was purchased by the Book-of-the-Month Club—and was still dominating best-seller lists when Selznick began to cast his production.

*The Lord of the Rings*, by contrast, was a cult favorite, not a popular best seller. Although it had long been kept in print by the Book-of-the-Month Club's hardcover editions—first of the three individual volumes originally published, then of the one-volume epic—it had never been a runaway best seller. At the time filming began, it was a fifty-year-old cult novel known largely to adolescents and fans of the modern quasi-medieval fantasy genre it had done so much to create. Although it was also framed as a historical account, Tolkien's tale of Middle-earth was both more and less self-serious than Mitchell's Civil War romance. Tolkien's history was as fictional as his geography; Middle-earth had no more basis in reality than the land of Oz. Frodo Baggins was an even more reluctant hero than Scarlett O'Hara. Like all Hobbits, he preferred an untroubled domestic life close to Bag End and was deeply disquieted by the mission thrust on him: to take the One Ring his uncle Bilbo had taken from the abhorrent creature Gollum to Mount Orodruin and throw it into the destroying fire lest it fall into the possession of Sauron, the Dark Lord, and enable him to consolidate his tyrannical power over all Middle-earth. The kernel of the story is no more than a fairy tale, its characters the stuff of animal fables, boys' adventures, and martial lore. Yet Tolkien created such a resonant and densely textured fabric of references for Middle-earth—a web of place names, family trees, interlocking generational histories, and (most notably) languages—that his fantasy assumes an epic richness. If Frodo and his friends and enemies fail to meet the minimal requirements for verisimilitude and complexity of character in the modern mainstream novel, Tolkien's achievement in creating a self-contained alternative world with its own cosmology, life forms, history, social customs, and languages seems at the same time dwarfed by being labeled a novel at all.

Amid all the differences between *Gone with the Wind* and *The Lord of the Rings* as source texts, one stands out as paramount: their very different status as texts. *Gone with the Wind* has been published in many editions since 1936, but its English-language editions all have the same words in the same order. There has never been any difficulty in establishing an authoritative text of Mitchell's novel. Tolkien's novel, by contrast, poses textual problems of several varieties whose combination is almost unparalleled in twentieth-century publishing. Like *Ulysses* and *The Sound and the Fury*, it has never appeared in an authoritative edition free of errors introduced by printers or editors; most editions, like those of Joyce and Faulkner, have corrected earlier errors only to introduce new ones.[13] Even if a single authoritative text of *The Lord of the Rings* were to appear, it is not clear exactly what that text would include and therefore what text any film adaptation would legitimately take as its original. As Tolkien notes in his prologue to *The Lord of the Rings*, the story of how Bilbo Baggins took the Ring from Gollum first appears in chapter 5 of *The Hobbit*

(1937), but the account of this episode that Bilbo gave to the Wizard Gandalf the Grey and his companions differed materially from the truth. Moreover, Tolkien introduced extensive textual revisions in the 1951 second edition of *The Hobbit* that deepened Gollum's depravity, emphasized Bilbo's loss of innocence, and inflated the monstrous power of the Ring.[14]

In addition, much of the elf queen Arwen's backstory is presented only in the voluminous appendices Tolkien first published in the 1955 edition of *The Return of the King*, not in the main line of the narrative itself, and most of her fellow visionary Galadriel's backstory appears only in Tolkien's posthumous novel, *The Silmarillion* (1977).[15] Finally, the twelve-volume *History of Middle-earth* begun by Tolkien and completed by his son Christopher (1986–96) provides a wealth of further information, taking sometimes critical, sometimes narrative form. Although Jackson's trilogy draws sparingly on this material, Tolkien Web sites buzz with debates over which details ought to be considered canonical, and there is no bright line between what is within the canon and what is not.

The final difference between *Gone with the Wind* and *The Lord of the Rings* as source texts is indicated by the word *canon*. For all its enduring popularity *Gone with the Wind* is finally a novel—certainly an immensely popular novel, perhaps a great novel, even a novel that gives unique expression to essential forces and contradictions in American history—and nothing more. For Tolkien's most devoted readers *The Lord of the Rings* carries an utterly different kind of authority. Orlando Bloom, who played Legolas in Jackson's films, has recalled that "we were incredibly lucky to have [Tolkien's book] as source material, as reference material, that kind of bible to keep turning back to."[16] The tireless concern to establish an accurate text, the widespread debate on apparent flaws and inconsistencies within the story, the willingness to extend speculation about the characters and their fates until it takes the form of narrative, the vast array of Tolkien scholarship in print and online all show that a substantial audience concurs with Bloom in regarding *The Lord of the Rings* in quasi-scriptural terms, as a particular kind of sacred writing whose adaptation demands unusual fidelity under unusually severe penalties. If Mitchell's novel provides a bible for filmmakers seeking to adapt it, Tolkien's provides a bible of a more literal and inspirational sort. It is both more problematic and more demanding for adapters than Mitchell's.

This is not to say that Tolkien's readers regard his stories of Middle-earth as literally true, any more than most contemporary biblical scholars regard every word of the Bible as literally true. The peculiar nature of Tolkien's authority would seem to place it somewhere on the spectrum that runs from the Bible to the Sherlock Holmes canon, which has also been the subject of so much quasi scholarship. As the example of Sherlock Holmes suggests, this sort of scriptural authority does not necessarily imply claims to literary value. But Tolkien's readers have not been shy about pressing such claims. Although most readers would probably dispute Tom Shippey's description of Tolkien as the author of the century,[17] it is even less likely that dissenters would propose Margaret Mitchell as an alternative.

The differences between the two source texts are magnified by the different approaches the filmmakers take in adapting them, differences framed by some remarkable similarities. It is a truism to point out that *Gone with the Wind* is the producer's film par excellence, its vision shaped by the creative, hands-on Selznick, who supervised the script, the budget, the hiring of cast members and key technicians, the production and postproduction, and the publicity for the film's initial release. Even though it is a convention of American film criticism to identify films as the products of their directors, virtually all commentators have agreed with Richard Harwell's verdict: "*Gone with the Wind* was David Selznick's film."[18] Yet *The Lord of the Rings* is in many ways a producer's film as well, since its director, Peter Jackson, also served as one of the films' principal screenwriters and producers. Jackson succeeded as completely as Selznick in creating an epic in his own image. For all their weight, both projects are fairly described as informed by a single overarching vision.

It is all the more surprising, then, that neither project was originally planned at the epic length it eventually reached. Although Sidney Howard's initial draft screenplay of *Gone with the Wind* totaled some 250 pages (not 400, as many commentators have reported),[19] that draft was no longer than Howard's initial screenplay for *Arrowsmith*, whose 1931 film version for Goldwyn ran less than two hours, and both writer and producer assumed it would be cut sharply. In reviewing Howard's first draft in January 1937, Selznick pronounced himself "prepared for a picture that will be extremely long in any case, perhaps as much as 14,000 feet"[20]—a few minutes over two and a half hours, nearly half an hour shorter than *The Great Ziegfeld* (1936). A week later Selznick wrote his treasurer, John Wharton, to assure him that "we are not approaching the picture with any foregone conclusion that it has to be enormous in size and has to have exceptionally high cost, even for big pictures."[21] In March 1937 he envisioned the film's budget as $1,500,000 "if we have stars, and $1,250,000 if we have not."[22]

In the meantime *Gone with the Wind* became the best-selling American novel in both 1936 and 1937, and it won the 1936 Pulitzer Prize for fiction, defeating, among other contenders, William Faulkner's *Absalom, Absalom!* As Mitchell's stock continued to rise, Selznick became more determined to film her book as faithfully as possible, even at unprecedented length. In August 1937 he asked United Artists general manager George Schaefer, whose company distributed Selznick International's films, about "the advisability of making 'Gone with the Wind' as two pictures," perhaps breaking them at Scarlett's marriage to Rhett.[23] Although Schaefer was enthusiastic, Selznick was not. But the speculation had encouraged him to think in even more expansive terms. A year later, facing a budget estimate of $2,800,000 for "the longest picture ever made,"[24] he wrote to Selznick International production manager Edward Butcher that "I am hopeful we can bring the picture in for $2,250,000 at the outside, and in cutting the script I will aim at a $2,000,000 cost."[25]

When Selznick signed Clark Gable for the role of Rhett Butler in August 1938, he committed himself to begin shooting the following January, even though he still had no shooting script. His solution was to hire writer after writer to rework the screenplay but to insist that each of them restrict himself to Mitchell's dialogue. F. Scott Fitzgerald, who worked on the screenplay for two weeks in January 1939, reported to his editor, Maxwell Perkins, that because he was forbidden from using any words but Mitchell's, "when new phrases had to be invented one had to thumb through [the novel] as if it were Scripture and check out phrases of hers which would cover the situation!"[26] Howard, who had returned to Hollywood briefly in January 1938 for an earlier rewrite, concurred: "It's not a movie script. It's a transcription from the book."[27] Although Selznick considered as late as January 1939 cutting, along with other introductory scenes, the O'Haras at prayer, the first scene between Scarlett and Mammy, and the barbecue, the finished film includes them all.[28] The final negative cost for Selznick's 222-minute epic transcription came to $4,250,000.

Peter Jackson's story provides a striking complement to Selznick's. Originally intrigued by the possibility of creating a screenplay for a *Lord of the Rings* with more heft and grandeur than Bakshi's cartoon, he; his wife, Fran Walsh; and their collaborator, Philippa Boyens, produced a ninety-page treatment covering Tolkien's entire story and persuaded Miramax to option the rights from Saul Zaentz, who had produced Bakshi's animated adaptation. But when Jackson took a draft screenplay of the two separate films his team planned, "using the end of Helm's Deep as the climax of Film One,"[29] which would correspond roughly to *The Fellowship of the Ring* and *The Two Towers*, leaving the events of *The Return of the King* for Film Two, Miramax demurred unless he could fit the entire story into a single two-hour feature. Given four weeks to shop their epic elsewhere before Miramax removed them from the project and made its own two-hour film, they pitched the two projected films to New Line, where CEO Robert Shaye had the opposite reaction; he wondered why Jackson was proposing two films and not the three that would parallel Tolkien's own three volumes. So Jackson, Walsh, and Boyens agreed to recast their epic as a trilogy. Like Selznick, they were backed into an epic length they did not begin by choosing.

Yet the parallel between each of Tolkien's three books and its corresponding film adaptation remained nominal. *The Two Towers* bears particular evidence of its origin as half of what Jackson calls Film One. Their concern for chronology, counterpoint, and dramatic effectiveness led Jackson, Walsh, and Boyens to move many of the events presented in the last four chapters of Tolkien's Book Three and the last four chapters of Book Four of *The Two Towers* to *The Return of the King*. The resulting lack of drama and incident in *The Two Towers*—Jackson complained that no major characters die in this second film—required the introduction of new dramatic developments. Faramir, who had easily resisted the temptation to take the Ring from Frodo in Tolkien, now takes Frodo, Sam, and Gollum captive and frees them only after much soul-searching. Frodo, inflamed by Gollum's innuendoes against Sam, turns against his old friend. The belief that the love between the warrior and future king Aragorn and the elf queen Arwen was less than compelling given the great geographical distance between them led Jackson to plan a new sequence in which Arwen rides to Helm's Deep to join Aragorn in battle. Liv Tyler, who played Arwen, took daily lessons in swordsmanship and martial arts for several weeks before the sequence was cancelled, partly because Internet rumors by Tolkien fans imagining Arwen as "Xena, Warrior Princess," had been so indignantly disapproving.[30] Instead, Jackson, Walsh, and Boyens decided to develop Arwen's love for Aragorn through a series of strategic flashbacks and to enlarge the siege of Helm's Deep to provide the film's major climax. The screenplay's unusually free reshuffling of incidents from Tolkien in the interest of simplified chronology, economy, and drama underlines Jackson's often repeated determination to remain faithful to Tolkien's epic as a whole rather than to any of its component parts—perhaps the only goal that remained consistent over the trilogy's production.

If both epics are accidental, they differ sharply in other ways. Selznick's target audience is adult females who have read *Gone with the Wind;*[31] Jackson's is adolescent males who are fairly steeped in *The Lord of the Rings.* Selznick's film plausibly assumes that the audience already has some general knowledge of the Civil War but none of Scarlett O'Hara's fictional story. Jackson, unable to assume viewers' knowledge of Middle-earth's history and languages, adds a drastically abbreviated prologue to *The Fellowship of the Ring,* paralleling Tolkien's prologue in introducing several major characters and dramatizing the recent history of the Ring but, again like Tolkien, makes no such concessions in his second and third films, whose lack of expository background in their opening movements would make them incomprehensible to viewers who had not already read Tolkien's books—or, better still, seen the earlier film versions of *The Fellowship of the Ring* and *The Two Towers,* whose climaxes mark unusually complete departures from their source text.

Though both film projects deal with the enormous size of their originals by making wholesale cuts, their strategies for cutting are different. Selznick, shoehorning a thousand-page novel into four hours, covers between four and five closely printed pages a minute. Jackson, dealing with a novel of similar length, takes nearly three times as long to tell his story. *The Return of the King* is nearly as long as *Gone with the Wind* all by itself. So Jackson needs to cover between two and three pages of Tolkien a minute—a daunting challenge, and far in excess of the standard shooting ratio of one minute of shooting time to one page of script but much less demanding than Selznick's ratio. Selznick's film takes just two minutes to cover the twenty-one pages of Mitchell's chapter 1; cuts large portions of chapters 8, 9, 11, 12, 16, 17, 18, 19, 26, 27, 28, 29, 30, 33, 35, 36, 37, 38, 39, 40, 41, 42, 43, 48, 49, 52, 55, 57, 58, and 60; and eliminates, among other characters, Ashley's sister Honey, Scarlett's brother-in-law and foreman Will Benteen, Scarlett's children Wade and Ella, the entire Tarleton family except for Scarlett's sparks Brent and Stuart, and all the O'Haras who do not live at Tara. In addition, the film frequently compresses time within scenes by the liberal use of wordless reaction shots and point-of-view shots to comment on the action without pausing for external dialogue or internal monologue. The film's inventions are correspondingly few, the most notable being Scarlett's stop at the ruined Wilkes plantation of Twelve Oaks in her flight from Atlanta to Tara.

Jackson's approach is much freer. Although he also cuts characters and episodes—from Frodo's and Sam's encounter with Tom Bombadil in *The Fellowship of the Ring* to the defense of the Shire in *The Return of the King*, along with virtually all the many songs Tolkien wrote for his characters to sing in prophecy or celebration—he is more likely to invent new characters like Háma's young warrior son Haleth, who speaks briefly with Aragorn in *The Two Towers*, and new incidents like Wormtongue's murder of Saruman and the duel between Aragorn and the troll in *The Return of the King*. Tom Shippey singles out three of Jackson's changes as crucial: Aragorn's near-death midway through *The Two Towers;* Faramir's decision to seize the Ring along with Frodo, Sam, and Gollum toward the end of *The Two Towers;* and Denethor's ruthless greed, selfishness, and remoteness from Faramir.[32] More generally, Jackson routinely balances his many cuts by dispersing and prolonging suspenseful sequences—like Faramir's struggle with his conscience and the journey of Frodo, Sam, and Gollum to the stairway at Cirith Ungol—and by inflating battle scenes like the siege of Helm's Deep and the defense of Osgiliath. A frequent sign of this sort of inflation is the substitution of Howard Shore's music for diegetic sound, frequently accompanied by slow-motion visuals.

A striking feature of Tolkien's writing is its subordination of the unity of individual units like chapters, episodes, or subplots in favor of a medieval-inspired interlace structure, "digressive and cluttered," that "seeks to mirror the perception of the flux of events in the world around us, where everything is happening at once."[33] Once the Fellowship of the Ring dissolves at the end of his first volume, most of *The Two Towers* and *The Return of the King* follow a given character or a small group of characters—Frodo and Sam, Merry and Pippin, Aragorn and his allies—for extended, often overlapping periods. More interested in fidelity to the larger design of Tolkien's epic than in fidelity to its component parts, Jackson develops a still more intricate interlace structure, reshaping and intercutting scenes and revising characters' actions and motivations while casting each of his three films as a dramatically satisfying experience on its own terms.

Unlike *Gone with the Wind,* which everywhere displays a fetishistic reverence for Margaret Mitchell's dialogue, *The Lord of the Rings* uses little of Tolkien's dialogue verbatim apart from a few obligatory speeches, from Frodo's ringing declaration, "I will take the Ring to Mordor!" (264) to Sam's quiet final line to his wife, "Well, I'm back" (1008). But if Jackson is so little concerned to preserve Tolkien's dialogue, the sequence of events in his story, the proportions among different events, his division of the story into three volumes of two books each, the actions or motivations of his characters, or even the climax—in which Gollum, instead of falling over the edge of Mount Doom as he celebrates his acquisition of the Ring, topples over the edge during Frodo's struggle with him— then exactly what is Jackson being faithful to? Shippey concludes that "the philosophical 'core of the original'"—"Tolkien's painstaking double analysis both of the dangers of speculation and of the nature of chance"—has "been lost in the movie version."[34] The response of eaalto, a fan rating *The Return of the King* on TheOneRing.Net, one of many Tolkien Web sites, is less sophisticated but in its way more revealing of the audience Jackson was clearly aiming to please: "An almost perfect finish . . . My only quibbles are that it's still too short (several scenes are obviously missing, Denethor/Eowyn/Faramir are short-changed, and the march on Mordor is rushed), and that the lime-green Army of the Dead looked a little fake on the battlefield. The siege was amazing, Mordor was perfect (ok, so the 'Lighthouse of Evil' effect seemed a little silly), and all the hobbits get strong roles this time around."[35] Though eaalto's criteria, like Shippey's, are based on fidelity, his notion of fidelity depends not on philosophical themes but on inclusiveness, decorum, pace, consistency with the first two films, serious and weighty treatment of the major characters, and a vision less philosophical than literal, a kind of ostensive realism in presenting Middle-earth and its denizens even though they never existed before Tolkien wrote about them.

More generally, the criteria of fidelity that Jackson and his cowriters set themselves involve first including all Tolkien's major characters and creatures. A distinctly defensive note enters their remarks on the omission of Tom Bombadil from *The Fellowship of the Ring*. Philippa Boyens explains that "we don't know that [the Hobbits] didn't go into the Old Forest. We don't know that they didn't meet Tom. We just don't mention it. It's just left untold."[36] Beyond including as many of Tolkien's characters as possible and apologizing for any omissions, the filmmakers strive to make obviously nonhuman characters from Treebeard to Gollum move and speak and act as realistically as possible, consistent with their status as otherworldly creatures. The touchstone of fidelity is Tolkien's imagined universe in all its physical fullness and the convincing staging of both large-scale battle scenes and intimate conversation.

Lynette R. Porter is certainly correct in noting that what makes Tolkien's heroes heroic is not simply their prowess in battle but "their ability to rise above their limitations—experientially, physically, mentally, spiritually, or emotionally—to perform a valiant act."[37] It is equally true, however, that Jackson's trilogy gravitates unmistakably in the direction of "an 'action movie,' even a 'special effects movie.'"[38] There is some justice to Jane Chance's complaint that "there are no quiet moments" in *The Fellowship of the Ring*.[39] Luckily for Jackson, his need to balance fidelity to Tolkien with commercial appeal is eased by the fondness of so many young male Tolkien fans for battle scenes far more extended than anything in the book. *Gone with the Wind* is similarly inflected by a popular genre outside its source text, this one more surprising. The velocity of Selznick's film, compressing a thousand pages and some fifteen years of fictional time into four hours, changed its pace and tone in ways Margaret Mitchell could hardly have predicted. James Harvey, observing that the film is "a 'romantic epic' that is neither especially romantic nor notably epic," calls it "a kind of ultimate tough comedy, its vitality more a development of thirties movie comedy than of any historical romance tradition."[40] Most of the film's often comic banter is merely implicit in the novel. Rhett's proposal of marriage in Mitchell is merely brusque: "I am asking you to marry me. Would you be convinced if I knelt down?" (831). Onscreen, his proposal takes a burlesque turn: "Forgive me for startling you with the impetuosity of my sentiments, my dear Scarlett—I mean, my dear Mrs. Kennedy. But it cannot have escaped your notice that for some time past the friendship I have felt for you has ripened into a deeper feeling—a feeling more beautiful, more pure, more sacred. Dare I name it? Can it be love?" The apparent contradiction between comedy and romantic epic—both genres aimed at female viewers—did not hurt Selznick's box office any more than the movement toward large-scale action set pieces hurt Jackson's.

One final difference in the attitudes the two filmmakers took toward adaptation—the need to censor many features of the source text—was forced on Selznick partly by the Hays office, the industry's self-censoring board that regulated the content of Hollywood films from 1934 to 1956, partly by the politics of mass-market entertainment. For all its popularity, Mitchell's novel amounted to a political minefield. The NAACP had been mounting boycotts of *The Birth of a Nation* for twenty years. *Gone with the Wind*, though avoiding the more obvious tokens of Griffith's racism, made no apologies for slavery and restricted its black characters to subservient roles both before and after Emancipation. Howard's screenplay accordingly walked a tightrope between verisimilitude and hindsight, cutting Mitchell's frequent use of the word *nigger* and occasional derivatives like *niggery* (427), even though as late as June 7, 1939,

Selznick was regretting this "blanket rule" and wondering if he could "salvage two or three of these uses."[41] All mention of sex disappeared from the film so that, for example, Rhett's line "The world is full of beds—and most of the beds are full of women" (896) became "The world is full of many things and many people. I shall find comfort elsewhere." The pain of childbirth was banished offscreen; Rhett no longer spoke of his lust for Scarlett, even when they were married; and Belle Watling's Atlanta bordello was changed to a saloon.

The one challenge that remained was Rhett's farewell speech, when Scarlett asked him what was to become of her: "Frankly, my dear, I don't give a damn." Howard had excised all Mitchell's other uses of "damn" from his screenplay. But Selznick, although he arranged to shoot alternate takes of this speech without the offending epithet, had emphasized Mitchell's own line—"My dear, I don't give a damn" (1035)—by adding the adverb *himself* shortly before shooting and was prepared to fight for the result. He confronted Joseph Breen, head of the Hays office, with the news that the earlier print screened for Breen, in which Rhett had said, "Frankly, my dear, I don't care," would not be the release print. When Breen threatened to cancel the Production Code certificate he had issued, Selznick argued vigorously and enlisted MGM president Joseph Schenck to enter the fray to protect his studio's investment in its most expensive property. Eventually Breen refused to authorize the use of *damn* and fined Selznick five thousand dollars for its use but did not rescind his approval: "In essence, the Hays office looked the other way."[42]

The resulting film, softening the racism, sexuality, and language of Mitchell's novel, still offered enough provocation to offend religious leaders from coast to coast. Nor was Selznick's attempt to distance himself from antebellum epics such as *The Birth of a Nation* and *So Red the Rose* wholly successful. On January 9, 1940, black dramatist Carlton Moss published a column in the *Daily Worker* that began: "Whereas 'The Birth of a Nation' was a frontal attack on American history and the Negro people, 'Gone with the Wind,' arriving twenty years later, is a rear attack on the same . . . The message of GWTW emerges in its final entity as a nostalgic plea for sympathy for a still living cause of Southern reaction."[43] Since fidelity to Mitchell offered no defense against any of these attacks, fidelity had to be compromised in a way that had become unnecessary by the time of Jackson's trilogy.

Once the celluloid versions of *Gone with the Wind* and *The Lord of the Rings* moved into production, the different kinds of fidelity they sought continued to lead to different problems. After repeatedly shooting Scarlett in the green muslin print dress Mitchell had prescribed for her in the opening scene, Selznick switched to a white dress to emphasize the virginal contrast with her behavior during and after the war. Although Mitchell had refused to participate in adapting her novel to the screen, she had urged Selznick to hire her friend Susan Myrick as voice coach and Atlanta historian Wilbur Kurtz as technical adviser. Both of them swiftly became embroiled in disputes about the film's period accuracy. The most important of these was the design of Tara and Twelve Oaks. Mitchell had described Scarlett's home as "a clumsy sprawling building" made of "whitewashed brick" (48, 47). Such a modest house would never do for Selznick, who envisioned a more imposing structure modeled on the trademark office building shown at the beginning of every Selznick International production. Years after the production, Kurtz recalled with pride his successful fight to "keep round columns off of Tara."[44] The discrepancy between Mitchell's Twelve Oaks and Selznick's was even more dramatic, as Myrick observed in writing to Mitchell about "the castle they have built" to serve as the Wilkes home and the barbecue setting, which "looked like the palace at Versailles."[45] Selznick turned Twelve Oaks, a "beautiful white-columned house that crowned the hill like a Greek temple" (25), into a monumental building Myrick compared to Grand Central Station. Determined to remain faithful to Mitchell's novel at so many points, Selznick could not resist the temptation to substitute an inflated myth of Southern domesticity for Mitchell's matter-of-fact descriptions.

Distinct albeit parallel discrepancies cropped up in the filming of *The Lord of the Rings*. Jackson's devotion to Tolkien's quasi-medieval mise-en-scène, which included set design, makeup, and especially the films' widely praised costume design, did not extend to dialogue, which is regularly less archaic in Jackson than in Tolkien. Without introducing obvious anachronisms, Jackson, Walsh, and Boyens unobtrusively disentangle the heroes' syntax and prune arcane references—except for references to names and places, which continue to carry the same musical value they do in Tolkien. In calling on cutting-edge special effects to animate Tolkien's creatures, Jackson insists on a theme of particular importance to Tolkien: the continuum between warriors, hobbits, elves, spirits, animals, plants, and inanimate minerals represented at their most sentient and malevolent by the Ring. As in Selznick's case, however, Jackson's desire for magnificence sometimes overcomes his quest for fidelity. The battles of Helm's Deep and Osgiliath are marvels of digital design, but not all the technical wizardry can disguise the obvious differences between the relatively small numbers of the live-action cast and the thousands of digitized extras who support them in overhead long shots. By all odds the most successful and highly praised of the films' many effects-dependent creations was the cringing, sniveling, menacing Gollum, a computer-animated composite based on Andy Serkis's live-action performance. Having created such a compelling villain in *The Two Towers,* however, Jackson could not resist tweaking him in *The Return of the King,* when new subdivision surface modeling technology allowed Weta Digital to construct a more flexible, expressive digital model that could serve as the basis for the character. By the time *The Two Towers* and *The Return of the King* were due for release on expanded DVD, Gollum CG supervisor Greg Butler explains, the character could be developed still further: "We incorporated subtleties that we had dropped when we ran out of time previously. We painted wrinkles on Gollum's forehead, on the sides of his nose, in the corners of his eyes and around his lips."[46] Hence Gollum's physical appearance changes more completely over the twelve-month diegetic period covered by *The Lord of the Rings* than Scarlett O'Hara's does over the fifteen-year period of *Gone with the Wind* because newly available technology allowed it to change, enabling Jackson to choose development over consistency. Both Selznick and Jackson repeatedly compromise their attempts at fidelity by their search for something more: more detail, more intensity, more expressiveness, more symbolic resonance, the larger scale appropriate to an epic canvas that, in the end, takes precedence even over their beloved source texts.

Sharper differences emerge in the ways the two epics were publicized. When a film is marketed as a faithful adaptation of a well-loved book, the most powerful spokesperson on the film's behalf is the book's author. Neither author was on hand to perform this task—Tolkien because he had died in 1973, Mitchell because she limited her participation to speaking at the Atlanta premiere of *Gone with the Wind.* But both exerted considerable indirect pressure on the films—Mitchell through her surrogates Susan Myrick and Wilbur Kurtz, Tolkien through the vast network of fans ready and eager to comment on the ongoing production on Tolkien Web sites, message boards, and blogs. The filmmakers' awareness of such powerful surrogates surely helped keep them steadfast in their dedication to the goal of fidelity.

Once more the difference between the recreated historical reality of *Gone with the Wind* and the created reality of *The Lord of the Rings* proved crucial. Selznick's publicity machine, treating its film as a window on a vanished past, concentrated as much on the details of that past as on the particulars of

Mitchell's novel. Its single most successful coup—the filming of the backgrounds for the burning of Atlanta a month before principal photography began, even before final casting had been established—married the cachet of epic filmmaking to the excitement of real-life contemporary spectacle. And its most ingeniously extended tactic—the year-long focus on casting the film, especially on the search for the perfect Scarlett, so as to "keep [the] public's interest in the project alive" while Selznick waited for January 1939, when Gable would be available to play Rhett and when Selznick's distribution contract with United Artists would have expired, freeing him to release the film through MGM[47]—treated the characters as if they were people as real as their Civil War background. Though he considered actors as different as Ronald Colman, Errol Flynn, and Gary Cooper for the role of Rhett Butler, Selznick soon assented to the hugely popular choice of Clark Gable, even though the terms on which he secured his services—MGM's payment of $1,250,000 and the loan out of Gable in return for distribution rights and 50 percent of the film's profits—would cost him millions. The search for Scarlett, however, ran on and on. At times it seemed that Selznick had tested every star in Hollywood. Norma Shearer, Bette Davis, Katharine Hepburn, Miriam Hopkins, Tallulah Bankhead, Jean Arthur, Loretta Young, Irene Dunne, Ann Sheridan, Lana Turner, Joan Bennett, Paulette Goddard, and Edythe Marriner (later Susan Hayward) all came under consideration before Selznick finally settled in January 1939, days before principal photography began, on Vivien Leigh.[48] Much less widely publicized were his search for the exemplary Technicolor cinematographer and set designer. His pursuit of William Cameron Menzies, the famed visual designer recently turned director of *Things to Come* (1936), did not end until he created the new term "Production Designer" to assuage Menzies's desire "not to get back to art direction as such."[49] At different points Selznick considered Tony Gaudio, Gregg Toland, Charles Lang, Hal Rosson, Oliver Marsh, Karl Struss, Karl Freund, and Rudolph Maté before choosing Lee Garmes. After shooting seven weeks worth of footage, amounting to "almost a third of the picture,"[50] Garmes was quietly replaced by Ernest Haller and denied screen credit for his work. In similar fashion George Cukor was replaced by Victor Fleming as the film's director a month into the production, a change effected as quickly and bloodlessly as possible in a brief, noncommittal memorandum issued jointly by Selznick and Cukor on February 13, 1939, and the signing of Fleming the following day—even though Cukor continued to rehearse scenes with both Vivien Leigh and Olivia de Havilland, who played Melanie Hamilton, on their days off for weeks afterward.[51] The pattern throughout was to publicize any decisions or nondecisions about personnel that could keep the glamour and imagined reality of the production in the public eye but to downplay any developments that might emphasize any conflicts or labor on the film as a manufactured product.

The contrast in the ways *The Lord of the Rings* was publicized could not have been greater, partly because film publicity had changed so much in the intervening sixty years, partly because of the very different nature of the film. The emphasis in the materials released by New Line and discussed endlessly by Tolkien fans fell almost entirely on two questions that had been central for Jackson since the project's inception: How faithful would the films be to their unfilmable source? And how adeptly could Jackson use recent developments in computer-generated effects to create Middle-earth and its creatures? Fans following the production were clearly interested in the film as a created object, an interest the publicity was equally clearly designed to quicken. New Line's official Web site for the film (www.lordoftherings.net), introduced by Jackson's brief vocal greeting, was heavy on lists of the characters and cultures of Middle-earth, effects footage and explanations, interviews that offered further production details, and downloads ranging from video clips to trailers to desktop wallpaper. While *The Fellowship of the Ring* was still in theaters, Jody Duncan published a fifty-page article demystifying its visual effects for specialists and hard-core fans.

Amid this copious media blitz, however, there was virtually no mention of casting. The monumental extended DVD release of *The Fellowship of the Ring* contains eleven featurettes discussing Tolkien's life and work, the process of adaptation, the film's storyboards, production design, location photography, visual effects, and postproduction, along with galleries including hundreds of still photographs. But although most of the principal actors, from Elijah Wood to Ian McKellen, turn up as talking heads or disembodied voices on a supplementary sound track to reminisce about the making of the film, there is never any discussion of why or how they were chosen for their roles. When Stuart Townsend was replaced in the role of Aragorn by Viggo Mortenson only a few days into the production, the recasting of the trilogy's romantic lead went largely unacknowledged by the studio and ignored by fans.

Instead of Selznick's well-publicized attempts to recreate a Civil War Georgia as accurately as possible—subject only to the competing imperatives of maximum dazzle and scale—New Line emphasized the creation of Middle-earth from nothing in a long series of glimpses inside the making of the trilogy. For the glamour of photos and interviews with the stars of the film, New Line substituted a thorough demystification of the digital wizardry required by the film's world of epic fantasy. The result was that many viewers arrived at theaters for the premieres of Jackson's three films not only knowing that vast numbers of the supporting cast did not exist outside CGI programs but prepared to enjoy that fact by watching the digital effects critically. If savvy viewers could no longer accept the Orcs and the Army of the Dead as real, they could enjoy them as distinct improvements over the digitized extras in *Titanic* and *Gladiator*. New Line's consistent emphasis, both before and after the film's release, on Web-based, often interactive, publicity features that took potential viewers inside the making of the films assumed that the target audience would approach the film not in a credulous spirit ("so that's what it looked like") but in a spirit of disavowal ("so that's how they ended up doing it") far deeper and more technically informed than the audience who delighted in recognizing Clark Gable in every one of Rhett Butler's scenes. At the same time, the making-of slant of New Line's publicity empowered viewers following the progress of the production online and often commenting on it on message and discussion boards as active collaborators in the filmmaking process. It was as if absorbing and understanding studio-fed information about the film's production and registering their reactions in a public forum made them consultants on the film.

This apparent feedback loop was completed by using the film to market other *Lord of the Rings* products. Marketing synergy, of course, was nothing new in Hollywood. For many years films, especially those produced by the Disney studios, had been used to market photographs, sheet music, recordings, figurines, commemorative brochures, and reprints of source books, just as they increased the circulation of the newspapers and magazines that covered their production and reception. Long before its filming began, *Gone with the Wind* had spawned commemorative bookends, lockets, and leather buttons and dress pins. When Margaret Mitchell refused to lend her name or image to any product endorsements, the enterprising M. T. Strommen Engineering Company hired another woman with the same name to advertise its device for rolling cigarettes.[52] Products marketed in connection with the film's release included paper dolls, collectible dolls, dress patterns, bonnets, hairnets, jewelry, perfume, postcards, board games, and chocolates. The cover of the July 1941 issue of *Progressive Farmer* features a publicity still from the film to illustrate Lillian Keller's article "Eighty Years of Southern Fashions," even though the issue contains no article on the film.[53] And, of course, images from the film were used to promote many reprint editions of Mitchell's novel, which was still selling briskly in 1939. In a final twist the phenomenon of *Gone with the Wind* has become the basis of numerous tributes and critical studies that fans consume not as books but as "collectibles."[54]

By the time of *The Lord of the Rings*'s release, marketing synergy had been raised to a high art. Like *Gone with the Wind* the film was used to sell photographs, figurines, games (now computer games in addition to the Monopoly Special Edition board game), clothing (headdresses and ornamental belt buckles rather than hairnets), tote bags, and jewelry (including numberless replicas of the One Ring), and autograph cards signed by the likes of Ian McKellen, Viggo Mortenson, Orlando Bloom, Liv Tyler, and Richard Taylor of Weta Workshop Design. Additional products included trading cards, calendars, wall scrolls, paperweights, bookmarks, jigsaw puzzles, pocket mirrors, cigarette lighters, refrigerator magnets, and decorative neon lights using the lettering of the trilogy's logo. The promotional tie-ins are vastly more varied and numerous than those for *Gone with the Wind*. A recent search of eBay disclosed 270 items under the category "Lord of the Rings—Knives, Swords, and Blades." Even the nefarious Gollum is represented on a computer mouse.

This explosion of tie-ins represents several important new developments Selznick never dreamed of. One is the enlisting of companies like Topps Trading Cards and The Franklin Mint, which exists for the express purpose of manufacturing commemorative memorabilia. Another is the possibilities for cross-pollination offered by franchises attuned to marketing synergy. Burger King promoted its own sales along with public awareness of the trilogy by tie-ins ranging from action figures for small children to commemorative glassware for their older siblings. After stopping for lunch, families could proceed to toy stores and purchase Barbie as Galadriel, Ken as Legolas, or the matched pair of Barbie and Ken as Arwen and Aragorn. The marketing blitz of Middle-earth naturally pushed the sales of Tolkien's work—not only *The Lord of the Rings* but *The Hobbit, The Silmarillion,* and lesser-known contributions to the saga— to new heights. Far more globally than in Selznick's case, the films were used to sell products, which in turn sold the film.

Yet one problem remained the same: the inevitable loss in fidelity such tie-ins insured. Herb Bridges points out that "as the years passed, through several versions of the painting of Rhett carrying the swooning Scarlett, Miss Leigh's décolletage plunged ever more deeply,"[55] updating the scene to accord with current mores. The makeover of Tolkien's characters has been even more rapid. Lynette R. Porter observes that "most action figures indicate that the heroes' action involves warfare":

> Even Hobbit action figures come with armor or swords in their individual or group toy packs. . . . In the books, Tolkien's most passive characters fight only under duress and the great necessity of saving Middle-earth. In contrast, the action figures often show Merry and Pippin in battle gear with swords, or at least carrying a sword. Even Frodo and Sam, who seldom used weaponry in either the books or films, and are not in large battle scenes, are portrayed in some toy sets as carrying swords. Frodo's sword Sting is a toy in its own right.[56]

Ironically, the limiting case in which fidelity bows to fashion concerns not the source texts but one of the films itself. In 1967 MGM rereleased *Gone with the Wind* in a widescreen print created by cropping the top and bottom from a 1939 master. For years nostalgic fans were outraged that the rerelease print, whose new format assumes that filling contemporary movie screens is more important than seeing the tops of characters' heads, was the only one available for exhibition.

Jackson took extraordinary pains to avoid outraging fans of his film by its posttheatrical releases, although his cautionary model was not *Gone with the Wind* but *Star Wars*, whose DVD release and coincident rerelease on VHS videotape sought to encourage fans who already owned videotapes of the film to purchase new versions which had been expanded with effects-rich sequences George Lucas claimed he had been prevented from filming because the necessary technology had not been available in the 1970s and 1980s. Lucas's plumped-up rereleases had been critically drubbed as shapeless and self-advertising. The extended edition DVD releases of Jackson's trilogy, each of them carefully timed for release a year after the initial bare-bones release of the corresponding film on videotape and DVD, included both extensive production materials and additional footage. As Jackson, Walsh, and Boyens tirelessly explained on the accompanying commentary track, however, this additional footage, ranging from brief exchanges to whole new scenes, had been planned from the beginning as part of the extended release and integrated fully into the theatrical release, right down to new music Howard Shore had composed for the additional material. The result was to cast the film's theatrical release far more convincingly than MGM had done in releasing the widescreen *Gone with the*

*Wind* or Lucas in releasing the augmented *Star Wars* as incomplete, a work-in-progress whose full expression awaited its posttheatrical release.

In certain strategic ways the extended editions of the trilogy looked even more deliberately back to Tolkien than the theatrical releases. They included basic information about the author's life and work and extensive discussions of specific points of adaptation. Just as important as the references to Tolkien, however, are the references to the institutional status of books. Each of the DVD extended editions is packaged in a slipcase whose shape, typography, and design (three different subdued colors with a faux-leather print and gold lettering) make it look like a book. The contemporaneous release of the four-DVD Collector's Edition of *Gone with the Wind* offers an instructive contrast. Like virtually all other video rereleases, this one trumpets its continuities with the original film, listing the principal cast members along with the director, producer, screenwriter, and composer on its slipcase and its ten 1939 Academy Awards inside, and including a carefully yellowed replica of the 1939 souvenir program. In addition, it announces its definitiveness as an act of conservatorship ("Hollywood's Most Beloved Epic Digitally Remastered for Its 65th Anniversary from Restored Picture and Audio Elements").[57]

In the four-disc release of each film in Jackson's trilogy, all cast and production credits apart from the title of each film and New Line's name were relegated to a loose packaging sheet obviously designed to be discarded, leaving each DVD volume encased in a pristine package as unsoiled by any traces of commerce as a deluxe edition of a book. Instead of advertising its continuities with Tolkien's book, Jackson's film, or the original video release of the film, the DVD clearly aspires to replace them all as the only definitive text, the one the film's auteur had in mind from the beginning.

Yet this definitive status is inevitably subject to dating. Each of the extended editions of the three films in Jackson's trilogy is more extended than the one before. Each ups the ante by adding more additional footage, more stills, and more elaborate featurettes. Despite Jackson's frequent assertions, the function of this additional material is not to bring the film closer to Tolkien's novel, though the additional footage often restores scenes from the novel that were cut in the films' theatrical release. If that were the case, the additional material would presumably track the extensive additional material Tolkien provided for his own epic in *The Hobbit, The Silmarillion,* the appendices to *The Lord of the Rings,* and *The History of Middle-earth.* But Jackson's additions do not borrow from this material. They do not even follow its primary impulse to deepen and intensify the apparent reality of Middle-earth by providing more details about its history, genealogy, cultures, and languages. Instead, Jackson's extras by and large seek to break the spell of Middle-earth, demystifying it by providing a bird's-eye view of its cinematic creation from raw materials whose most important suppliers included both Tolkien and Weta Digital.

It would be a mistake, then, to call any extant version of Jackson's film text definitive, when it was clearly planned from the beginning as a variorum text, an epic that would be shot in a single fifteen-month burst, carved into three outsized features, and then released in ever-more-comprehensive posttheatrical releases (and, one can only assume, theatrical rereleases). The marketing and publicizing of *The Lord of the Rings* everywhere suggests that the film demands an interactive response. Viewers have not truly experienced Middle-earth unless they have played the video game, worn the jewelry, acquired the action figures, or posted their reactions and suggestions to an online site for the filmmakers' presumed scrutiny. The single longest addition to each of Jackson's three films in its extended DVD incarnation is a final credit crawl lasting twenty minutes that lists all the charter members of the *Lord of the Rings* fan clubs, implying that they, too, are contributors to the films. Yet the actual contribution the films ask is the purchase of something—photographs, souvenirs, commentaries on Tolkien, and, of course, later editions of the films. The Extended DVD Edition of *The Return of the King* is packaged with two coupons that offer rebates to anyone purchasing both the original video release of the film and either the Extended Edition or the Collector's DVD Gift Set. The planned obsolescence that invites even consumers of the Extended Edition to rush out and buy the original release as well suggests that the ultimate goal of any adaptation that works toward an ever-more-comprehensive fidelity is an invitation to the audience to spend without end.

# CHAPTER SEVEN

# Traditions of Quality

Though it seems an unlikely companion to *Gone with the Wind* and the *Lord of the Rings* trilogy as an example of transmedia synergy, the 1995 BBC television miniseries *Pride and Prejudice* has been greeted just as rapturously, and in much the same terms, by respondents to the Internet Movie Database (www.imdb.com). Apart from a few curmudgeons who express reservations about Jane Austen or a fondness for the 1980 BBC adaptation of *Pride and Prejudice*—not a single respondent prefers the 1940 MGM adaptation with Greer Garson and Laurence Olivier—the hundreds of comparisons of the 1995 series to Austen's novel are so consistently enthusiastic that the most common observations are "perfection!" and "what more can I add?" Writing on March 31, 2005, cymanasseh says, "This film is better than perfect." Redheadliz25 avers on September 4, 2004, "The movie IS the book and is truly wonderful! 11/10!"—a rating stpete48, writing on February 26, 2003, suggests is too modest: "10 out of 10; No! 20 out of 10 . . . do I hear 30!" Even the few respondents who find Austen tough going are impressed by the adaptation's fidelity to her novel. In accord with the laws of synergy, Austen's sales rose dramatically in the wake of *Pride and Prejudice*, the 1995 BBC *Persuasion*, Douglas McGrath's 1996 *Emma* (starring Gwyneth Paltrow), and *Sense and Sensibility*, whose screenwriter and star, Emma Thompson, accepted her Academy Award for Best Adapted Screenplay of 1995 with the wish that Jane Austen could know how well she was doing in Uruguay.

There is, of course, a darker side to the question of fidelity to a beloved literary source, a side exposed most influentially by François Truffaut. In his landmark essay "A Certain Tendency of the French Cinema," Truffaut described the "Tradition of Quality" of Claude Autant-Lara, Jean Dellannoy, René Clement, Yves Allegret, and Marcel Pagliero as defined by their screenwriters rather than their directors. Asserting that "I consider an adaptation of value only when written by a *man of the cinema*," Truffaut brusquely dismissed Autant-Lara and Dellannoy, whose films staked their aesthetic claims on the literary respectability of their sources. His insistence that "I do not believe in the peaceful coexistence of the 'Tradition of Quality' and an '*auteur's* cinema'" shaped by directors like Jean Renoir, Robert Bresson, Jean Cocteau, Max Ophüls, and Jacques Tati turned the Tradition of Quality into a term of contempt even as such traditions continued to flourish, for example, in the hands of the BBC.[1]

The distinction that has most often been abstracted from Truffaut between adaptations willing to reinvent their sources and adaptations condemned to servile imitation implies that all members of the Tradition of Quality are interchangeable. To the Internet Movie Database commentators on *Pride and Prejudice*, however, evaluative distinctions between different adaptations of *Pride and Prejudice*, even among different BBC adaptations of Austen's novel, are instinctive. Evidently there is not a single Tradition of Quality but several competing traditions. Even when a film's avowed aim is simply to reproduce the experience provided by a celebrated novel, different films may try very different strategies—a truth acknowledged by Truffaut in his remarks about different screenplays adapting Georges Bernanos's *Journal d'un curé de campagne*.

Indeed, Truffaut's broadside, usually read as a simple denunciation of literary rather than cinematic values, a cornerstone in the *politique des auteurs*, is remarkably helpful in distinguishing several different Traditions of Quality. The aesthetic of the BBC miniseries that include *Pride and Prejudice* is best approached by contrast with earlier aesthetics that also invoke associations with literary respectability. Moreover, one of those earlier traditions, the one associated with Hollywood studio adaptations of the 1930s and 1940s, has been unfortunately neglected and vilified for many years, squeezed to death between the specifically antiliterary bias of the nascent discipline of film studies thirty years later and the casting of these studio films as villainous antitypes by still later generations of adaptations and fans who hailed the BBC miniseries precisely because it was not the MGM version.

The 1995 *Pride and Prejudice* offers itself less as a new achievement than as a transparent, nondistorting window through which viewers can see Jane Austen's story, characters, and world. As a careful reading of Truffaut reveals, however, the quest for fidelity is always a fetish. The differences among the three Traditions of Quality this chapter will examine—Hollywood adaptations from the first two decades of synchronized sound, BBC television miniseries that began some forty years later, and the films produced by Ismail Merchant and directed by James Ivory, to which the BBC series are so often compared—are marked by the three different fetishes on which they focus.

The choice of these three traditions is inevitably arbitrary because there is no single period or national cinema in which adaptations of literary classics has historically predominated. Trends like the Jane Austen year of 1995–96 or the more muted Henry James year that followed with *The Portrait of a Lady* (1996), *The Wings of the Dove* (1997), and *Washington Square* (1997) do not translate into dominant literary periods or cinemas. A quick tabulation of results from the Internet Movie Database—a rough comparative guide, even if it omits some films and makes no attempt to register the relative importance of the ones it lists—suggests that the number of films based on classic novels and plays remains relatively constant from decade to decade. Thackeray adaptations peak in the 1910s with four films, Charlotte Brontë adaptations in the same decade with five, and Dickens adaptations in the 1920s with thirty-five. But no Trollope adaptations appear before the 1974 BBC miniseries *The Pallisers*. Hawthorne adaptations reach a high-water mark (6) in the 1920s; Melville adaptations (7), Faulkner adaptations (6), and Hemingway adaptations (11) in the 1950s; Cooper adaptations (7) and Poe adaptations (26) in the 1960s. The 1970s see an uptick in adaptations of Defoe (7), Hardy (8), Wilde (20), Flaubert (7), and Henry James (18, during a period no one called the Henry James years). The biggest decade for Tolstoy films (21) is the 1920s, for Gogol films (13) the 1960s, for Chekhov films (41) the 1970s, for Dostoevsky films (20) the 1990s. There is no more a single Period of Quality than a single Tradition of Quality.

Even so, the first two decades of Hollywood talkies, for better or worse, have gone down in film history as a floodtide of literary adaptation during which studio heads rushed to film properties whose inimitable dialogue had hereto-

fore been confined to intertitles. No producer from this period was more as-
siduous in fashioning a Tradition of Quality from established literary sources
than David O. Selznick. Selznick's well-known attraction for novels and plays
that guaranteed box-office potential through association and his resistance to
wanton departures from his sources make him a stellar example of one particular aspect of Truffaut's description: depending on literature and its trappings
for cultural capital is "like giving oneself a good address."[2]

Selznick had worked at MGM, Paramount, and RKO since 1926, but it was
not until his return to MGM as a vice president and unit head under his father-
in-law, Louis B. Mayer, that he became firmly associated with literary adaptations. Even at Metro and as the head of Selznick International, his own company, beginning in 1936, Selznick's adaptations of classic novels—*David
Copperfield* (1935), *Anna Karenina* (1935), *A Tale of Two Cities* (1935), *Little Lord
Fauntleroy* (1936), *The Prisoner of Zenda* (1937), *The Adventures of Tom Sawyer*
(1938)—regularly alternate with adaptations of contemporary best sellers and
other projects: *Dinner at Eight* (1933), *Viva Villa!* (1934), *Vanessa: Her Love Story*
(1935), *The Garden of Allah* (1936), *A Star Is Born* (1937), *Nothing Sacred* (1937),
*The Young at Heart* (1938), *Gone with the Wind* (1939), *Rebecca* (1940), *Since
You Went Away* (1944), *Duel in the Sun* (1946). Selznick's cinema is a paragon
of what Dwight Macdonald calls midcult, a purveyor of middle-class values
through variously aristocratic and proletarian heroes that "pretends to respect
the standards of High Culture while in fact it waters them down and vulgarizes
them."[3] For Selznick a source novel's cultural cachet is important largely because it helps presell its film adaptation, and his definitive articulation of his
point of view—"We bought *Rebecca,* and we intend to make *Rebecca*"—is as-
serted on behalf of a contemporary best seller, not a literary classic. Selznick's
elaboration of his position to Alfred Hitchcock, who supervised the free treatment of Daphne du Maurier's 1938 novel that so exercised his producer, is especially revealing:

> The few million people who have read the book and who worship it would very
> properly attack us violently for the desecrations which are indicated by the treat-
> ment; but quite apart from the feelings of these few million, I have never been
> able to understand why motion-picture people insist upon throwing away some-
> thing of proven appeal to substitute things of their own creation. . . .
>
> I have made too many classics successfully and faithfully not to know beyond
> any question of a doubt that whether a film is narrative or dramatic it will suc-

ceed in the same manner as the original succeeded if only the same elements are captured and if only as much as possible is retained of the original—including alleged faults of dramatic construction. No one, not even the author of an original work, can say with any degree of accuracy why a book has caught the fancy of the public. . . . The only sure and safe way of aiming at a successful transcription of the original into the motion-picture form is to try as far as possible to retain the original.[4]

As his memo to Hitchcock makes clear, the matrix for Selznick's films is reliable middlebrow entertainment, whether it draws on classic novels like *David Copperfield*, minor classics like *The Prisoner of Zenda*, or contemporary best sellers like *Rebecca*. Fidelity to the source is not an end but a means, not an aesthetic but an economic imperative.

This attitude persists in the flexible definition of literary classics variously embodied in such contemporaneous projects as *Dracula* (1931), *Frankenstein* (1931), *Dr. Jekyll and Mr. Hyde* (1931), *Grand Hotel* (1932), *Little Women* (1933), *Treasure Island* (1934), *The Old Curiosity Shop* (1934), *The Scarlet Letter* (1934), *The Scarlet Pimpernel* (1934), *The Count of Monte Cristo* (1934), *Crime and Punishment* (1935), *Becky Sharp* (1935), *Mutiny on the Bounty* (1935), *The Informer* (1935), *The Last of the Mohicans* (1936), *Romeo and Juliet* (1936), *Anthony Adverse* (1936), *The Prince and the Pauper* (1937), *Captains Courageous* (1937), *A Christmas Carol* (1938), *Pygmalion* (1938), *Wuthering Heights* (1939), *The Hound of the Baskervilles* (1939), *The Hunchback of Notre Dame* (1939), *The Wizard of Oz* (1939), *The Letter* (1940), and *Pride and Prejudice* (1940). Despite the occasional recourse to American and Continental classics, this list strongly emphasizes an Anglophilic tropism toward subjects formerly considered too big for the movies. The resulting films most often present crowded canvases replete with incident, providing opportunities for Hollywood to show off the dozen stars of *Grand Hotel* or the hundreds of extras who storm the Bastille in *A Tale of Two Cities* in properties most amenable to tested Hollywood genres like the costume romance, the swashbuckler, or the children's story. The patron saint of this tradition is Dickens, whose extroverted, overstuffed novels provide an ideal armature for midcult entertainment.

The Tradition of Quality championed by Selznick is not a revolution or even a turn toward literary subjects; it is the mixture as before, with the added seasoning of a brand-name property that can provide largely conventional period melodramas with a literary-historical imprimatur. At their most ambitious these films follow *Ben-Hur* (1925) and the silent epics of Cecil B. DeMille in marrying epic scale, represented by important characters making consequential moral choices in a lavishly appointed world over a period of months or years, to the intimacy of period fairy tales like *The Prince and the Pauper,* which suggests that the fate of nations may hang on the doings of a few forgotten private citizens. Like D. W. Griffith the directors of these films typically impart a larger scale to their domestic stories by motivic contrasts between the dark, confined interiors in which the heroes and heroines live their private lives and the bright, grand, minutely detailed exteriors that provide a public context that amplifies each personal decision.

The Dickens adaptations Selznick produced for MGM were particularly successful at melding the novelist's aesthetic to the studio's proclivity for wholesome, star-studded spectacle. Dickens was the ideal candidate for the MGM treatment, since he was at once sentimental, wholesome, and entertaining. Eschewing tightly constructed works like *Bleak House* and *Great Expectations,* which had yet to find wide critical favor even among literary critics, Selznick chose instead Dickens's episodic coming-of-age story *David Copperfield* and *A Tale of Two Cities,* the most melodramatic of all his novels and the one offering the most obvious possibilities for period display. The adaptations by Hugh Walpole and Howard Estabrook *(David Copperfield)* and W. P. Lipscomb and S. N. Behrman *(A Tale of Two Cities)* consistently subordinate Dickens's dialogue, apart from the obligatory tags like Sydney Carton's final speech, to pictorialism while emphasizing obligatory scenes—the arrival of the Murdstones and their donkeys at Aunt Betsey Trotwood's, the assassination of the Marquis of Evremonde—and ruthlessly cutting transitional scenes along with subplots and minor characters.

Writing to Kate Corbaley, an assistant story editor at MGM, Selznick remarked, "It is amazing that Dickens had so many brilliant characters in *David Copperfield* and so few in *A Tale of Two Cities.*"[5] This mysterious judgment— surely Carton is more deeply conceived than any character in *David Copperfield*—cuts to the heart of Selznick's interest in Dickens. He is attracted to what E. M. Forster called Dickens's flat characters, the caricatures like Aunt Betsey and Micawber, whose incarnation of some singular humor makes an immediately powerful impression without their doing anything in particular, characters who can be made iconically powerful onscreen through intelligent casting, costuming, and makeup.[6] The primary function of Selznick's adaptations is to display these characters as fully and entertainingly as possible. Unlike the 1933

*Oliver Twist,* which dutifully unfolds its story with little attention to displaying any of its characters' histrionic range, Selznick's Dickens adaptations put their gallery of characters through their paces instead of harnessing their potential for change and development.

Whatever the vagaries of their stories, studio adaptations released during the Depression could rely on garnering the sympathies of many viewers for downtrodden heroes and heroines, from Hester Prynne to Little Nell. Like the gangster cycle that had crested a few years earlier, these literary adaptations offered their principals rescue from their travails through either the fantasy of fabulous wealth *(Treasure Island, The Count of Monte Cristo)* or reliance on an extended surrogate family *(Captains Courageous, The Wizard of Oz)*. Despite the care Selznick took to capture Dickens's tone, the value of his work was less in Dickens's distinctive voice than in his stories, which offered assurances that contemporary misfortunes were nothing new and could be overcome by hard work and domestic virtue.

Even if adaptations of the period sacrifice the controlling narrative voice on which stylists like Dickens (and Austen and James, whose work goes largely unadapted during this period) depended for their most distinctive effects, it does not follow that they consider language unimportant. Far from it. Kamilla Elliott, noting that "some silent film editing, far from freeing film from its dependence on verbal language, is based in it," has argued that the supposedly noncinematic intertitles of silent films were an essential ingredient of an emerging aesthetic: "Aspects of montage developed from the words of intertitles rather than in opposition to them. Cuts between intertitles and filmed scenes constitute one of the earliest forms of montage."[7] Instead of freeing cinema from its dependence on the verbal language of intertitles, early sync-sound adaptations develop a fascination with printed words, books, and authors that amounts to a fetish.

It is only natural that film adaptations pay special attention to the words of the literary texts on which they are based. But this attention, however regularly it is justified in the name of fidelity, often goes in quite different directions, suggested by an analogy with the codes of musical language. The 1933 *Oliver Twist,* for example, runs its credits over an orchestration of the trio from the third movement of Schubert's G-major piano sonata that is appropriate in several ways: because it is old—roughly contemporaneous, in fact, with the events of the story—because it is appealingly simple and childlike, and because it sounds like the lullaby that might well form the backdrop to the film's opening scene.

The fact that the sonata, like Schubert himself, was unknown in England at the time simply shifts its textual status from historically accurate background music to parallel classic that helps secure the film's status by association.

Literary classics already associated with classical music offer more obvious opportunities to borrow cultural capital. Not content with using Felix Mendelssohn's incidental music throughout *A Midsummer Night's Dream* (1935), Max Reinhardt and William Dieterle begin the film with a drawing of the fairy queen Titania accompanied by a six-and-a-half-minute overture incorporating music from five sections of Mendelssohn's score. Herbert Stothart's music for *Romeo and Juliet* (1936) periodically yields to themes from Tchaikovsky's *Romeo and Juliet Fantasy Overture*. A bolder attempt to trade on the status of classical musical texts appears at the end of the opening scene of the 1940 *Pride and Prejudice*, when the Bennet and Lucas families race their carriages home to determine which family shall be the first to call on that eligible new arrival Mr. Bingley. The music, an excerpt from the overture to Smetana's *Bartered Bride*, is both anachronistic and utterly out of keeping with Austen's range of tones—an appropriate complement to an episode that, after all, has no counterpart in her novel—but its status as a musical classic that is at once venerable, accessible, and fun establishes the same sorts of claims for the film.

Studio adaptations of the period use associations with literary classics in the same ways they use associations with musical classics: as a claim at once to historical resonance, cultural cachet, and popular appeal. One of the enduring clichés of adaptations that seek to trumpet their literary associations is running their opening credits over a shot of the book under adaptation. Even films not generally remembered as literary adaptations—*The Thin Man* (1934), *Leave Her to Heaven* (1945), *The Postman Always Rings Twice* (1946)—often press their source novels into this service. It is hardly surprising that when Gottfried Reinhardt, who produced *The Red Badge of Courage* (1951), was confronted by largely hostile responses to early preview screenings, one of the first retrenchments he ordered was to run the credits over a shot of Stephen Crane's novel.[8] The opening of the much-revised release print of the film provides a compendium of techniques for claiming literary cachet. A shot of the novel, whose cover is labeled "Stephen Crane's great novel of the Civil War / THE RED BADGE OF COURAGE / A John Huston Production," opens to reveal turning pages combining the principal credits with period-style drawings of which the last is Stephen Crane, over which a voice-over, written by Dore Schary and delivered by James Whitmore, begins the transition to the film's opening shots:

*The Red Badge of Courage* was written by Stephen Crane in 1894. From the moment of its publication, it was accepted by critics and public alike as a classic story of war, and of the boys and men who fought war. Stephen Crane wrote this book when he was a boy of twenty-two. Its publication made him a man. Its story is of a boy who, frightened, went into a battle and came out of it a man with courage. More than that, it is the story of many frightened boys who went into a great civil war and came out a nation of united, strong, and free men. The narration you will hear spoken consists of quotes from the text of the book itself.

Most credit sequences establish their claims to literary cachet more subtly. Selznick's production of *Anna Karenina* allows "Count Leo Tolstoy" to share the title credit screen with director Clarence Brown. Credits can be presented as if against the parchment pages of an open book, as in *Daisy Miller* (1974) and *Mickey's Christmas Carol* (1983), or on the turning pages of a book, as in *Jane Eyre* (1944) and *Marnie* (1964), fetishizing the film's literary associations.

The credits for the 1936 *Romeo and Juliet* display a full-screen credit for "Literary Consultant: Professor William Strunk, Jr. of Cornell University." The credits for the 1935 *A Tale of Two Cities*, which include a bibliography of historical works on the French Revolution, must mark the only time in Hollywood history that either Thomas Carlyle or the word *bibliography* has appeared in a film's credits. The credit sequence of *Scrooge* (1951) focuses not only on its source text but on Dickens's career by opening with a shot of a hand taking down a fat volume marked *A Christmas Carol* from a shelf of identically bound books, obviously Dickens's collected works, even though no actual volume of *A Christmas Carol* would be nearly as hefty as *David Copperfield* or even *A Tale of Two Cities*. *Nicholas Nickleby* (1947) invokes another textual frame, the physical properties of the book, at one remove, by literally framing its credits with designs based on Phiz's drawings for the novel's original monthly installments and its first one-volume publication in 1839.

The credit sequence to the 1935 *David Copperfield* makes it plain exactly what is at stake in this reference to the physical appearance of the source novel. Although the central design of the film's ungainly main title—"The Personal History, Adventures, Experience, & Observation of David Copperfield the Younger"—is copied almost word for word and stroke for stroke from the title page of Dickens's original monthly numbers, the decorations around the screen's border are more general and winsome than Phiz's metaphoric and portentous invocations of figures from the hero's life. Like the credit sequence to

*Oliver Twist* (1933), which improves its original more unobtrusively by repro-ducing the opening page of the novel but introducing a new paragraph break after the first sentence, *David Copperfield*'s credits imply that textual fidelity is less important than fidelity to the image or idea of a Dickens text, an image that the film explicitly textualizes, though it does not correspond precisely to any specific source text.

Since it is obvious that no film adaptation of Dickens can replicate the vi-sual style of his first illustrator all the way through, the MGM *Copperfield*, hav-ing launched its claims to replicate the Dickens world by the look of its credit sequence, establishes its claims to prestige and entertainment value in quite different terms. Instead of claiming close fidelity to Dickens's text—a claim that would be sorely undermined by the casting of Edna May Oliver, Basil Rath-bone, and W. C. Fields—the film plays its trump card immediately following the credits: a final card that reproduces the closing sentence of the introduc-tion to the Charles Dickens Edition of 1869—"Like many fond parents, I have in my heart of hearts, a favorite child, and his name is David Copperfield"—complete with the author's holograph signature, as if to guarantee the exper-tise and authenticity of this endorsement of the novel's value.

This displacement of fidelity to a particular literary text by self-validation through textualized appeals to literary associations—from the physical look of the original text to a testimonial from the author—becomes in other adapta-tions a more generalized, but equally textualized, appeal to the canons of liter-ature itself. *The Woman in White* (1948) closes its credits, which feature the cus-tomary open book and turning pages listing cast and crew members, with a card forthrightly announcing, "This famous story of mystery was written by Wilkie Collins nearly a hundred years ago. It is recognized as a classic and has set a pattern for this entire field of literature"—the perfectly coercive prepara-tion for the final credit: "ENGLAND 1851." Even before the story has begun, the film has told viewers that they are not just seeing a movie but enjoying the cul-tural benefits of secondhand literature, and not just any literature but a mys-tery classic that presumably combines the appeal of *Anna Karenina* and *The Big Sleep*.

*Jane Eyre* marks the logical endpoint in this progression from fidelity to a source novel as a guarantee of value to reliance on the prestige and entertain-ment value of English history, the idea of the author, and the institution of lit-erature. Its credit sequence ends with a page headed "Jane Eyre. Chapter I," and continuing: "My name is Jane Eyre. I was born in 1820, a harsh time of change in England. Money and position seemed all that mattered. Charity was a cold and disagreeable word. Religion too often wore a mask of bigotry and cruelty. There was no proper place for the poor or the unfortunate. I had no father or mother, no brother or sister. As a child I lived with my aunt, Mrs. Reed of Gateshead Hall. I do not remember that she ever spoke one kind word to me."

The actual first page of Brontë's novel begins both more quietly and more abruptly: "There was no possibility of taking a walk that day. We had been wandering, indeed, in the leafless shrubbery an hour in the morning . . ."[9] The new and improved opening, as Jeffrey Sconce has observed, "invoke[s] the cultural capital of *Jane Eyre* as novel and legitimate[s] the interpretive authority of the film's adaptation" by using "a hallucinatory page of text" inscribed, in an act of literary back-formation, on a textual simulacrum of the novel as fictional as the fat volume containing *A Christmas Carol,* as fictional as the England in which coaches race through country roads to report the arrival of eligible suitors and starving orphans are serenaded by Schubert sonatas.[10]

Along with written texts (whose dangerous power is explored in the stories of *The Scarlet Letter, A Tale of Two Cities,* and *The Letter*), the author's collected works, and the historical period in which classic novels are set—even if that world was contemporary for the original readers of *Frankenstein* or *Pride and Prejudice*—studio adaptations show a distinct tendency to fetishize the figure of the author. *The Prince and the Pauper* includes in its credits not only Mark Twain's name but a head-and-shoulders drawing of the famous author. Herbert Marshall, having starred in different roles in both adaptations of W. Somerset Maugham's play *The Letter* and having played Geoffrey Wolfe, a thinly disguised version of Maugham in *The Moon and Sixpence* (1942), returned to play Maugham as author in *The Razor's Edge* (1946), paving the way for Maugham himself to introduce the stories in the anthology films *Quartet* (1949) and *Trio* (1950). *Devotion* (1946) deserves special mention not only for its wholesale romanticizing of the Brontë family but for introducing a brief London street scene in which the dialogue is limited to the following exchange:

"Morning, Dickens."

"Morning, Thackeray."

The tendency toward recasting authors of the literary properties under adaptation as celebrities had been sent up as early as *The Bride of Frankenstein* (1935), which slyly casts Elsa Lanchester as both the prim Mary Shelley at the beginning of the film and the monster's mate, whose performer was identified in the credits only as "?" at the end.

Such an obsessive emphasis on books, words, written documents, the author's collected works, historical period, and literal incarnation may seem to demote the filmmaker to the author's servant. But the reverence for words and books and authors is a fetish that sanctifies the power of the adaptation's true auteur. As Selznick contends in one of his last letters, "Great films, successful films, are made in their *every* detail according to the vision of one man, and through supporting that one man, not in buying part of what he has done."[11] This formulation makes the struggle for fidelity to an author's book into the quest of the producer as auteur, the creator whose ultimate goal is not fidelity but Quality.

Selznick's visionary approach to adaptation is poles apart from the approach of Ismail Merchant and James Ivory, the production-direction team responsible for some two dozen features released over a period of fifty years. If Selznick represents the producer as the auteur seeking to ennoble his showmanship by cloaking it in the fetishized figure of the original author, Merchant Ivory represents a different aspect of Truffaut's Tradition of Quality: the drive toward a stylistic and thematic consistency that overrides the differences in their sources. In one of his most scathing passages Truffaut accuses screenwriters Jean Aurenche and Pierre Bost of treating adaptation as "an exact science" in which "equivalences," inventions presented in the name of fidelity to the spirit of the original, are "only timid astuteness to the end of getting around the difficulty, of resolving on the soundtrack problems that concern the image, plundering in order to no longer obtain anything on the screen but scholarly framing, complicated lighting effects, 'polished' photography, the whole keeping the 'Tradition of Quality' quite alive."[12] The resulting homogeneity, which Truffaut considers evidence of a poverty of cinematic imagination, is a hallmark Merchant Ivory's films deliberately cultivate.[13]

It is hardly surprising that the team's films would look and sound so much alike given their fondness for a relatively unchanging core of collaborators. They have worked repeatedly with a repertory company of favorite actors like Shashi Kapoor, Madhur Jaffrey, Nancy Marchand, Wesley Addy, Madeleine Potter, Christopher Reeve, Vanessa Redgrave, Greta Scacchi, Maggie Smith, Denholm Elliott, Helena Bonham-Carter, Sam Waterston, Simon Callow, and Nick Nolte. Most of their films have been photographed by Satyajit Ray's cinematographer Subrata Mitra or by Walter Lassally, Tony Pierce-Roberts, or Pierre Lhomme. All their features since 1979 have been scored by Richard Robbins. And the screenplays for virtually all of them have been written by Ruth Prawer Jhabvala, alone or together with Ivory.

In many ways it is Jhabvala rather than producer Merchant or director Ivory who is the true auteur of the collaboration and whose leading concerns set its course. Born in Cologne of German-Jewish parents, she emigrated at twelve to England with her parents and at twenty-four to India with her husband. Most of her many novels and stories, beginning with *To Whom She Will* (1955), dramatize cultural differences within Indian society and between India and its British residents and observers. It was exactly her eye for cultural conflict that drew Merchant and Ivory to her 1960 novel *The Householder* as a property for their first feature film in 1963. Although she had had no experience as a screenwriter and little exposure to films, Jhabvala agreed to write the adaptation and remained as the team's most durable and important collaborator.

Merchant Ivory's earliest features focused on contradictions in Indian culture. In *The Householder* a newlywed, troubled by his bride's independence, seeks advice from a variety of sources. *Shakespeare Wallah* (1965) follows the adventures of a traveling English theatrical troupe in the last days of the Raj. *Bombay Talkie* (1970) explores the doomed romance between a self-dramatizing American author and an equally narcissistic married Indian movie star. Beginning with *Savages* (1972), a rare Merchant Ivory film in which Jhabvala took no part, the team began to intersperse its films about Anglo-Indian relations (*Autobiography of a Princess* [1975]; *Hullabaloo over George and Bonnie's Pictures* [1978]; *Heat and Dust* [1983], based on Jhabvala's Booker Prize–winning 1975 novel) with an equally critical examination of American cultural values and institutions (*The Wild Party* [1975]; *Roseland* [1977]; *Jane Austen in Manhattan* [1980]). It was not until 1979 that they undertook their first adaptation of a literary classic, Henry James's *The Europeans*.

Merchant Ivory's literary adaptations, the body of work for which they are best known, thus emerge from a matrix of earlier studies of cultural conflict. The novels they choose to adapt focus similarly on the clash of cultural values in settings whose exotic appeal is as carefully evoked as the Raj. *Quartet* (1981) follows Jean Rhys in stranding its heroine without money or prospects in Jazz Age Paris. *Mr. and Mrs. Bridge* (1990) holds a magnifying glass to the airless marriage of a self-contained Kansas City lawyer, Walter Bridge (Paul Newman), and his tellingly named wife, India (Joanne Woodward), as they move from the

American 1930s to the 1940s. *Slaves of New York* (1990) and *Le Divorce* (2003) examine cultural dislocations in contemporary New York and Paris. In each of these adaptations, no matter how recent its source novel, Merchant, Ivory, and Jhabvala serve as cultural anthropologists less interested in telling a story than in faithfully rendering an exotic milieu. In their hands even contemporary subcultures become foreign. It is no wonder that one of their most notable successes, *The Remains of the Day* (1993), is based on a novel by the equally dispassionate cultural pathologist Kazuo Ishiguro, who also provided the original screenplay for their final collaboration, *The White Countess* (2005).

The team is best known, however, for its adaptations of E. M. Forster and Henry James, two novelists noted for their civilized studies of cultural conflict. The Forster adaptations hew more closely to their originals' construction and dialogue. *A Room with a View* (1985) celebrates the liberating potential of a trip to Florence on a repressed English rose. *Maurice* (1987) traces the romance between two Cambridge undergraduates in the days before World War I, when homosexuality indeed dared not speak its name. *Howards End* (1992) uses the conflicts within the landed Wilcox family and the disruptive Schlegel sisters to press Forster's question of who shall inherit England. If *A Room with a View* and *Maurice* provide their heroes and heroines with liberating romances, *Howards End*, like *Heat and Dust, Mr. and Mrs. Bridge*, and *The Remains of the Day*, is a study of the costs of cultural repression.[14]

Liberation and repression form the dialectic of Merchant Ivory's James adaptations as well. *The Europeans* uses the incursion of a pair of charming, dubious European cousins to shake up a staid New England town. *The Bostonians* (1984) recasts this transatlantic conflict into a tug-of-war between Boston suffragette Olive Chancellor (Vanessa Redgrave) and reactionary southern gentleman Basil Ransom (Christopher Reeve) over Verena Tarrant (Madeleine Potter), the impressionable young public speaker they both love. *The Golden Bowl* (2000) uses a quartet of unholy lovers—an American father and daughter and their new spouses, who have secretly been lovers in the past and have secretly resumed their affair—to focus questions of responsibility, ownership, and cultural imperialism.

The keynote of Merchant Ivory's adaptations is decorum. Indeed, the filmmakers seem to take the boisterous studio adaptations represented by Selznick as an antitype. The style of all their films, often borrowing their blocking and lighting from Indian, European, or American paintings, aims for quietly glowing surfaces. *The Europeans* and *The Bostonians*, both influenced by the canvases of Sargent and Winslow Homer, are set in a series of historic properties duly catalogued, like the grander interiors of *The Golden Bowl*, in the end credits. The time frame of *The Europeans* is compressed from James's several months to a few weeks in order to allow the entire film to be bathed in the warm hues of a New England autumn. Like John Ford's westerns, these adaptations are always ready to put the narrative on hold while they revel in pictorial or auditory effects. Richard Robbins's musical scores combine period pastiches with period pieces chosen to be more thematically apt and less anachronistic than the Schubert and Smetana excerpts in *Oliver Twist* and *Pride and Prejudice*. And the inviting visuals in *A Room with a View* and *Howards End* have made a generation of American filmgoers avid for trips to Italy and England.

It would be misleading, however, to describe Merchant Ivory's visuals as merely decorative. Even their black-and-white films are crowded with eye-catching details that disrupt the flow of the story, and the visuals of color films like *Jane Austen in Manhattan*, *Slaves of New York*, and *Le Divorce* suggest decorous carnivals. Generally speaking, in fact, the widely noted decorum of Merchant Ivory's adaptations functions as a frame that strains to contain the most brutal and far-reaching cultural conflicts imaginable. *The Golden Bowl* dramatizes the disparity between these deep-running conflicts and the film's decorous surfaces by the disturbingly self-excusing refrain by which Charlotte (Uma Thurman) and Prince Amerigo (Jeremy Northam) justify keeping their adulterous affair secret from their spouses: "It wouldn't be fair to them." Just as the breathtaking selfishness of the lovers Vikram (Shashi Kapoor) and Lucia Lane (Jennifer Kendal) destroys the family members and friends who are sucked into their obsession in *Bombay Talkie*, the sexual battles in *The Bostonians* and *Howards End* are over nothing less than the fate of nations. Although *The Bostonians* follows James in having Ransom win Verena away from Olive, it eliminates the muted ending, tinged with pessimism, that James gave his novel and substitutes a rousing impromptu speech Olive gives to her suffragette followers at the Boston Atheneum, urging their place in history despite the heroine's defection. It is as if the film, showing Olive losing the battle over Verena, could not forbear a reminder that she ended up winning the war.[15]

The seductive decorum of Merchant Ivory's lovingly rendered period surfaces conceals the stark dualities to which the films obsessively return: East/West, North/South, past/present, country/city, America/Europe, simplicity/worldliness, expressiveness/conformity, female/male, feeling/intellect, patriarchy/romance, sincerity/artifice. Jhabvala's great subject both in her novels and in her films is the costs of cultural conflict. It is a subject that allows her to boil down even as forbiddingly long and obscure a novel as *The Golden Bowl* to two hours by discarding almost all of James's dialogue and interior analysis in favor of an exteriorized development of its central conflict: the determined attempt of the American Maggie Verver (Kate Beckinsale) to reclaim her titled European husband from her friend Charlotte Stant while protecting her father, who has married Charlotte, by never letting the two adulterers know that she is on to them.

Virtually all Jhabvala's films for Merchant Ivory, whether or not they are adaptations, focus on the costs their conflicts exact on a similarly lost lady, a heroine who finds herself torn between two cultures, neither of which commands her wholehearted allegiance. Lizzie Buckingham (Felicity Kendal), pulled from the orbit of her parents' Shakespearean troupe by her romance with the Indian playboy Sanju (Shashi Kapoor), returns to England at the end of *Shakespeare Wallah,* waving good-bye not only to her parents but presumably to memories of a culture from which she will eternally be barred full entry. Eugenia (Lee Remick), unsuccessful in her coy pursuit of Robert Acton (Robin Ellis), similarly returns to Europe having succeeded in shaking up her staid New England relatives without being able to join her life to theirs. Respectable memsahib Olivia Rivers (Greta Scacchi), forced into an abortion after her affair with the rebel Nawab (Shashi Kapoor) leaves her pregnant in *Heat and Dust;* India Bridge, passing year after stifling year in a loveless marriage in *Mr. and Mrs. Bridge;* the extraordinary pair of sad, noble heroines Emma Thompson plays in *Howards End* and *The Remains of the Day;* Maggie Verver, slowly sinking into the awareness that her European husband has resumed his affair with her best friend; even Roxeanne de Persand (Naomi Watts), abandoned by the love-stricken husband suddenly demanding a divorce on his terms—all of them become battlegrounds for irreconcilable cultural differences.

The most lost of all these ladies is penniless Marya Zelli (Isabelle Adjani), who drifts through *Quartet* in the company of her protector and married lover H. J. Heidler (Alan Bates), gliding through a recreation of Montparnasse most notable for "the violent disparity between the quarter's gilded surfaces, with its pretension to sensitivity and emotional refinement, and its underlay of meanness."[16] The contrast between polished surfaces and the turbulent emotions and moral dilemmas beneath remains the defining feature of the Merchant Ivory franchise, even to *The White Countess.* The allure of the films' period trappings is so great that many commentators have followed Geoffrey Macnab's dismissive comment on the retro glamour of *The Remains of the Day:* "On the page, perhaps, Darlington Hall may seem a vast mausoleum of a house which keeps servants and toffs alike manacled by propriety. On screen, however, the sheer visual relish with which the place is depicted can't help but undermine the mordant irony in Ruth Prawer Jhabvala's script."[17] But James Ivory has defended the films vigorously against this accusation: "Our English films are criticized by the British newspapers for being too nostalgic. . . . They even call *The Remains of the Day* a piece of nostalgia. But nostalgic for whom? Are the tasks of swabbing parquet floors and polishing brass in the Old Manor so very wonderful to recall?"[18]

If Merchant Ivory's films invoke glamorous period veneers only to expose the passions they conceal, why have they so frequently been described as merely decorative? Three reasons come to mind. The first decade of English commentary on Merchant Ivory's films could not help assessing them as an adjunct of Margaret Thatcher's political retrenchment from British socialism. Hence Cairns Craig, contending that "Forster and Waugh have proved popular because the world in which their works are set—the world just before film became the dominant modern medium, just before the modernist experiment in literature—is the last great age of the English *haute bourgeoisie,*" concludes that "these films engage with the idea of crossing the border between cultures, but in the knowledge that there is a safe haven to retreat into. They can allow their audiences to experience the tensions of an interrelatedness which contemporary British culture—*pace* Mrs. Thatcher and the Bruges group—will have to live with, but within the profoundly safe context of the past."[19] Ivory's reply that his films, far from wallowing in nostalgia, use the past to explore the costs of cultural interpenetration seems disingenuous when it is embedded in the foreword to a coffee-table book of color photographs from his English films. Even the franchise's most ardent defenders have tended to blur its differences from the BBC aesthetic it helped inspire, as in Robert Emmet Long's list of films, from *Sense and Sensibility* (1995) to *The Age of Innocence* (1993), "sometimes said to be riding Merchant Ivory's coattails."[20] Critics and complicit aftermarketers alike repaint Merchant Ivory's critique of monoculturalism as nostalgia.

An even more likely reason, however, for the frequent neglect of Merchant Ivory's cultural critique in favor of its embalming of beautiful dead cultures is that the passions that swirl beneath the films' postcard-perfect imagery so seldom surface. Lee Clark Mitchell observes that the film adaptation of *The Golden Bowl* "shifts from epistemological melodrama, in its excesses of thought beneath the social surface, back to phenomenal melodrama, with its excesses of action played out onscreen."[21] Yet the propensity for avoiding melodrama in staging cultural conflict is Merchant Ivory's most distinctive fetish. So determined is this avoidance that in the rare moments melodrama does erupt, as in the climaxes of *Bombay Talkie* and *The White Countess*, it feels misshapen and irrelevant, as if it had been imported from some other movie. Far more characteristic is *Mr. and Mrs. Bridge*, which constantly flirts with melodrama—most notably in the tornado that threatens the restaurant dinner Walter Bridge stubbornly refuses to abandon and in his secretary's stammering attempt to confess her love for him—but frustrates it every time.

Although their preference for a world in which virtually nothing happens is an inversion of the Selznick Tradition of Quality that elevates the earlier Hollywood tradition to an antitype, it is not unique to Merchant Ivory. Indeed, it is precisely the quality that draws them to the novels of James and Forster in the first place, though it reaches its apotheosis not in any of their James or Forster adaptations but in *The Remains of the Day*. The cautionary tale of Mr. Stevens, the butler (Anthony Hopkins), adds to James's story "The Beast in the Jungle," which dissects a life spent in the unconscious avoidance of love, an equally determined though equally unconscious avoidance of political commitment. When the primary focus of the film is the tight-lipped success of Stevens and Miss Kenton (Emma Thompson) in repressing their attraction to each other as a figure for England's prewar success in repressing its resistance to Hitler, it is no wonder that so many critics have discounted its unexpressed passions as irrelevant or negligible.

A final reason that so many critics have dismissed Merchant Ivory's analysis of the necessary costs of cultural cross-pollination is their fetishistic fondness for metaphors that dramatize these conflicts without resolving them. In *Shakespeare Wallah* Sanju's jealous lover Manjula (Madhur Jaffrey), coming to the Buckinghams' theater to disrupt a performance of *Othello*, is, despite herself, so moved by the final scene between Othello and Desdemona—at once an imperishable classic of the British stage and an earlier exploration of the costs of crossing cultural boundaries—that tears come to her eyes. But this momentary weakness does not alter her disruptive tactics or her long-range plan for coming between Sanju and Lizzie Buckingham. Merchant Ivory's later films are virtual anthologies of metaphors for unresolved cultural conflict, from the hunt outside Darlington Hall in *The Remains of the Day* to the museum Adam Verver is raising in American City to house the treasures he has acquired in *The Golden Bowl*. Perhaps the most resonant of all is the climactic image of India Bridge's Lincoln stuck halfway out of her garage in a snowstorm so that, unable to open the doors and get out, she can only call forlornly, "Is anybody there?" Typically, however, this image of India's eternal stasis between immersion and escape from her husband's stifling repression is inconsequential. As the film's closing titles, run under some black-and-white home-movie footage, announce: "Yes, Mr. Bridge arrived in time to save Mrs. Bridge. Much irritated, he telephoned a towing service, and the Lincoln was soon dislodged. They went on as before for quite a few years."

The film that stages Merchant Ivory's trademark dualities most schematically and reveals most clearly their investment in staging conflicts rather than resolving them is *Jane Austen in Manhattan*. Taking off from a fact-based auction in which two bidders compete fiercely to purchase a manuscript of a scrap of Austen juvenilia, her stage adaptation of a brief sequence from Samuel Richardson's novel *Sir Charles Grandison*, it proceeds to the fictional tale of two rival stage directors equally determined to produce the dramatization. The traditional staging planned by Lilianna Zorska (Anne Baxter) represents reverence for history, received culture, and the classic literary text. The experimental production planned by Lilianna's ex-lover Pierre (Robert Powell), which seeks to return the story to its primitive, passionate roots, represents the drive toward reinvention, contemporary relevance, and cultural evolution. As in *Bombay Talkie*, both antagonists are equally wily, ruthless, charismatic, controlling, and uncompromising, and both use loving relationships as tools for getting what they want. The film offers both Pierre's seduction of his follower Ariadne (Sean Young) and Sir Hargrave Pollexfen's forcible abduction of Harriet Byron in Austen's play as metaphors for cultural appropriation. The running debate between Lilianna and Pierre uses their different attitudes toward Austen (is her play an artifact to be preserved or a property to be used?) as a figure for the moral questions of how to treat the past and one another.

There is never any possibility of resolving these conflicts. Because the two antagonists tilt with each other almost entirely through intermediaries, each one has unlimited opportunities to make self-aggrandizing speeches without having to answer the other's most provocative charges. The production of *Sir Charles Grandison* Lilianna stages at the end of *Jane Austen in Manhattan* allegedly combines elements that express both her attitude and Pierre's toward literary classics. But it is actually a traditional staging accompanied by Richard Robbins's quasi-Mozartian score, marked only by a few timid disruptions in its dramaturgy as the actors break the fourth-wall convention and symbolically burn the book over which all the fuss has been made. The cultural conservatism of this apparent synthesis is confirmed by the film's constant reference to the play as Austen's, beginning with the title *Jane Austen in Manhattan,* despite the fact that it is itself a fragmentary dramatic adaptation of an episode in Richardson's epistolary novel by an apprentice author whose reputation rests on her future work. In the struggle for control of literary history, defending Austen's text is simply a more likely starter than defending Richardson's.

Just as they prefer to stage cultural conflicts rather than resolve them, Merchant, Ivory, and Jhabvala are fetishistically attached to the figure of the lost lady who is threatened and often destroyed by them. Not only do they keep bringing her back for encores in film after film, but they also multiply her dilemmas. In adapting *The Bostonians,* a novel that already features Verena Tarrant in this role, they recast Olive Chancellor in it as well by making her more sympathetic and more central than James did and by adding a rousing speech at the end that makes her both a victim and an agent of the rising tide of women's rights. *Jefferson in Paris* (1995) similarly presents two lost girls orbiting the American ambassador to France, his daughter Patsy Jefferson (Gwyneth Paltrow), who feels rootless and desolate in Paris, and his slave and unacknowledged mistress, Sally Hemings (Thandie Newton), whose issue with him will be unacknowledged for a century to come. *Heat and Dust,* following Jhabvala's novel, follows two lost ladies, Olivia Rivers (Greta Scacchi) and her greatniece Anne (Julie Christie), fifty years apart, both torn between East and West, both pregnant with the children of their Indian lovers, the second surviving because she is able to profit from her knowledge of her relative's mistakes in too readily accepting the abortion that is the final mark of the repressive yoke of her husband and the Raj. *Surviving Picasso* (1996) sets the success of its narrator/heroine François Gilot (Natascha McElhone) in standing up to the sexually rapacious painter (Anthony Hopkins) against the previous failures of Olga Koklova (Jane Lapotaire), Marie-Thérèse Walter (Susannah Harker), and Dora Maar (Julianne Moore). It seems likely that what attracted Merchant Ivory to Diane Johnson's novel *Le Divorce,* whose contemporary setting and lack of literary cachet made it an apparently uncharacteristic choice for them, was its focus on two sisters, Roxeanne de Persand (Naomi Watts) and Isabel Walker (Kate

Hudson), caught between American and French cultural norms of marriage and romance.

Throughout all these films the leading questions remain constant. What is most deeply at issue in the divisions between competing or cross-pollinating cultures? Can these divisions ever be bridged? In any pairing of cultural oppositions—Indian/English, European/American, female/male—what gives one member of the pair power over the other? What can the past teach the characters and the audience about the requirements of the present? What are the costs of repression and the possibilities of compromise? Merchant, Ivory, and Jhabvala have no need to import these questions into the novels they adapt; they choose the novels specifically for the prominence they already have there. Adaptation is for them, as for Pierre in *Jane Austen in Manhattan*, less a matter of honoring a past literary tradition than of finding earlier works that address contemporary problems within a decorum of manners, visuals, and music that will make them palatable, even seductive—so seductive that many commentators have dismissed them to concentrate on the décor.

Despite their restriction to the small box, it is in the BBC television adaptations that décor takes over, and admirers of Merchant Ivory might be forgiven for thinking that their heroes had been crucified for the BBC's sins. Ginette Vincendeau has distinguished "heritage cinema," which aims "to depict the past, but by celebrating rather than investigating it," from studio costume drama like Selznick's by emphasizing its "careful display of historically accurate dress and decor, producing what one might call a 'museum aesthetic.'" Vincendeau uses heritage cinema as an umbrella category that includes not only "the British quality television adaptations of the 1980s" but films produced by Merchant Ivory, European period films of the 1980s (*Chariots of Fire* [1981]; *Babette's Feast* [1987]), recent costume films based on "'popular classics' (Forster, Austen, Shakespeare, Balzac, Dumas, Hugo, Zola)," and films, like *1492: Conquest of Paradise* (1992) and *Artemisia* (1998), that "draw on a wider popular cultural heritage that includes historical figures and moments, as well as music and painting."[22] This definition, although it seems both restrictive (are James adaptations to be excluded because *The Golden Bowl* is not a popular classic?) and elastic (is Artemisia Gentileschi really part of the popular cultural heritage?), applies very precisely to the general run of adaptations and quasi adaptations produced for the BBC. Many of these adaptations first aired for American audiences on *Masterpiece Theatre*, whose creators, Frank Marshall and Herb

Schmertz, described its focus in similar terms twenty years later as "quasi-literary masterpieces. . . . Not even the BBC realized that there was a theme to what they were doing. They never identified it. They just thought of it as books to drama."[23]

More closely than either studio adaptations or the work of Merchant Ivory, BBC television adaptations exemplify a third aspect of Truffaut's Tradition of Quality. They are *"scenarists' films"* created not by producers or directors but by screenwriters: "When they hand in their scenario, the film is done; the *metteur-en-scène,* in their eyes, is the gentleman who adds pictures to it."[24] The best-known BBC adaptations take the form of dialogue with visuals obbligato. Studio adaptations fetishize the apparatus of literature: printed words and books, authors and their collected works. The films of Merchant Ivory fetishize the lost lady figuring the costs of cultural conflict against an exotically handsome background. The BBC adaptations dismiss the fetishized author in favor of a textual transparency that aims to give access not to the figure of Austen the author but more directly to the Austen world in which the cultural conflicts incarnated in Merchant Ivory's lost ladies, far from being unresolvable, are never presented as serious disturbances to anyone but the individual characters on whom they bear.[25] These television adaptations treat their backdrops in purely pictorial terms in order to fetishize two different elements they treat as complementary: the original text's dialogue, which is replicated as fully and literally as possible, and a carefully rendered set of period illustrations that are staged in cinematic terms but have the function of tableaux vivants, illustrations to a deluxe edition of a classic literary text.

The period emphasis of the BBC adaptations distinguishes them from Merchant Ivory productions, for which period accuracy goes hand in hand with geographical exoticism. In the BBC adaptations, by contrast, exoticism is a function of historical nostalgia, a longing for another time rather than another place. The decorum of these adaptations, instead of serving as a frame for cultural conflicts that threaten it, becomes itself an unthreatened and unquestioned value. Because the BBC adaptations, again unlike Merchant Ivory, are based overwhelmingly on English novels and set in England, they valorize at once England's past through pictorial nostalgia and English literature through a faithful replication of their chosen authors' dialogue.

Fans of the 1995 *Pride and Prejudice* have identified three leading sources of pleasure they take in the adaptation: its fidelity to Austen's dialogue (which they largely conflate with fidelity to Austen); its presentation of a mise-en-scène that in its details of architecture, fashion, and musical styles is taken to represent something like the world she and her characters would have known; and dramatization of a romantic fantasy that appeals directly to a large contemporary audience. Even fans who prefer the 1980 BBC dramatization generally acknowledge that its production values are more modest, its staging generally more mannered and deliberate than that of the later version, and David Rintoul more stiff as Darcy than Colin Firth, though they defend the production on the grounds that all these differences make it more faithful to Austen's novel.

Sarah Cardwell's traversal of BBC adaptations notes several crucial departures the 1995 *Pride and Prejudice* makes from its celebrated predecessor *Brideshead Revisited* (1981).[26] Still more important, however, are the contrasts between *Brideshead Revisited* and the 1980 *Pride and Prejudice*, which preceded it by little more than a year. The performers in the earlier Austen adaptation declaim their lines as if onstage, rarely move any parts of their bodies apart from their hands and heads, and hardly ever move while speaking. The blocking of dialogue scenes seems all the more stolid given the persistence of two-shots that frame pairs of motionless speakers and the homogeneity of interior spaces and costumes, which are both typically restricted to pale, neutral, or monochrome colors. The sparing exterior sequences are marked by even, diffused lighting, and the production is recorded on videotape rather than 35 mm film. Although music accompanies the dance episodes and the framing credits, there is no background music. The effect, as in other BBC Austen adaptations of the period—*Persuasion* (1971), *Emma* (1972), *Sense and Sensibility* (1981)—is of a bare-bones Austen dominated by a theatrical aesthetic. If it were not for their sparse musical tracks, indeed, these adaptations would seem even more dominated by a radio aesthetic, in which rooting the characters in a particular place and time is subordinated to establishing relationships and moods through the enunciation and inflection of dialogue and the strategic use of sound effects like the canned birdsongs that invariably accompany outdoor scenes.

*Brideshead Revisited* was the first of the BBC miniseries to establish an aesthetic distinct from either the radio or the theatrical aesthetic of its television predecessors. Although the articulation of its stage-trained performers was as plummy as anything heard in the earlier Austen adaptations, their voices were only part of a symphony that included a wider range of sound effects and a far more liberal use of music. *Brideshead Revisited* seems more extroverted than the earlier Austen adaptations not only because it spans more places and years but because it follows its hero's introduction to a new world, a world that is slowly changing, and because the surfaces of that world are rendered, as in Merchant Ivory, with loving attention to detail. Locations from Oxford University to Castle Howard were chosen for maximum visual splendor and sumptuously photographed, and exterior shots carefully planned to include notable or recognizable architectural monuments. *Brideshead Revisited,* originally envisioned on the same scale as the early BBC Austen adaptations, grew from the six hours scripted by John Mortimer to eleven, for, as director Charles Sturridge has noted, "the scenes had begun to expand based on the realization that the potency of the story evaporated without the detail."[27] The epic treatment of what had by no means been an epic novel amounts to a fetish with fidelity as comprehensiveness that would become closely identified with BBC adaptations.

Unlike feature films, which are tailored to a two-hour time slot that they overflow at their peril, a television miniseries can run indefinitely, since the medium always requires new programming and does not prefer untried new material to familiar and well-loved fare. The BBC had already produced *The Pallisers,* a twenty-two-episode version of Trollope's six political novels, in 1974. But the most revealing success in expanding a property was the Independent Network's *Upstairs, Downstairs,* which charted the fortunes of the aristocratic Bellamy family and its domestic staff through the years of World War I and beyond through what turned into a total of sixty-eight episodes whose microcosm of English social history riveted viewers and left them hungry for more.

*Brideshead Revisited* profited from an equally important lesson *Upstairs, Downstairs* had taught: a classic adaptation did not require a classic original. In the case of *Upstairs, Downstairs,* as Alistair Cooke notes, it did not require an original of any sort, for it was "a work made for television without any collateral debt to the theatre, to the cinema, or to a published work of fiction."[28] The case of *Brideshead Revisited* is more peculiar. Although Cardwell remarks that "it is rather curious . . . that the programme which, more than any other, established the generic identity of the traditional television classic-novel adaptation was based upon a book written during the Second World War," and adds that "it is possible that the adaptation of *Brideshead* itself helped to reinforce a popular perception that the source novel is a modern classic,"[29] she never points out that before the airing of its television adaptation, Evelyn Waugh's best-selling, middlebrow 1945 novel was no more widely considered a classic than Dorothy L. Sayers's detective novels about Lord Peter Wimsey. The BBC period adaptations of *Clouds of Witness* (1972), *The Unpleasantness at the Bellona Club* (1972), and *Murder Must Advertise* (1973) helped elevate Sayers from a genre classic to a middlebrow classic. Similarly, the classic status of Waugh's novel, among his least highly regarded during his lifetime, was secured not by any consensus among experts or by its status as a subject of academic study. Instead, *Brideshead Revisited* was canonized by a television adaptation that embalmed in exhaustive detail and epic length the narrator's achingly nostalgic attitude, at once disillusioned and enduringly romantic, toward a vanished idyllic past and the fugitive promise of social mobility in an English society defined by class-consciousness. Because all these factors were a function of historical rather than literary perspective, it was equally easy for the BBC to assimilate nonliterary projects from *The First Churchills* (1969) to *Reilly: Ace of Spies* (1983) into its evolving Tradition of Quality.

The 1995 *Pride and Prejudice* benefits from a new aesthetic nearly as far removed from the theatrical/radio aesthetic of earlier BBC miniseries as from the melodramatic aesthetic exemplified by Selznick. Cardwell has aptly described the hushed long shots that frame architectural treasures like Pemberley and turn exterior views into landscape as "televisual."[30] H. Elisabeth Ellington contends that even in Austen's novels, a place like Pemberley is treated as a fetish that makes readers "consumers of landscape as much as of love story."[31] More generally, such transformations of buildings and grounds into deluxe landscapes go far toward establishing a miniseries Tradition of Quality—that is, a tradition that defines itself specifically by contrast with other television programming. A miniseries in the Tradition of Quality can spend as much money for location shooting as a feature film, even taking the trouble, according to production designer Gerry Scott, to show "real exteriors outside the windows of the rooms,"[32] and devote even more screen time to shots in which literally nothing happens.

Austen's unrivaled mastery of domestic comedy that can be scaled down for television viewers makes her as obvious a patron author for this new Tradition of Quality as Dickens, Forster, and James are for earlier such traditions. A constant challenge, as in adaptations of James, is to find strategies that will compensate for the loss of the variable-focus wit of the author's own voice. In Austen's case, however, the task is simplified by the fact that so many of her characters can plausibly speak exactly as she does. Since the target audience would be keenly disappointed to lose Austen's immortal opening line—"It is a truth universally acknowledged, that a single man in possession of a good fortune, must be in want of a wife"[33]—it can be moved from Charlotte Lucas's mouth, where screenwriter Fay Weldon had placed it in 1980, to Elizabeth Bennet's.

Just as Truffaut associated the French Tradition of Quality with aesthetic and political conservatism, Deborah Cartmell identifies Austen as "a conservative literary icon" because adaptations of her novels, like those of Shakespeare's plays, "tend to perpetuate their assumed conservative ideology in spite of critical readings which suggest otherwise."[34] The 1995 *Pride and Prejudice* is no more faithful than the 1980 miniseries, but it is consistently more colorful and lively, creating its own modest echo of Selznick's bustling *David Copperfield*. Characters are constantly in motion in nearly every shot; the camera itself is more mobile without ever calling attention to itself; framings vary more dramatically from shot to shot; lighting effects are more varied as well; and quasi-period music is used liberally throughout. The result is longer and less intense scene by scene than a two-hour movie adaptation like *Persuasion* (BBC, 1995) or *Emma* (ITV, 1997) but more strongly characterized both psychologically and visually than its miniseries predecessors. Like all television, it is still illustrated radio but more vigorously illustrated.

A miniseries like the 1995 *Pride and Prejudice* invokes several generic contexts: other television programs, other miniseries, other costume dramas, other Austen adaptations, and of course Austen's novel. The goal of the miniseries Tradition of Quality is to establish its market appeal within each of these contexts while giving special emphasis to the most culturally upscale of them. Television viewers may indeed be more interested in their format of endless continuity than in the structure of any given program, but the Tradition of Quality demands a higher degree of structural integrity, not only for the entire story but for each fifty-minute segment. So the six episodes of *Pride and Prejudice* focus respectively on the arrival of Mr. Bingley at Netherfield, the arrival of Mr. Collins at Longbourn, Darcy's abortive first proposal to Elizabeth, Elizabeth's visit to Derbyshire, Lydia's elopement with Wickham, and Darcy's second proposal—each telling a relatively self-contained story even as the first five whet the appetite for more.

Other compromises confirm the adaptation's position within the miniseries Tradition of Quality. The dialogue is kept as faithful as possible to Austen, but the Bennet sisters can deliver it while striding or running across the countryside or tucking each other into bed, and lines and speeches can be added, cut, or reassigned in the interests of clarity or period verisimilitude. Although it is too much to expect, as the British tabloids hoped, that even the most contemporary adaptation would include "full frontal nudity and daring sex scenes,"[35] the adaptation adds an obligatory kiss between Elizabeth and the accepted Darcy and earlier views of Darcy sitting in a bathtub and emerging from the pond at Pemberley in a wet, clinging shirt in order to appeal to "a very specific audience—late twentieth-century Western female spectators"—by "construct[ing] a model of masculinity far removed from Austen's in its emphasis on physicality and emotional expression."[36] The adaptation follows Austen in remaining closer to Elizabeth than any other character, even though it presents occasional scenes, especially at Netherfield, from which she is absent. But although it never presents the equivalent, for instance, of Austen's observation that "in Darcy's breast there was a tolerable powerful feeling towards her, which soon procured her pardon, and directed all his anger against another,"[37] it focalizes Darcy by repeatedly presenting Elizabeth as she appears to him so that viewers can watch him falling in love with her humor, wit, and ebullience. It softens Austen's tone by omitting her harsher judgments of Mrs. Bennet—"a woman of mean understanding, little information, and uncertain temper"— and Mr. Collins—"a mixture of pride and obsequiousness, self-importance and humility"[38]—but intensifies the turbulence of Darcy's first proposal by having Darcy nervously pace, sit, then stand again as Elizabeth refuses to meet his eyes until she delivers her wounded, cutting response.

The net result of all these calculations is an adaptation that can be marketed during its initial broadcast release as quality television and in its video incarnations as a sumptuous period romance. Against the Edenic backgrounds of Longbourn, Netherfield, and especially Pemberley, the heroine and hero can play out a decorous yet spirited mating ritual designed to appeal as a romantic fantasy to modern viewers who welcome less jaundiced alternatives to their own views of courtship and society. Austen's more sociological observations on the rise of the English middle class, a cultural conflict played out in generational time rather than Merchant Ivory's dramatized space, are subordinated to the psychology of her romantic leads.

Small wonder, then, that in 2002 the series was released on two DVDs as part of A&E Television Network's "Romance Collection: A&E Literary Classics." The fourteen-disk set included adaptations of the classic novels *Tom Jones* (1998), *Emma* (1997), and *Jane Eyre* (1997), the unread classic *Ivanhoe* (1997), the minor classic *Lorna Doone* (2000), the swashbuckling period nonclassic *The Scarlet Pimpernel* (1998), and the nonadaptation *Victoria & Albert* (2001). Regardless of their provenance, all eight were now equally certified romantic classics by virtue of their period settings, visual style, and homogenized marketing, so that Baroness Orczy and Queen Victoria met Austen on equal ground.

Apart from showing that Austen could assume a dazzling variety of guises, from the Beverly Hills update *Clueless* (1995) to the Bollywood adaptations *Kandukondain Kandukondain* (*I Have Found It;* based on *Sense and Sensibility* [2000]) and *Bride and Prejudice* (2004), the most important legacy of the miniseries Tradition of Quality, in connection with the earlier Traditions of Selznick and Merchant Ivory, is the revelation that since Quality depends less on any particular literary antecedents than on the invocation of an exotic or Edenic history, a particular visual style, and shrewd merchandising, anything with a historical basis—*The Red Badge of Courage, The Remains of the Day, Victoria & Albert*—can be marketed as a Quality adaptation. As Truffaut saw half a century ago, fidelity in adaptation is not an end but a fetishistic means, for every adaptation that aims at fidelity is really aiming at Quality.

# CHAPTER EIGHT

# Streaming Pictures

Of all the canards that have bedeviled adaptation studies, the most persistent is the belief that film adaptations involve a transfer from words to images. This assumption, passed off as an observation, takes many different forms. Noting that novels and films are united in their quest "to make you see," George Bluestone begins his study of adaptation by emphasizing the difference between verbal images, which involve conceptual thinking, and visual images, which are perceived rather than conceived, and by announcing that "between the percept of the visual image and the concept of the visual image lies the root difference between the two media."[1] Writing more than twenty years later, Keith Cohen considerably complicates Bluestone's analysis but summarizes film adaptation still more simply as "words changed into images."[2] Dudley Andrew elaborates the "absolutely different semiotic systems of film and language" in similar terms: "Generally film is found to work from perception toward signification, from external facts to interior motivations and consequences, from the givenness of a world to the meaning of a story cut out of that world. Literary fiction begins oppositely. It begins with signs (graphemes and words) building to propositions which attempt to develop perception."[3]

More recent theorists have been wary of such an absolute distinction between verbal and visual media. W. J. T. Mitchell contends that "the interaction of pictures and texts is constitutive of representation as such: all media are mixed media, and all representations are heterogeneous; there are no 'purely' visual or verbal arts."[4] And Kamilla Elliott argues that "visual/verbal categorizations break down at every level in the hybrid arts of illustrated novels and worded films: at the level of the whole arts, at the level of the whole signs, and at the level of pieces of signs."[5]

As Elliott acutely observes, contemporary adaptation studies resists a categorical distinction between verbal and visual texts in theory while reinscribing it in practice. Brian McFarlane provides a representative example. He notes that interpreting a film depends on several different kinds of signifying codes: "language codes," "visual codes," "non-linguistic sound codes," and "cultural codes." But he labels all these codes—even the visual, which "goes beyond mere 'seeing' to include the interpretive and the selective"—"extra-cinematic," as if the essence of cinema were seeing without hearing, selecting, or interpreting.[6]

The leading proposition of Elliott's attack on the categorical distinction between verbal novels and visual films is that words are crucial to most movies and pictures to a surprising number of novels. If we enlarge the range of texts under adaptation to include comic books and picture books, as well as illustrated books, the distinction becomes still more untenable. But commentators have rarely considered such adaptations, either because they undercut a categorical distinction that seems essential to adaptation theory or because adapting texts that are largely visual to begin with seems so easy, simple, or natural that the process has limited theoretical interest. This chapter will consider several kinds of allegedly visual-to-visual adaptations. Far from providing uncomplicated transfers of visual information from one medium to another, such adaptations pose distinctive problems of their own. My discussion will consider a broad range of strategies that movies have had to adopt in dealing with such texts. The particular solutions they develop to the problems that arise from apparently unproblematic visual-to-visual adaptations, however, are less important than the problems they reveal.

The challenge of adapting illustrated novels is especially great when the illustrations have a canonical status adapters ignore at their peril. Despite Lorraine Janzen Kooistra's observation that "*fin-de-siècle* first editions consistently faced their publics with illustrative contexts,"[7] however, the number of novels whose illustrations are still regarded as canonical is surprisingly small. It might seem that the illustrations and illuminated chapter headings Thackeray supplied for *Vanity Fair* would be widely considered canonical. Yet Elliott has shown that the status of Thackeray's illustrations gradually declined throughout the nineteenth century until "the *only* value accorded the illustrations [was] through analogy to literature and language. Their pictorial value [was] summarily dismissed."[8] As the twentieth century wore on, the novel with canonical illustrations—pictures provided by the author or by an artist working together with the author on the novel's first edition—became a virtually lost art, and the few exceptions had no impact on filmmaking practice. Jane Langton's detective stories about retired police chief Homer Kelly, illustrated with the author's line drawings of New England settings, have never been adapted as movies, and Alan Rudolph's 1999 adaptation of Kurt Vonnegut's *Breakfast of Champions* (1972) found no visual inspiration in the willfully schematic squiggles with which Vonnegut had illustrated his novel. The tendency to treat illustrated novels as verbal texts readily detached from the illustrations attached to them persists even in the case of John Gardner, whose *Nickel Mountain* (1973), like most of his fiction, had been published with illustrations—in this case, etchings by Thomas O'Donohue—that left no trace on Drew Denbaum's 1984 film adaptation. L. Frank Baum, whose plucky heroine Dorothy Gale, played by Judy Garland in Victor Fleming's *The Wizard of Oz* (1939), looks nothing like either the comically squat heroine imagined by W. W. Denslow in his illustrations to Baum's 1900 novel or the Gibson Girl devised by John R. Neill for the sequels beginning with *The Marvelous Land of Oz* (1904).

It is no wonder, then, that studies of illustrated books have most often focused not on the kinds of illustrated volumes most familiar to twentieth- and twenty-first-century readers—gift editions that add a series of drawings or paintings by a well-known illustrator to a canonical text written many years earlier—but on Victorian novels that were commonly illustrated on their first publication in serial or book form by artists who typically enjoyed a more intimate or interactive relationship with their authors.[9] The late nineteenth century, the period between the rise of the technology for mass-producing pictorial images and the rise of the cinema, was by common consent the high-water mark of the illustrated book in English. The illustrations John Leech supplied for *A Christmas Carol* have been the subject of perhaps the most sustained attempt by any film to adapt a single set of illustrations, the animated version of

*A Christmas Carol* directed by Richard Williams in 1971. But a better-known test case from the late nineteenth century, John Tenniel's line drawings for Lewis Carroll's children's fantasy *Alice's Adventures in Wonderland* (1865), suggests, as well, that film adaptations have been at least as preoccupied with remaining faithful to Tenniel as to Carroll, even though complete fidelity to the illustrations is impossible.

Carroll's first version of his story, *Alice's Adventures Under Ground* (1864), was a manuscript book of ninety-two pages illustrated by the author himself. His friend Tenniel's illustrations have eclipsed Carroll's own to become canonical, appearing in the first book publication of *Alice's Adventures in Wonderland* and in many reprint editions and inspiring both subsequent illustrators and cinematic adaptations. Even a brief glance at Carroll's illustrations shows that he provided Tenniel with many of his most memorable ideas. Tenniel's image of Alice disconcerted but not quite discomposed by her alarmingly stretched neck (26) closely mirrors Carroll's (12).[10] When Tenniel's suddenly giant Alice strains at the boundaries of the frame designed to contain her image (45)—one of the few rectangular frames Tenniel provides—the effect is anticipated by Carroll's even more claustrophobic rendering (37). And *Alice's Adventures Under Ground* provides a preliminary example of the most thorough melding of verbal and visual achieved by Carroll: the mouse's woeful tale of his encounter with a cat, whose rhymed text continues to be shaped like a mouse's tail in *Alice's Adventures in Wonderland* (40), although the words of the tale are completely different from those in *Alice's Adventures Under Ground* (28).

For all these similarities, virtually all film adaptations of *Alice* draw on Tenniel's illustrations rather than Carroll's, borrowing the blonde hair and apron Tenniel had provided for the heroine rather than the more nondescript dark hair and dress Carroll gave her. Even here, however, the quest for fidelity to Tenniel's illustrations is highly selective. Although film Alices are almost invariably blonde, none of them has the high, broad forehead, the deep-set, melancholy eyes, or the eternal pout Tenniel envisioned.[11] The search for typological similarities rather than psychological similarities—Alice as a visual icon of Victorian childhood rather than an individual personality—is reflected in other ways as well. Although film adaptations largely take cues for blocking Alice's first tentative observations and explorations from Tenniel's illustrations for chapter 1 (17, 21, 23), most of them are henceforth more attentive to the general look of characters than to the particular positions they assume in Tenniel. And most adaptations copy the look of the grotesque creatures Alice meets, from the Mock Turtle to the Queen of Hearts, more closely than of the heroine herself. Wherever the adaptations do follow Tenniel, however, the illustrations become cruxes, however incomplete they remain as models. Although Tenniel's drawings do not move in the manner of motion pictures, many of them, as Perry Nodelman points out, already "show moments either just before or just after strenuous action and create tension by implying action."[12] Some adaptations have gone beyond this invitation to represented action to use specific motifs from Tenniel as signatures. Tenniel's image of Alice meeting the hookah-smoking Caterpillar (53) has become a virtual synecdoche for Walt Disney's 1951 animated adaptation, directed by Clyde Geronimi, Wilfred Jackson, and Hamilton Luske. The character who is easiest to copy from Tenniel—the Mad Hatter, whose distinctive look depends neither on individual physiognomy nor on special effects—is, not surprisingly, the one who remains the most constant from one film to the next, even though no adaptation copies Tenniel's subtle trick of making his top hat grow from image to image, beginning as a realistically oversized hat (76) and gradually assuming ever greater proportions (79, 83) until it comically dwarfs his head (118, 120).

Nor do most of the film adaptations follow Tenniel's frequent play between the two dimensions of the printed page and its flat illustrations and the third dimension of Wonderland they imply. Unlike his drawing of Alice watching the White Rabbit vanish through a series of ever-smaller archways (28), most of Tenniel's pictures, like the one showing the Fish-Footman delivering a letter to the Frog-Footman (64), imply a relatively shallow space, with three-dimensional cues provided by facial modeling, cross-hatched shadows, or lightly sketched backgrounds. Live-action adaptations of *Alice,* by contrast, typically unfold in a consistently naturalistic three-dimensional space that has neither the need nor the ability to represent a third dimension by the stylized codes of Tenniel's pen-and-ink drawings. Only animated versions like the Disney cartoon and Jan Švankmajer's surrealist 1988 adaptation have the capacity to show the two-dimensional space Tenniel pictures in some of his illustrations of the court of the King of Hearts.

Tenniel's first illustration of the playing cards who are painting the flowers (85) shows Two, Five, and Seven as having the flat torsos of playing cards but three-dimensional heads and limbs. When Alice meets the King and Queen of Hearts, Tenniel's illustration (87) shows the court cards to be far flatter than she is, as befits their two-dimensional facial models, though the Queen's expression in profile is far from anything found on a court card. Even the disembodied head of the Cheshire Cat floating over the court cards (94) looks more three-dimensional than they do. In his two illustrations showing the presentation of the tarts to the King (16, 128), Tenniel wittily combines two-dimensional cues (for example, the foursquare blocking of the characters and the strong profile of the Knave) with suggestions of a third dimension (for example, the three-quarter view of the King's face in 128, a pose that suddenly makes him seem milder and more human) before using a three-dimensional picture of Alice beset by a torrent of cards to provide a transition back to her normal waking world. Despite their often wild visual inventions, neither the Disney nor the Švankmajer adaptation explores this particular sort of play.

The one adaptation that consistently quibbles on the differences between two and three dimensions, and indeed between color and black and white, is Kirk Browning's 1983 television version for National Educational Television. A prologue showing several featured actors sitting around the stage discussing the erratic actress who plays Alice and then the actress herself (Kate Burton) smoking nervously in her dressing room uses diagonal blocking, movement away from the camera, and tracking movements to emphasize the realistically three-dimensional space. As the dark-haired Burton, nervously reviewing her lines for "Jabberwocky," raises her hands to her head in anguish, the film cuts to a shot of Tenniel's drawing of Alice crowning herself queen, in a two-dimensional pose that precisely mirrors Burton's, as the opening credits run. Back in her dressing room, Burton gazes anxiously from a mirror bordered on the left by a series of Tenniel drawings. As the camera tracks in to a drawing that shows Alice emerging from the other side of the looking glass, the shot wavers and dissolves to a similarly wavy head-on shot of Burton in Alice's pinafore and blonde wig. This new shot, which places the three-dimensional heroine in an initially ambiguous space, pulls back to show her emerging from the looking glass into a world whose sets, beginning with the looking glass and the ornaments on the mantel on which Alice is sitting, consistently have the look of black-and-white or pastel monochrome drawings. Burton's Alice proceeds throughout the adaptation to interact with characters whose stiff movements, flat makeup, and stylized, often black-and-white, costumes give them a decidedly two-dimensional look—all within a three-dimensional space whose visual cues are almost entirely two-dimensional.

Norman McLeod's 1933 film adaptation of *Alice in Wonderland* suggests why even adaptations that have the freedom to copy Tenniel's drawings quite closely seldom do. McLeod and William Cameron Menzies, who supervised the film's visual design and coauthored its screenplay, are at such pains to copy the look of Tenniel's illustrations that they muffle an all-star cast that includes Gary Cooper as the White Knight, Edna May Oliver as the Red Queen, and Cary Grant as the Mock Turtle behind plaster masks that render their well-known voices virtually unrecognizable. Only W. C. Fields as Humpty Dumpty emerges as both a Tenniel (and a Carroll) grotesque and a character star.

He does not, however, emerge as a character from *Alice in Wonderland* because Humpty Dumpty appears only in *Alice's* sequel, *Through the Looking-Glass* (1871). The Paramount adaptation, like a surprising number of other film adaptations, freely blends characters and episodes from both stories, adding Tweedledum and Tweedledee, the White Queen and the Red Queen, and the White Knight to *Alice's* cast of characters. The result is more faithful to the series of drawings Tenniel produced for the two books than to the structure Carroll worked out for them, a structure both nonsensical and tightly woven in *Through the Looking-Glass.* Many another screen *Alice* is actually a compendium of both stories, with *Alice in Wonderland* invariably giving the adaptation its name. The Internet Movie Database lists twenty-three film adaptations of *Alice in Wonderland* but only five adaptations of *Through the Looking-Glass,* all five entitled *Alice through the Looking Glass* in order to include the identifiable franchise heroine, and two additional films entitled *Through the Looking Glass,* neither one an adaptation of Carroll's story.

Despite Kamilla Elliott's careful taxonomy of *Alice* adaptations—those that rely on literalized analogies, structural analogies, psychoanalytic analogies, and looking-glass analogies between the adaptations and their originals[13]—most film adaptations of Carroll's story treat it and its sequel as a series of set pieces or episodes as subject to selection, abridgment, or rearrangement as the acts on a television variety program of the 1950s, held together only by the abiding presence of Alice, whose role is scarcely more well-defined than that of a television emcee. These adaptations, although they make no serious attempt to reproduce Tenniel's visuals exactly, are structurally closer to his vivid but discontinuous illustrations than to the nonsensically overdetermined logic of Carroll's writing.[14] Apparent exceptions to this rule only end up proving it. Apart from *Alice through the Looking Glass,* a 1996 entry in the "Fairy Tales on Ice" series skated by Morgan Ballard as Alice and Nancy Kerrigan as the White Queen, the two leading adaptations that most explicitly address the problem of performance—a problem whose neglect buries the stars of the 1933 Paramount adaptation under inexpressive masks—are Willing's 1999 adaptation and Disney's 1951 cartoon. Peter Barnes's teleplay for Willing frames Carroll's story by a realistic Victorian tale in which Alice, whose parents want her to sing for their friends, finds herself substituting nonsense for the song she is supposed to have learned. Only a trip through Wonderland can cure her of her stage fright and assimilate her into the adult world as a seasoned performer.[15] In Carroll, by contrast, Alice makes a mess of everything she recites, cutting through the moralizing surface of Victorian drawing-room culture to reveal a deeper nonsense logic beneath.

The Disney film resolves the Paramount version's problem of how to stage grotesque performances that are both subordinate to the story's logic and recognizable as star turns by casting several performers whose voices are well known but subordinating those voices to the animated visuals. Instead of being buried, as he was in his 1933 role as the Frog, Sterling Holloway is now instantly recognizable as the Cheshire Cat, a cartoon figure whose image is perfectly consistent with the rest of Disney's visual menagerie. Yet the Disney film also inverts Carroll at another point with equally radical results by giving Alice the goal of escaping Wonderland and returning home. When she is most discouraged about her prospects, Disney's Alice sings "Very Good Advice" to herself as darkness falls over Wonderland, sadly acknowledging her failures to conform to adult rules and reducing herself and her animated auditors to tears. Like Willing, Disney seems less interested in celebrating the invincible power Carroll had invested in childhood innocence, confidence, and adventurousness than in punishing Alice for being a child. The result in each case is to avoid the series of static tableaux implied by Tenniel's drawings by superimposing a new structure on Alice's adventures that makes them both more clearly coherent and less like Carroll's.

The challenges in adapting picture books, books whose illustrations are at least as prominent and important to their interpretation as their words, is still greater because the relationship between word and image is more obviously dialectical. The *New Yorker*'s weekly back-page feature, which offers a prize for the best caption to a wordless cartoon, is only the latest evidence that the pictures in these texts may take precedence over their words. James Thurber, whose peerless scrawls enlivened the *New Yorker* for many years, claimed that the caption "That's my first wife up there, and this is the *present* Mrs. Harris" was intended to explain a woman perched atop a bookcase who "was originally designed to be a woman crouched on the top step of a staircase" and that the caption "What have you done with Dr. Millmoss?" was added, like the images of a pipe, shoe, and hat, to a drawing of a hippopotamus when "something about the creature's expression when he was completed convinced me that [he] had recently eaten a man."[16] Collections of cartoons by Saul Steinberg, Charles Addams, and Gary Larson depend at least as much for their impact on their visual styles as on their verbal wit.

There are of course no film adaptations of such collections. Surprisingly, however, there are no purely visual adaptations of books that tell stories through their pictures either—at least not of children's books like Fernando Krahn's *The Mystery of the Giant Footprints* (1977) or John S. Goodall's *The Surprise Picnic* (1977) or Mitsumasa Anno's *Anno's Journey* (1978), all of which eschew words entirely apart from their titles. Even the animated short film based on Raymond Briggs's *The Snowman* (1978) adds the song "Walking in the Air," though no spoken dialogue, to Briggs's wordless fable. Although it might seem natural for cinema to gravitate to such purely pictorial sources, the obstacles to making, marketing, and exhibiting such adaptations would be formidable because the books in question never dispense with dialogue; they merely relegate their dialogue to an adult reader who helps guide young children through the books. Indeed, children reading wordless picture books on their own often replicate their parent's earlier dialogue aloud in an attempt to provide interactive commentaries that can scarcely be duplicated in a theater or even on a videotape. Perry Nodelman has observed that "television is not merely a visual medium. Words (and music, and just plain noise) pour out of television sets as rapidly and aggressively as pictures do."[17] Given the clamorous media that shout, whistle, and buzz for attention, no child would sit still for a wordless, soundless display of images unaccompanied by any interaction or commentary. And even the addition of a musical track to a wordless book like *The Snowman* makes the experience, no longer entirely visual, entirely different. No wonder the 1991 television program *Where's Waldo?* added both musical cues and a series of voices to its source, a series of picture books inviting viewers to find the hero's striped shirt and stocking cap in pictures crowded with obscuring detail.

Nor have there been any film adaptations of picture books designed for adults who can navigate them on their own, like of Frank Masereel's woodcut novel *Passionate Journey* (1919), Max Ernst's fantastical collage *A Week of Kindness* (1934), or the graphic fiction of Lynd Ward. *Gods' Man* (1929), the first of

Ward's novels in woodcuts, suggests why not. Ward's story—a poor artist accepts the gift of a fabled brush from a masked benefactor and experiences first great success, then romantic betrayal, and finally happiness and apparent redemption before his benefactor returns, demands that the artist paint his portrait, and removes his mask to reveal that he is Death—unfolds in a series of 120 woodcuts unaccompanied by any words except for the novel's title and five chapter titles ("The Brush . . . The Mistress . . . The Brand . . . The Wife . . . The Portrait"). Despite its striking visual design, *Gods' Man* would be exceptionally difficult to adapt as a film that sought to preserve its original impact. Translating Ward's woodcuts into live-action visuals would reduce the story to one more Faustian parable, depriving it of all Ward's somber power. Animating the woodcuts would pose special problems. Ward's graphic style, unlike, say, Walt Disney's, is designed to increase the impact of each picture, not encourage maximum fluidity between pictures. Each picture is designed as a tableau, and each depends for its force on its pictorial distinctness. Ward's often subtle narrative cues—a character easily recognizable in one picture must be the same tiny character in the next, a hand entering the frame in one picture belongs to a new character shown in the next—are consistently subordinated to the iconic and emotional power of each picture. Narrative cinema, by contrast, consistently subordinates pictorial qualities to narrative flow. And continuity editing, as apprentice editors swiftly learn, risks losing the audience if it does not subordinate pictorial similarities among successive shots to temporal sequence and narrative causality—just the opposite of Ward's procedure.

The alternative, of course, would be to photograph each of Ward's woodcuts as a still picture and edit the results together, in the manner of Kenneth Clark's television miniseries *Civilisation* (1969) and Ken Burns's PBS documentaries. But it is highly unlikely that many viewers would sit and watch a series of still photographs of black-and-white woodcuts presented without the music or voice-over commentary that would prevent the adaptation from being purely visual, especially since the scale that Ward varies so dramatically from picture to picture anticipates Burns's ubiquitous zoom-ins and zoom-outs so completely that further zooming would be superfluous. For better or worse, modern film audiences have come of age in an audiovisual culture that prescribes and promises saturation of two senses, not just one, by complementary, often heavily overdetermined, auditory and visual cues. These audiences would find any purely visual experience of cinema incomplete. Hence the kinds of picture books that make the best movies are the ones to which extrapictorial elements can most readily be added.

Movies offer no examples of purely pictorial adaptations of purely pictorial books. Instead, they offer multichannel examples of equally multichannel word-and-picture books like the work of Beatrix Potter, Charles M. Schulz, and Dr. Seuss, the pseudonym of Theodor Seuss Geisel. Adaptations of Seuss's *How the Grinch Stole Christmas!* (1957) illustrate the range of problems involved in bringing word-and-picture books to the screen.

The box-office success of Ron Howard's adaptation *How the Grinch Stole Christmas*, which sold more tickets than any other film released in 2000, has little to do with the specifics of Seuss's story and still less with his language. Although narrator Anthony Hopkins faithfully recites Seuss's rhymed couplets, most of the film's words—all the nonrhyming dialogue among Howard's characters—are the product of screenwriter Jeffrey Price. In the same way, the effects-heavy 104-minute film adds a great deal of new material to Seuss's fifty-six-page book: an earlier meeting between the Grinch and Cindy Lou Who (Taylor Momsen), an abortive childhood romance with the new character Martha May Whovier that explains how the Grinch became the misanthropic enemy of the Whos, and numberless bits of comic business for the film's star, Jim Carrey. Stripping Seuss's story to the bones of its fable of Christmas conversion and revealing more clearly the story's roots in *A Christmas Carol,* the film abandons Seuss for the conventions of latter-day adaptations of Dickens's story to make the Whos recklessly materialistic in their frenzy to decorate their homes and pile up gifts for one another. So complete are these changes that the ending requires a conversion of the Whos along with the Grinch.

It is Howard's visuals, however, that depart most decisively from Seuss's. Although he had authorized two earlier animated films based on *How the Grinch Stole Christmas!* Seuss had long resisted offers for a live-action adaptation. It was not until his widow, Audrey Seuss Geisel, saw a live staging of the story at San Diego's Old Globe Theater that she authorized the project. Howard follows Seuss in depicting the Whos as basically human, the Grinch as basically non-human, and the Grinch's dog Max as basically a dog. But his Grinch, a vision in chartreuse fur with piercing yellow eyes, is not only more verbal and more antic but more colorful than Seuss's, and Howard invents many secondary characters: Martha May Whovier (Christine Baranski); Cindy Lou Who's parents, Lou Lou (Bill Irwin) and Betty Lou (Molly Shannon); Mayor Maywho

(Jeffrey Tambor); and Whobris (Clint Howard). In addition Howard stages his highly unrealistic story in a thoroughly realistic three-dimensional space, transforming Seuss's lightly sketched backgrounds and perfunctory third-dimensional cues into a riot of color, movement, and sound that is often just as important as the foreground action. The result is an extravaganza whose main point of similarity to Seuss, its status as a fable of Christmas redemption, has already been eclipsed by the December 2003 release of *The Cat in the Hat,* an equally effects-heavy live-action showcase for another anarchic star, Mike Myers, that attempts to turn the Seuss franchise into a Christmas tradition even though the story of *The Cat in the Hat* has nothing to do with Christmas.

Far more determined in their attempts to remain faithful to Seuss's visuals are the two earlier animated short films of the same title. The first of them, made with Seuss's active participation, was directed by animation veteran Chuck Jones in 1966. Although it closely follows Seuss's story and language, adding only a few rhymed couplets and two songs written by Seuss, Jones's animated visuals are very different from Seuss's.[18] Even though Seuss includes a new picture on virtually every page of his book, his pictures alone do not tell the story; like Tenniel's, they provide a series of tableaux that illustrate the story, mark its dramatic high points, add important visual information, and modulate its potentially threatening story by their consistently absurdist tone. It is only from Seuss's illustrations, for example, that we can tell the Grinch is less human than the Whos, who wear clothing (including in some cases eyeglasses), have last names (though those names are always "Who"), and are often (though by no means always) conventionally gendered in appearance.[19] Jones distinguishes the Grinch from the Whos in auditory terms as well, giving the Whos soft, high voices; the Grinch narrator Boris Karloff's gravelly voice, its higher overtones electronically removed; and the song "You're a Mean One, Mr. Grinch" to the deepest voice of all, the uncredited Thurl Ravenscroft, the trademark voice of Tony the Tiger.

Jones replaces Seuss's world of lines and shapes with a world of distinctly colored spaces. Instead of borrowing the black-and-red look of Seuss's book, Jones uses color much more freely for backgrounds as well as foregrounds like the Grinch's bilious green hue, which becomes a settled fact beginning with this adaptation. In addition to dissolving Seuss's tableaux into a stream of conventionally smooth animation, Jones provides the occasional nod to the specific conventions of Warner Bros. cartoons, as when Max and the Grinch's sleigh run over a curl of snow until they are upside-down and then fall—all but the

Grinch's hat, which hangs in midair for a moment before following. A still drawing could have portrayed this moment but not the trademark comedy of its flouting of physics.

Unlike Howard, Jones follows Seuss in setting his story in a largely two-dimensional drawn world whose backgrounds are sparse and whose third-dimensional cues are limited to essential functions like indicating relative distances. But he faces further problems in animating Seuss's figures, whose black outlines are far too textured to allow easy animation. In the series of theatrical films and television specials based on Charles M. Schulz's *Peanuts* comic strip, the animators follow Schulz's wavering outlines as closely as possible in each animation cel, making the animation itself less smooth.[20] Jones makes the opposite decision, smoothing and simplifying Seuss's line in each cel in order to facilitate animation. The result is a more idiomatic cartoon that looks less like Seuss's drawings.

Children would have to wait until 1992, a year after Seuss's death, for an animated adaptation of *How the Grinch Stole Christmas!* whose visuals truly looked like Seuss's. And for a very good reason: the twelve-minute film, directed by Ray Messecar and narrated by Walter Matthau, follows the conventions established by Kenneth Clark and Ken Burns for making a movie based on still pictures. Each shot holds on an image of a single still drawing from the Seuss book, often zooming in or out, and adding only occasional touches of limited animation. The Grinch's eyes shift back and forth in one shot as he imagines the Whos' Christmas; his fingers nervously drum in another. The compromise between fidelity to Seuss and smooth animation becomes clearest when the Grinch goes down the chimney of Cindy Lou's house, and the image shows a cutout Grinch emerging from his sleigh and jumping down the chimney without ever changing the position of his arms and legs.

Even this version, however, finds it necessary to punch up Seuss's visuals. If the limited animation barely qualifies Messecar's adaptation as an animated film, his use of color is quite different from that of his model. *How the Grinch Stole Christmas!* was the last of Seuss's large-format picture books to be printed in only two colors, and its use of red is sparing and strategic.[21] The Grinch's red eyes are angry; the red bows surmounting the Whos' Christmas wreaths are festive; the Grinch's red Santa Claus costume and the enormous red sack of booty on his sleigh are ironic; and the red suffusion around the Whos' climactic song is joyous.[22] Messecar uses a limited but still wider array of pastels, adding blue, green, peach, and pink to most of the drawings in the manner of

Seuss's later books. Instead of indicating backgrounds with impressionistic swirls of color, as Seuss does, Messecar uses color to fill in background spaces completely. The result is to push Seuss's drawn world of black outlines and red highlights closer to Jones's animated world of distinct, brightly colored spaces. The attempt to reproduce the exact lines of Seuss's drawings while improving them with the color suggests an attempt to reconcile Jones's elaborate, expensive, and unfaithful streaming video with the discrete, discontinuous pictures of Seuss's book. The result is not so much an animated cartoon as an approximation of a private reading by a crusty grandfather who simply makes his gruff voice a little gruffer when he voices the Grinch.

Mention should also be made of two related animated shorts written by Dr. Seuss: Gerard Baldwin's *Grinch Night* (1977), in which the Grinch tries to do for Halloween what he has tried unsuccessfully to do for Christmas, and Bill Perez's *The Grinch Grinches the Cat in the Hat* (1982), in which the Grinch meets his match when he tries to spoil the Cat's picnic. Both may seem more faithful to Seuss's visual than his verbal conception, but in fact both are sequels deliberately unfaithful to the events of Seuss's earlier story but equally faithful to the character of the Grinch (and its narrative implications) in visual and verbal terms. Neither film attempts to duplicate the story of *How the Grinch Stole Christmas!* but inconsistencies arise only for viewers who wonder how sincere and lasting was the conversion of the Grinch, last seen carving the Roast Beast that was the highlight of the Whos' Christmas dinner. His deplorable preference for continued mischief, however, is perfectly consistent with the common use of the epithet "Scrooge" to describe an incorrigible miser, not the converted benefactor of Tiny Tim.

Taken as a group, the Grinch adaptations raise five problems in adapting picture books to the screen. The first is the impossibility of translating a child's private, interactive experience of having a picture book read aloud by a specific reader to cinema, which is restricted to a single public voice (Anthony Hopkins, Boris Karloff, Walter Matthau). Another is the problem of fitting voices to characters without speaking roles in the book. A fundamental problem of *Peanuts* adaptations is how old-sounding to make the voices of children who in Schulz's comic strip are constantly saying things too mature for their age. The animated Grinch films by Jones and Messecar duck this problem by having the narrator voice both the speaking roles, but Howard's live-action adaptation meets it head-on, inviting the complaint that quite apart from his look, Jim Carrey doesn't sound like the Grinch.

A third problem is the need to translate the lines of Seuss's drawings into the colored masses of animated cartoons or the three-dimensional space of Howard's live-action film. And a related but distinct problem involves the different depth cues pen-and-ink drawings and movies deploy. This last difference is not between a two-dimensional and a three-dimensional medium, for the space of both book illustrations and movie screens is flat. The difference, as Tenniel's witty drawings of the court of the King of Hearts show, is more precisely between the ways the two different media conventionally imply a third dimension.

More fundamental than any of these differences is the problem of translating the discontinuous tableaux of Seuss's drawings into the continuously streaming images common to cinema. Perry Nodelman has observed that "almost every picture in most books represents a different scene. The whole point of film montage is that we come to understand action by means of the various ways the action has been broken down into smaller bits. But that does not happen in picture books."[23] The Messecar adaptation is an exception to this rule. The precise correspondence between shots and drawings rules out the possibility of continuity editing that might analyze space or action. Jones and Howard, however, are both obliged to reconstitute Seuss's discontinuous images into a flow in which the shot rather than the frame is the smallest unit of perception by representing motion as process rather than selecting only the most crucial moments to portray and implying the movements in between.

It might seem from this summary that the simplest cinematic adaptations of picture books, and those with the greatest ability to remain faithful to their progenitors, were animated films based on comic strips or comic books. Like movies themselves, comic books are multimodal texts that typically combine an image track and a dialogue track, confined in the case of comics to dialogue or thought bubbles hovering over the characters' heads (or, in the case of *Prince Valiant*, run decorously beneath the panels). Unlike children's books, neither comic strips nor comic books imply the presence of an absent narrator who will guide their readers but disappear from film adaptations. Although the example of *Peanuts* shows that animated adaptations must translate characters' dialogue into auditory terms that are often problematic, the success of the *Peanuts* franchise indicates that after a certain number of entries, the voices of Charlie Brown, Lucy, and Linus will become normative for the film franchise and provide a reassuring point of reference for each new entry. Animated adaptations raise fewer problems than live-action adaptations in translating two dimensions into three, line into shapes in space, and black-and-white into color, especially if, like *Peanuts,* their comics have already appeared in color on Sunday mornings. The Messecar adaptation of *How the Grinch Stole Christmas!* shows that animated adaptations have the option of forgoing the continuity editing by which filmmakers and viewers make narrative sense of streaming video. And a final difficulty specific to feature adaptations of comic strips—the need to impose a single coherent story on what originally appeared as a succession of three- or four-panel jokes—can be readily overcome in the case of *Peanuts,* which often develops a story over an arc of a dozen or more strips, or a noncomical comic like *Superman,* whose primary allegiance is to a continuing melodrama with cliffhanger endings.

Certainly comic-book adaptations are far more important to the film industry than picture-book adaptations. Unlike economically marginal adaptations of Lewis Carroll and Dr. Seuss, which are aimed at niche markets and are rarely released theatrically, comic-book adaptations are a billion-dollar business. Ever since *Superman* (1978) and *Batman* (1989) gave superhero adaptations respectability, as well as major box-office clout, Hollywood has pinned some of its fondest financial hopes to films like *The Phantom* (1996), *Hulk* (2003), and *The Fantastic Four* (2005), pitched to an audience of twelve- to seventeen-year-old boys, the unmarked clientele that constitutes Hollywood's only nonniche demographic. As these last three films suggest, however, comic-book adaptations are not guaranteed blockbusters. For every *X-Men* (2000) and *Spider-Man* (2002), the industry releases more than its share of comic-strip disappointments, even disasters.

These misfires might seem mysterious in view of the assumption that comic books with a built-in fan base are easy to adapt to the cinema. Despite their pictorial similarities, however, important differences remain between comics and movies. Movies are an audiovisual medium; comics a lexicovisual medium. Comics and movies both use a two-dimensional medium that has the ability to imply a third dimension. But comics and movies deploy color very differently, since comics are normally limited to six colors (eight, counting black and white), whereas the most rigidly controlled movies usually exploit the resources of a much wider color palette. Most important, comics, though their individual panels are more likely to correspond to individual shots than to the scenes implied by book illustrations, comprise discontinuous tableaux rather than streaming video.

Scott McCloud deals briefly with several of these problems in *Understand-*

*ing Comics,* a tour de force that uses the format of a comic book to analyze the form. Beginning with Will Eisner's definition of comics as "sequential art" and refining it as "sequential *visual* art," McCloud argues, through a dialogue with imaginary interlocutors, that comics require a more specific definition to distinguish them from animated films, another mode of sequential visual art. Because "you might say that *before* it's projected, film is just a very very very very *slow* comic," he suggests a more precise definition: "*juxtaposed* sequential visual art."[24] This definition takes into account the fact that the multiple static frames of movies, projected onto the same space in rapid succession, are designed to produce the illusion of a seamless flow while the equally static frames of comics are designed to remain discontinuous and simultaneously available in space. In Jean-Louis Baudry's terms, cinema "lives on the denial of difference: differences are necessary for it to live, but it lives on their negation" because, unlike the successive frames of comics, "adjacent images [within a given shot] are almost exactly repeated, their divergence being verifiable only by comparison of images at a sufficient distance from each other."[25] Cinema therefore involves a peculiar form of disavowal, which Christian Metz has summarized in the formula "I know very well, but all the same . . ."[26]

As McCloud points out, however, comics involve a similar disavowal of their own. McCloud focuses his discussion of this phenomenon on the gutter, the space between successive panels that encourages readers in search of narrative to supply intermediate actions, transitions, and programmatic spatial, chronological, or thematic continuities that the comic never explicitly provides. Glossing a succession of shots in which a man and a woman gradually ease out of the frame as they kiss, McCloud remarks: "Filmmakers *long ago* realized the importance of allowing viewers to use their *imaginations.* But while *film* makes use of audiences' imaginations for *occasional effects, comics* must use it far more often!"[27] This pardonable bit of medium chauvinism cannot be defended. The "gaps" Wolfgang Iser finds in novels as cues that invite readers to supply narrative and thematic connections and speculations that are not spelled out have their analogies in every discursive form, from shopping lists (each of which is headed with the unwritten line, "buy these items") to representational and, indeed, nonrepresentational painting.[28] Even the formula of disavowal that Metz pronounces constitutive of cinema is borrowed from Lacanian psychoanalyst Octave Mannoni's discussion of theater.

Translating comics to the movie screen, then, does not so much introduce or close gaps that invite the audience's active participation as translate certain kinds of gaps to other kinds. The way both modes often encourage speculation about offscreen (or off-panel) space suggests that programmatic omissions are crucial to both of them. Instead of gutters between every frame, movies provide imperceptible changes between successive shots. The straight cuts within movies correspond more closely to the gutters in comics, but the simultaneous availability of successive frames in comics and not in movies will always make the terms of their reception different. Both modes are successive, narrative, and visual, but neither is purely visual or, as McCloud's own book attests, necessarily narrative.

The very real differences between comics and movies as signifying systems is less likely to play out in medium-specific politics or ontologies ("What Comics Can Do That Movies Can't [and Vice Versa]") than in myriad decisions about specific representational codes. Conflicts between the different ways comics and movies portray color and three dimensions, for instance, are front and center in *Who Framed Roger Rabbit* (1988), which freely mixes two-dimensional "toons" like Roger and Jessica Rabbit with live-action characters like private eye Eddie Valiant (Bob Hoskins). As soon as it switches from the two-dimensional space of its opening Maroon Cartoon to the three-dimensional space in which the birds hovering around Roger's face take on depth and Baby Herman is revealed as a cigar-chomping palooka, the film sets up a series of quibbles between two and three dimensions, as when R. K. Maroon (Alan Tilvern) opens the blinds over his office window to reveal an enormous image of Dumbo hovering just outside. For much of the film Roger and Eddie are linked by handcuffs that are unmistakably three-dimensional and therefore ought not to hold a two-dimensional figure like Roger. But Roger, although he is drawn with a typical animator's outline and costumed in red overalls whose bright, even color gives little hint of three-dimensional modeling, frequently implies a third dimension as well. He can fall off a three-dimensional crate, get knocked unconscious by the three-dimensional frying pan wielded by a shadowy figure who turns out to be his two-dimensional wife, and get tied along with Jessica to a three-dimensional hook and hoisted off the floor. The scene in which Jessica knocks out her husband deftly combines cartoon imagery (Roger's foolish attempts at silence and secrecy, the choice of the frying pan as blunt instrument) with the noir visual vocabulary appropriate to the film's nominal genre and fictional setting (the atmospheric shadows cast over Roger's face, darkening his overalls, and in the darkened alley by his unknown assailant). The result is a double visual matrix that produces not a coherent noir

cartoon but a running series of comical quibbles on the inconsistencies between the worlds of noir and comics, as different in their ways as 1947 Los Angeles and Toon Town.

*Who Framed Roger Rabbit* could freely indulge in such pleasantries because
its source, Gary K. Wolf's *Who Censored Roger Rabbit?* (1981), was not a comic
book but a novel with no explicitly visual component the film had to follow,
challenge, or abandon. Adaptations based on comic-book franchises, lacking
the luxury of visual freedom, are often strongly criticized for their infidelity to
their sources. Even when adaptations escape this charge, their visual fidelity is
sharply limited. When *Batman* opened, many critics who disliked it still praised
its visual style. The film's Gotham City, wrote Roger Ebert, "is one of the most
distinctive and atmospheric places I've seen in the movies"; it "discards the recent cultural history of the Batman character—the camp 1960s TV series, the
in-joke comic books—and returns to the mood of the 1940s, the decade of film
noir and fascism. The movie is set at the present moment, more or less, but
looks as if little has happened in architecture or city planning since the classic
DC comic books created that architectural style you could call Comic Book
Moderne."[29] As Will Brooker has pointed out, however, the film's production
design, though certainly striking, owes little to Bob Kane's 1940s comics, which
were "mostly gung-ho romps against Hitler's minions," and not much more to
its other most frequently cited source, Frank Miller's darkly revisionist graphic
novel *The Dark Knight Returns* (1986): "Only a few moments in the film could
be read as referring explicitly to Miller's work. . . . It would take a stretching of
the term to define [Tim] Burton's film as an 'adaptation' of the mid-1980s
comics."[30]

Ebert, again speaking for many reviewers, rhapsodizes in similar terms
about the opening sequence of *Dick Tracy* (1990):

> Another of the movie's opening shots establishes, with glorious excess, the Tracy
> universe. The camera begins on a window, and pulls back, and moves up until
> we see the skyline of the city, and then it seems to fly through the air, turning as
> it moves so that we sweep above an endless urban vista. Skyscrapers and bridges
> and tenements and elevated railways crowd each other all the way to the distant
> horizon, until we realize this is the grandest and most squalid city that ever was.
> It's more than a place: It's the distillation of the idea of City—of the vast, brood-
> ing, mysterious metropolis spreading in all directions forever, concealing mil-
> lions of lives and secrets.[31]

This is well said, but Ebert's evocation of "the Tracy universe" has nothing to do with the look of Chester Gould's comic strip, which takes virtually no interest in exteriors, brooding or benevolent. The film's widely acclaimed production design remains faithful to Gould's visuals at only a few key points: its fondness for grotesque villains in elaborate makeup, the generic quality of its nondescript interiors, the restriction of its production design to the seven colors of Gould's strip, and its costuming of its hero in a brilliant yellow trench coat and matching fedora. There is no attempt to present the stylistic hallmarks that set Gould's visuals apart from those of other comics: the shallow spaces, the absence of mediant grays or other cues of facial modeling, the heavy use of profiles (especially for Tracy), the facial inexpressiveness of Tracy and his prey, the underplaying of motion cues that make Tracy seem solid and immobile even when he is walking down the street. The similarities the film does emphasize, like its grandly artificial exteriors, all depend less on pictorial resemblance than on a search for iconic or conceptual equivalences. What's the most striking thing about Dick Tracy? His yellow trench coat. So put Warren Beatty in a yellow trench coat, and he'll look just like Dick Tracy, though it's hard to imagine an actor as little like the clipped, frozen hero, whose jaw is so square it could open cans.

Beatty's film raises another problem crucial to the difference between comics and movies, one that has already arisen several times in this chapter: the nature of performance. The Grinch masquerades as Santa, and Carroll's Alice plays many roles and participates in many performances in Wonderland, but performance is not central to novels or illustrations or comic books as it is to the cinema. Fictional films, like the theater, are inescapably a performative medium in which real people pretend to be fictional characters. Whatever the character is doing, the actor is simultaneously performing, as most viewers are constantly aware. Cinema multiplies the question behind illustrated books for prereaders—how best to read this book aloud?—to innumerable questions about how to play the characters (from the performers' point of view) and what relation a given performance has to all the others each performer has given. One result is to make casting, quite apart from either the economic impact of well-known performers and the performances they actually give, essential to discussions of movies. (What will happen if we cast Warren Beatty as Dick Tracy? Dustin Hoffman as Mumbles? Madonna as Breathless Mahoney?) Another is to foreground questions of tone—not just the tone of the original franchise but the tone the performers adopt toward that franchise.

Superhero adaptations are distinguished by an impressive variety of performative tones. The casting of the unknown Christopher Reeve already implied that Warner Bros.' four *Superman* adaptations (1978–87) would play their stories as straight melodrama, with occasional forays into epic pretension (the weighty prologue of *Superman*) and Rube Goldberg comedy (the opening sequence of *Superman III* [1983]). Casting Michael Keaton as Batman linked Tim Burton's film to the Burton-Keaton *Beetlejuice* (1988), whose dark comedy overrode its ghoulish premise. When Keaton was replaced after two films by Val Kilmer in *Batman Forever* (1995) and George Clooney in *Batman and Robin* (1997), the franchise seemed headed toward a more generic approach until it was rescued by Christian Bale's intensity in *Batman Begins* (2005).

Bale's performance adds a new layer of self-seriousness to the Batman franchise. More often, superhero adaptations kid their superheroes by having the performers deliver outrageous dialogue perfectly straight (Adam West in the television series *Batman* [1966–68]), allowing them to make fun of their roles (Lynda Carter in *Wonder Woman* [1976–79]), or exploring tonal contradictions within the comics themselves. Tobey Maguire's wide-eyed innocence as Peter Parker poignantly emphasizes the psychological contradictions implicit in his relation to his unwilling alter ego in *Spider-Man* (2002) and *Spider-Man 2* (2004), whereas Patrick Warburton's drolly clueless superhero reveals a deeper vein of absurdism in the live-action television series *The Tick* (2001–2) that is equally traceable to the film's forebears in the comics and an earlier animated series (1994–97). Like the visual choices they make, comic-book adaptations' performative styles depend less on any medium-specific comic-book look than on the individual style of their particular source and the relation they seek to establish to that source. None of them to date has chosen to duplicate it.

The reasons why are clear. Even though reviewers and fans routinely praise comic-book adaptations for their fidelity to their original franchises, it does not follow that fidelity alone can ensure an adaptation's popularity or even that the most faithful adaptations are the best. Nor are most comic-book adaptations centrally concerned with fidelity—at least not with fidelity to the visual design of their progenitors. If they were, they would be animated, since animated films can come much closer to the look of comics than live-action films. But of all the most financially successful comic-book features, only *The Incredibles* (2004) has been animated. The film's computer-generated Pixar graphics, which are based on shapes rather than lines, nowhere suggest the two-dimensional space of comic books. Nor is there any reason why they should, since *The Incredibles,* unlike virtually all superhero films, is not an adaptation of an earlier franchise. Although it alludes at many points to viewers' assumptions about superheroes in general, the film, based on an original screenplay, is under no pressure to look like anything in particular.

Animated superhero adaptations, by contrast, have been relegated to Saturday morning television, and although animated television adaptations like *Batman* (1992–95) have garnered critical praise, no Hollywood feature has followed its lead into animated adaptation. The closest that the Disney studio, long the dominant force in feature-length animated films, has come to a superhero feature is *Hercules* (1997), a story based on a nonvisual original. Despite the apparent ease of adapting comic books to the cinema, it is as if there were a proscription on such adaptations.

The proscription, of course, is economic rather than judicial. Ever since the 1933 *Alice in Wonderland,* Hollywood filmmaking has remained star-driven, unlike the production of television programming for children. In *Hercules* Disney can hide character stars like Danny DeVito, James Woods, and Amanda Plummer behind animated visuals partly because the stars have been chosen for their distinctive voices but mainly because Walt Disney himself, dead for thirty years, is the real star, the brand name that assures parents that the film will be safe for children and amusing for parents. Although Superman and Batman are brand names that carry similar box-office clout, the Flash, Green Lantern, and Xena, Warrior Princess, do not. No wonder then that most comic-book adaptations make no serious attempt to capture the visual qualities of their models' drawn universe. As a genre, comic-book adaptations concentrate less on visuals than on concepts like the hero's personality, the morality of his or her world, and the nature of the trademark villains who distinguish so many superhero franchises.

The adaptation that has made the most sustained attempt to date to replicate the look of any comic-book source is *Sin City* (2005). Robert Rodriguez, who conceived the film and persuaded author Frank Miller to approve it, was so intent on following Miller's visuals as well as his narrative situations and dialogue that he gave Miller sole writing credit and codirecting credit on the film, even though it meant resigning from the Directors Guild of America, which had ruled that "only 'bona fide teams' could co-direct films."[32] Although Miller had designed *Sin City* specifically to resist adaptation to the screen, Rodriguez followed his action and visuals as closely as possible by using Miller's dialogue as his screenplay and taking the individual panels of the three comic-book stories he had chosen to adapt—"Sin City," "The Big Fat Kill," and "That Yellow Bastard"—as his storyboards. Jody Duncan reports that "Miller . . . was more inclined than Rodriguez to suggest deviations from his original work. 'I didn't want to change anything,' Rodriguez noted, 'and I didn't want to let Frank change anything, either. During the shoot, he'd occasionally come up to me and say, "Why don't we try a black silhouette shot here?" And I'd say: "Look what you did in the book, Frank. It's a white silhouette. I think we should do that."'"[33] The result—fidelity as fetish—parallels with amusing precision Gus Van Sant's equally fetishistic refusal to let screenwriter Joseph Stefano improve his literal 1998 remake of Alfred Hitchcock's *Psycho* (1960). Stefano recalled that Van Sant dismissed his suggestion for sharpening the film's notoriously talky final scene by showing the psychiatrist conversing directly with Mrs. Bates with the remark that "it was a shame we didn't do it that way the first time."[34]

Apart from his devotion to his source, sharpened by his determination to woo the author, there were several reasons Rodriguez could copy the look of Miller's comic with unprecedented fidelity. Miller's visuals did not look like other comic-book visuals. Their stylistic signature—high-contrast blacks and whites with a sparing use of deeply saturated color for talismanic objects and details, itself deeply influenced by the live-action visuals of film noir—was easier to reproduce than the visuals of *Superman* or *Dick Tracy*. Well-known actors like Mickey Rourke and Benicio del Toro were willing to submit to prosthetics that made their faces unrecognizable. And although *Sin City* was technically a live-action film, it was shot against digitized backgrounds that could be manipulated as completely as Miller's own visuals.

The film does not and could not replicate Miller's visuals precisely. Even though Rodriguez uses Miller's panels as his storyboards, there is always a world of difference between the way storyboards and the movies made from them look. Rodriguez's streaming video is constantly showing movement Miller's discontinuous tableaux can only imply. And Rodriguez ended up sacrificing visual fidelity to his source in the interests of more expressive performances. As Duncan notes: "Originally instructed to match the pure whites and blacks of Miller's drawings, Hybride—along with the two other effects vendors [each of whom produced the visuals for a different episode]—eventually introduced some tonality into the shots to soften their stark quality and to retain performance nuances in the actors' faces."[35] Even the most resolute attempt at fidelity to the text is compromised, as usual, by the fact that there is always more than one text to be faithful to.

The problem of remaining faithful to multiple, often competing inter-texts—some visual, some verbal, some generic, some historical and cultural—is displayed in greater complexity in Peter Webber's 2003 film adaptation of Tracy Chevalier's novel *Girl with a Pearl Earring*. Although Chevalier's fictional tale of the relationship between Johannes Vermeer and the servant girl who became the subject of one of his most enigmatic paintings had been published to widespread acclaim in 1999, the film met with a decidedly more mixed reception. Reviewers repeatedly criticized Olivia Hetreed's screenplay as laborious and slow—several of them agreed with Phil Hall that it was "as exciting as watching paint dry"[36]—even as they praised Dien Van Straalen's costumes, Christina Schaffer's art direction, and Eduardo Serra's cinematography, all of which were nominated for Academy Awards.

Why were reviewers so much harsher toward the film than toward Chevalier's novel, despite the obvious visual strengths it added to the novel? It would be tempting to assume that film reviewers are simply philistines who demand constant melodramatic action or that the film made Vermeer's images too accessible and determinate. The real reason, however, is that the film unavoidably reveals problematic contradictions among its many sources that the novel is more successful at concealing. In attempting to specify a visual track for a novel whose images had all been evoked by words, the film runs into problems faced by many another adaptation of apparently cinematic novels by Ernest Hemingway, Dashiell Hammett, and James M. Cain that turn out to be surprisingly hard to film.[37] Adaptations like *Who Framed Roger Rabbit* address the formidable challenges involved in bringing an allegedly cinematic novel to the screen with a resourcefulness and a playful energy that makes the problems seem well worth solving. The value of *Girl with a Pearl Earring*, by contrast, is to show how intractable such problems can be.

Webber's film is a visual adaptation of a special kind. Its ostensible source text, Chevalier's novel, is purely verbal except for the reproduction of details of two Vermeer paintings, *Girl with a Pearl Earring* and *View of Delft*, on its hardcover book jacket and its paperback cover. Yet the novel itself, an attempt to provide a fictional backstory to an actual painting, depends in turn on visual sources—not only the title painting but nine other paintings that Griet, the servant girl who narrates the story, describes, almost always without naming them.[38] In attempting to explain how Vermeer's servant girl came to collaborate actively in one of his best-loved paintings, Chevalier attempts to be faithful to both the paintings and the few known facts of the painter's life. But she assumes other imperatives as well.

When her father asks her to describe the story behind Vermeer's latest picture, *Woman with a Water Jug*, Griet replies that "his paintings don't tell stories" (91). Chevalier's premise, however, is that every picture does indeed tell a story of a very particular sort. Her novel, an unconsummated love story between the painter and his subject, hearkens back to two models: the obligatory romance that must explain the creation of every great painting of a woman by a man, and the tale of passion renounced or transcended in the name of art. The novel is at once a protofeminist parable and a celebration of class mobility. Griet consistently presents herself as unusually sensitive both visually and psychologically, able to tell in a moment that Vermeer's wife, Catharina, and his daughter Cornelia both dislike her. Her sensitivity to psychological nuance foreshadows her eye for color and composition, which is consistently equal, often superior, to Vermeer's own. For his part the painter, struggling to provide for a large family headed by a wife who does not understand his work and a mother-in-law who sees only profit in it, gradually increases his demands on her. He bids her purchase his pigments, grind them, make suggestions concerning the composition and blocking of his paintings, and finally pose for the title painting. In all this behavior he shows a historically apt air of command, most obviously when he casually demands that she pierce her own ears to accept the earrings he has decided the painting demands, combined with an anachronistic respect for the gifts of a servant and a woman. This respect blossoms into a shared passion for painting that is increasingly sexualized but never sexually consummated.

Buried still deeper within Chevalier's revisionist fable of the creative power of female servants is the assumption that public expressions of aesthetic accomplishment have their roots in private experience defined by both individual psychology and socioeconomic forces. According to Chevalier's narrative, *Girl with a Pearl Earring*, which seems so idealized that it is almost abstract, is very much of its time and place, a bustling Dutch provincial center in 1666. Griet and Vermeer are implicated in a conventional domestic melodrama that requires the artist to create art within the matrix of his family's contradictory demands for paternal authority, parental nurturing, and economic support. But they are also implicated more specifically in an economic system that values them only for their work but emphasizes their unequal power by sharply limiting a female servant's presumed work to the most demeaning and least expressive tasks of cleaning, running errands, and (although Griet narrowly escapes this demand) forced sex at the pleasure of wealthy patrons. The novel therefore invokes several generic models: period realism, period romance, feminist rediscoveries of female forebears' often thwarted power, and Jamesian fables of passion renounced or transcended for art's sake. These models pull the story in several different directions. Vermeer is both prodigious and dilatory, weak and assertive, sensitive and obtuse, devoted and indifferent to his wife. Griet is at once Vermeer's servant, his muse, his victim, his double, his active collaborator, and his Cinderella. She is a typical figure of the seventeenth-century Dutch servant class who also happens to embody the most progressive attitudes of late twentieth-century feminism. None of these contradictions undermine the novel, however, because the tensions they express, especially the tension between private experience and public creation, between individual genius and active collaboration, are its subject.

Webber's film inherits all these productively contradictory models without abating any of them. In addition, it takes on several others, some of them even more contradictory. Unlike Chevalier, Webber assumes the responsibility of setting his story in a place that looks at every moment like seventeenth-century Delft. In addition, he needs to show paintings that look like real Vermeers and to indicate in some way some visual continuities between the world on Vermeer's canvas and the world he painted. But the film cannot simply show an external world that looks like a series of Vermeer paintings; to do so would be to trivialize the artistic achievements it is celebrating. Webber compromises by showing far fewer actual Vermeer paintings than Chevalier's Griet describes but lingering longer over the visual particulars of the studio in which he creates them. Not surprisingly, the film was widely praised for its success in creating the interlocking worlds of Vermeer and his paintings.

In showing how Vermeer's complex relationship with a specific young woman produced a timeless masterpiece, Webber follows Chevalier's romantic impulse in eliminating all possible artistic influences apart from that relationship. Neither the novel nor the film, for example, considers any model of influence as prosaic as Albert Blankert's suggestion that Frans van Mieris's more realistic contemporaneous portrait of a similarly posed woman may have provided a "source of inspiration" for Vermeer's more idealized portrait, which "only indicates the rhythmic beautiful contour of the face, and keeps detail to a minimum."[39] Although Webber is at pains to limn the gradual stages in the development of Vermeer's growing intimacy with his maid, the film never shows the celebrated painting itself under development. There are very few shots of Vermeer actually painting and none of his works-in-progress. Despite its rich visual texture, the film throws away what viewers might have taken as its promise to show the visual growth of its title painting more explicitly and comprehensively than Chevalier's novel does. The film's Vermeer comes across as just as contradictory as the masterpiece over which he slaves unseen, since he is both deeply implicated in the demands of his family and the mercantile economy of Delft and apparently immune from any influence by the paintings with which he has surrounded himself, or indeed any artistic impetus beyond his muse of the moment.

In addition to exposing these contradictions more fully than the novel, the film is implicated in several discourses that are not nearly so exigent in the novel. Its situation within the genre of biopic romance demands that the relationship between Vermeer and Griet be consummated or at least acknowledged as such. Yet its high-art tone undermines this promise in the name of artistic and emotional transcendence, and its painstaking period settings require Griet to withdraw from the relationship in the name of realism. Hence the adaptation cuts Chevalier's epilogue, which shows Griet, married ten years later to Pieter the butcher, inheriting the pearl earrings on the painter's death and pawning them instead of wearing them, because even though viewers can predict that Griet will end up with her persistent working-class swain, showing them together at the end would unacceptably dampen the matter-of-fact yet romantically noble renunciation with which the film concludes. By omitting this epilogue, however, the film is unfaithful to still another text, Chevalier's novel, one more model that exerts a pressure on the adaptation that it never exerts on itself.

Finally, Webber's film, like all fictional films, is a performance text that requires the copresence not only of the historical Vermeer and the fictional Vermeer, as Chevalier's novel does, but of the actor who plays Vermeer. Scarlett Johansson drew high praise for her performance as Griet. Reviewers spoke so warmly of her expressive stillness that none of them seemed to miss the narrator of the novel, who was always explaining things Johansson's Griet had to pass over in silence. The consensual view was that Johansson's quietly smoldering intensity made a virtue of the film's challenge to make Griet strong, sympathetic, and complex even though she rarely spoke.

Reviewers gave decidedly more mixed notices to Colin Firth's Vermeer. Jay Antani suggests in the *L.A. Alternative Weekly* that "Webber's movie never quite overcomes the well-trodden trope and cliché, leaving two wonderful actors, Colin Firth and Tom Wilkinson, in desperately shallow waters. As Vermeer . . . Firth is just another taciturn, brooding artist."[40] James Christopher aptly encapsulates reviewers' ambivalence toward the performance when he writes in the *Times* (London) that "Firth smoulders like a damp rag."[41] A good deal of this sentiment seems to be impatience with the unheroic painter, who makes mounting demands on Griet without ever treating her as an equal or giving her the support she craves to stand up to his more powerful wife and mother-in-law. The character is faithfully copied from Chevalier, but in the novel there was no one to blame for his moral failings but the painter and the absent novelist. The film, by contrast, provides two ready scapegoats: Firth, who could have created a stronger character, and Webber, who could have directed him to give a more appealing performance. Criticisms of Firth, however, overlook the ways in which both his character and his performance are riven by unavoidable contradictions. Chevalier's Vermeer is a cowardly, sensitive visionary. To this contradiction the film adds the casting of Firth, the closest the genre of literary adaptation has yet come to a matinee idol, as the world's least demonstrative romantic lead, a hero whose genius is meant to anchor the story but who seems, apart from his work, not worth caring about.

The myriad problems that arise in Webber's film show that it is not a visualization of a verbal novel or even a streaming version of Vermeer's still paintings. And it is an illustration of Chevalier's novel only in the sense that the novel itself is an illustration of Vermeer's painting. Instead of following the customary twentieth-century procedure of providing a visual adjunct to a verbal text, Chevalier produces a text intended not to subordinate Vermeer's painting to the status of an illustrative visual but to illustrate a hypothetical set of circumstances under which it may have been created. J. Hillis Miller has noted the pun hidden in the word *illustration,* which means both visual texts attached to verbal texts and examples drawn from an earlier text that explain how that text works.[42] Chevalier's novel invents an illustrative backstory for Vermeer's masterpiece under the pretense of restoring the private history Vermeer's public work has repressed. In the same way, Webber's film invents a highly selective set of visual contexts for the novel under the pretense that Chevalier's verbal text has necessarily repressed them. Neither set of inventions is any more reducible than the problems implicit in adapting *Alice in Wonderland* or *How the Grinch Stole Christmas!* or *Sin City* to an attempt to copy visual images from one medium to another, or to make still pictures stream.

# CHAPTER NINE

# The Hero with a Hundred Faces

Sherlock Holmes is not the fictional character who has been played by the largest number of performers in film adaptations. That honor goes to Count Dracula, played to date by 121 actors, followed by Tarzan at 108, and Franken-stein's monster at 102. Holmes lags comparatively far behind. The Internet Movie Database lists seventy-six movie Holmeses, though it omits such early Holmeses as Maurice Costello (1905), Holger Rasmussen (1911), Georges Tré-ville (1912), H. A. Saintsbury (1916), Hugo Flink (1917–18), Ferdinand Bonn (1918), Kurt Brenkendorff (1919), and the unknown performer who first brought the great detective to flickering life in *Sherlock Holmes Baffled* (1903). Even though his film incarnations are outnumbered by those of Dracula, Tarzan, and Frankenstein's monster, however, Holmes represents a fictional franchise that poses such unusual problems for adaptation study that he de-serves special attention.

The Holmes franchise shares several of these problems with the Dracula, Tarzan, and Frankenstein franchises. All four cases are organized around larger-than-life figures whose mythopoetic appeal is iconic rather than psy-chological. If Holmes is a more complex character than Tarzan or perhaps

Dracula, he is surely simpler than Frankenstein's monster. All four span several media, so that their many film adaptations represent only a fraction of the number of adaptations on stage, radio, and television.[1] And all four draw their iconography not merely from their literary originals but from a mixture of visual texts, from illustrations to earlier film and television versions. Indeed, this mixture is so rich that, as André Bazin has said of *The Three Musketeers* and *Les Misérables,* their heroes "enjoy in some measure an autonomous existence of which the original works are no longer anything more than an accidental and almost superfluous manifestation."[2] All four are therefore hybrid adaptations that depart from their putative originals at any number of points, often choosing instead to remain faithful to unauthorized later versions. To take the most obvious example, Mary Shelley's novel relegates the night when Frankenstein brings his monstrous creation to life to a brief paragraph of summary, but every film adaptation follows the early theatrical adaptations of Richard Brinsley Peake and Henry M. Milner in transforming this episode into a pivotal scene.[3]

Sherlock Holmes's movie life is similarly complicated by the need to pick and choose which progenitor texts to follow, which to modify, and which to ignore. Everyone knows that Holmes is tall and lean, with piercing eyes and a hawklike nose, because that is the way his friend and amanuensis, Dr. John H. Watson, describes him in *A Study in Scarlet,* the first of the four short novels and fifty-six short stories in which Arthur Conan Doyle introduced him to the world. But the iconic image of Holmes in deerstalker and inverness cape, a calabash clutched in his lips, owes little to Conan Doyle, who never mentions either the cape or the deerstalker by name—the closest references to the latter are to a "close-fitting cloth cap" in "The Boscombe Valley Mystery" (1:103) and an "ear-flapped traveling cap" in "Silver Blaze" (1:388)—and describes Holmes as variously smoking a briar-root pipe, a cherrywood pipe, a black clay pipe, and a metal opium pipe but never a calabash.[4] Movie audiences know that Watson wears a mustache and Holmes is clean-shaven, but they do not know this because Conan Doyle ever says so.

The unforgettable iconography of Holmes is drawn largely from his illustrators and, indeed, from a small selection of them. Holmes's first illustrators, D. H. Friston, Charles Kerr, George Hutchinson, and William H. Hyde, are much less influential in establishing his look than Sidney Paget, whose 356 drawings for the periodical publication of *The Adventures of Sherlock Holmes* (1891–92), *Memoirs of Sherlock Holmes* (1892–93), *The Hound of the Baskervilles* (1901), and *The Return of Sherlock Holmes* (1903–4) began with the publication of "A Scandal in Bohemia," the first of Holmes's shorter adventures, in the *Strand Magazine* in July 1891; and Frederic Dorr Steele, who provided illustrations for the magazine publications of the stories in *The Return of Sherlock Holmes, His Last Bow* (1908–17), and *The Case-Book of Sherlock Holmes* (1921–27). It was Paget who rejected Doyle's description of Holmes's "thin razor-like face [with] a great hawk's bill of a nose, and two small eyes, set close together," in favor of the striking good looks of his model, Paget's brother Walter, to make Holmes a good deal more handsome. And it was Paget who first gave Holmes a deerstalker, the artist's own favorite hat.[5]

Further details, like Holmes's calabash and the signature dialogue line "Elementary, my dear Watson," are added by William Gillette, the American actor and director whose play *Sherlock Holmes* (1899) provided him the opportunity to play the detective in more than thirteen hundred performances. In his essay "Sherlock Holmes in Pictures" Steele acknowledges basing his drawings on Gillette: "I did not need to be told to make my Sherlock look like Gillette. The thing was inevitable."[6] Yet Steele, like Paget, retained the clay pipe described by Doyle, never the curved pipe that entered his iconography because Gillette, finding it impossible to deliver his lines with a straight pipe between his teeth, "adopted a curved pipe that he could clamp between his teeth and still be understood."[7] The calabash was duly copied in the series of forty-five short films and two features for Stoll (1920–23) starring Eille Norwood and took root for good in the series of fourteen features Basil Rathbone made for 20th Century–Fox and Universal (1939–46).[8] Gillette's most unexpected influence was on Doyle himself, for Holmes's chronicler borrowed the character of Billy, the Baker Street page Gillette had invented for his play, for two of his own dramatizations of Sherlock Holmes and retained him in *The Valley of Fear* (1915), "The Adventure of the Mazarin Stone" (1921), and "The Problem of Thor Bridge" (1922). This act of back-formation insured canonical status for Billy.[9]

To make a distinction between more and less canonical illustrators and adapters of Holmes touches on the most distinctive feature of the Holmes franchise: its status as a literary canon that has produced not only many film, radio, and television adaptations and a wealth of variously canonical illustrations but a torrent of imitators in its original medium. In purely literary terms, Holmes has enjoyed the most vigorous afterlife of any fictional character. In this regard he is less like Dracula or Tarzan or Frankenstein's monster than like James Bond, who returned to life following his creator Ian Fleming's death in a series of pastiches written by Kingsley Amis, John Gardner, and others.

Bond's robust literary afterlife pales beside the staggering number and variety of Holmes's unauthorized adventures. Even before Doyle's death in 1930, August Derleth had begun a series of stories about the Holmes-inspired Solar Pons that eventually outnumbered Doyle's own. *The Exploits of Sherlock Holmes* (1954) presents a dozen adventures written by Doyle's son Adrian Conan Doyle, half of them coauthored by John Dickson Carr. Holmes has met Jack the Ripper in London, the Phantom of the Opera in Paris, Sigmund Freud in Vienna, and the Wizard of Oz. His clients have included Lewis Carroll, Enrico Caruso, and Oscar Wilde. He has solved the mysteries of Edwin Drood (courtesy of Edmund Pearson) and Little Red Riding Hood (courtesy of Anthony Boucher), and Manly Wade Wellman has shown him repelling a Martian invasion. His love life, expressly denied in "A Scandal in Bohemia," has been explored by Sena Jeter Naslund in *Sherlock in Love* and by Laurie R. King in a series of pastiches beginning with *The Beekeeper's Apprentice.* He has been cryogenically frozen and defrosted, presented as incompetent, and unmasked as a traveling violinist, a British agent, and a woman. In recent years the appetite for new permutations of Holmes has only grown. *The New Adventures of Sherlock Holmes*, edited by Martin H. Greenberg, Jon L. Lellenberg, and Carol-Lynn Rossel Waugh, has sold more than one hundred thousand copies since its publication in 1987, and the anthology *Holmes for the Holidays* (1996), which in pairing Holmes with Yuletide might have seemed rather specialized in its appeal, sold well enough to spin off a sequel, *More Holmes for the Holidays* (1999).

Nor is it Holmes alone who has enjoyed such a hardy afterlife. Scotland Yard's Inspector Lestrade, invariably bested by Holmes in the canon, solves twelve mysteries, usually at Holmes's expense, in a series of novels by M. J. Trow. Irene Adler, whom Holmes describes as "*the* woman" (5), returns triumphantly in eight novels by Carole Nelson Douglas, from *Good Night, Mr. Holmes* (1990) to *Spider Dance* (2004). Holmes's brother Mycroft, briefly identified as doing intelligence work for the Crown in "The Adventure of the Bruce-Partington Plans," deals with continental intrigue in a series of novels by Quinn Fawcett. Gerard Williams has given Dr. James Mortimer, the physician who set Holmes against the Hound of the Baskervilles, two cases of his own.[10] Even Mrs. Hudson, the housekeeper at 221-B Baker Street, has solved a pair of book-length mysteries by Martin Davies.[11] Short-story pastiches of Holmes have starred nearly every continuing character Watson ever mentions, from Wiggins, the street urchin who leads the Baker Street Irregulars, to Billy, the pageboy introduced by Gillette.[12] Holmes's pastiches have been chronicled not only from the point of view of nearly every eligible character mentioned in his adventures but in the voices of Thorne Smith, H. P. Lovecraft, Theodore Dreiser, P. G. Wodehouse, Dashiell Hammett, and Mickey Spillane.[13]

The vast corpus of Holmes's noncanonical adventures has several peculiar features. Almost from the moment of Holmes's first popular success in the pages of the *Strand,* he was widely parodied by such diverse writers as Bret Harte, Mark Twain, O. Henry, and Doyle himself (in "How Watson Learned the Trick" [1924]), and the parodies have continued apace. The great detective has been satirized in print and onscreen as Padlock Bones, Jawlock Jones, Holmlock Shears, Shamrock Jolnes, Picklock Holes, Sherlock Boob, Sherlock Pimple, and Sherlockz Holmz, this last opposed by the nefarious Professor Moratorium.[14] Holmes is remarkable not only for the number of parodies he has inspired (on this score he leaves Dracula, Tarzan, and the Frankenstein monster in the dust) but for the unusually thin line between parodies and pastiches of the great detective.

The frequent difficulty in distinguishing between imitation and parody extends to the franchise's most distinctive feature: the vast array of Sherlockian pseudoscholarship that has grown around the canon. In *Sir Arthur Conan Doyle,* a 1927 Fox Movietone interview, Doyle professed his bemusement that so many correspondents had treated Sherlock Holmes as if he were a real person: "I get letters addressed to him. I get letters asking for his autograph. I get letters addressed to his rather stupid friend, Watson. I've even had ladies writing to say that they'd be very glad to act as his housekeeper."[15] In this regard Holmes is less like Dracula, Tarzan, or Frankenstein's monster than like King Arthur and Robin Hood, with one important difference. Scholars may disagree about whether and to what extent Arthur or Robin of Locksley is based on some historical person. Everyone agrees that Holmes is based on a real person—Dr. Joseph Bell, one of the young Doyle's teachers at the University of Edinburgh—and most readers are well aware that he is a fictional character. But a large number of readers pretend to believe that Holmes is as real as Joseph Bell even though they know perfectly well that he is not.

This disavowal of Holmes's fictional status goes well beyond the willing suspension of disbelief that Coleridge equated with poetic faith. Even 150 years after the presumed date of his birth, Holmes continues to receive mail at 221-B Baker Street, an address that did not exist when he is supposed to have lived there but was created a century later as a tourist attraction. A global network of fans thrives under the umbrella of the Baker Street Irregulars, beginning in the 1930s as a drinking club in which bets testing members' knowledge of Holmes were settled by consulting the Sacred Writings, as the Irregulars called them, with the loser buying the next round. Leslie S. Klinger's monumental *New Annotated Sherlock Holmes* lists some three hundred active Holmes societies around the world. Much of the work of these societies is devoted to debating apparent inconsistencies within the canon (for example, the location of Watson's war wound, described in *A Study in Scarlet* as his shoulder and in *The Sign of the Four* as his leg, or the first name of Professor Moriarty and his brother, both given as James in "The Final Problem"), which are invariably treated not as slips by Conan Doyle but as invitations to ingenious scholarly exegeses, many of them published in periodicals like *The Baker Street Journal* and *The Sherlock Holmes Journal.* Throughout his extensive commentary on the stories, Klinger himself, like his predecessor William S. Baring-Gould, "perpetuate[s] the gentle fiction that Holmes and Watson really lived and that (except as noted) Dr. John H. Watson wrote the stories about Sherlock Holmes, even though he graciously allowed them to be published under the byline of his colleague and literary agent Sir Arthur Conan Doyle."[16]

When fans reinvent themselves as scholars not by praising the Holmes canon in aesthetic terms or analyzing its presentational strategies but by proceeding as if its every sentence were literally true and applying themselves to resolving the resulting problems, many of their researches will naturally take the form of hypothetical narratives. Innumerable commentators have speculated about the so-called Great Hiatus between Holmes's apparent death in 1891 at the hands of Professor Moriarty at Reichenbach Falls and his stunning return three years later or have attempted to reconcile Dr. Watson's tantalizing hints about his several marriages.[17] The result is a uniquely seamless blend of critical commentary, mock-exegesis, hypothetical or supplemental adventures, pastiche, and parody that has no close analogue in any other fictional franchise.[18] The blurring of generic lines was already underway by 1933, when Vincent Starrett published his influential study *The Private Life of Sherlock Holmes,* a collection of critical and biographical essays on Holmes and Conan Doyle that also included a sonnet on Holmes and a pastiche, "The Unique Hamlet."[19] And it is this rich stew of variously authored and authorized stories and commentaries, already well underway before Holmes ever came to the screen, to which all adaptations make primary reference. The Holmes adaptations, in other words, take as their primary referent not the particular story they are ostensibly adapting—*A Study in Scarlet, The Hound of the Baskervilles,* and so on—but the franchise as a whole. The prodigious extent and variety of that franchise makes the Holmes films a case study in adaptations whose precursor text is both greater and smaller than the text they explicitly identify.

Adaptations that have felt free to take the entire Holmes franchise rather than any particular adventure as a source text have generally set themselves against the wishes of the Doyle estate, whose preference for close adaptations is reflected in the 1942 contract with Universal Pictures that "called for a certain number of the Universal films to be taken directly from Conan Doyle's works."[20] But these adaptations do not ignore the ideal of fidelity; they merely displace its subject from a specific adventure to a larger or smaller text. Every Sherlockian movie, for instance, takes pains to set apart its hero by means of a series of iconic visual signatures, an especially pressing necessity in silent films in which Holmes does not sound like Holmes or parodies in which Holmes does not act like Holmes. In *The Mystery of the Leaping Fish* (1916) Douglas Fairbanks establishes his hero, Coke Ennyday, as a burlesque of Holmes by means of his smoking, his dressing gown (surprisingly more prominent in early screen depictions than the deerstalker and inverness cape), his propensity for disguise, and the comical fondness for self-injected drugs that gives the film its distinctive flavor. While he is waiting for a client in the opening scene, the intrepid detective determines his next action by spinning a dial marked "EATS/ SLEEP/SMOKE/DOPE." In *The Limejuice Mystery, or Who Spat in Grandfather's Porridge?* (1930) Herlock Sholmes, though like the rest of the cast only a puppet, is again easily identified by his violin playing, his drug use, his outrageous disguises, his deerstalker and cape, his magnifying glass, and his triumph over a row of police officers in puppet lockstep.

The replacement of the original adventure by the franchise as the material for each new adaptation means that a given film often combines elements from several Holmes stories. Gillette's 1899 play, cannily billing Doyle as coauthor, had added bits of business from *A Study in Scarlet* and "The Boscombe Valley Mystery" to a plot cobbled together from "A Scandal in Bohemia" and "The Final Problem." In the most notable film example, *Murder at the Baskervilles* (British title: *Silver Blaze* [1937]), Holmes returns to Baskerville Hall, where he is reminded by Watson that it has been "twenty years since you disposed of the

Hound of the Baskervilles." Sir Henry Baskerville plays host to Holmes and Watson, and his daughter Diana's fiancé, Jack Trevor (Arthur Macrae), replaces Fitzroy Simpson as the police suspect. Not to be limited by only two sources, *Murder at the Baskervilles,* like many other Holmes films, also introduces Professor Moriarty as the criminal mastermind behind the theft of the racehorse Silver Blaze.[21]

In addition to roaming at will among Doyle's oeuvre, Holmes adaptations often borrow from other quasi-canonical sources. Gillette's 1899 play supplies not only Holmes's calabash but his most enduring dialogue tag, "Elementary, my dear Watson," which appears nowhere in Doyle. Despite their fidelity to Doyle's physical descriptions of Holmes and Watson, the Granada television adaptations starring Jeremy Brett often depart from Doyle's descriptions of minor characters. Melas (Alkis Kritikos), in "The Greek Interpreter" (1984), for instance, is anything but "a short, stout man whose olive face and coal-black hair proclaimed his Southern origin" (1:645), nor is burly Jonas Oldacre (Jonathan Adams) in "The Norwood Builder" (1985) "a strange little ferret-like man" (2:836). But they are often surprisingly faithful to Paget's illustrations, which provide a frequent source for the blocking of noteworthy tableaux, most clearly in "The Speckled Band" (1984), whose shot of Holmes and Watson in a railway car is copied from one of the most famous of Paget's drawings, an illustration for the corresponding scene in "Silver Blaze" (1:390).

Of course, many adaptations look far outside the Holmes stories for inspiration. Apart from outright parodies, the most amusingly wide-ranging films are probably two Arthur Wontner vehicles, *The Triumph of Sherlock Holmes* (1935) and *Murder at the Baskervilles,* both of which provide Professor Moriarty with machine-gun-toting henchmen imported from contemporaneous American gangster films. These additions, invariably described as making the film unfaithful to its original, are more accurately described as an attempt to be faithful to multiple originals. In their own way the Universal films starring Rathbone and Bruce often keep greater faith with the imperatives of wartime propaganda and the visual style and narrative structure of the Universal monster films than with the Holmes franchise. So freely do the Universal films mingle their Sherlockian motifs with extracanonical elements that only the sharpest sleuths in the audience would know that *The Spider Woman* (1943), *Terror by Night* (1946), and *Dressed to Kill* (1946), all credited as "based on" or "adapted from a story by Sir Arthur Conan Doyle," take off from material introduced respectively in "The Adventure of the Devil's Foot," "The Disappearance of Lady Frances Carfax," and "The Adventure of the Six Napoleons," which Universal had already adapted more recognizably as *The Pearl of Death* (1944).

In addition to freely mixing elements from inside and outside the canon, the Holmes adaptations make a point of avoiding elements that might threaten the timelessness of Holmes's world, its resistance to anything like progression or historical development. Even though the third and fourth series of Granada adaptations, *The Case-Book of Sherlock Holmes* (1990–91) and *Memoirs of Sherlock Holmes* (1994), unobtrusively update their period setting from the Victorian to the Edwardian era, the producers depart from Doyle and follow the example of practically all other adaptations in keeping Watson single so that he can remain at Holmes's disposal indefinitely. The 2001 Muse adaptation with Matt Frewer marries Mary Morstan (Sophie Lorain) to her benefactor Thaddeus Sholto (Marcel Jeannin). The 1987 Granada adaptation teases viewers with the possibility that Watson (Edward Hardwicke) will propose but ends instead with him watching Mary (Jenny Seagrove) pensively on the street below and repeating for the last time his refrain, "What a very attractive woman." Out of all the adaptations of *The Sign of the Four,* only the 1934 version with Arthur Wontner allows Watson (Ian Hunter) to propose to Mary (Isla Bevan).[22] More surprisingly, the historic first meeting between Holmes and Watson, which Doyle makes into such a memorable scene in *A Study in Scarlet,* is dramatized in only two adaptations: "The Case of the Cunningham Heritage," the pilot episode of the 1954–55 television series *Sherlock Holmes,* produced by Sheldon Reynolds; and *Young Sherlock Holmes* (1985), in which Holmes (Nicholas Rowe) and Watson (Alan Cox) first meet as schoolboys in a scene whose obvious playful echoes of Doyle make his own original scene, in which they do not yet know each other as adults, logically inconsistent.

Most unusual of all is the presence of borrowings from Conan Doyle in adaptations that do not acknowledge them. Although only one of the Sheldon Reynolds television episodes, "The Red-Headed League," is explicitly based on a canonical source, "The Case of the Night Train Riddle" borrows much of its plot from "The Adventure of the Priory School." "The Case of the Shoeless Engineer" is a generally close adaptation of "The Adventure of the Engineer's Thumb," which provides not only the first half of its story but the names of two its principal characters, Victor Hatherley (David Oxley) and Colonel Lysander Stark (Richard Warner). And "The Case of the Pennsylvania Gun" devotes its twenty-five minutes to a remarkably efficient compression of the first half of *The Valley of Fear,* a source that also provides the central mystery in Terence

Fisher's otherwise original German film *Sherlock Holmes und das Halsband des Todes* (*Sherlock Holmes and the Deadly Necklace* [1962]).

This freedom with which adaptations treat the Holmes canon raises obvious questions about the relations between authorship and authority. Every adaptation wants to claim the authority of Sherlock Holmes, even if it ridicules that authority. But they often disagree with each other, and sometimes with themselves, in aligning that authority with Doyle's authorship, generally focusing instead, like biblical adaptations, on either some microtext (the figures of Holmes and Watson, who are assumed to be malleable within certain limits) or some macrotext (the franchise as an enterprise larger than Doyle). The result is an attitude Laura Miller has recently described: "The world is full of frivolous things people insist on taking very seriously (like fashion and professional sports), but Sherlock Holmes is not one of them. It may be a labored game to pretend to believe in him, but it will always be a game. He is constructed out of the stuff and spirit of pure play."[23] Holmes's movie career, like the mountains of print commentary his adventures have spawned, indicates more clearly than any other multimedia franchise the special character of that play.

Pace Miller, there are times that Sherlockian play is thoroughly pragmatic and indeed serious. Why is it that Sherlock Holmes, out of all the fictional characters ever created, should have enjoyed such a sumptuous afterlife in print and other media? The answer most often given—he and his world are figures of pure wish-fulfillment, the expression of an unquenchable longing for a world that was already disappearing as Conan Doyle wrote—is both clearly correct and clearly inadequate. Why should Holmes and not other impossible heroes such as Superman or James Bond or Tarzan or Frankenstein's monster assume an aura of historical actuality that allowed him to survive the death of his author, spin off half a dozen fictional series starring his supporting characters, spawn hundreds of fan clubs in every corner of the globe, and provoke reams of commentary seeking to reconcile apparent factual inconsistencies in his adventures? What makes the figure of Holmes not only distinctive but unique?

Surely the feature that most clearly distinguishes Holmes from other heroes of fantasy is that unlike them, he literally died and was reborn. Holmes's fans know that Conan Doyle, chafed by his hero's popularity and eager to devote himself more fully to historical romance, sent him to his death, locked in the arms of Professor Moriarty, in "The Final Problem," the concluding story in *Memoirs of Sherlock Holmes*. For nearly seven years Doyle, besieged by requests for more stories about his most enduring fictional creation, stoutly resisted, and it was not until *The Hound of the Baskervilles,* originally conceived as an independent tale of horror, that "the structure . . . required some powerful protagonist on the 'good' side worthy of its 'evil' opponent; and so he decided to resurrect Sherlock Holmes."[24]

"Resurrect" is accurate here in only a limited sense, however, because the events of the story seem to take place in 1889, two years before Holmes's recorded death.[25] The most remarkable feature of Holmes's resurrection is that his audience was not satisfied with more posthumous fictional adventures of the hero. Instead of what looked like a posthumous reminiscence by Watson (the story was serialized in the *Strand* under the subtitle "Another Adventure of Sherlock Holmes," and the last of its fifteen chapters titled "A Retrospection"), they demanded the specific assurance that Holmes had not died. From a very early point in Holmes's reception he seems to have crossed a boundary in the popular imagination between fiction and history.

This boundary was smudged even further by the October 1903 publication of "The Adventure of the Empty House," which informed a stupefied Watson, along with hordes of avid readers, that Holmes had never died in Reichenbach at all. Though he had indeed sent Moriarty to his death, he had only pretended his own in order to remain at large to pursue his efforts against the evil professor's criminal organization at the cost of keeping his old friend in the dark for the three years before his return in 1894. Holmes's death and resurrection have no obvious precedent or parallel in fiction. It is as if Shakespeare revealed in *The Winter's Tale* not that Perdita, conceived specifically as a character to be rescued from apparently certain death, but Ophelia or Desdemona, long assumed by their author as well as their audience to be dead and buried, were still alive and had been alive all along. The closest parallel is movie monsters like Michael Myers or Freddy Krueger, who are repeatedly but ineffectually dispatched by the heroes so that their deaths become rituals that do nothing to defuse their threat. The grandfather of these monsters, Holmes's contemporary Count Dracula, is something of an anti-Holmes, an eternally undead monster who threatens to turn innocents into his undead accomplices as well. If Dracula is associated with ageless superstition, animism, and mortality, Holmes offers the reassuring, albeit improbable, promise that scientific rationalism can defeat the forces of violence, mystery, and death itself.

It is a pardonable exaggeration to suggest, as Samuel Rosenberg does, that Holmes's return from the grave constitutes "a serio-comic travesty of the Death and Resurrection of Jesus."[26] Holmes's resurrection may not give him the gravitas of the dying and reborn god, the hero with a thousand faces, whose modern task, according to Joseph Campbell, is to plumb the mystery of humankind, "that alien presence with whom the forces of egoism must come to terms, through whom the ego is to be crucified and resurrected, and in whose image society is to be reformed."[27] But it does give him at least three kinds of special privilege. It makes him a hero with a hundred faces whose resilience is such that he can be impersonated by dozens of actors who resemble each other in nothing but their ability to play Sherlock Holmes—actors who found themselves to their frequent chagrin confused with the character they played.[28] It ensures that he will never die, for a hero once risen from the grave has surely established that he is impervious to any new threat, especially if he can be incarnated anew by performers of every generation. Finally, it makes this most secular of mythopoetic figures endlessly adaptable in the specific sense that he is endlessly available for use. And that is what adaptations of Holmes do: use him and his franchise in ways that, for all their various pretenses of fidelity, are often remote from the purposes of Conan Doyle.

Not that Doyle's purposes were consistent. He expressed his indifference to Sherlockian adaptations as early as 1899, when he told William Gillette, who had inquired whether he could rework Doyle's own five-act play in order to end it with Holmes's marriage, "You may marry him or murder him or do anything you like with him."[29] At least one early modernization, *The Copper Beeches* (1921), announced in its opening credits that it was "produced under the personal supervision of Sir Arthur Conan Doyle." Yet Doyle was opposed to the electric lights and automobiles in the Stoll films starring Eille Norwood.[30] Upon Doyle's death in 1930 the administrators of his estate, whose control shifted many times over the years, became both more activist and less consistent in their attempts to control the content of the franchise. Richard Valley reports that the estate's "disapprov[al] of Fox's handling of the canon" in the extremely free adaptation *The Adventures of Sherlock Holmes*, which borrows the title of a volume of twelve short stories for an adventure based on none of them, "led to Fox dropping the series."[31] Yet the films that followed at Universal were even freer. The aesthetic criterion of fidelity to the original author, already problematic during Doyle's life, was replaced soon after by a pragmatic criterion of utility.

The Universal adaptations, starring Basil Rathbone as Holmes and Nigel

Bruce as Watson, are stellar examples of adapting a franchise in order to put it to new use—in this case, by bringing Holmes and Watson back to life once more. Years after his retirement from professional life to keep bees in Sussex, years after even his presumed death (the best evidence indicates that Holmes was born in 1854, and "His Last Bow," the latest case recorded by Doyle, can be dated to 1914), he miraculously joined Tarzan, Abbott and Costello, and the Invisible Man to fight the Axis Powers in World War II. In a series of twelve films that Universal released between 1942 and 1946 Holmes and Watson assumed modern dress to battle enemy agents, master criminals, and continuing evil in a distinctly contemporary world.

Even among fictional characters volunteering on behalf of the Allies, Holmes's case is special. Unlike Captain America, he was not created specifically to fight the war; unlike that of Superman, Tarzan, or Abbott and Costello, Holmes's wartime service was not simply a continuation of his variously eccentric peacetime life. Holmes had been created sixty years earlier as a detective, not a warrior. Entering him in the lists against the Axis required both his resurrection and his retooling—a series of guarantees that he was fit to serve in the greatest generation, despite being a fictional character some ninety years old.

Holmes's quasi-historical reality might have seemed to pose a second stumbling block to his resurrection. How could Universal bring back a hero so firmly pegged to a long-past historical period? The studio's job was made easier partly by the long-running convention of updating Holmes for the movies. Of all Holmes's scores of screen appearances before 1942, only two, the Fox films starring Rathbone and Bruce, had been period pieces. It was only natural for Universal to ignore what must have looked like Fox's temporary detour back to the nineteenth century and return Holmes to the twentieth, where movie audiences had been watching him for years.

Still more fundamental was the fact that resurrection was nothing new in Holmes's career. An immortal hero offered such obvious advantages in the fight against the Nazis that Universal would no doubt have been willing to waive Holmes's lack of war service. But in fact Holmes had served in World War I, briefly but with distinction. When Conan Doyle had visited the Argonne front in June 1916, its director, General Georges-Louis Humbert, asked him, "*Sherlock Holmes, est ce qu'il est un soldat dans l'armée anglaise?*" Doyle reported in *A Visit to Three Fronts* that "the whole table waited in an awful hush. '*Mais, mon général,'* I stammered, *'il est trop vieux pour service.'* "[32] Nonetheless, Doyle sent Holmes and Watson into the field against the German agent Von Bork a year later in "His Last Bow."

It is not surprising that Holmes was suited for counterespionage, for he had already retrieved vital government documents in "The Naval Treaty" (1893), "The Adventure of the Second Stain" (1904), and "The Adventure of the Bruce-Partington Plans" (1908). What is more surprising is that Universal, in returning Holmes to wartime service, did not draw on any of these tales of international intrigue. Although the credits for the first of the Universal films, *Sherlock Holmes and the Voice of Terror,* give "His Last Bow" as its source, the film retains only three elements from the story: the wartime milieu (though that of a different war this time); Holmes's prophetic final speeches about an east wind coming, which are taken almost verbatim from the story; and the name Von Bork for the spy Holmes unmasks. Not only Holmes but his plots must be retooled to fight the Axis.

The executives at Universal were clearly aware that Holmes was a problematic wartime hero, for the opening scene of *Sherlock Holmes and the Voice of Terror* takes his fitness as its central issue. When Sir Evan Barham (Reginald Denny) suggests to the other members of the Intelligence Inner Council, under heavy public pressure to stop the faceless saboteur whose radio broadcasts herald terroristic attacks, that their best hope may be Sherlock Holmes, Sir Alfred Lloyd (Henry Daniell) argues, "This isn't a case for a private detective! This is a problem of state!" and Admiral Prentiss (Olaf Hytton) adds, "What's happened within these walls has always been secret. We don't want any outsiders here." Sir Evan's reply—"In this emergency, we should take advantage of everyone's peculiar gifts. Mr. Holmes is the most subtle and extraordinary private investigator of our time"—finesses Holmes's biggest problem, that he's really the most subtle and extraordinary private investigator of a time long past, by displacing it onto the readily resolvable problems of Holmes's status as a private detective and private citizen. When Holmes and Watson arrive, Sir Evan turns what ought to be their impossibly advanced age into a joke by telling Watson, "Bowser, you've put on a little weight since you left school," provoking the response, "You don't look any younger yourself, Dimples."

Sir Evan's defense of Holmes's suitability and, even more important, his timeliness is amplified by an opening title addressed to the movie audience: "Sherlock Holmes, the immortal character of fiction created by Sir Arthur Conan Doyle, is ageless, invincible and unchanging. In solving significant problems of the present day, he remains—as ever—the supreme master of deductive reasoning." All three of Holmes's Universal war adventures finesse his updating and his sudden exigent historical actuality in other ways as well. *Sherlock Holmes in Washington* displaces his temporal dislocation from the 1890s to the 1940s onto a dislocation in space, packing him off to the United States, where Watson can attempt to master American slang ("What's cooking?" he asks at one point), try his first milkshake, and encounter such comic-strip heroes as Flash Gordon ("Seems a very capable fellow," says Watson judiciously). This spatial dislocation is just as jarring as Holmes's temporal dislocation, but it disarms any criticism of implausibility by providing a constant stream of jokes. *Sherlock Holmes and the Secret Weapon* joins the other two, and indeed the two Holmes films Rathbone had made for 20th Century–Fox, by giving him frequent opportunities for disguise, further displacing his transformation by allowing him to change from an eccentric art collector or a Swiss bookseller-cum-Axis spy back to a Holmes that seems by contrast doubly authentic.

This authentic Holmes is modernized in ways that allow him to retain subtle tokens of both his nineteenth-century roots and his universalism. The opening credits of all the Universal Holmes films begin with a tilt up from Holmes and Watson's legs to show them standing in the fog in coats and hats that are neither clearly period wear nor clearly modern. The opening of *Sherlock Holmes and the Voice of Terror* shows its World War II atrocities in long shots with the title character's hectoring radio voice-over, making it impossible to see what the victims are wearing or hear how they are speaking, and then presents the Inner Council in formal wear and military uniforms that are impossible to date precisely. *Sherlock Holmes in Washington*, beginning with the same title card describing Holmes as "ageless, invincible and unchanging," adopts a more obviously contemporary setting in its airfield opening. There follows a more crucial seriocomic Washington-bound train sequence, whose echoes of *The Lady Vanishes* (1938) and *Night Train to Munich* (1940) place it not in contemporary wartime but in Movie Neverland. And the Swiss sequence that opens *Sherlock Holmes and the Secret Weapon* is more redolent of Alpine fairy tales than of midcentury political neutrality.

Holmes, Watson, and their milieu can be selectively modernized despite the obviously contemporary situations in which they are placed because they have the luxury of drawing on many different sources: Conan Doyle's stories, the illustrations of Paget and Steele, the Golden Age whodunits of Agatha Christie and Ellery Queen that provide an influential model for Holmes's wartime mysteries, earlier movie versions of Holmes, and movies of international intrigue that do not feature Holmes. The most obvious progenitors are the two Fox films starring Rathbone and Bruce. In many ways, however, an even more powerful influence is *Murder at the Baskervilles*, whose additions to Doyle's "Silver Blaze" expanded an intimate story about domestic crime and expected justice to the realm of international criminal conspiracy. Although the film made it clear from the beginning that Moriarty was behind the plot to steal Silver Blaze, it still preserved the mystery of who had killed John Straker, the racehorse's trainer. After that mystery was cleared up in an episode that followed Conan Doyle's story surprisingly closely, the film added a wholly new conclusion in which Watson, attempting to gather information about Moriarty's nefarious criminal organization, is captured and about to be thrown down an elevator shaft when he is rescued by Holmes and Lestrade.

Such a farrago of sources and modes might seem unrepeatable. Yet *Murder at the Baskervilles* establishes a formula the Universal films follow closely. Holmes's rare flirtations with international politics in Conan Doyle had always posed small-scale problems—typically the disappearance of some vital document—on which the fate of nations hung. Although the consequences were enormous, the scale of each adventure was intimate. In "The Adventure of the Bruce-Partington Plans" the appearance of Holmes's brother Mycroft, who evidently holds some unspecified post in the Foreign Office, insulates Holmes from the necessities of government work; in "The Adventure of the Second Stain" matters of international security turn on the domestic relations between the Right Honorable Trelawney Hope and his wife. In *Murder at the Baskervilles* the situation is reversed. Even the most small-scale crimes turn out to implicate American gangsters, international crime lords, and characters from Holmes's other adventures. In addition to making lightning deductions, Holmes is therefore required to become a fearless nemesis of crime, a good man with a revolver, and a heroic figure of decisive physical attainments—in short, an action hero to rival Flash Gordon.

This is exactly the hero of the Universal franchise. Unlike Conan Doyle's Holmes, whose proud ignorance of the fact that the earth orbited the sun made his limitations almost as notable as his accomplishments,[33] the Universal Holmes is a thinking machine who is also a master of disguise, a connoisseur of the arts who knows how to treat a lady even though he will never settle down with one, and a politically astute consultant who can survive repeated brushes with violent death. Fans who have deplored Nigel Bruce's buffoonish Watson, the most distinctive figure in the Universal films, have ignored the extent to which the paragon of Rathbone's Holmes makes such a counterweight necessary.

Holmes returns as a paragon who can do all things well and a timeless hero whose resurrection is so certain that he can now ritualistically be captured by enemies determined to put him to death, even employing, in *Sherlock Holmes and the Secret Weapon,* a sadistic method proposed by Holmes himself. His status as the beau ideal of the British stiff upper lip reaches a climax in his merging with another English hero who unites the man of thought and the man of action: Winston Churchill. Holmes sounds just like Churchill in quoting the end of "His Last Bow" at the fadeout of *Sherlock Holmes and the Voice of Terror.* He quotes *Richard II*'s Churchillian description of England at the end of *Sherlock Holmes and the Secret Weapon.* And he concludes *Sherlock Holmes in Washington* by quoting Churchill himself in praise of America. All three speeches are designed to give the fictional private detective a nonfictional public face by affirming the United States' links to the motherland and prophesying that Churchill's intellect and indomitability will triumph over world-class thugs like Hitler and Professor Moriarty.

Along with Holmes and Watson, Universal followed *Murder at the Baskervilles* in resurrecting one of the least-used features of Conan Doyle's stories: the master criminal as the image of the Third Reich. Whether he was called the Voice of Terror, Heinrich Hynkel in *Sherlock Holmes in Washington,* or Professor Moriarty in *Sherlock Holmes and the Secret Weapon,* this figure had several distinctive roots: the Nazi menace, the Universal monster films of the 1930s, and the Moriarty franchise. George Zucco, who had played Moriarty in *The Adventures of Sherlock Holmes,* was cast as Richard Stanley, né Hynkel, in *Sherlock Holmes in Washington.* And Lionel Atwill, whose iconic appearances in such Universal horror films as *Dr. X* (1932), *The Mystery of the Wax Museum* (1933), and *The Vampire Bat* (1933) had made him the most menacing Dr. Mortimer imaginable in the Fox *Hound of the Baskervilles,* reverted to type as Moriarty in *Sherlock Holmes and the Secret Weapon,* where the miraculous return of a man Holmes had thought "dead these many years" is used as a darkly comic mirror of Holmes's own, as when Moriarty sneers at the nemesis he thinks he is about to kill: "Just like old times, eh?"

Moriarty dies himself minutes after this taunt, but he duly returns, evergreen as Dracula or Holmes himself, in *The Woman in Green* (1945), one of a long line of master criminals who continue to flourish after Universal's Holmes had turned his attention from counterintelligence to ostensibly domestic mysteries with a strong flavor of international intrigue. *The Scarlet Claw* and *The House of Fear* (both 1944) add Canada and Scotland to the list of Commonwealth nations that come under Holmes's unifying protection. *The Spider Woman*, *The Scarlet Claw*, and *The Woman in Green* all identify serial killers, a new staple of the Universal franchise, as master criminals, aspiring Moriarties. *Pursuit to Algiers* (1945) and *Terror by Night* apply the plot conventions of the Golden Age whodunit—small cast of characters, intimate setting isolated from the outside world, red herrings that misleadingly implicate innocent suspects, strict observance of clues to the unknown perpetrator, double-twist endings, all conventions quite remote from Conan Doyle's stories—to tales of international intrigue, suggesting that the science of deduction can vanquish universal evil as surely as it had defeated the Third Reich.

Once Holmes had gone to war, he never truly reverted to peacetime investigations at Universal. Perhaps the most economical indication of the series' intention to claim transnational moral authority for Holmes's most private investigations, the authority he has achieved by facing down the Axis Powers, is his closing speech in *The Pearl of Death*, whose resolutely nonpolitical master criminal he describes as "no more than a symbol of the greed and cruelty of lust for power that have set men at each other's throats throughout the centuries. And the struggle will go on, Watson, for a pearl, a kingdom, perhaps even world dominion, till the greed and cruelty have burned out of every last one of us. And when that time comes, perhaps even the pearl will be washed clean again."

For many years Rathbone's Holmes, forged in Hollywood's attempt to strengthen American support for the motherland and the Allied cause, was considered definitive. At the height of Rathbone's fame in the role, however, Vincent Starrett, in his 1942 sonnet "221:B," had suggested a completely different approach to the resurrection of Holmes and Watson, "Who never lived and so can never die": a nostalgic return to "that age before the world went all awry . . . Where it is always eighteen ninety-five."[34] Although dozens of Holmeses, many in full period regalia, sprouted after Rathbone relinquished the role in 1946, it was not until forty years later that a new Holmes, his world modeled on Starrett's lines, was hailed as equally powerful: Jeremy Brett, in a series of thirty-six segments and five features Granada made for British television. Purists recoiling from Bruce's doltish Watson and the textual freedom of the Universal adaptations welcomed the new series as the most faithful of all Sherlockian adaptations. But that very fidelity, neutral as it might have seemed, indicated a program for turning Holmes to new uses through new kinds of play with the franchise.

The most striking innovation of the Granada adaptations is Brett's performance as Holmes. If Eille Norwood and Arthur Wontner had suavely underplayed the great detective and Rathbone had wrapped his steel in faultless diction, catlike grace, and unfailing courtesy, Brett played him as hectic and hectoring, a clinical case of manic-depression who frequently fell into illnesses from which only the challenge of new adventures could rouse him. Unlike Rathbone, whose keynote was iron-willed consistency in every situation, Brett showed Holmes constantly swinging between moody self-absorption and full-throated ridicule of the suspects, the police, and even his clients. Although his alarming mood swings were anything but faithful to Conan Doyle, they carried the electrifying potential to make every conversational exchange into high drama without bursting the boundaries of television. The thirteen episodes in *The Adventures of Sherlock Holmes* (1984), Brett's first season in the role, moved more quickly and surely than any other Holmes adaptations to date.

Two other casting choices raised more questions about fidelity than Brett's performance. One was Edward Hardwicke's replacement of David Burke as Watson beginning with the second series of adventures, *The Return of Sherlock Holmes* (1986–88). Despite a few telling differences between the two performers—Hardwicke radiated greater kindness and geniality than the more reserved Burke—both were convincing Watsons with strong physical similarities. The problem arose in making the transition, especially since "The Empty House," the first of Hardwicke's appearances, included a key flashback to "The Final Problem," the last of Burke's. Howard Baker, who directs the episode, takes care during the flashback to keep Watson at such a great distance that it is impossible to tell whether it is Burke or Hardwicke. Even so, the irony remains that in "The Empty House," a story that turns on Holmes's reappearance to Watson in a disguise so convincing it fools him, it is Watson, not Holmes, who is making the more miraculous return, incarnated by a new performer Holmes cannot acknowledge. Here the episode chooses fidelity to the imperatives of a continuing television series over fidelity to Doyle.

Another casting decision, however, was clearly motivated by Granada's desire for greater verisimilitude: the refusal to repeat performers in different roles in the series. Although Inspector Lestrade was always played by Colin Jeavons, Mrs. Hudson by Rosalie Williams, and Mycroft Holmes by Charles Gray, other performers were restricted to a single appearance. The obvious point of contrast is the Universal series, in which menacing figures like George Zucco, Lionel Atwill, and Henry Daniell could be freely recycled in order to infuse menace into a range of different characters. The repertory casting of the Universal films and the Sheldon Reynolds television series made their stock characters seem even more similar and their drama more ritualistic.[35] An unspoken premise of the Granada series was that every episode was a completely new adventure for its continuing hero.

An important feature that did remain the same throughout the Granada productions was the period setting. Unlike the Universal films, which had gone to considerable lengths to present Holmes as a timeless hero, the Granada episodes emphasized his period milieu from their opening images, a montage subordinating Holmes (who does not appear until the end of the sequence) and Watson (who does not appear at all) to a series of London exteriors emphasizing the excitement and exotic appeal of Victorian crime. The stories that follow are punctilious in their attention to exterior detail. Jeremy Paul, who wrote the screenplay for the feature-length *The Last Vampyre* (1992), recalled that art director Colin Pocock had insisted the title of the episode be changed from Doyle's original, "The Adventure of the Sussex Vampire," because knowledgeable viewers would recognize the village exteriors as Gloucestershire rather than Sussex.[36] Unlike earlier screen Holmeses, Brett is careful throughout the series to wear Holmes's signature deerstalker and inverness cape only in excursions to the country.[37] More generally, the individual episodes of the series stay resolutely in a given period, avoiding anachronisms like those in the Muse *Hound of the Baskervilles* (2000), in which the dialogue given the young Sir Henry (Jason London) includes such jarring lines as "Call me Henry," "Why not?" "Sure," "Like a bear," and "Shouldn't rush into anything, huh?" Victorian (later Edwardian) surfaces are a source text quite as important for the series as Conan Doyle. The first eleven episodes in *The Adventures of Sherlock Holmes* run their end credits over a series of the drawings Sidney Paget made for their particular story, emphasizing the series' roots in both classic art and literature and a historical period sanctified by distance and sentiment.

Yet all is not sentiment here. Beginning with "The Blue Carbuncle," the Granada adaptations consistently work to broaden the emotional range of their originals, presenting, for example, the dark side of Victorian Yuletide in "The Blue Carbuncle," the depth of feeling in the closing reunion of Neville St. Clair and his wife in "The Man with the Twisted Lip" (in *The Return of Sherlock*

*Holmes*), and the unresolved pathos of the title character's climactic return to life in "The Disappearance of Lady Frances Carfax" (in *The Case-Book of Sherlock Holmes*). Even as the series remains faithful to the exterior details of Holmes's world, it constantly seeks to improve Doyle's stories by making them more realistic, suspenseful, heartfelt, or mysterious.

The most immediately obvious of these improvements are the teaser prologues added to most of the first two dozen episodes. Unlike Doyle's stories, which almost invariably begin with Holmes and Watson in Baker Street, the Granada episodes typically begin with a glimpse of the malefactor at work, the discovery of a body, or a flashback or prelude that arouses expectations of more criminal behavior. This subordination of Doyle's text to the conventions of television drama is matched by the series' attempt to expand Watson's role. Since no Holmes adaptation makes more than intermittent use of Watson's first-person narrative voice, Watson is always in danger of becoming a tangential character. In *The Copper Beeches* (1921) he is indeed so minor that he is never identified as Watson. The Universal films had addressed this problem by casting Nigel Bruce and giving him a strong, if widely execrated, profile of his own. The Granada films address it by giving Watson more of the dialogue that Doyle assigns to other characters, especially Holmes, breaking Holmes's often long monologues into more dramatic dialogues even as they give Burke and Hardwicke more to do than nod silently.

The Granada films take pains to remain faithful to an even more important text than the conventions of television drama: Jeremy Brett's star persona. Brett's approach to Holmes is the opposite of Basil Rathbone's. Instead of making himself into Holmes, Brett recreates Holmes in his own image as a theatrical manic-depressive whose histrionic outbursts repeatedly sacrifice fidelity to Conan Doyle for the sake of dramatic effectiveness. Yet the series' legion of followers have agreed that these departures from Conan Doyle do not count as infidelities, even when the hero embarks on a long trajectory of psychological and physical maladies that mirror the star's own illnesses. By the time he appeared in *The Case-Book of Sherlock Holmes*, Brett was noticeably more aged and febrile. During his final season in *The Memoirs of Sherlock Holmes*, a title that seems to apply more closely to Brett than to Holmes (who had already come back from the dead to begin *The Return of Sherlock Holmes*), Brett broke down during the filming of "The Three Gables" and again after completing the prophetically apt "The Dying Detective." Accordingly, Charles Gray's Mycroft Holmes, who had already taken on the role of his brother's sidekick in "The

Golden Pince-Nez" when his commitment to *Shadowlands* (1993) prevented Edward Hardwicke from playing Watson, substituted for Holmes himself in "The Mazarin Stone." These substitutions do no more to undermine Granada's claims to fidelity than the excising of Inspector Lestrade from this final series because Colin Jeavons was unavailable. The well-being and scheduling of stars are invisible imperatives more exigent than any attempt at textual fidelity.

A more general imperative involves Granada's decision to supplement its short episodes with five feature-length films, for any series that includes both short and long films must grapple with problems of stretching and compressing. *The Hound of the Baskervilles* (1987) and *The Sign of Four* (1987) follow their short-novel-length originals more or less closely, but *The Master Blackmailer* (1991), *The Noble Bachelor* (1992), and *The Last Vampyre*, all features based on short stories, perforce add a great deal of new material. Indeed *The Last Vampyre* shelves its original's plot for one almost entirely new. The status of the short episodes would seem to be more straightforward. "The Second Stain," an episode from *The Return of Sherlock Holmes* that is line by line perhaps the most faithful of all the Granada adaptations, suggests that fifty minutes is an ideal length for adapting a Holmes short story. Thus additions and deletions at this length are not commonly dictated by the procrustean length of the episode but by some other imperative. *The Adventures'* episode "The Greek Interpreter," for instance, adds a fifteen-minute pursuit aboard a carefully Victorian train to a story without many incidents of its own. "The Final Problem," the last episode in *The Adventures*, pads its simple but powerfully affecting story by adding a prologue in which Holmes advises the administrators of the Louvre on Moriarty's theft of the Mona Lisa. "The Red-Headed League," which immediately precedes "The Final Problem" in *The Adventures*, adds Moriarty as the sinister brains behind the plan to rob the City and Suburban Bank in order to establish a narrative arc that will anticipate Moriarty's fatal return in the following episode. *The Case-Book*'s adaptation of "The Creeping Man" changes so many elements in Conan Doyle's story of a scientist's unwise experiments with monkey glands that it raises the question of why the producers, with so many candidates for adaptation, chose the story in the first place.

This question goes to the heart of the Granada adaptations' obsessive but narrow attention to fidelity. No matter how much had to be changed in the screenplay, "The Creeping Man," like "The Final Problem," must have seemed irresistible because the attractions of its particular scenes, despite its inadequate premise, are so strong. In rewriting Doyle, the adaptations are choosing fidelity to the appealing macrotext of the Victorian milieu and to a selection of powerful microtexts like the shadow of the apelike figure outside Edith Presbury's room and the tableau of Holmes and Moriarty hurtling over Reichenbach Falls (an image well represented in the inconography of Sherlockian illustrations even though it depicts an event that never happened) over fidelity to the texts Doyle wrote.

The need to be faithful to multiple and often competing texts makes the Granada adaptations highly ambivalent in their approach to cruxes in Conan Doyle. At times the episodes simply repeat Doyle's errors or inconsistencies. The snake that bites Julia Stonor and her stepfather in "The Speckled Band" episode of *The Adventures* is still identified as a swamp adder, even though there is no such snake.[38] Richard Valley notes that "Silver Blaze" "retained the several errors Conan Doyle admitted making in racing rules and regulations."[39] Sometimes the episodes sidestep these errors by strategic omissions. Instead of replicating Watson's obviously erroneous attribution of the events of "The Adventure of Wisteria Lodge" to March 1892 (2:1233), a time when Holmes was presumed dead, the corresponding episode in *The Return*, like virtually all the Granada adaptations, passes over the date in silence. In the opening of "The Crooked Man," an episode in *The Adventures*, Watson drops the inconvenient reference to his marriage (1:582), and "The Man with the Twisted Lip" avoids one of the most famous cruxes in Doyle, the moment when Mrs. Watson refers to her husband as James, by the simple expedient of omitting her from the episode.[40]

From time to time, however, the Granada episodes adopt a more activist attitude toward their sources. *The Adventures* episode "The Norwood Builder" responds to the criticism of many Sherlockians that no coroner would have mistaken charred rabbit bones for the human bones of Jonas Oldacre by inventing a sailor who can serve as an unwitting human accomplice in Oldacre's scheme to escape his creditors by having himself declared dead.[41] In *The Casebook* "Shoscombe Old Place" seeks to make its complementary tale, of death concealed rather than pretended, more palatable to contemporary viewers by omitting Doyle's identification of Sir Robert Norberton's creditors as "the Jews" (2:1715, 1731). Occasionally the adaptations even correct Doyle on factual points. "The Red-Headed League" changes the date on which the League is dissolved from October 9, 1890, to June 28, 1890.[42] Three episodes in *The Return* are equally forthright. "The Musgrave Ritual" takes sides among different editions of the story by omitting a couplet from the formula of the Ritual—"What was the month? / The sixth from the first"—that appears in the first English edition of the *Memoirs* but not in the *Strand* publication or in any American editions.[43] "Silver Blaze" cuts a notorious line of dialogue—"I stand to win a little on this next race" (1:415)—which broadly suggests that Holmes is illegally profiting from his private knowledge that the missing Silver Blaze will be running after all, though it later shows him smirking as he collects his winnings.[44] And "The Bruce-Partington Plans" corrects Doyle's failure to give chief clerk Sidney Johnson the keys to his office door, without which he would have no way to lock up after he leaves.[45]

Such an inconsistent attitude toward the source to which the Granada films are professing fidelity suggests three pivotal conclusions. First, fidelity to a franchise is impossible when the franchise is as riddled with contradictions as Doyle's corpus. Second, in the same way that much of Sherlockian commentary veers into narrative, many details in Granada's narrative adaptations cross over willy-nilly to textual or interpretive commentary. Third, and most important, the attitude the Granada adaptations take toward Doyle's text is not so much faithful as fetishistic, giving the appearance of fidelity by concentrating on certain kinds of details but neglecting, correcting, or improving others. The best example of this fetishism is the titles Granada chose for its four series of episodes: *The Adventures of Sherlock Holmes, The Return of Sherlock Holmes, The Case-Book of Sherlock Holmes,* and *The Memoirs of Sherlock Holmes.* All four of them refer to titles of Doyle's books, but not one of them actually contains all the adventures, or even nothing but adventures, from the book to which it allegedly corresponds. The Granada adaptations are determined to remain faithful to Doyle except at those points where they are determined to depart from him.

The true aspiration of the Granada adaptations is the same as that of all adaptations of any canonical fictional franchise. They do not want to be faithful to any particular members of the franchise. They do not even want to be faithful to the franchise in general. What they want is to become canonical members of the franchise themselves, as definitive as the progenitor texts they take as their point of departure. Just as M. J. Trow's novels about Inspector Lestrade or Carole Nelson Douglas's about Irene Adler make a case for these characters as unsung heroes invidiously marginalized by Conan Doyle, just as the voluminous researches of the Baker Street Irregulars concerning Watson's wives and war wounds seek to establish what Watson really meant by his apparently contradictory references, adaptations of Holmes aim to present a

Holmes more definitive than Conan Doyle's. Every aspirant is urged to this goal by the example of Basil Rathbone and Jeremy Brett, each hailed as the definitive Holmes despite their enormous differences. If there can be two definitive Holmeses, surely there can be a hundred.

The Universal adaptations pursue this goal by treating Holmes frankly as a resource to be pressed into service, a timeless hero who, once resurrected, can never die or age. The Granada adaptations pursue it through selective fidelity, presenting more dramatically compelling versions of Holmes's adventures set in an expanded universe bound by Victorian times and mores yet more rounded and emotionally comprehensive than Doyle's. The Universal films transplant the Holmes myth so that it can be deployed for a moment of supreme cultural extremity; the Granada films refurbish the myth to make it more resonant as a specifically historical myth for an audience seeking refuge in nostalgia.

Still more openly revisionist treatments of the myth seek entrance to the canon by rewriting the myth wholesale. Billy Wilder's insouciant *The Private Life of Sherlock Holmes* (1970), for example, poses as a long-hidden narrative that promises to reveal "matters of a delicate, sometimes scandalous nature." It begins with a long, structurally gratuitous prologue in which Holmes (Robert Stephens), pressed to provide stud service for a childless prima ballerina (Tamara Toumanova), demurs on the grounds that he prefers the company of men like Watson. The mystery that follows, which involves missing dwarfs, bogus Trappist monks, and a meeting between Queen Victoria and an undersea monster, shows Holmes matching wits with his brother Mycroft (Christopher Lee), getting hoodwinked by his own client (Genevieve Page), and ending his mission in failure, along with Mycroft and the client. The film seems intended as the ultimate send-up of the Holmes myth. Yet it recalls nothing so much as Conan Doyle's very first Holmes short story, "A Scandal in Bohemia." Not even Wilder's incongruous wisecracks—when a carriage pulls up outside 221-B late one evening, Watson (Colin Blakely) suggests, "Maybe Mrs. Hudson is entertaining," prompting Holmes's reply, "I have never found her so"—can puncture the fabric of the myth, which is so resilient that it softens the most resolute parody to affectionate pastiche.

Herbert Ross's *The Seven-Per-Cent Solution* (1976), based on the first of Nicholas Meyer's series of Sherlockian pastiches, is even more frankly revisionist. Beginning with the revelation that a bug-eyed Holmes (Nicol Williamson) is so deluded that he imagines himself opposed by Professor Moriarty (Sir

Laurence Olivier), his inoffensive former tutor, it packs the great detective off to Vienna so that he can be cured by Sigmund Freud (Alan Arkin). The cure, which ultimately reveals that Moriarty was the lover of Holmes's mother, is evidently so complete that by the fade-out, which finds Holmes off on a holiday with Lola Deveraux (Vanessa Redgrave), the courtesan he has rescued from white slavery, he has overcome both his persecution mania and his distrust of women. The film strikes an aggressively playful note from its opening credits, which identify Lola as "an Irish charlady's daughter. (Details of her private life can be found in *The Private Correspondence of Clemenceau*)" and gravely suggest of the abductor Lowenstein (Joel Grey) that "there is reason to believe this character is totally fictitious." Yet its goal is not to invert the Holmes myth but to explain it point by point, from Holmes's drug use to his hatred of Moriarty to his activities during the Great Hiatus (when Watson asks the departing Holmes how he should explain his absence to his legion of fans, Holmes replies ebulliently, "Tell them I was murdered by my mathematics tutor! They'll never believe you anyway"). Even as Holmes's heroic credentials are debunked, his detective methods are held up as a mirror of Freud's, though it is never entirely clear which figure influenced the other more decisively. And Williamson's outrageously stylized portrayal of Holmes, widely snubbed by reviewers as exaggerated and even insulting, has emerged over the years as the likely model for Jeremy Brett's reputedly definitive Holmes.

Just as *The Seven-Per-Cent Solution* uses Holmes to dramatize Freud's early experiments in hypnotherapy even as it provides fictional explanations for some of the detective's most famous tics, *Murder by Decree* (1979) uses Holmes to dramatize specifically contemporary anxieties about politics and the treatment of women. By following James Hill's film *A Study in Terror* and Nicholas Meyer's novel *The West End Horror* (1976) in setting Holmes against Jack the Ripper, Bob Clark's film asks the hero to solve a crime more real than he is. If the Universal films showed that Holmes could be recalled to battle the Nazis, *Murder by Decree* substitutes a famous series of unsolved Victorian crimes for a contemporary war. Yet Holmes (Christopher Plummer), duly endowed with the nostalgic force proper to the elaborate period production, is as anachronistic in his way as the twitching, cocaine-addicted Holmes of *The Seven-Per-Cent Solution*. Moving through a landscape shaped at once by the conventions of the political thriller, the horror film, and an earnest pastiche of Victorian London, Holmes follows the Universal films in unearthing large-scale public intrigues behind apparently private crimes. His compassion for the prostitutes who become the Ripper's victims and his final revelation that the Ripper was working to cover the traces of the British Establishment's search for Prince Edward's unacknowledged Catholic child reveal a staunchly protofeminist, post-Watergate sensibility. Just as the Universal films expressed a fervent wish that Holmes could return as a paragon of British starch and resourcefulness to fight the Axis, *Murder by Decree* expresses an equally fervent wish that Holmes the right-minded feminist champion of the disenfranchised could return to put the Establishment in its place. Yet even this anti-Establishment attitude is not so much an inversion of Conan Doyle's Holmes as a logical extension of the anti-Establishment credentials he registers in "A Scandal in Bohemia," "The Boscombe Valley Mystery," and "The Adventure of the Second Stain."

After the self-seriousness of *Murder by Decree*, *Young Sherlock Holmes* (1985) feels like a romp. The title of Barry Levinson's film says it all: What if Holmes and Watson had actually met as schoolboys? What sort of boys would they have been, what sort of relationship would they have had, and what sort of crimes would they have solved? The answers to these questions are not especially inventive. Holmes (Nicholas Rowe) would have been intellectual, aloof, and superior; Watson (Alan Cox) would have been eager, puppyish, and physically shy; they would instantly have established a salt-and-pepper friendship; and their school's little town would have been plagued by a string of murders. A far more interesting question concerns the film's marketing strategy: How do you make a film appealing to a target audience of twelve-to-eighteen-year-old boys who have barely heard of Sherlock Holmes? Levinson and screenwriter Chris Columbus add a girl (Elizabeth Hardy) for Holmes to romance, a series of ghoulish, effects-heavy homicides, a rising curve of action scenes, and an extended climax in which the three schoolchildren improbably defeat the evil schoolmaster and scores of underlings headquartered in a clandestine Egyptian temple in the neighborhood. In prophesying the men Holmes and Watson are to become and explaining how Holmes acquired his fondness for pipes and his fear of commitment to the fair sex, the exuberantly revisionist film makes a hash of Conan Doyle, but the Sherlockian canon is already so rife with contradictions that it seems able to absorb any new light whatsoever.

This rule applies even to the most metafictional and radically revisionist outrage yet visited on the canon, Thom Eberhardt's *Without a Clue* (1988), which replaces the blundering Watson beloved of Sherlockian commentary with a blundering Sherlock Holmes. Watson (Ben Kingsley), in this version of events, is the real brain behind the franchise; he has invented the character of Holmes and then invited down-at-heels actor Reginald Kincaid (Michael Caine) to apply for the position only in order to deflect unwanted publicity. In coming to the aid of still another helpless, comely, and ultimately treacherous client, Leslie Giles (Lysette Anthony), Watson and Holmes quarrel and separate over the terms of their secret agreement but finally solve the mystery when Watson is lost at sea, presumed drowned, and the witless Holmes is forced to investigate on his own. It would be hard to imagine a more complete inversion of the Holmes myth. Holmes is incompetent, incapable even of protecting his pocket watch from Wiggins (Matthew Savage), who repeatedly pinches it from him. In fact, he is a wholly fictitious invention of the slyly masterful Watson, whose every reference to the Holmes canon inverts its force and whose only sorrow is his failure to establish his reputation under the sobriquet "The Crime Doctor." Up to the very last scene, the odd couple never appear together without bickering, and their arguments have a distinctly anachronistic flavor. Yet the film is not merely a satirical commentary on the lopsided hero worship of the Holmes stories but a correction of it that purports, like all revisionist adaptations, to set the record straight once and for all. Its success in those terms can be gauged by the online reaction of Spleen, an Australian respondent to the Internet Movie Database who maintains that the film is payback for the inaccuracies and inconsistencies for which generations of commentators have blamed Watson in the Holmes canon: "How does this get us around all the inconsistencies that have puzzled Sherlock aficionados over the past century? To be frank, it doesn't. But no theory does. There are just too many inconsistencies to be fended off and this theory is about as likely to be right as any other."[46] In a stellar illustration of Kamilla Elliott's "de(re)composing concept of adaptation," in which "novel and film decompose, merge, and form a new composition,"[47] each new version of Holmes's adventures challenges the authority of all previous versions so that no version of events, including Watson's or Doyle's, is definitive, and any new version is as likely to become definitive as any other.

The paradoxical goal of all these revisionist adaptations is the same goal all adaptations of a successful franchise share. The more playfully freewheeling they are in their inventions, the more care they take to root them in a historical context that seems real, from the painstaking Victorian surfaces of *Murder by Decree* to Lola Deveraux, the courtesan who appears nowhere but *The Seven-Per-Cent Solution* and *The Private Correspondence of Clemenceau*. The more vigorously they insist on the historical and documentary reality of Conan

Doyle's fictional canon, the more forthrightly they pose as explanations, corrections, or revelations about that canon more real than the canon itself. New adaptations are admitted as canonical only to the degree that they both acknowledge the primacy of earlier texts and succeed in establishing their own reality as superior, whether they are combining elements from several Doyle adventures; enlisting Holmes to fight Hitler; showing that he was really manic-depressive, pathetically addicted, protofeminist, and anti-Establishment; mixing Sherlockian plots with elements from the gangster, monster, horror, or action genres; or assuming the form of mock-scholarly commentaries capable of recasting the canon as thoroughly as any fictional adventures.

In 1962 Basil Rathbone, looking back ruefully over his eight-year tango with the great detective, ventured the hilariously wrongheaded assertion that "the Sherlock Holmes stories are dated and their pattern and style, generally speaking, unacceptable . . . . The only possible medium still available to an acceptable present-day presentation of Sir Arthur Conan Doyle's stories would be a full-length Disney cartoon."[48] On the contrary, the franchise has proved more vigorous and various, more hospitable to dozens of new Holmeses, than its definitive exponent—or at least one of its two definitive exponents—realized because of its ability to absorb into itself all the many adaptations that have drawn their inspiration from it. It is all in play, of course, but that does not mean the stakes cannot be high: the enshrining of a perfect Victorian museum of London, the vindication of Freudian therapy, the indictment of the British Establishment, the morale of the English-speaking world in time of war, and of course still another corporation's ability to wring another few million dollars out of the most protean of all fictional franchises.

# CHAPTER TEN

# The Adapter as Auteur

It is ironic that François Truffaut's seminal essay "A Certain Tendency of French Cinema" bequeathed the term *auteur* to critical discourse, since the central subject of Truffaut's withering survey was the *metteur-en-scène*, the mere scene-setter who functioned as the auteur's opposite. Unlike Jean Renoir and Robert Bresson, who create their own cinematic worlds, metteurs-en-scène merely furnish and photograph what Truffaut calls the literary worlds of their screenplays. Since Truffaut the term has largely fallen into disuse, replaced by the term *adapter*, even though adapters ought logically to be screenwriters rather than directors.

Although it might seem that the metteurs-en-scène who create Jane Austen adaptations for the BBC and the auteurs who seek to create films in their own image represent polar opposites defined in absolute contradistinction to one another, many directors whose films are based almost entirely on literary adaptations have nonetheless established a reputation as auteurs. Several of Ernst Lubitsch's greatest films, from *Trouble in Paradise* (1932) to *The Shop around the Corner* (1940), are adaptations of a series of forgotten Hungarian plays. Orson Welles, who wrote or cowrote all his screenplays, rarely tackled an original subject after *Citizen Kane* (1941). Even most of Bresson's key films are adaptations of novels. Why do some adapters remain metteurs-en-scène while others avoid or outgrow the label?

Many filmmakers make contributions so definitive to the films on which they collaborate that their hand is instantly recognizable. Contract directors like Joseph H. Lewis, Jacques Tourneur, Max Ophüls, and Douglas Sirk have created films that could not possibly be mistaken for each other's or anyone else's. So have cinematographers like Rudolph Maté, Lee Garmes, Karl Freund, Gregg Toland, John Alton, and James Wong Howe; production designers like Hans Dreier and Richard Sylbert; editors like Dede Allen and Thelma Schoonmaker; sound designers like Walter Murch; choreographers like Busby Berkeley; special-effects wizards like John Dykstra and John Gaeata; and composers like Max Steiner, Erich Wolfgang Korngold, Miklós Rózsa, Bernard Herrmann, and John Williams. All these filmmakers are well known to film scholars and film students; all have some claim to authorship of their films. But although several of them are more widely recognized than the authors whose work their films adapted, none except perhaps for Berkeley is a household name commonly recognized by a more general audience.[1] Given the difference between film authorship (playing a leading role in creating a film) and auteurship (establishing a claim to authorship that is widely recognized), how do adapters establish themselves as auteurs outside the film industry and the academy? What determines who is to count—director Simon Langton? screenwriter Andrew Davies? novelist Jane Austen? the BBC?—as the auteur of the 1995 miniseries *Pride and Prejudice?* The careers of three unquestioned auteurs whose body of work consisted almost entirely of adaptations—Alfred Hitchcock, Stanley Kubrick, and Walt Disney—suggests that the auteur status of filmmakers depends at least as much on their temperament and working habits, their triumphs in conflicts with other aspiring authors, and their success at turning themselves into brand names as on their artistic aspirations or any textual features of their films.

Audiences long accustomed to Hitchcock's signature traits—his close identification with a single genre, his cameo appearances, his cherubically corpulent figure tricked out in a series of outrageous costumes for the prologues and epilogues to *Alfred Hitchcock Presents*—may well have forgotten that most of Hitchcock's films were adaptations. Among his fourteen films before his breakout thriller *The Man Who Knew Too Much* (1934), only two—*The Ring* (1927) and *Champagne* (1928)—were based on original screenplays. Many of his early credits cast him as the metteur-en-scène of such properties as *Easy Virtue, The Manxman, Juno and the Paycock,* and *The Skin Game,* whose credits billed it as "a talking picture by John Galsworthy." Despite the prophetic freedom with which *Sabotage* (1937) adapted its great original, Joseph Conrad's *The Secret Agent,* David O. Selznick, after luring England's star director to America, consistently treated Hitchcock as a metteur-en-scène rather than an auteur.

The resulting conflict over Hitchcock's notorious first treatment for *Rebecca,* which began with a farcical scene in which a cigar-smoking Maxim de Winter made his shipboard guests seasick, seems inevitable only because we think of Hitchcock as an auteur. But the freedom Hitchcock had taken with Daphne du Maurier's best-selling novel left Selznick "shocked and disappointed beyond words." In a stinging memo to Hitchcock, Selznick, who would assure du Maurier of "my intention to do the book and not some botched-up semioriginal [like] . . . *Jamaica Inn,*" laid down the formula that distinguishes auteurs from metteurs-en-scène: "We bought *Rebecca,* and we intend to make *Rebecca.*"[2] Years later Hitchcock summarized his own auteurist attitude toward adaptation equally trenchantly in his interview with Truffaut: "There's been a lot of talk about the way Hollywood directors distort literary masterpieces. I'll have no part of that! What I do is to read a story only once, and if I like the basic idea, I just forget all about the book and start to create cinema."[3]

Hitchcock's graduation from the metteur-en-scène of *Juno and the Paycock* to the auteur of *Strangers on a Train* (1951), *Rear Window* (1954), and even *Dial M for Murder* (1953), whose screenplay by Frederick Knott follows Knott's play almost line for line, was a slow and laborious process. The process begins in Hitchcock's films of the 1940s, especially his loan outs from the literary-minded Selznick, which include both more free adaptations like *Foreign Correspondent* (1940) and *Suspicion* (1941) and more original screenplays like *Saboteur* (1942), *Shadow of a Doubt* (1943), *Lifeboat* (1944), and *Notorious* (1946). Surprisingly, *Rope* (1948) and *Under Capricorn* (1949), the two films for which Hitchcock served as an independent producer for his own company, Transatlantic Pictures, are not notable for any striking departures from their sources; indeed, the long takes that are the principal innovation of both films might be described as an attempt to be as faithful as possible to the claustrophobia of Patrick Hamilton's stagebound play and the romantic period detail of Helen Simpson's novel. By the time Transatlantic folded in 1950, however, Hitchcock, bound for a series of new studio contracts that gave him far greater freedom than he had enjoyed under Selznick, was evidently determined to make and market his films as Hitchcock originals.

To establish himself as an auteur, however, Hitchcock had to wrest authorship of his films away from another plausible candidate: the author of the original property. Here he was helped by his close identification with a powerful Hollywood genre and the obscurity of his literary sources, an obscurity he deliberately cultivated by his refusal to make films based on classic novels like *Crime and Punishment*, whose authorship would leave no room for his own. Avoiding brand-name authors like Dostoevsky, Hitchcock created his own brand-name franchise by steamrolling authors whose work he coveted. By bidding through intermediaries who kept his name secret, he was able to purchase the rights to *Strangers on a Train*, *The Trouble with Harry*, and *Psycho* cheaply, to the considerable chagrin of all three novelists. Once he had purchased their properties, he banished the authors; only Frederick Knott and Leon Uris, the best-selling author of *Topaz*, were invited to work on the screenplays based on their books. Instead the films were retooled as Hitchcock originals that promised not the literary values of their properties but the reliable generic thrills, set pieces, and ironic yet reassuringly familiar markers of the Hitchcock universe: mysterious doubles, icy blondes, staircases, brandy snifters, and the explosion of self-references in *Frenzy*. Even though Hitchcock continued to rely on literary sources—among all his films after *Rope*, only *North by Northwest* and *Torn Curtain* are based on original screenplays—he methodically avoided literary cachet as an area in which he could not successfully compete and instead embraced a generic identification that he was able to promote through his carefully crafted public image, as well as his films. His success in turning his own corporeal presence into a trademark in his cameo appearances, his witty endpapers to *Alfred Hitchcock Presents* and *The Alfred Hitchcock Hour*, the monthly mystery magazine and the board game to which he lent his name and image, even the signature eight-stroke silhouette with which he often signed autographs established him as the quintessential directorial brand name, an auteur capable of eclipsing authors whose claim to authority was simply less powerful.[4] Hitchcock's unquestioned success in casting himself as the auteur of his films, however, should not hide the fact that his auteurship is less a norm than an aberration. His success in establishing his credentials is largely a function of his identification with a single genre and the relative obscurity of most of the authors he adapts. Auteurism abhors a vacuum.

Hitchcock, so averse to conflict that he once left Ingrid Bergman's tirade on the set of *Under Capricorn* twenty minutes before Bergman noticed his absence, preferred to finesse the authors he eventually eclipsed beneath the success of his generic branding. Stanley Kubrick, by contrast, earned his auteur status the old-fashioned way: by taking on authors directly in open warfare. Just as the crucial period in the rise of Hitchcock the auteur was the 1940s and 1950s, the much shorter pivotal period for Kubrick was the 1960s, the very period that film studies were first entering the academy under the banner of auteurism. At the beginning of the decade he was a moderately successful genre director associated with war and crime films; by decade's end the release of *2001: A Space Odyssey* (1968) and *Clockwork Orange* (1971) confirmed his status as one of the most strikingly individualistic auteurs in or out of Hollywood. Kubrick transformed himself from metteur-en-scène to auteur mostly by his work, and his increasingly skilled infighting, on three films: *Spartacus* (1960), *Lolita* (1962), and *Dr. Strangelove or: How I Learned to Stop Worrying and Love the Bomb* (1964).

Weeks before arriving on *Spartacus* at the request of its executive producer and star, Kirk Douglas, Kubrick had parted ways with another powerful star, Marlon Brando, who, having hired him to direct *One-Eyed Jacks*, clashed with him over the story's shape and casting and ended up directing the film himself. Douglas was eager to hand the project over from Anthony Mann, whom he dismissed after three weeks of shooting, to Kubrick, who had directed him in *Paths of Glory* (1957) as the first of a projected multipicture deal. But the atmosphere on the set of *Spartacus* was just as combustible. Testosterone-fueled prima donnas like Laurence Olivier, Charles Laughton, and Peter Ustinov—"guys who are bigger than any director," Kubrick's friend Norman Lloyd recalled—jousted with the famously volatile Douglas over blockings and line readings.[5]

Ustinov observed years later that authorship of virtually every aspect of the film was so unsettled that he could take a shot at reworking his own material. Noting Laughton's sensitivity to the overbearing Olivier, he recalls, "I rewrote all the scenes I had with Laughton, we rehearsed at his home or mine, often slogging away into the middle of the night. The next day, we rearranged the studio furniture to conform with what we had engineered at home, and presented the company with a *fait accompli*. Kubrick accepted what we had done more or less without modification, and the scenes were shot in half a day each."[6]

Remarkably, the screenwriters managed to be equally disputatious. Because principal screenwriter Dalton Trumbo was still blacklisted and scorned by

Howard Fast, author of the novel under adaptation, his authorship was hidden by the front writer Edward Lewis and the fictitious "Sam Jackson," the two credited on the shooting script. When Lewis indicated his unwillingness to accept either that credit or sole credit for the screenplay, there seemed no solution but to credit the screenplay under a pseudonym—a tactic Douglas deplored—until Kubrick, who had taken a screen credit for writing each of his earlier features, suddenly suggested, "Use my name." When Douglas asked, "Stanley, wouldn't you feel embarrassed to put your name on a script that someone else wrote?" Kubrick, looking puzzled, said that he wouldn't.[7] Although a "revolted" Douglas resolved the problem by crediting Trumbo under his own name, Kubrick had made his point: the brains behind the film were, or ought to be, his. Yet editor Robert Lawrence reported that Kubrick "never really would agree to the concept that this was his movie," and Kubrick told Gene Phillips that "*Spartacus* is the only film on which I did not have absolute control" and described his status to Joseph Gelmis as "just a hired hand."[8] The lesson he drew from this experience was to avoid projects on which a strong producer or star could withhold the control he craved.

It might seem paradoxical, then, that his next film, which Norman Kagan describes as "probably the biggest creative watershed in Kubrick's career,"[9] was based on a well-known novel by an author who received sole screen credit for the screenplay—the only time in his career Kubrick voluntarily relinquished such a credit. But the withdrawal was merely a strategy by Kubrick and his partner, producer James B. Harris, who had amused Kirk Douglas throughout *Paths of Glory* by posting "HARRIS-KUBRICK" signs throughout the production.[10] Having sold their rights to *The Killing* (1956), Kubrick's first success, in order to raise the $75,000 Vladimir Nabokov asked for the screen rights to his censor-baiting novel, Kubrick and Harris had every intention of capitalizing on the author's name as a cardinal selling point in marketing *Lolita*. When Nabokov resisted their invitation to write the screenplay himself, they pressed him further for several months until he finally agreed, turning out an adaptation that ran to four hundred typescript pages. Enjoined to cut his work to filmable length, Nabokov obliged with a highly original two-hundred-page version whose general outline Kubrick followed even though, according to Ed Sikov, "Harris, uncredited, ended up revising it,"[11] often restoring material from the novel Nabokov had carefully deleted or transformed in his screenplay. Throughout the production Kubrick swore the performers to secrecy about these changes, lest the author discover what was happening to the screenplay he had submitted. His concern was abundantly justified. When the completed film was screened privately for Nabokov, he realized that "only ragged odds and ends of my script had been used" and complained in the foreword to his screenplay, published with still further revisions in 1973, that "most of the [newly invented] sequences were not really better than those I had so carefully composed for Kubrick, and I keenly regretted the waste of my time while admiring Kubrick's fortitude in enduring for six months the evolution and infliction of a useless product."[12]

Kubrick's experience on both *Spartacus* and *Lolita* illustrates a revealing split among the different functions of authorship that does not arise in Hitchcock. In *Spartacus* Kubrick grasped at the most obvious mark of the cinematic auteur, the credit as writer-director, which would stamp the film as a Kubrick property rather than the property of Kirk Douglas, Dalton Trumbo, or Howard Fast, without being able to assume the primary task of shaping the dramatic material into a distinctive world. *Lolita,* by contrast, shows him attempting to appropriate the opposite functions of authorship—the right to invent new scenes, revise dialogue, and approve Peter Sellers's on-set improvisations as Clare Quilty—while just as deliberately farming out its most visible sign of public attribution to an author who could furnish the kind of literary cachet that would help head off the censors' most high-handed objections to the whole nature of the story of a middle-aged man with an irresistible lust for his prepubescent stepdaughter. Whether the press thought Nabokov's novel was a literary classic or a pornographic fantasy, it would be far better to have Nabokov's name on the screenplay, even if Harris and Kubrick had essentially rewritten it, even to the point of removing the cameo appearance Nabokov wrote himself as a butterfly collector[13] and substituting Kubrick's own authorial signature, a pair of framing references in which Quilty is first seen pretending to be Spartacus, waiting for someone to "come to free the slaves or something," and is last described as "on his way to Hollywood to write one of those spectaculars."

Kubrick took time in the middle of shooting to assure a *Sight and Sound* interviewer that "to take the prose style as any more than just a part . . . is simply to misunderstand what a great book is. . . . Style is what an artist uses to fascinate the beholder in order to convey to him his feelings and emotions and thoughts. These are what have to be dramatized, not the style."[14] Twenty-five years after Nabokov's screenplay earned the film's only Oscar nomination, however, Kubrick acknowledged his failure to find a cinematic equivalent for Nabokov's voice when he told an interviewer for *Der Spiegel:* "If it had been written by a lesser author, it might have been a better film."[15] Kubrick's search for greater control led him to produce as well as write and direct all his subsequent films, in support of his argument that since film directing was "[no]thing more or less than a continuation of the writing . . . a writer-director is really the perfect dramatic instrument."[16] His search for a lesser author took him first to Peter George, whose 1958 novel *Red Alert* provided a textbook illustration of what Kubrick called "people's virtually listless acquiescence in the possibility—in fact, the increasing probability—of nuclear war."[17]

Originally cast in the form of straightforward antiwar melodrama like *On the Beach* (1959) or *Fail-Safe* (1964), or indeed like *Paths of Glory,* the film, as Kubrick explained to Joseph Gelmis, assumed a life of its own:

> I started work on the screenplay with every intention of making the film a serious treatment of the problem of accidental nuclear war. As I kept trying to imagine the way in which things would really happen, ideas kept coming to me which I would discard because they were so ludicrous. I kept saying to myself, "I can't do this. People will laugh." But after a month or so I began to realize that all the things I was throwing out were the things that were most truthful. . . .
>
> So it occurred to me that I was approaching the project in the wrong way. The only way to tell the story was as a black comedy or, better, a nightmare comedy where the things you laugh at most are really the heart of the paradoxical postures that make a nuclear war possible.[18]

Once he had reached the decision to turn *Dr. Strangelove* into a nightmare comedy, Kubrick brought satirist Terry Southern in to pump up the sex jokes and outrageous proper names (Jack D. Ripper, Lionel Mandrake, Buck Turgidson, Merkin Muffley, Dmitri Kissoff, Bat Guano) that increasingly displaced George's emphasis on serious ideological opposition to the Red Menace and fear of death as the engine of the film's race to destruction. The Doomsday Machine, designed to counter any nuclear attack with retaliatory worldwide destruction beyond the possibility of human intervention; General Ripper's reflexive ascription of his temporary impotence to a communist plot to fluoridate drinking water; and Dr. Strangelove, whose artificial arm keeps rising reflectively in a Nazi salute, all became metaphors for the characters' attempts to purge themselves of all humanity in order to embrace a system of lockstep beliefs and actions they foolishly believed would save them from the mortal frailties that made them human.

The catastrophic embrace of dehumanization, once Kubrick uncovered it, became the formative theme of all his later films, from *2001* to *Eyes Wide Shut* (1999), and the one that most surely enshrined him as an auteur. Greg Jenkins has enumerated eleven touchstones of Kubrick's adaptations, from his introduction of each film by *"a heavily visual sequence that immediately and purposefully seizes our attention"* to occasional moments when *"Kubrick invents his own material outright, and imposes it on his new narrative."*[19] Yet Kubrick's auteur status depended less on his thematic or technical consistency as an adapter than on the work habits these films showcased: his obsessive attention to detail, his domination of every aspect of production from screenwriting to special effects editing, his need to stamp every one of his films as his regardless of the competing claims of writers, producers, and stars. Although Kubrick was every bit as dictatorial as Hitchcock in his temperament, his auteurist persona was different in crucial ways. Unlike Hitchcock, who turned his public persona into a voluble trademark for a transmedia genre franchise, Kubrick, retreating to England to produce a series of nongenre films marked by thematic affinities and ever-lengthening intervals in between, became identified with individual craftsmanship. Norman Kagan could admiringly observe in 1972: "He writes, shoots, directs, edits, and often handles his own publicity. He has, in fact, sought ever more control as his career [has] progressed; his films are probably as close to personal works of art as any in the commercial cinema."[20]

The image of the last solitary romantic artist who embraced the technology of cinema only to recoil from its chilling institutional implications was promoted equally by Kubrick's films and the filmmaker's public persona, based paradoxically on the resolute avoidance of public appearances, and perfectly calculated to appeal to the emerging academic field of film studies. The reaction of Andrew Sarris, the dean of American auteur-hunters, to Kubrick is instructive. Relegating the director to the lowest circle of his auteurist hell, "Strained Seriousness," in 1968, he dismissed the pretensions of *2001: A Space Odyssey* with a sneer: "Kubrick's tragedy may have been that he was hailed as a great artist before he had become a competent craftsman."[21] Returning to the film in 1970 "under the influence of a smoked substance," he pronounced it "a major work by a major artist" that "express[es] its director's vision of a world to come seen through the sensibility of a world past. Even the dull, expressionless acting seems perfectly attuned to settings in which human feelings are diffused by inhuman distances."[22] What changes here is Sarris's assessment of Kubrick's technical competence and its adequacy to his intentions; what remains constant is the unquestioned assumption that for better or worse,

Kubrick is the sole creator of his films. Concluding his highly critical review of *Marnie* in 1964, Sarris could lament, "The master of suspense has struck out in his own park."[23] His similar response to *2001: A Space Odyssey* indicates the extent to which he acknowledges the director, even at his worst, as an auteur.

If Hitchcock represented the adapter-auteur as generic trademark and Kubrick the adapter-auteur as solitary artist, Walt Disney managed to combine both figures in his rise to auteur status, a path that was longer, more twisted, and altogether more interesting than either Hitchcock's or Kubrick's. It might seem odd to consider Disney as either adapter or auteur, since he neither wrote nor directed any of the features for which he is best remembered. Yet Disney is clearly both adapter and auteur, since all the Disney features before *The Lion King* (1994) were based on earlier stories or novels, and they were all marketed as products of Disney and no one else.

The rise of the Disney trademark can be measured by two pivotal reversals in Disney's ascent. The first is his loss of control in 1928 of Oswald the Lucky Rabbit, an animated hero Disney had brainstormed and Ub Iwerks animated, to Universal Studios and distributor Charles Mintz, who had hired most of the animators away from Disney's studio. Furiously refusing to accept Universal's offer to finance the Oswald shorts in return for half the profits and recognition of their copyright to the character, Disney, who had forthrightly renamed the Disney Brothers Studio the Walt Disney Studio as early as 1925, broke with Mintz, renounced all rights to Oswald, and worked with Iwerks to create Mickey Mouse, whose third short, *Steamboat Willie* (1928), used innovative sync-sound techniques to make him a star. Still stung by the memory of his failure to share any of the royalties from Oswald's reproduction on badges or candy boxes and by the distributors who had written to the studio asking for Oswald's autograph instead of his creator's,[24] Disney vowed that he would never again create a character or a film whose name could be separated from his own.

This stance may seem paradoxical in view of the fact that Disney's shorts had depended from the beginning—*Little Red Riding Hood* (1922), *The Four Musicians of Bremen* (1922), and *Jack and the Beanstalk* (1922)—on adapting familiar stories. Even Disney's best-known pre-Oswald franchise, the fifty-seven "Alice Comedies" (1923–27), took off from a short, *Alice's Wonderland* (1923), whose heroine's live-action/animated visit to an animation studio and Cartoonland, traded on the title and premise of Lewis Carroll's children's classic. Not until Mickey Mouse's coattails had made Walt Disney a household name did the studio attempt such original shorts as *Flowers and Trees* (1932) and *The Old Mill* (1937), now trading on Disney's name instead of Mickey's. The studio's first feature, *Snow White and the Seven Dwarfs* (1937), remained within the genre of the fairy tale less because of its literary cachet than because of its familiar genre.

Disney's one early flirtation with frankly upscale cultural values marked a second pivotal reversal in his career. Following the success of *Snow White and the Seven Dwarfs*, the studio embarked on a project called *The Concert Feature* whose premise, the attempt to provide animated visuals for such classical musical selections as Bach's *Toccata and Fugue in D Minor* and Beethoven's *Pastoral Symphony*, marked the only time in his career when Disney would act as a metteur-en-scène. The result, released as *Fantasia* (1940), was a financial flop that belied Disney's prediction that the film "makes our other pictures look immature, and suggests for the first time what the future of the medium may well turn out to be" and stopped his plans "to make a new version of *Fantasia* every year" or at least to update the film by constantly shuffling different sequences into and out of its loose continuity.[25] Instead, the studio returned to free narrative adaptations of fairy-tale properties whose authors, unlike Beethoven and Leopold Stokowski, could not compete with Disney because they were indeterminate (*Snow White* and *Cinderella* [1950]), defunct (*Alice in Wonderland* [1951]; *Peter Pan* [1953]), or as obscure as the novelists Hitchcock's expanding trademark effaced (*Pinocchio* [1940]; *Dumbo* [1941]; *Bambi* [1942]).

Although he did not write or direct any of these features, or indeed more than a handful of his animated shorts after 1930, Disney maintained his status as their auteur by the simple expedient of claiming their most prominent credits. When his employees at the Walt Disney Studios, whose numbers had grown from 150 to 750 during the production of *Snow White*, demanded fuller credits on completed film, Disney, who had suppressed all but Iwerks's names on the credits of his silent shorts, added so many names in such tiny type that his own name was the only one that stood out. Nor did the seventy-two contributors credited include either Jakob and Wilhelm Grimm, whose version of the story served as the film's basis, or any of the performers who supplied the characters' voices. Adriana Caselotti, the young Italian soprano who voiced Snow White, was not only uncredited but forbidden, according to persistent rumors, to accept an invitation from Jack Benny's radio program because Disney did not wish to demystify his animated character.[26]

What may seem like Disney's dictatorial control over his productions' marketing should be seen in the light of two mitigating factors. One is the general invisibility of children's authors, whether or not their work was adapted by Disney, between the death of L. Frank Baum, the "Royal Historian of Oz," in 1919 and the fame Theodor Geisel won as Dr. Seuss not with his first picture book, *And to Think That I Saw It on Mulberry Street* (1937), but with a pair of books he did not write till twenty years later, *How the Grinch Stole Christmas!* and his innovative primer for new readers, *The Cat in the Hat* (both 1957).[27] Throughout the period of Disney's early animated features, the bylines of the best-known children's franchises were either subordinated to those of their publishers (for example, Golden Books, the early-childhood picture books whose gold bindings were their most distinctive feature) or actually created by the publishers (most notably the Stratemeyer Syndicate, which produced among many other series Nancy Drew and the Hardy Boys).

The other mitigating factor is Disney's paternalism toward his employees, whose unionizing efforts he staunchly resisted because he saw their enterprise as a utopian "community of artists . . . where work and leisure—perhaps even family life—could be totally integrated to the benefit of all."[28] Disney subsumed the work of hundreds of creators and craftsmen under an individual signature as imperious as the writing credit Kubrick offered to take on *Spartacus* and as graphically recognizable as Hitchcock's silhouette. In this way the studio head presented himself as an artisan or craftsman in the Kubrick mold who could recount homespun tales of his youth drafting cartoons in a Kansas City garage, in an eerie prefiguration of the founders of Hewlett-Packard, while still following the general tendency of children's mass-produced entertainment to emphasize the centralized, paternalistic creation of a utopian imaginative world whose trademark had the widest possible application. His animators and artists would not be credited on Disney's shorts until a strike in May 1941 ensured that "Disney would no longer have the monopoly of credits on the short cartoons."[29]

By this time Disney had already begun the slow and often painful evolution from the auteur as individual craftsman, the inventor and animator of Mickey Mouse, to the auteur as corporate franchise, an evolution that would take nearly fifteen years to complete. Shut out of his cartoons' profitable European markets by the coming of World War II, Disney had allowed his brother, Roy, to talk him into a public stock offering in April 1940, raising much-needed capital that kept their company afloat even though "Walt despised the idea of having outsiders share in the decisions that he had made by himself throughout the company history."[30] Although *Dumbo* (1941) earned half a million dollars for the studio, both *Pinocchio* and *Fantasia* failed to recoup their considerable expenses. Pressed for the cash he needed to complete *Bambi*, Disney slapped together two completed cartoon shorts, "How to Ride a Horse" and "The Reluctant Dragon," and a third, "Baby Weems," that existed only as a series of storyboards. Connecting the three animated films with a story in which the humorist Robert Benchley visits the Disney studio to try to sell a children's book that his wife (Nana Bryant) has read to him and ends up getting a behind-the-scenes studio tour, Disney produced *The Reluctant Dragon* (1941), a project that marked his first mostly live-action feature.

Benchley plays something of a reluctant dragon himself, since the idea of pitching the book to Disney is his imperious wife's rather than his character's, and he shows every sign of diffidence when she drops him off at the studio, book in hand, and leaves. Even though Benchley has no appointment to see Disney, however, he is greeted cordially, given a visitor's pass, instantly admitted, and assigned an officious guide (Buddy Pepper) who spouts statistics about the studio as Benchley, trying to avoid him, ducks into an art class, an orchestral performance, and a sound effects studio. The contrast with the studio's earlier self-promotion short, *How Walt Disney Cartoons Are Made* (1937), is instructive. The earlier short, made in conjunction with *Snow White* and recut as a promotional trailer for Disney's first animated feature, took viewers, as an anonymous voice-over narrator announced, "behind the doors of the famed Walt Disney Studios in Hollywood, doors usually barred to all visitors." The personnel in the earlier short, from Disney's "hard-boiled directors" to the "pretty girls" who traced animated drawings onto celluloid, were equally anonymous and mute. They were all subordinated to Disney—"no picture goes into production without Walt's personal okay"—who had the only speaking role apart from the narrator. In *The Reluctant Dragon*, by contrast, studio personnel were warm, personable, and welcoming, as well they should have been, since they were played by the likes of Frank Faylen, Frances Gifford, and Alan Ladd. Everyone Benchley meets smilingly stops working to help him, and nearly everyone seems to know his name. The film reinvents the studio as a big, happy family whose three leading loyalties are to producing quality product, welcoming visitors, and remaining faithful to Disney's vision.

*The Reluctant Dragon* is pivotal not only in recasting the public image of a studio no longer privately owned by the Disney brothers but in putting the studio's work-in-progress center stage. Beneath Benchley's tour of the studio, spiced with his increasingly determined attempts to evade his minder and his numerous encounters with caricatures of his own comical face, was the subtext that it was at least as amusing to watch cartoons being made as it was to watch the cartoons themselves. Indeed, none of the three cartoons embedded in the film turned out to be a work-in-progress after all. "The Reluctant Dragon," based on the children's book by Kenneth Grahame, was never released separately. "How to Ride a Horse" was released without any changes as a short subject in 1950. And "Baby Weems," so successful in storyboard stills with voice-over narration, was never made at all. *The Reluctant Dragon* was the first hint that the Disney studio could be more saleable than its products.

The end of 1941 launched the studio into a still more turbulent period. On December 8, the day after Pearl Harbor, Disney arrived at work to find that a U.S. Army unit had taken control of his studio—the only Hollywood studio to be so treated—to convert its facilities in support of antiaircraft forces. During the eight months the unit remained on the premises, the federal government began to order an unprecedented number of informational live-action shorts from Disney. Within a year the studio's production had rocketed from thirty thousand feet to three hundred thousand feet annually.[31] Under his new mandate Disney mothballed his plans to produce *Alice in Wonderland* and *Peter Pan*, focusing first on *Bambi* and then developing a new wartime role for animated cartoons. The studio joined Warner Bros. and MGM in making its continuing characters available for military service in dozens of shorts from *Donald Gets Drafted* to *Der Fuehrer's Face* (both 1942).[32] But Disney went a step further. Instead of creating the generic "Mr. Taxpayer," which Treasury Secretary Henry Morgenthau had suggested as an animated model emphasizing the importance of prompt and accurate tax filing, Disney placed Donald Duck in the role, and Donald's spluttering antics in the result, *The New Spirit* (1942), managed to be both effective propaganda and great fun for viewers who felt as exasperated as Donald. In addition, Disney, shut out of European markets for his product, embarked on a goodwill tour of Latin America and released two live-action/animated compilations recording the results: *Saludos Amigos* (1942) and *The Three Caballeros* (1944).

The most substantial of the studio's wartime cartoons, however, was an adaptation based on a most unlikely source: Major Alexander P. de Seversky's *Victory through Air Power*. Seversky was an army officer, a veteran flier, and an expert who held numerous patents in aeronautical engineering. His 1942 book argued that attacking the Axis Powers by land and sea played into Axis strengths, allowing their U-boats and land-based aircraft to wreak havoc on Allied ships while the shorter supply lines of both Germany and Japan could be redirected or contracted to counter Allied threats. Only by building many more long-range land-based planes and organizing the air force as a separate military service, Seversky contended, could America hope to convert its statistical advantage in service personnel and materiel into victory.

Impressed by the book and convinced by its logic, Disney was determined to adapt it as an animated feature. The decision might have seemed perverse, for there is nothing at all funny about Seversky's book and precious little about Disney's 1943 film. In lieu of the customary pleasures of Disney cartoons—unforgettable grotesques, anthropomorphic animals, magical transformations—the film dispenses entirely with sharply drawn individual characters and with speaking roles apart from Seversky, presented in live action, and a voice-over narrator. In fact, once Disney has finished his bravura introductory sequence covering forty years of aviation history, no more faces are presented. Aggressors and casualties alike are shown only from behind, in shadow, as disembodied arms, or from a great distance in order to figure both the Axis and the Allies as massed forces rather than collections of typical individuals. When the Japanese bomb Pearl Harbor, they destroy numberless ships and planes, but no human casualties are shown.

Instead, the film uses the iconography of diagrams and editorial cartoons to press its case for air power. The Axis supply lines are represented as spokes in a cartoon wheel that can change thickness or circumference at will. Animated graphics make the case against attacking Japan from China, Siberia, or short-range airplanes launched by aircraft carriers. The Aleutian Islands, a potential site for airbases, become a rifle barrel pointing at Japan. The result is an impressive demonstration of cartoons' transformative power as propaganda.

Bold and original in design, *Victory through Air Power* might have marked a new direction for the Disney studio. But the end of the war eliminated the need for wartime propaganda, though not Disney's sense of urgency about speaking for America. Nor did the reopening of European markets give the studio's finances the expected boost. Disney films could now safely be shipped to Great

Britain, but whatever profits they amassed had to be spent in Britain. So Disney decided to shoot a live-action film in England. *Treasure Island* (1950), his first live-action feature adaptation, was a rousing financial success. So were the series of nature films that grew out of Disney cartoonists' long and careful studies of the animals they were to animate. Beginning with *On Seal Island* (1948) and the Oscar-winning *Beaver Valley* (1950), the studio released a series of two-reel "True-Life Adventures" about animals in the wild.

It was fortunate, indeed, that these new ventures into live-action filmmaking were so popular because Disney's feature cartoons continued to lose money. Although *Cinderella* was a major success, *Alice in Wonderland* lost a million dollars, and *Peter Pan* barely eked out a profit in its initial release. By 1953 more than half of the studio's fully animated features since *Snow White and the Seven Dwarfs*—*Pinocchio, Fantasia, Bambi, Victory through Air Power, Alice in Wonderland*—had lost money. The very films that had established their creator's auteur status were becoming impossible to market successfully.

It was at this point that Disney, buffeted so long by financial shortfalls, made the decisions, once again driven by financial need, that put his auteur status on a new and immensely more successful footing. In return for a commitment from the fledgling ABC Television Network for $500,000 cash and loan guarantees of $4.5 million toward the construction of Disneyland, a theme park the producer planned to open in Anaheim, Disney agreed to supply the network with a half-hour weekly television segment originally called *Disneyland* (later redubbed *Disney's Sunday Movie, Walt Disney Presents, Walt Disney's Wonderful World of Color,* and, after Disney's death, *The Wonderful World of Disney*) when it premiered on October 27, 1954. The program did not mark a detour in Disney's plans to open his amusement park, for it provided him with an outlet "on which he would be free to promote liberally not only his amusement park but his films."[33]

Introducing the DVD release of the program's premiere episode, Leonard Maltin has observed:

> Although he was a visionary in the truest sense of the term, Walt Disney was not eager to embrace the new medium of television. He didn't want to compromise the standards of quality he'd set for his motion pictures by having to churn out new material every week. But ironically, that was the tradeoff he had to make in order to raise the financing for his theme park. . . . Up to this time Walt had not been much of a public figure. He appeared in the occasional newsreel or pro-

motional film. He did agree to go on camera for a couple of TV specials in the early 1950s. But it was this weekly series that made him a familiar figure to viewers young and old. . . . He was like a surrogate uncle with the keys to a magic kingdom.[34]

These remarks only extend the mythmaking Disney had begun in earnest in his television premiere. It is true that Disney's exposure to the cameras had been limited before he agreed to host *Disneyland*. Although he had the only speaking role in *How Walt Disney Cartoons Are Made*, his appearance was brief and scripted. He appeared for scarcely longer in *The Reluctant Dragon*, a film that figured him as both the grail of Benchley's quest and the presiding spirit of the studio. Maltin is correct in observing that *Disneyland*, together with *The Mickey Mouse Club*, which premiered in 1955, established Disney firmly as a public figure.

It is disingenuous, however, to say that Disney resisted television because he did not want his standards of quality compromised by weekly deadlines. As the premiere demonstrates, the program was designed specifically as a showcase for projects that would not have to be prepared anew each week. The opening sequence of the episode, which pans from a framed still of Mickey Mouse to frame the photo together with Disney before tracking over to a much larger aerial plan of the theme park the program was designed to promote, shows Disney shifting from the artisanal auteur who devised Mickey Mouse to the impresario auteur. Introducing his yet-unfinished theme park, the television host told his audience, "Disneyland the place and *Disneyland* the TV show are all part of the same." Disneyland's four subdivisions became, in their presenter's view, "the inspirational America of the past century" (Frontierland), "a wonder world of nature's own design" (Adventureland), a technological utopia of space travel and exploration for "our own common man" in 1986 (Tomorrowland), and "the happiest kingdom of them all" (Fantasyland).

What Disney neglects to say is that the four lands are shrewdly designed as receptacles for the studio's recycled back product and future work in the same genres: homespun tall tales, nature documentaries, high-tech tours, and animated cartoons. At the same time, Disneyland's emphasis on an idealized American past whose capital is Main Street, Hometown USA, circa 1900, and an American future whose sole emphasis is on benevolent technology completely elides the American present, the world of politics, ideology, social problems, and anything else that might undermine visitors' or viewers' experience of "the happiest place on earth."

In addition Disneyland elides Disney's own present, reconfiguring the host as an archivist auteur whose reputation is based on his retrospective achievements and his future promise rather than on his current projects.[35] He repositions himself from creator to host with preternatural deftness. After assigning the introductions to three of Disneyland's worlds to other hands, Disney introduces Fantasyland himself, reminding his audience that "I hope we can never lose sight of one thing: that it was all started by a mouse. That's why I want this part of the show to belong to Mickey: because the story of Mickey is truthfully the real beginning of the story of Disneyland." This nostalgic introduction to clips from *Plane Crazy* (1928) and *The Pointer* (1939) and the complete short *Lonesome Ghosts* (1937) tactfully skips over the fact that Mickey Mouse is a museum piece. Mickey's last appearance in *The Simple Things* (1953) had marked the beginning of a drought that would not end, apart from brief animated appearances in *Disneyland* and *The Mickey Mouse Club*, until *Mickey's Christmas Carol* (1983). Disney's own active connection to the character had ended even earlier with his refusal to voice Mickey in *Mickey and the Beanstalk* (1947). He revealed the peculiarity of his new auteur status in a story he told about himself:

> I was stumped one day when a little boy asked, "Do you draw Mickey Mouse?" I had to admit that I do not draw any more. "Then do you think up all the jokes and ideas?" "No," I said, "I don't do that." Finally he looked at me and said, "Mr. Disney, just what do you do?" "Well," I said, "sometimes I think of myself as a little bee. I go from one area of the studio to another and gather pollen and sort of stimulate everybody. I guess that's the job I do."[36]

Disney's rebirth as an auteur, in short, was preceded by his complete withdrawal from all the tasks directly associated with the figure on whom his initial auteurship had been based: brainstorming, drawing, storyboarding, animating, voicing. Instead he had become, like Hitchcock, a television persona in whose name decisions were made by creative underlings who constantly asked each other, What would Walt say?

The opening of Disneyland on June 17, 1955, faithfully chronicled on "Dateline Disneyland," a live segment of *Disneyland*, completed Disney's transformation from creator to impresario. The cartoon characters on whom Disney's initial reputation had been based have now made the transition to live action, impersonated by actors and actresses whose costumes efface their own personalities and who are contractually forbidden to speak. Indeed the only animation on offer in the episode's ninety-minute length is a segment of a few seconds showing the railroad train Casey Jones Jr. Instead Disney announces, reading from the park's dedicatory plaque, "Disneyland is dedicated to the ideals, the dreams, and the hard facts that have created America." Ideals and dreams are supplied in plenty, but the hard facts are drowned out, at least in "Dateline Disneyland," by an endless procession of guests from Danny Thomas and Gale Storm to California governor Goodwin Knight, and an even more seamless musical track that turns European settlers' wars against Native Americans into a Davy Crockett song ("Bang! Went Old Betsy") and provides a heavenly chorus for an obviously faked rocket liftoff.

The emergence of this new Disney, the visionary impresario as auteur, does not eclipse Disney the adapter. It merely redirects the focus of his adaptation from specific texts like *Bambi* and *Treasure Island* to America past and future, completing Disney's shift from the creator of Mickey Mouse to the caretaker of nostalgic and visionary Americana, the man who became the face of a project to repackage the nation's history and technology as wholesome family entertainment.

The resulting transmedia synergy ended the studio's financial strain for good. Disney was a natural for television, not because his programming was consistently brilliant but because it was consistently family friendly. Once the authority of the 1930 Production Code began to collapse in the 1950s, millions of filmgoers came to rely on Disney's negative cachet, the guarantee that his films would contain nothing to offend any member of the family. Bolstered by both the prestige from the Emmy-winning *Underseas Adventure* (1955), Disney's account of the difficulties in filming underwater, and its more direct promotion through *Disneyland*, *20,000 Leagues under the Sea* (1954) became the studio's highest-grossing live-action film to date.[37] After years of financial struggle Disney was suddenly rich and famous, free to supplement his trademark animated films with a long series of live-action films whose principal trademark would be their family-friendly innocuousness. Disney thus became both the perfect television presenter in the 1950s and the perfect counterweight to the rising tide of Hollywood sex and violence in the 1960s.

Both *Disneyland* and *The Mickey Mouse Club* gave Disney an onscreen television presence that made him quite as visible as, and ultimately more influential than, Hitchcock. *The Mickey Mouse Club* had many more unifying features—a relatively constant cast, ongoing stories like *Spin and Marty*, themed days of the week like "Exploring Day," "Circus Day," and "Anything Can Happen Day"—than *Alfred Hitchcock Presents*, which depended on Hitchcock as its main continuing feature. But Disney's smiling face and avuncular manner were the sole features that linked *The Mickey Mouse Club*, whose afternoon airtime aimed at an audience of children, to *Disneyland*, whose prime-time hour aimed more generally at family audiences.

By this time, the maintenance of the brand name had become routine and its power imperialistic. The studio, which had always had a sharp ear for the distinctive voices of character actors, from Billy Gilbert to Sterling Holloway, buried the identities of the performers who supplied its cartoon characters' voices in interminable lists of newsprint credits unless their fame could promote the films rather than the other way around. Disney's reach would soon extend to a truly distinguished list of authors whose work the studio had adapted, including J. M. Barrie, Jules Verne, Rudyard Kipling, and T. H. White. New authors would be considered for adaptation only if they agreed to make their characters available to the company's merchandising arm and agreed to forgo any future claims concerning the results, and Disney attorneys became legendary for their vigilance in detecting possible infringements of the company's valuable copyright of material it had more often adapted than created. When Cynthia Lindsay described Disney in 1960 as "the well-known author of *Alice in Wonderland*, the *Complete Works* of William Shakespeare, and the *Encyclopaedia Britannica*,"[38] she was only confirming popular belief in his status as the author of the films he neither wrote, directed, nor produced and, in an unparalleled back-formation of marketing, of their original properties, now frequently reissued in children's versions as *Walt Disney's 20,000 Leagues under the Sea* or *Walt Disney's The Jungle Books*.

The opening of Walt Disney World in 1971 and EPCOT Center, a true merchandising utopia, in 1982, marked a triumphant demonstration of the franchise's ability to survive the demise of its namesake in 1966. As Disney's direct involvement in his properties had diminished, the imperialistic power of his status as auteur had steadily increased, even though he functioned less as creator than as coordinator, impresario, merchandiser, enforcer, and ultimately, through his still-recognizable signature, corporate logo. The widely remarked renascence of the studio's animation unit with *The Little Mermaid* (1989), *Beauty and the Beast* (1991), and *Aladdin* (1992) marked still another triumph of transmedia corporate hegemony, flooding the marketplace with *Aladdin* storybooks, costumes, lunchboxes, action figures, video games, and Happy Meals under the guise of individual craftsmanship (returning to Walt's values and vision).

Yet it would be a mistake to think of the corporate model of Disney's continuing success as an exception to the general rules of authorship whereby adapters can aspire to the condition of auteurs. No less than Disney do Hitchcock and Kubrick imply corporate models of authorship that seek to hide any signs of corporate production beneath the apparently creative hand of a single author whose work—that is, whose intentions, whose consistency, whose paternal individual care for the franchise, even if that franchise is as suspenseful as Hitchcock's, as prickly as Kubrick's, or as horrific as Stephen King's—can be trusted. Auteurs of this sort are made, not born; they emerge victorious in battle with competing auteurs, whether writers, producers, or stars; and their authorial stamp is less closely connected with original creation than with brand-name consistency and reliability, from Hitchcock's suavely amusing scares to Disney's wholesome family entertainment. Rising from the ranks of metteurs-en-scène to the status of auteur depends on an alignment of several marketable factors: thematic consistency, association with a popular genre, an appetite for the coordination and control of outsized projects, sensitivity to the possibility of broad appeal in such disparate media as movies, television, books, magazines, and T-shirts. Perhaps the most indispensable of these factors is a public persona—Hitchcock's archly ghoulish gravity, Kubrick's fiercely romantic quest for control, Disney's mild paternalism—that can be converted to a trademark more powerful than the other authorial trademarks with which it will inevitably compete.

# CHAPTER ELEVEN

# Postliterary Adaptation

Recent Hollywood adaptations have strayed far from what observers seem to have assumed are their God-given roots in classic and contemporary novels. *Superman* (1978), *Batman* (1989), *The Phantom* (1996), *X-Men* (2000), *Spider-Man* (2002), and *Hulk* (2003) are all based on comic books. *Die Another Day* (2003), like the last several James Bond adventures the Academy of Motion Picture Arts and Sciences has deemed eligible for the Best Adapted Screenplay competition, is based on a franchise character, not any particular novel by Ian Fleming or anyone else. *Pokémon: The First Movie* (1999) is an adaptation of a card game, *Dungeons and Dragons* (2000) of a role-playing game, *American Splendor* (2003) of a reality-based comic strip. *My Big Fat Greek Wedding* (2002), nominated for an Academy Award for Best Original Screenplay, is based on Nia Vardalos's stand-up comedy sketches. Even *Adaptation* (2002), nominated the same year in the Best Adapted Screenplay category, turns its ostensible source into a wildly self-reflexive parable by grafting onto Susan Orlean's nonfictional 1998 book *The Orchid Thief* a preposterous fictional story about its screenwriter's inability to adapt that source.

This tendency away from using novels as sources seems likely to continue.

Recent figures in "Literary Hollywood," the *Hollywood Reporter*'s monthly summary of script, book, and pitch sales for film and television development, show that novels consistently account for less than 15 percent of such sales.[1] Video games are increasingly replacing novels as fodder for Hollywood movies. As communication scholar Stephen Kline observes in "Learners, Spectators, or Gamers?" the video industry is an economic force that dwarfs Hollywood: "U.S. game revenues swelled to $10.6 billion in 2001, a figure which surpasses total annual box office for movies and matches the amount spent on computers for schools."[2] Jonathan Dee adds: "Globally, the industry earned $28 billion in 2002, and in the United States, it's growing at around 20 percent a year. According to *Fortune* magazine, Americans will spend more time playing video games this year—about 75 hours on average—than watching rented videos and DVD's. A nationwide survey found that the percentage of last year's college students who had ever played video games was 100."[3] So far, however, neither reviewers nor theorists have developed a way of talking about postliterary adaptations that has progressed much beyond sarcasm or outrage. The problem is especially acute in the case of movies whose sources are not only nonliterary but nonnarrative. Michael Wilmington, reviewing *Pirates of the Caribbean* (2003) for the *Chicago Tribune*, observed that "this is a movie based not on a novel, history or even another old movie, but on a theme park ride . . . and that means we're lucky if we get any wit, imagination or character at all," as if such a source placed the film beyond the pale of civilized discussion.[4] The summary dismissal of such adaptations is evidently based partly on a literary bias that assumes cinema should adapt only originals more culturally respectable than cinema itself and partly on a narrative bias that assumes that stories are the ingredients that make the best movies.

Yet there is much to be gained by considering the peculiar problems raised by postliterary adaptations—that is, movies based on originals that have neither the cachet of literature nor the armature of a single narrative plot that might seem to make them natural Hollywood material. Even if many more of them were not gathering on the horizon, they would warrant a closer look because they throw a new light on the subject of adaptation and suggest a possible alternative to the chimerical quest for fidelity.[5]

The most reassuring observation to make about nonliterary and, indeed, nonnarrative adaptation is that it is nothing new. It is framed first of all by a long tradition of nonnarrative paintings based on narrative originals drawn from biblical or classical or mythological subjects. Paintings like Mantegna's *St.*

*Sebastian* (c. 1460), Correggio's *Jupiter and Io* (c. 1532), and Poussin's *Rape of the Sabine Women* (c. 1636) not only essentialize the stories on which they are based to nonnarrative tableaux but also, because they presumably feature the faces and bodies of living subjects, narrativize those subjects even as they provide a socially accepted context for the display of the human body. Films like *From the Manger to the Cross* (1912) and *The Birth of a Nation* (1915) can draw on nonnarrative paintings and photographs for much of their imagery under the aegis of restoring a narrative the paintings and photos had merely suggested. In the long history of adaptation, the unmarked model of Hollywood adaptation—a narrative original is converted into a narrative adaptation—is nothing more than a blip of the single century during which two fictional narrative modes, the novel and narrative cinema, dominated their respective media. Because nonnarrative sources or adaptations, or both, have been the norm for most of human history, the current prejudice in favor of a literary narrative–to–cinematic narrative model of adaptation is arbitrary and parochial.

Hollywood offers many earlier examples of adaptations that are neither literary nor narrative. Setting aside the large number of movies based on nonfictional narratives, usually histories or memoirs, there have been such notable adaptations of nonfictional, nonnarrative books to the screen as *Mean Girls* (2004; based on Rosalind Wiseman's *Queen Bees and Wannabes*), *Sex and the Single Girl* (1964; based on Helen Gurley Brown's best-selling guide of the same name), and *Everything You Always Wanted to Know about Sex *but Were Afraid to Ask* (1972; based on a highly selective series of questions from David Reuben's question-and-answer book).

These last two examples, borrowing little more than their provocative titles from their nominal originals, might seem marginal adaptations if they were not so much like many other ostensibly straightforward adaptations that borrow no more. Even before the James Bond franchise floated free of Ian Fleming's novels—interestingly, none of the Bond adventures written by Fleming's authorized successors has been adapted to the screen—nominal adaptations like *The Spy Who Loved Me* (1977), *Moonraker* (1979), *For Your Eyes Only* (1981), and *A View to a Kill* (1985) had long since parted company with the plots, characters, and other non-Bond features of their alleged sources. The same is true for virtually all Hollywood sequels, from *The Godfather: Part II* (1974) and *The Godfather: Part III* (1990) to *The Matrix Reloaded* (2003) and *The Matrix Revolutions* (2004), that were not planned at the time of the original film. Borrowing the continuing cast and the milieu of their originals but freely inventing new adventures and supporting characters, these sequels are still widely considered adaptations. So are Hollywood franchises like *Superman* and *Batman*, whose borrowings are mainly restricted to their heroes' origin stories and roster of enemies, and free adaptations like *V. I. Warshawski* (1991), which is based so loosely on Sara Paretsky's first two novels, *Indemnity Only* and *Deadlock*, that it amounts virtually to a new case for its eponymous heroine.

The tradition of loose adaptations that either narrativize or denarrativize their originals goes back to such primitive films as *King John* (1899), whose single shot shows Sir Herbert Beerbohm Tree's monarch in the sudden and unmotivated throes of death, and *Sherlock Holmes Baffled* (1903), whose outmatched hero would certainly be impossible to identify as Sherlock Holmes if not for the title. Fifty years later, *Singin' in the Rain* (1952), "suggested by the song 'Singin' in the Rain,'" follows in this tradition. Such adaptations challenge the received wisdom that what adaptations borrow is the plots and characters, or some unspecified essence, of their originals. Whatever particular features they borrow, the feature that is most important is the marketing aura of the original, whether that aura is indicated, for instance, by the title *(King John* and *Singin' in the Rain)* or the franchise character *(Sherlock Holmes Baffled)*. Whether or not this aura invokes literary cachet, it always betokens commercial value from whatever associations are most likely to be profitable.

*Clue* (1985), one of the earliest postliterary adaptations, provides a helpful model of how adaptations work when they ignore their originals' narrative functions or invent their own in the absence of a preexisting narrative. The film, "based," as its opening credits point out, "on the Parker Brothers' board game," seems designed not so much to use the rules of the game to frame its original whodunit story as to entice players of the game into movie theaters by rising to the challenge of converting such an interactive, rule-bound activity to the conventions of Hollywood narrative.[6] John Landis and Jonathan Lynn, who devised the film's story, take off from the narrative of the game's backstory, in which Mr. Boddy has been murdered, and players, each of whom plays a different suspect, compete to ascertain which of six suspects has killed him, using which of six weapons, and in which of nine rooms. The solution depends on a random selection from among cards representing each suspect, weapon, and crime site chosen unseen at the beginning of the game before the remaining cards are distributed evenly among the players. Players who move from room to room making suggestions that require other players to show them cards refuting their hypotheses can solve the mystery by the process of elimination or by a canny reading of the evidence other players do and do not share with them or with each other.

The film is compelled both to omit several distinctive features of the game—the cards, the interactive pursuit, the questioning they make possible—and to specify many details the game leaves blank (the expressions on suspects' faces, the look of the mansion in which the murder takes place, a definitive solution out of hundreds of possible solutions). Accordingly, one of its chief pleasures is the recognition of so many elements from the game. The film retains the game's nine rooms, six weapons (all of which are eventually used in its six murders), and six suspects, all true to the rudimentary personalities suggested by their color-coded names—Colonel Mustard (Martin Mull), Professor Plum (Christopher Lloyd), Mr. Green (Michael McKean), Mrs. Peacock (Eileen Brennan), Miss Scarlet (Lesley Ann Warren), Mrs. White (Madeline Kahn)—and adds only one additional suspect, Wadsworth the butler (Tim Curry). The secret passages that allow movement between rooms in opposite corners of the game board play an important role in the film. Faithfully, albeit even more improbably, characters in the film are just as uncertain as are players in the game about which room Mr. Boddy (Lee Ving) was killed in and whether the fatal wound was inflicted by a knife, candlestick, revolver, rope, lead pipe, or wrench. In its most widely remarked innovation, the film even manages three different solutions to the mystery, each featured in one-third of the release prints, so that patrons who wanted to see all three solutions had to return to the theater at least three times. The playful pleasure to be derived from the ingenuity with which these features of the game are preserved in a new medium is quite distinct from the more accustomed pleasure of recognizing Elizabeth Bennet and Mr. Darcy in an adaptation of *Pride and Prejudice.*

To these familiar features the film adds a linear narrative. Lacking the card play that makes the game depend on interactivity and the process of elimination, it is compelled to invent new clues to a new mystery. Yet it would be a mistake to say that the film adds a narrative to a nonnarrative original, for the game itself is narrative in the sense that it provides a starting point, a single foreordained solution, and myriad possible paths by which that solution may be reached. In activating some of these paths and suppressing others, the film does not narrativize the game but converts its multifoliate narrative structure into a somewhat more Cartesian or Aristotelian structure with a single middle to complement the game's single beginning and end. It is no coincidence that Clue, with its strong narrative implications, was the first board game to become the basis for a fictional film. Yet even a brief consideration of other popular contemporary board games—Monopoly, Candy Land, Chutes and Ladders, Mille Bornes, Life—will indicate how many of them are cast in a narrative form equally adaptable to the movies.

Of course, neither Clue nor any of these other games provides anything like enough circumstantial detail for a feature-length film, but movies have been rising to the challenge of filling out skeletal outlines since the earliest days of adaptation. *Clue* specifies a setting—1954 New England—that evokes both the era of the board game's early success in America and the specific historical associations of the decline of McCarthyism, reflected in the film's casting of Washington insiders as Mr. Boddy's blackmail victims and pseudonymous dinner guests.[7] The film's subdued lighting and muted color scheme are inspired by innumerable dark-and-stormy-night Hollywood predecessors. Its staging of group scenes borrows wholesale from the blocking of *Murder on the Orient Express* (1974), to which it is also indebted for the extended retrospect (a long series of brief flashbacks in the earlier film, a jauntily literal reenactment this time) of the murder. Finally, its generally facetious tone, pointedly at odds with its high body count, follows that of the mystery spoof *Murder by Death* (1976), whose cast also includes Eileen Brennan.

These conventions—the playful use of familiar elements from the original source whose recognition in a new context will evoke pleasure, the activation of narrative potentialities already implicit in the source text, the filling out of circumstantial detail by evoking resonant historical settings or piggybacking on established narrative texts or genres, a generally and often incongruously lightsome tone suggesting that this sort of adaptation is fundamentally more whimsical than the serious adaptation of novels or plays or stories—remain surprisingly constant throughout the realm of postliterary adaptation. All four of them are generally preserved intact, and when any of them is varied, the reasons why are explicitly set forth within the adaptation, even when the original that is being adapted is not a board game but a role-playing game, a card game, or a video game.

It is not surprising that video games have so far been the most frequently adapted of all postliterary sources.[8] They have an enormous target audience of gamers, especially if they are adapting a game that extends beyond a single unit to an entire franchise, like *Resident Evil* (2002), based on "Resident Evil I and II"; *Doom* (2005), based on "Doom 1–3"; and *Wing Commander* (1999), based on "Wing Commander I–V." So great is the possible payoff for a successful film adaptation of a video-game franchise that the widely reviled Uwe Boll, undeterred by the critical drubbing that greeted *House of the Dead* (2003), signed on to direct the equally execrated *Alone in the Dark* (2005), even though he was passed over to direct the *House of the Dead 2: Dead Aim* for television (2005). The undisputed queen and king of such franchises, however, are Final Fantasy, which has so far spawned thirty-one video games and six films, and Pokémon, a children's card game whose track record includes nine video games and thirty-six television segments, short films, and theatrically released features.

Few films based on video games have attracted much of an audience outside the gaming community. But video games have obvious attractions as postliterary source material. They look much more like movies than board games do, even sharing the same home-theater screen. Their framing stories and backstories—the attempt to rescue a kidnapped princess or survive in a perilously remote outpost or defeat a series of enemies in hand-to-hand combat—are themselves the stuff of Hollywood narrative. More specifically, their characteristic agon, in which a plucky hero who is clearly standing in for the player at the joystick overcomes a series of increasingly impassible obstacles en route to a distant goal, corresponds closely to the unvarying formula of the contemporary action film. The principal differences between video games and their cinematic incarnations, as in *Clue,* are the loss of interactivity and the substitution of a single linear narrative for a multifoliate narrative. The movie audience cannot choose among different actions and strategies as video-game players can, but their fictional avatars are much less likely to die before reaching their goals. For the reset button that restores the questing hero to life at the lowest level of the quest, movies based on video games substitute the near-death cliffhangers and hairsbreadth escapes familiar from 1930s serials and Saturday-morning cartoons.

Within this context video-game adaptations generally observe all four of the conventions of postliterary adaptations, beginning with the playfully ingenious recycling of elements from the original game. *Super Mario Bros.* (1993), for example, not only retains but constantly emphasizes the title characters' absurd names, Mario Mario (Bob Hoskins) and Luigi Mario (John Leguizamo)—"How many Marios between you?" a suspicious official demands at one point—their professional status as plumbers, their unlikely credentials as heroes, and their quest to rescue a kidnapped princess. The film's wittiest reference to the game comes in its final moments, after the credits have run, when a pair of Japanese businessmen make "a very exciting proposal" to Iggy (Fisher

Stevens) and Spike (Richard Edson), the feckless cousins of the evil King Koopa (Dennis Hopper), for "a video game based on your adventures. What would you call it?" After considering "Iggy's World" and "The Indomitable Spike," the two cry in unison, "Super Koopa Cousins!" playing not only with the game's title but with the unexpected sequence of game-into-movie.

Although few settings apart from a monochrome silver elevator interior evoke the game's visuals directly, the film's emphasis on primary colors and strong visual contrast gives it a look similar to that of *Double Dragon* (1994), whose two heroes, often acting and speaking in cartoonish unison, sport ever-brighter outfits in red and blue monochrome as the film nears its climax. So does a sovereign disdain for the customary primacy of horizontal movement in cinema. The Brothers and their enemies are constantly jumping, falling, and swinging through a series of unusually vertical sets. Their freedom from a single horizontal plane is never as complete as that of the characters in a Road Runner short. But the film's Gravity Lite approach to physics, adopted as well by *Mortal Kombat* (1995), suggests the ability of video game heroes to surmount obstacles and enemies by the simple expedient of jumping over them.

Like other video-game adaptations, however, *Super Mario Bros.* is at pains to distance itself from the source it invokes. The film begins with a prologue of primitive-looking animated shots that purport to show "Brooklyn 65 million years ago" over the game's ineffably upbeat computer-generated music but then moves swiftly to establish a more sophisticated and realistic mix of present-tense sound and image. In the same way, General M. Bison (Raul Julia), when he uses remote-controlled bombs to blow up the boat captained by Colonel Guile (Jean-Claude Van Damme) in *Street Fighter* (1994), exults, "GAME—OVER!" indicating the ways the enemies' combat both is and is not like a video game. *Mortal Kombat,* which looks and feels more like a video game than any other video-game adaptation to date, stages a series of ritualized man-to-man (occasionally woman-to-man) combats in a series of two-dimensional spaces (announcing before the last of them, "Let Mortal Kombat *begin!*") and accompanies them by the exaggerated percussive sounds common to *Super Mario Bros.* and *Street Fighter.* But these scenes are interspersed with a series of dialogue scenes played out in a more clearly three-dimensional space, like the continuity scenes that separate production numbers in an MGM musical. By the time of *Doom*'s release, explicit references to its source text are largely restricted to a single five-minute sequence in optical point-of-view shots imitating the game franchise's most influential feature and numerous ironic references to games, as when Sarge (The Rock), announcing a new mission to his team of Marines, says, "We got us a game," and, on their landing at the Ark that will take them to Mars, enjoins them: "Look alive, men. Game time." Most forthright of all in disavowing its video-game roots is *Lara Croft: Tomb Raider* (2001), which eschews ritualized two-dimensional combat and primary colors altogether. *Lara Croft* is most reminiscent of its video-game origins in the opening battle between its title character and an implacable dino-robot that turns out to be simply a training exercise whose ending is announced when the heroine sees the screen "GAME OVER/Consult your dealer." Thereafter it stages a series of half a dozen increasingly elaborate action sequences that still take up a relatively small amount of the film's running time.

Although *Lara Croft, Resident Evil,* and *Doom* move further from their video-game roots than other such adaptations, the requirements of linear narrative force them all to frame what would otherwise be an endless cycle of quests for talismanic objects or duels against obstacles or enemies within a single larger narrative borrowed from a source outside the game. By far the favorite such narrative is the threat to destroy Earth as we know it, whether from genetically reengineered Martian mutant zombies in *Doom,* the parallel world of Dinohattan in *Super Mario Bros.,* the Altworld in *Mortal Kombat,* or the baleful power of Koga Shuko (Robert Patrick), the mystic who seeks both halves of the medallion that will allow him absolute power over both body and soul in *Double Dragon.* As their mentor Lord Rayden (Christopher Lambert) tells the three questing heroes of *Mortal Kombat:* "The fate of billions will depend upon you." Even in *Street Fighter,* in which the threat is merely to the Allied Nations from the renegade warlord General Bison, the AN are clearly identified with Earth as we know it. The ubiquitous baby-blue helmets stenciled "AN" and the AN's Security Council are an obvious reference to the United Nations, and the AN values of one-world utopianism personified by Colonel Guile are opposed by Bison's aggressive militarism. When Dr. Dhalsim (Roshan Seth), the imprisoned physician ordered to convert Guile's captured friend Carlos Blanka (Robert Mammone) into "the perfect genetic soldier," is seeking to reverse the process, he substitutes footage of a baby cooing and Martin Luther King's "I Have a Dream" speech for the images of nonstop violence with which Carlos has been bombarded.

A similar pattern emerges in *Dungeons and Dragons* (2000), based on a roleplaying game that is potentially even more open-ended than any video game. Although the political struggle that frames the film's quest for a magical rod is restricted to the kingdom if Izmer, the embattled Empress Savina (Thora Birch), challenged by what looks like nothing so much as a wildly insurgent Congress, responds by affirming the traditional American—that is, in the customary logic of Hollywood, universal—values of freedom and equality. And since the film nowhere leaves Izmer or its concerns, the kingdom becomes coterminous with the world. Even the animated *Pokémon: The First Movie* (1998) picks up this motif, its series of ritualized battles on New Island framed by the evil Mewtwo's dreams of defeating the most accomplished Pokémon masters in the world.

Not surprisingly, *Lara Croft: Tomb Raider* is also the most determined of all video-game adaptations to date to flesh out its adventures by invoking a series of narrative contexts outside its original. Lara herself is clearly a combination of James Bond and Indiana Jones. The training combat that opens the film alludes to *From Russia with Love* (1963) and *Never Say Never Again* (1983), and both her occupation and the film's handling of enclosed spaces recalls *Indiana Jones and the Temple of Doom* (1984). The film's preference for exotic settings combines the appeal of both franchises. For the video game's presentation of an endless series of explorations of interchangeable tombs in search of valuable artifacts, the film substitutes a moment virtually unique in human history: a planetary alignment, the last in five thousand years, that will allow some intrepid quester to unite both halves of a triangular talisman and control time.

Other adaptations, though less determined than *Lara Croft* to disavow their video-game roots, fill out their games' atavistic narratives by invoking other, more respectable, narratives from generic borrowings from Hollywood action films to more specific references. The James Bond and Indiana Jones films provide the inspiration for much of the films' framing narratives, structure, and visual design, although *Double Dragon* is more clearly influenced by *Blade Runner* (1982) and *Robocop* (1987); *Doom* by *Alien* (1979), *Aliens* (1986), and *The Matrix* and its sequels (1998–2003); and the computer-animated *Final Fantasy: The Spirits Within* (2001) and *Final Fantasy VII: Advent Children* (2004) by earlier CGI films. The goals, gestures, and iconography of General Bison's regime in *Street Fighter* are obviously patterned after the public image of the Third Reich; the film's celebration of natural versus mechanized combat prowess echoes *Star Wars* (1977); and its climactic sequence, the reactor failure that blows up the villain's stronghold, is lifted from *Dr. No* (1962). The Thieves Guild sequence in *Dungeons and Dragons* borrows liberally from the conscription of Han Solo at Sy Snootles's cantina in *Star Wars*. Casting the improbably slight

Robert Patrick as Koga Shuko allows *Double Dragon* to invoke at once the indestructible T-1000 Patrick had played in *Terminator 2* (1991) and the postapocalyptic Los Angeles landscape *Double Dragon* shares with the earlier film, while adding a witty edge to Patrick's running battle with the LAPD, whose numbers had concealed his disguised villain in *T2*. For viewers with longer memories *Double Dragon* even adds a reference to *The Maltese Falcon* (1941) in Koga Shugo's observation that although he may have lost a son in pursuit of the Dragon medallion, "I can always have another." *Super Mario Bros.* drops facetious references to *The Wizard of Oz* (1939) ("I got a feelin' we're not in Brooklyn no more"), *Star Wars* ("Mario! Take my belt! Trust the fungus!"), and *Doctor Zhivago* (1965) (whose sentimental title song, "Somewhere My Love," twice reduces Koopa's goombahs to tears).

Although most video-game adaptations are less broad in their comedy and parody than *Super Mario Bros.*, most of them, with the notable exception of the self-serious *Doom*, aim for a self-mocking tone that punctures the potential seriousness of their imperiled-Earth scenarios. Lara Croft never goes into combat without tossing a disdainful smirk at her adversaries—an eminently natural reaction, considering the essentially ludic nature of each agon—and the byplay between Ridley (Justin Whalin) and Snails (Marlon Wayans) in *Dungeons and Dragons* remains lightsome right up to the scene in which Snails is killed. Despite targeting a younger audience, *Pokémon: The First Movie* assumes viewers will understand a constant stream of in-jokes, from the heroes' description of vengeful Mewtwo ("Sounds like a real Pokenstein!") to Mewtwo's order to release his army of clones ("Send in the clones!"). Perhaps most surprising of all is the Volkswagen advertisement invoked by one of the Nordic rowers who ferry the Pokémon masters to the site of combat: "We'll get you to New Island before you can say Fahrvergnügen."

Most facetious of all is *Double Dragon*, whose Mohawked henchmen (who end the film carrying signs that read "Will hench for food") are as broadly burlesqued as its guilelessly winsome heroes and whose action is repeatedly interrupted by a pair of newscasters played by George Hamilton and Vanna White. The result, quite different from the genial self-mockery of Jackie Chan, which becomes a part of the game heroes he plays in his action films, is a fundamental lack of seriousness, as if no one involved in such an unlikely adaptation could possibly maintain a straight face through it all. Even *Street Fighter*, whose no-nonsense efficiency in setting up and knocking down its archvillain is markedly at odds with the in-jokes common to video-game films, takes time after the main event for climactic references to *Who Framed Roger Rabbit* (1988) in its dead villain's alarming return to life, looking more than ever like Christopher Lloyd's glazed Judge Doom, and *Terminator 2* ("Lieutenant, take a note. I need a vacation," its exhausted hero tells his aide-de-camp on his own return from presumed death).

It might seem from these elements—playfully inventive references to their video-game originals, selective narrativizing of the games' narrative hints or implications, filling out those hints with borrowings from other fictional or historical narratives, and a generally unserious tone ironically at odds with the violent high-level threats the stories present—that video-game adaptations establish a very loose or uneven relationship to their originals hardly worthy of the name adaptation. In fact the opposite is the case. The leading features determined by the strategies required to adapt video games to the movies have so far been so formulaic that in fewer than fifteen years video-game films have established their own distinctive genre that both acknowledges a debt to their originals and maintains a distance from them.

The fundamental marker of the video-game film genre is a formulaic plot, whereby a single hero or a small group of isolated heroes wards off the threatened destruction of the civilized world and its way of life through a series of battles designed to neutralize the menacing aspirations of a villain equipped with magical powers. Unlike the heroes of actual video games like *Grand Theft Auto*, who are often aggressive in their explorations, their film avatars are almost always defensive, seeking the magical tokens that give them power only in order to thwart their evil adversaries' quest for them. The struggle for world domination simultaneously inflates the importance of individual physical contests and provides a trajectory for them. Attempts to overcome obstacles are generally translated into interpersonal terms, and battles between heroes and villains are calibrated not by increasing difficulty, as in video games, but by ever-more-fearsome opponents and rising stakes, as heroes from *Pokémon*'s Ash and Pikachu to *Mortal Kombat*'s Johnny (Linden Ashby), Liu (Robin Shou), and Sonya (Bridgette Wilson) make last-ditch stands against megalomaniac sorcerers. The combat may involve the clash of armies, as in *Street Fighter*, which subordinates individual fights to the continuity of spectacle by cutting freely during the assault on General Bison's Shadaloo stronghold among different fights involving Colonel Guile, his behaviorally altered friend Carlos, his aide-de-camp Cammy (Kylie Minogue), a Sumo wrestler, a martial-arts expert disguised as a television news reporter, and a pair of equivocal soldiers of fortune. But even in *Doom*, whose weapon of choice is the Bio-Force Gun (a piece of hardware whose initials had been understood to stand for slightly different words in the games), the climax to which it leads is always a hand-to-hand clash between a single hero and his or her archenemy, both of them equipped not with guns but with nothing more than traditional martial-arts weapons, magical talismans, or their bare hands. The fate of the civilized world depends on the outcome of this last battle.

Although the target audience of twelve-to-eighteen-year-old boys—*Pokémon: The First Movie* aims for an even younger audience—cannot interact with the heroes in this struggle as completely as they can in a video arcade by making them choose specific paths, weapons, or strategies, the genre does everything possible to establish an intimacy between viewers and their heroes. The heroes are invariably figures of male fantasy, either identification figures like Billy and Jimmy Lee in *Double Dragon* or hypersexualized females like Lara Croft, and they are invariably young, attractive, and physically fit.[9] Placed in a world in which they are initially either estranged from power like the Mario Brothers or the teenaged principals of *House of the Dead* or limited to localized displays of game-playing prowess like the heroes of *Pokémon* or *Double Dragon*, they rise to power by increasingly assured displays of combat skills that depend on wisdom, focus, and strength. Yet their films, from *Pokémon* ("I'll promise never to fight again if you will") to *Mortal Kombat* ("It's not about death; it's about life") always condemn the violence that drives their plots. Even *Street Fighter*, the most belligerent of them all, reserves its firepower for defensive actions against villains who can be defeated in no other way.

The contrast between the lofty mission of these heroes and their decidedly adolescent credentials helps motivate the distinctively facetious tone of their adaptations. The heroes' uncertainty about their own fitness for epic battle and their discomfort with the formal rhetoric of individual combat by a stream of in-jokes balances the video-game genre's wholesale inflation of testosterone-fueled conflict with a determined lack of seriousness. Video-game adaptations joke about the postapocalyptic devastation in "New Angeles" in 2007, "after the Big One" *(Double Dragon)*, the unlikeliness of romance between heroines and villains *(Lara Croft: Tomb Raider)*, and the bodacious sexual temptations of alternative worlds *(Super Mario Bros.)*. Mostly, however, they joke about themselves, their mixture of fantasy and violence, their relation to the more established genres of the video game, the action film, and the sword-and-sorcery epic, and the adolescent discomfort of heroes who seem not quite ready for prime time.

One reason the heroes of these films may be so uncomfortable is the costumes they are obliged to wear. After the circus explosion of color in *Super Mario Bros.*, later entrants in the video-game genre reserve bright, stylized colors for costumes that help set the combatants off from a world whose color is generally desaturated *(Street Fighter)* or monochrome *(Double Dragon)*. *Super Mario Bros.* had established a correlation between Luigi's bright primary colors and romantic naïveté that *Double Dragon, Mortal Kombat,* and *Dungeons and Dragons* all pick up. Even *Street Fighter,* whose color scheme is far more naturalistic, maintains a contrast between the red associated with General Bison and his thugs and the baby blue of the Allied Nations. The heroes' garb is not only brightly colored but anachronistically flowing and abbreviated, especially in *Double Dragon, Mortal Kombat,* and *Dungeons and Dragons,* all of which demand extensive martial-arts combat that restrictive clothing would inhibit. It is hardly surprising that Lara Croft, the least facetious of video-game heroines to make the leap to the big screen, favors neutral colors for her wardrobe, since it's hard to act serious about what you're doing when you're doing it in a red toga.

The world through which these characters move takes off from the world of video games but seeks to improve on its often primitive graphics and two-dimensional sense of space. Most video-game adaptations contain sequences showing a video-game universe (the facetious prologue to *Super Mario Bros.;* the more realistic, but still stylized, prologue to *Lara Croft: Tomb Raider;* and the long-awaited five-minute point-of-view sequence in *Doom*) in order to contrast their more realistic, detailed, or elaborate space. Throughout *Mortal Kombat* the arenas in which one-on-one contests are played out are strikingly reminiscent of the two-dimensional combat screens of video games, but the scenes in between take place in a more fluid, realistic three-dimensional space. The strong verticals in the production design and blocking of *Super Mario Bros.* provide many reminders of its heroes' relative freedom from gravity. The main reason that the space of *Lara Croft* can seem so much more naturalistic than that of earlier video-game films is that the game on which it is based already presents a much more conventionally three-dimensional space. It is easier to adapt video games to the cinema when they look more like movies to begin with.

A more distinctive feature of the video-game genre is the radical discontinuity of space, not from shot to shot but from scene to scene, and occasionally
within scenes. Both the Mario brothers and the Koopa cousins are frequently
catapulted from one space to another apparently noncontiguous space with all
the suddenness of an ascent to a new level of play or the discovery of one of the
secret passages in *Clue*. Later films that might be expected to naturalize these
abrupt transitions instead heighten the discontinuity of space by visual effects
that toss combatants fighting in a forest onto the deck of a rotting ship *(Mortal Kombat)* or allow spells that open a watery portal from one space to another
*(Dungeons and Dragons)*. The result is a world in which magic is to some degree naturalized and accepted by characters who are still impressed and bewil-
dered by other magical feats. This carefully maintained balance of credulity and
skepticism—the acceptance of some magical manifestations and the capacity
to be awed by others—stands in contrast to the world of video games, in which
all magic is equally naturalized for players who must accept magical help
against magical threats in order to survive.

This partial naturalizing of magic is the rationale for the leading technical
features of the genre. Their visual design sets heroes and villains off from a
monochrome background that invokes both the future and the past. Their
sound design depends on the heavy use of ostinato musical figures stripped of
any harmonic progression that recall the endlessly repeating computerized
loops of video-game sound tracks. *Doom* adds a constant stream of sound
effects in three-dimensional space, creating an aural space that envelops audience members who cannot enter the visual space as completely as they could
in the games. In nearly every case the films' visual effects are pyrotechnical and
far more important than characters or casting. It hardly matters what form
these effects take as long as they are inventive, unrealistic, and self-advertising.
The Dinohattan of *Super Mario Bros.* features animatronic beasts, *Double
Dragon* elaborate prosthetic makeup, *Dungeons and Dragons* digitized backgrounds and virtual camera movements. Even *Street Fighter,* along with *Doom*
the most consistently naturalistic of these films, ends by giving its resurrected
villain a bolt of "superconductor electromagnetism" that endows him with supernatural powers for his final battle with Colonel Guile. These effects are designed not to be uncritically accepted but to impress.

These common features of video-game adaptations allow each new adaptation to refer not only to its progenitor game but to a video-game genre whose
distinctive features, separating it from both action films and video games, con-

stitute a self-contained universe whose rules and boundaries are familiar to the target audience yet constantly subject to change. The ability to recognize and negotiate such a system amounts to a genre literacy that depends not on literature or literariness but on the ability to master a parallel set of conventions that establish the genre and to recognize transformations that make change possible. The two most interesting test cases of genre literacy video-game adaptations have produced to date, *Street Fighter* and *Lara Croft: Tomb Raider*, are those that fit the genre's conventions least well. Both films expand the possibilities of video-game adaptations by combining elements of the genre with elements of other genres. Both therefore seek to identify themselves with the video games on which they are based while making unusually strenuous attempts to disavow those identifications.

Even though it is more ambitious in its cross-pollination of genres, the case of *Lara Croft: Tomb Raider* is simpler because its tactics are more familiar. Simon West, the director who admits that "I'm as much of a snob about video games as anyone," clearly sought to create a crossover film that would appeal to a much larger audience than the game's demographic without alienating any of that demographic. Accordingly, he announces in "Digging into *Tomb Raider*," an interview featurette on the DVD release of the film, that "the way to make it work is to take it seriously." Angelina Jolie, his star, adds: "Not cartoony. Not camp." Like *Super Mario Bros.*, then, the film apparently invokes its video-game model, "Tomb Raider," only in order to disavow it as subliterary and unserious. Unlike *Super Mario Bros.* and its elder offspring, however, the film maintains its distance from its equivocal model not by facetiousness but by grafting on a plot and tone borrowed from the relatively respectable models of James Bond and Indiana Jones and the kind of naturalism West ascribes to location shooting. "It looks totally real, because you're there," he says of scenes shot in Iceland and at Angkor Wat, quite as if he were directing a biblical adaptation.

At the same time, Mike McGarvey, CEO of EIDOS Interactive, avers on another, equally self-congratulatory featurette—"Are You Game?"—that he and Jeremy Heath-Smith, EIDOS Head of Global Development, "were very involved in looking at the script and the cast and the characters and making sure, once again, that the integrity of the product would be maintained. We felt we didn't really want to compromise." For McGarvey, compromise evidently involves not infidelity but cultural slippage, and casting Academy Award winner Jolie is a stand against the compromise of the game's integrity. The ultimate purpose of this confluence of genres is a marketing synergy that will boost the stock of the film, the game, and any possible sequels and spin-offs.

*Street Fighter* shows how this synergy can operate in the virtual absence of textual markers. The film takes its title from a video game, and its opening credits duly note that it is "Based on the 'Capcom' video game 'Street Fighter II.'" Yet the film borrows almost nothing from the game beyond the names of its leading characters and their inclination to battle each other with every weapon at their disposal. Its geopolitical outlook, its brusquely professional tone, the militaristic trappings of hero and villain, the series of battles it dovetails involving different combatants often fighting simultaneously in separate locations—all of these owe less to its nominal source than to the Jean-Claude Van Damme action/kickboxing franchise (*Universal Soldier* [1992], et al.). What Universal gets from the game "Street Fighter" is not any structural or thematic elements the Van Damme franchise lacks but rather the addition of a new trademark that will increase the size of Van Damme's audience and extend it further among younger males even as it boosts the sales of the game series. Hence a promotional video for a new video game, "Street Fighter: The Movie" that introduces the videotape release of the film freely intercuts screens from the video game with live-action footage from the movie over the announcement: "Battle head to head with the stars of the movie!" The supreme token of genre literacy, it seems, is the appetite for new versions of a familiar story in whatever mutually supporting medium generates them.

The ultimate example to date of this channeling of genre literacy into marketing synergy is a pair of movies that do not fit the relatively narrow genre of video-game adaptations because they are based on theme-park attractions. The leading and practically the sole player in this area is the Disney Company. Having tested the possibility of bringing the attractions of Disneyland and Walt Disney World to the screen with the 1997 TV film *Tower of Terror,* the company has since released three features based on theme-park attractions. The first of these, *The Country Bears* (2002), is little more than a rehash of *The Blues Brothers* (1980) and *The Blues Brothers 2000* (1998) refitted for live-action versions of the animatronic characters of the "Country Bear Jamboree" at Disneyland (since torn down and replaced by "Winnie the Pooh") and Walt Disney World. *Pirates of the Caribbean* and *The Haunted Mansion* (2003), however, are worth a closer look. Both their originals would seem to represent formidable challenges to any attempt at adaptation. Yet both adaptations reflect familiar strategies driven not by duplication but by expansion, inflation, and mutual commercialization, strategies that illuminate the corpus of postliterary adaptations and the apparently antithetical group of more traditional adaptations as well.

Neither attraction offers anything like a fully formed narrative that can serve as the basis of a feature film. "Pirates of the Caribbean" offers a tour of a series of animatronic pirate tableaux from boats carrying two dozen visitors, "The Haunted Mansion" a voice-over-guided tour of a haunted house from moving pods carrying two or three. But both of them, like board games and video games, provide narrative cues that can be developed, a succession of images, scenes, and set pieces with clear narrative implications. "Pirates of the Caribbean" features the torture of new prisoners, a bride auction, the sacking of a town, and the attempt of several pirates to escape their prison cells by enticing a dog who is holding the keys. Visitors to "The Haunted Mansion" are shut in a room with no apparent means of escape, driven through scenes of dissolution, and taken through a haunted attic, an animated graveyard, and a "swinging wake." Both attractions imply not a single coherent backstory that would explain all the sights and sounds with which visitors are bombarded but hints of a hundred different backstories, all redolent of conventional associations (the pirates are always swaggering, vulgar, and drunk, the ghosts always amusingly scary), with no attempt to reconcile them.

Although both attractions seek to immerse visitors in an all-embracing world strikingly similar to the world presented onscreen in a darkened movie theater, neither provides the well-formed narrative that adapters would expect from a source novel. Instead, they are more closely analogous to a far more immediate antecedent of Hollywood movies: pitch sessions in which writers toss out dozens of ideas for specific images or characters or scenes that could be incorporated into a film. When a pitch is based on an original concept, the film that follows is less likely to arise from an armature of narrative than from a series of obligatory episodes for which the narrative will provide the excuse. Even when the pitch is based on a novel, however, Hollywood filmmakers know all too well that its success is as likely to be based on the opportunities it provides for moving or exciting scenes as on the novel's plot or characters or thematic nexus. In this light "Pirates of the Caribbean" and "The Haunted Mansion" are less like atavistic prenarratives than like second-generation properties shorn of any literary pretensions and ready for pitching.

A second obstacle to adaptation, the fact that both films are based on multiple sources, separate attractions in Disneyland and Walt Disney World, is largely overcome by Disney's penchant for standardization, which subordinates minor differences in the sequence and details of the tableaux presented to visitors in California and Florida to a larger homogeneity. But a third presents opportunities that the two attractions handle in very different ways. Although both "Pirates of the Caribbean" and "The Haunted Mansion" present many human or formerly human figures, neither features anything that could be called a character, certainly not a hero. In both cases the main characters in the tour, as in point-of-view video games like "Doom," are the visitors themselves. True, the visitors are assigned passive roles rather than the strenuously active roles they are expected to take on in "Doom." They are expected simply to react with condign amusement and fear to the much more active animatronic figures presented to them. Nor do the visitors, whose reactions may differ sharply, constitute anything like a single pivotal character, heroic or not. The challenge of each film, like that of video-game films like *Doom*, is to invent characters who will be satisfactory substitutes or supplements for the visitors. This time, however, the challenge is less demanding because the visitors to theme-park attractions are less interactive than video gamers, more like movie audiences already; even their movements from one space to the next are tightly scripted by vehicles they cannot control and a voice-over commentary that cues their reactions.

Both film adaptations take the opportunity to cast stars in performances so characteristic that performance becomes one of their films' principal pleasures. Johnny Depp, the star of *Pirates of the Caribbean*, is cast as Captain Jack Sparrow, the pirate in the thick of the action. Depp and Geoffrey Rush, who plays Barbossa, flesh out the roles the attraction had implied, though both are in their own ways very different pirates from those back in Disney World. The roles of the audience's surrogate, the characters who experience the spectacle and adventure of the movie, are assumed by Keira Knightley as Elizabeth Swann and, to a lesser extent, Orlando Bloom as Will Turner, though both are more active than any audience would be. In *The Haunted Mansion*, by contrast, the featured ghosts and creeps played by Terence Stamp, Wallace Shawn, and Jennifer Tilly are subordinated to the family of real-estate agent Jim Evers, who are trapped in the mansion in much the same way visitors to the attraction are trapped. The casting of Eddie Murphy as Jim allows audiences the luxury of believing that they would be just as insouciant if they were trapped in a haunted house. At the same time, the film motivates its spooky complications and their eventual resolution by an appeal to the sort of family values with which Disney has long been associated. Jim is an incorrigible workaholic who never has time for his family. Their stop at the mansion is a detour of "twenty minutes, tops," in a long-promised family outing. The family is quickly separated by the determination of Master Gracey (Nathaniel Parker) to reclaim Jim's wife Sara (Marsha Thomason) as the reincarnation of the bride who killed herself long ago, plunging Gracey's predecessor into suicidal grief. And the Evers family's only hope for escaping the mansion is to work as a team, incorporating especially the skills and suggestions of their daughter Megan (Aree Davis) and their son Michael (Marc John Jefferies), the obvious stand-ins for the attraction's target clientele. In their different ways, then, both adaptations seek to improve on their sources by offering viewers the opportunity to identify with attractively idealized versions of themselves as participant spectators while they regard spectacles populated by larger-than-life character stars.

Both films provide just enough specific allusions to their originals to remind veteran visitors of their earlier experiences. *Pirates of the Caribbean* uses the attraction's key-carrying dog as the basis for the pirates' attempted escape from prison and scatters a host of visual references from the dunking of the mayor and the roped line of slave women to the design of its trademark medallion. *The Haunted Mansion* borrows the visual design of its library, corridor, ballroom, graveyard, and many of its supporting spooks, as well as the tagline "There's always *my* way" to indicate an unlikely way to escape the mansion. Both films recycle the theme songs associated with their respective sources, "Yo Ho! The Pirate's Life for Me" and "Grim Grinning Ghosts." Yet these allusions form only a minor part of a network of references that broaden both the scope and the tone of their originals, even as they multiply the number of extras, effects, and explosions in the attractions. *Pirates of the Caribbean* adds expository sequences on land, relatively virtuous pirates to balance the attraction's drunken bullies, and heroic pomp, from the redcoats in formation to the pirates' defeat, to balance its orgies of malfeasance. *The Haunted Mansion* sets off its spooky apparitions by Jim Evers's misbegotten pragmatism ("Phew! Oh, man!" he exclaims in distaste on opening a moldering casket), the unbridled comedy of the plaster casts following "Grim Grinning Ghosts" with a succession of tags from the barbershop quartet repertory, and allusions to dozens of other films (Mike tells Jim, "I see dead people," and the fiery end of Terence Stamp's butler, Ramsley, recalls the death of the title character in *Saboteur*) and the Disney brand name itself (a Mickey Mouse padlock on the mansion's front gate). Both films take every opportunity to add computer-generated visual effects to their sources' animatronic creations. And of course both intersperse

their attractions' nonstop action with scenes designed to provide greater re-
pose, relief, or emotional intimacy.

For all these reasons it would be an obvious mistake to see either film as a
straightforward adaptation of a single source text. Not only was neither attraction originally intended as a source text for a narrative film, but neither attraction was ever intended to provide an isolated or discrete textual experience.
Although both "Pirates of the Caribbean" and "The Haunted Mansion" present
self-enclosed worlds, those worlds depend in turn on the larger and even more
self-enclosed world of Disneyland or Walt Disney World. Visitors waiting in
line for either attraction are bombarded with images of nearby attractions in
locations (Adventureland or New Orleans Square) designed to integrate individual attractions into a larger can't-miss experience; visitors emerging from
either one exit to a gift shop filled with attraction-themed merchandise. Like
every other attraction in Disneyland or Walt Disney World, they are designed
not just to provide entertainment but to sell something else—postcards, T-
shirts, related attractions, return trips to the Magic Kingdom, and sequels like
*Pirates of the Caribbean: Dead Man's Chest* (2006) and *Pirates of the Caribbean:
At World's End* (2007).

The DVD releases of *Pirates of the Caribbean* and *The Haunted Mansion* extend this pattern even more expertly than the releases of video-game adaptations. *The Haunted Mansion* includes an audio commentary, a deleted scene, a
music video, a virtual tour of the mansion, a featurette on the making of the
graveyard sequence, and a history of the theme-park attraction. The whole
package is supplemented by fliers offering discounts on other Disney DVDs
and a sweepstakes promoting the Disney Resort's Twilight Zone Tower of Terror. The two-DVD "Collector's Edition" of *Pirates of the Caribbean* is even more
heavily loaded with extras, ranging from multiple voice-over commentaries,
deleted scenes, and production featurettes to a television segment from *Walt
Disney's Wonderful World of Color* promoting the new attraction and DVD-
ROM links to an online history of the attraction and an image gallery docu-
menting its creation.[10] Such a complete edition could have been superseded
only by a three-DVD edition including "The Lost Disk," with eight new featurettes ranging from "Becoming Captain Jack" to "Spirit of the Ride," every element of the presentation expressly designed to increase traffic to every other
element of the Disney franchise by a combination of inflation, amplification,
gigantism, market broadening, and just enough duplication to evoke the absent alternative incarnation to which access is readily available for a small fee.

Indeed, the main reason more recent films and television programs have not been based on theme-park attractions is probably that so many of the attractions, located in parks owned by entertainment conglomerates like Universal Studios or tied to television franchises like *Sesame Street*, are already based on films or television programs themselves.

This market-driven approach to adaptation may seem poles apart from Jane Austen. For all the crass frankness of its determination to strip-mine nominal sources for their commercial potential without regard for any intrinsic value that might justify closer textual fidelity to them, however, *The Haunted Mansion* is not so far from *Pride and Prejudice* after all. When Hollywood moguls first fastened on classic novels (as opposed to sensational classics like *Frankenstein*, which had begun inspiring cinematic adaptations a generation earlier), their publicity departments' trumpeting of the adaptations' artistic cachet was equally a market-driven argument for the adaptations' commercial value as parasites or substitutes for commodities whose prestige demonstrated their proven appeal. Underlying contemporary theorists' assumptions about the normative value of novelistic adaptation is the ability of an earlier generation of film producers to appeal to a tradition whose prestige value not only extended into the past but depended on the originals' pastness. Now that the target audience for movies has shifted from families to teenaged boys indifferent to the distant past and its alleged classics, nothing is more natural than that producers would seek a similar cachet among experiences that its new target audience already values. Whether the medium under adaptation is prose fiction, video games, or theme-park attractions, the bottom line remains the ability of the original to presell the adaptation.

The most important twist postliterary adaptations have added to this well-established system is the ability of adaptations to return the favor by selling their originals in quantity, sending players and visitors back to video games and theme parks waiting in turn to advertise still other entertainment products. The most efficient synergy yet is the case of video games like "Aladdin," "Finding Nemo," and "The Matrix," which are increasingly developed in tandem with their mutually supporting feature-film avatars, so that all three of these films, for instance, incorporate action sequences specifically designed to transfer readily to the video game.[11] A new day may be dawning with the 2007 release of Threshold Entertainment's premiere film, *Foodfight!* an animated tale of after-hours high jinks in a supermarket that features some eighty characters associated with brand names like Uncle Ben, Mrs. Butterworth, Charlie the Tuna, and Mr. Clean. Although Eric A. Taub quotes Threshold chief Larry Kasanoff as insisting that a cast of newly invented leading characters would prevent the film from being "one long product commercial," Kasanoff acknowledges that he "expect[s] the packaged goods manufacturers featured in the movie to spend heavily to promote it."[12] Even before its release, the film raises provocative questions concerning the relation between the manufacturing industries that supply brand-name products to supermarket shoppers and the culture industries that supply brand-name authors and novels to the book-buying public. For all the obvious points of contrast with the gentility of literary adaptation as process and industry, postliterary adaptation seems like one more version of business as usual—with the emphasis, as usual, on business.

# CHAPTER TWELVE

# Based on a True Story

This survey of problems in adaptation has considered a wide variety of films, from silent shorts aiming at epic weight to heritage adaptations of canonical English novels to adaptations that choose video games or theme-park attractions as their source texts. It might seem that postliterary adaptations mark a vanishing point in adaptation studies. But one last kind of adaptation is still more problematic and more seldom treated as adaptation: films that profess to be based on no source text at all but on a true story.

The label "based on a true story" seems to have come into common use only during the 1990s. The earliest films I have been able to find that carry the label are *Awakenings* (1990) and *GoodFellas* (1990). If the label is recent, however, the concept is much older. *Dog Day Afternoon* (1975) begins with the title, "What you are about to see is true—it happened in Brooklyn, New York, on August 22, 1972." A film may establish its credentials as based on a true story by the detailed historical prologues that begin *Empire of the Sun* (1987), *Schindler's List* (1993), or *Kundun* (1996) or the epilogues that indicate the fate of the leading characters at the end of *The French Connection* (1971), *Amistad* (1997), and *The Insider* (1999). But the presence of such titles is no guarantee that the film has any basis in a true story. Tobe Hooper introduces his wholly fictional film *The Texas Chain Saw Massacre* (1974) with the announcement: "The film which you are about to see is an account of the tragedy which befell a group of five youths, in particular Sally Hardesty and her invalid brother, Franklin. . . . The events of that day were to lead to the discovery of one of the most bizarre crimes in the annals of American history, the Texas Chain Saw Massacre." Hooper's claim is echoed and sharpened twenty years later in the opening title to *Fargo* (1996): "This is a true story. The events depicted in this film took place in Minnesota in 1987. At the request of the survivors, the names have been changed. Out of respect for the dead, the rest has been told exactly as it occurred." Only when the film's screenplay was published the following year did Ethan and Joel Coen acknowledge what hundreds of Web commentators had been arguing for months: *Fargo* only "pretends to be true."[1] Its claim to be a true story—or, more accurately, to be based on a true story, with a few identifying details changed as a gesture of respect for the dead—was itself untrue. *Animal House* (1978) ends with a far more transparently duplicitous montage sequence that freezes on the leading characters over subtitles that identify, for example, Bluto (John Belushi) and the coed he has just grabbed as "Senator and Mrs. John Blutarski."

Even though they lack any such overt identifying labels as the legend "based on a true story" or the contextual titles that seek to situate them in history, films recognizably based on true stories go back still further, to *I'll Cry Tomorrow* (1955), *Rope* (1948), *The Great Moment* (1944), *Mutiny on the Bounty* (1935), and *Kameradschaft* (1931). All of Sergei Eisenstein's films from *Strike* (*Stachka* [1925]) to *Ivan the Terrible* (1946) could reasonably be described as based on a true story. Of course none of Eisenstein's films carries any such label, and not only because it would not become fashionable for another fifty years. Each of them poses as history (*Strike* and *Battleship Potemkin* [1925] as chamber history, *October* [1927] and *Ivan the Terrible* as epic history), and their historical claims would be reduced, not elevated, by the claim to be based on a true story. So would the claims of *From the Manger to the Cross* (1912), *Intolerance* (1916), or any biblical adaptation that plays fast and loose with history by filtering it through variously reliable intermediate sources or inventing new incidents in the interest of dramatic impact. These examples suggest that "a true story" has a unique status among source texts.

"Based on a true story" indicates a source text that both is and is not a text, one that carries some markers common to most source texts but not others. Most source texts have authors and publishers who have sold the adaptation rights in return for a given amount of money and a screen credit. But "a true story" is authorless, publisherless, agentless. Because the description may be claimed or not at the filmmakers' pleasure, it appears only when it is to the film's advantage. There is no need for Steven Spielberg or Clint Eastwood to claim that *Schindler's List* or *Midnight in the Garden of Good and Evil* (1997) is based on a true story when the credits can include the more ambitious claim, "Based on the [best-selling] book by Thomas Keneally" or "by John Berendt." But if the label does not appear in the screen credits, it can always be added to the packaging. The cover to the DVD release of *Hotel Rwanda* (2004), "written by Keir Pearson and Terry George," announces that it is based on a true story. So does the DVD cover of *City of God* (*Cidade de Deus* [2002]), even though its credits clearly indicate that it is based on a novel by (*"do romance de"*) Paulo Lins.

Given that the claim to be based on a true story is always strategic or generic rather than historical or existential, what exactly does it mean? One thing it does not mean is that the film is an accurate record of historical events. Commentators on documentaries and docudramas have long decreed that historical reenactments in cinema, no matter how carefully researched, are not historical records but fictionalized reenactments of historical events. Even when Audie Murphy is cast in the starring role of *To Hell and Back* (1955), a World War II film based on his own war memoir, he is only playing himself, not reliving the stresses, risks, and dangers that made him the most decorated enlisted soldier in the war. Movies can become historical records of staging, performance, costuming, set decoration, and even representations of history. But they can no more be accurate records of the historical events they purport to represent than a film adaptation can be an accurate record of any particular source text.

Nor does the label appear in written histories, whose truth claims, by and large, are considerably more ambitious and exigent. If each volume of Jacob Burkhardt's *Civilization of the Renaissance in Italy* or Will and Ariel Durant's *Story of Civilization* had been accompanied by the line "based on a true story," it would have acted as a disclaimer rather than the opposite. The claim is made only on behalf of movies (and, in principle, of television and radio programs) whose representational conventions are so similar to those of recordings of historical events that audiences might well take those representations as themselves historical if it were not for counterconventions like the casting of actors and actresses as historical figures.[2] The boundary between documentary and realist audiovisual fiction is notoriously problematic, as Orson Welles demonstrated in his 1938 radio broadcast "The War of the Worlds," whose novel form—a musical program interrupted by increasingly urgent news bulletins, interviews, and eyewitness accounts—fooled thousands of listeners into believing Martians had invaded New Jersey, even though the program never claimed to be based on a true story and began by identifying itself explicitly as based on H. G. Wells's 1898 science-fiction novel.

But the claim, when it does appear, is still more narrow than that. Movies presenting themselves as based on a true story are not simply claiming to tell the truth. Nor are they claiming a specifically educational function, as in instructional films like the *Why We Fight* series (1943–45) that Frank Capra produced and directed for the War Department or his later science films (1956–58) for Bell Labs. The difference between making true statements and presenting a true story explains why the claim is made only for films that have a historical rather than a pedagogical basis.

Moreover, films presenting well-known events from public history tend to avoid the tag as well, and for good reason. If Ronald Maxwell's *Gettysburg* (1993) were described as being based on a true story, the claim would be both too modest, since the film sets out to dramatize a chapter of public history rather than being based on one, and too inflated, since the film is actually based on a novel by Michael Shaara. Nor is the claim attached to biblical spectacles like *The Ten Commandments* (1956), historical epics about Queen Elizabeth or Christopher Columbus, audiovisual compendiums like Ken Burns's *Baseball* (1994), animated cartoons like *Pocahontas* (1995) or *The Prince of Egypt* (1998), or films whose version of real-life events has been refracted by a source novel, like *Psycho* (1960) or *The Silence of the Lambs* (1991).

The claim to be based on a true story is both vaguer and more circumscribed. Oliver Stone prefaces his film *Salvador* (1986) with a title indicating that "this film is based on events that occurred in 1980–1981. Characters have been fictionalized." The claim may be misleading, but the distinction is clear: at least some of the events the film portrays actually happened but not necessarily to the film's characters. The phrase "based on a true story" begins with an ambiguous verb—just what does it mean to be "based" on a true story? what sort of fidelity to the historical record is offered?—and ends with the implication that even before the film was made, a story was circulating that was not only about actual events but was a true account of them, as if extracting a story from actual events or imposing a story on them was unproblematic. The result is not exactly a truth claim; it is not an invocation of either the conventions of realist fiction or Roland Barthes' reality effect; and it is not made in films about well-known events in public history like *Mutiny on the Bounty* or *Pearl Harbor* (2001) but of forgotten events, like the 1839 slave revolt aboard the *Amistad* or the heretofore private history of citizens like the amateur bank robbers of *Dog Day Afternoon,* whose stories have never been told before.

The stakes in the claim to be based on a true story are perhaps best illustrated by a parallel claim made in *Stan Mack's Real Life Funnies,* for years a staple of the *Village Voice.* Although Mack's drawings were presented in strip form like *Peanuts* and *Doonesbury,* they did not tell a continuous story from week to week or, sometimes, even from panel to panel. Mack simply attended some promising event like a casting call for *Oh! Calcutta!* or the Modern Language Association convention, jotted down the more outrageous remarks he overheard, and then enshrined them in speech bubbles surmounting drawings of their speakers. Although Mack maintained that "I try to draw the people who actually said the lines,"[3] this resemblance is less important to his strip's effect than its trademark guarantee: "All Dialogue is Reported Verbatim."

Oftentimes this guarantee is not particularly important, since a good deal of the dialogue in Mack's strip carries the same weight that it would in a fictional TV comedy. Take this exchange between a man and a woman at lunch:

—So, how's your love life, Larry?
—Do I ask you about *your* love life?
—You never did when we were married.

Its joke is funny and the story it tells complete in itself, as in the even shorter confidence from one woman to another, "John's easy to entertain. . . . I just take him to bed."

In other cases, however, the claim of accurate reporting is indispensable. When a bearded man in a head kerchief and a long robe proclaims, "I'm ready to face the world—*at long last,*" or when a press photographer complains, "*You're* depressed! My estranged wife's lover is here with a *floor pass!*" their speeches do not quite amount to self-contained jokes. The first joke depends on two contrasts, one between the remark's generic self-help rhetoric and the exaggerated self-seriousness of its concluding qualification, and another between the gravity of the speaker's announcement and his absurd appearance. The second joke depends on a contrast between the photographer's presumed professionalism and his neurotic self-concern. But none of these contrasts is quite strong enough to justify either pronouncement as a freestanding joke. What makes them funny enough to repeat is their revelation of characters they do not exhaust, and the assurance that somebody out there really talks like this, so that real life, which readers might expect to be part of Mack's setup lines, becomes part of his punch lines. In cases like these the claim that the dialogue is being reported verbatim is essentially a claim to authority. Like Bakhtin's "authoritative word,"[4] or the divine Book of Life that serves as the model for so many eighteenth-century novels, it acts as a transcendental intertext, a master text that establishes the value of the discourse at hand. In this case the transcendental intertext assures readers that the quoted speech is representative of a particular individual's or subculture's way of thinking and talking. It is these implied habits rather than the discourse itself that can be put on display.

In the same way, the claim to be based on a true story appeals to the master text of the true story—a secularized, authorless Book of Life not to be confused with reality or history or the truth—for specific kinds of textual authority, all of them having only an incidental relation to historical accuracy. Like Stan Mack's guarantee, the claim turns the represented people and situations into a series of setup lines whose punch line is that everything the film is showing, or at least a tantalizingly undefined part of it, actually happened. In chapter 6 I argued that Hollywood adaptations of best sellers, from *Gone with the Wind* (1939) to *Lord of the Rings* (2001–3), are marketed in ways that seek to trade on the authority of their progenitor texts. Like the novels that inspired them, the claim implies, they will be sweeping, or incisive, or emotionally transporting— but, in any case, worthy of similar commercial success as entertainment. As Dudley Andrew has pointed out, however, "the notion of a transcendent order to which the system of the cinema is beholden in its practice goes well beyond the limited case of adaptation." Andrew points to the "city symphony" as one example of "an adaptation of a concept by the cinema."[5] He has recently identified a far more pervasive example: the case of historical films. Since "the debt owed to the traces of the past by the historian is analogous to the onus felt by the filmmaker to respect some text from the cultural storehouse," Andrew asks, "why not treat historical films as adaptations?"[6]

As Andrew demonstrates, the relation between history and fiction as intertexts is complex. But they have at least one obvious similarity: their availability as transcendental authorities that can advance claims for a film's value, not as an accurate reproduction but as an entertaining experience, from a transcendental position apparently outside the film and the filmmaking industry.

The point of claiming that a film is based on a true story is not to establish truth or fidelity to the truth as a predicate of the discourse but to use the category of the true story as a privileged master text that justifies the film's claims to certain kinds of authority—ideally by placing them beyond question.

Although they pretend to be transcendental, the truth claims of the tag "based on a true story" are always strategic and instrumental. The film's relation to a true story is used to support claims about its value as entertainment that are the real point of its ostensible truth claims. These claims can take many forms. In *Dog Day Afternoon*, for example, the shapeless inconsequence of the botched bank robbery attempted by Sonny (Al Pacino), and especially its abrupt and disconcertingly off-key conclusion, are excused by the implied claim: Don't blame us; we didn't make this up. A similar claim is implied on behalf of the tantalizingly inconclusive ending of *Midnight in the Garden of Good and Evil* and the sad return of Leonard Lowe (Robert De Niro) and his fellow sufferers to incapacitating illness at the end of *Awakenings*.

By invoking its roots in a true story, *Awakenings* employs another strategy that depends on its presumed fidelity to the factual basis of its events: Isn't this sad? It would be wonderful, the film implies, if the miraculous recovery Leonard and the other patients of Dr. Malcolm Sayer (Robin Williams) enjoyed could have been permanent rather than temporary. But it was not to be, as we know from consulting the record. In the same way, films as different as *Shadowlands* (1993) and *The Diary of Anne Frank* (1959) prepare and justify their somber endings as required by biographical or historical record, even though improving history has always been an option for fictionalizations in any medium. A related claim—Isn't this inspiring?—is urged by films like *Born Free* (1966), *Stand and Deliver* (1988), *My Left Foot* (1989), and *Antwone Fisher* (2002), which assure their viewers that nothing is impossible even for people who do not happen to be the heroes of fictional movies. Given the endless search for real-life heroes who fit the mold of Hollywood genres, it is not surprising to find films like *Norma Rae* (1979), *The Right Stuff* (1983), *Erin Brockovich* (2000), *Schindler's List*, and both versions of *Walking Tall* (1973, 2004) depending on still a third related claim: that heroism is possible even under the most adverse circumstances. Isn't this heroic? they ask, inviting admiration rather than emulation. All three questions muster truth claims as a support for stories that might well have trouble standing on their own without them.

In *The Wrong Man* (1957) the convenient coincidence of the robber being captured just as Henry Fonda, whose life has been ruined by his being mistaken for him, starts to pray is excused by a more specific claim: truth is stranger than fiction. It can show the real robber telling the store owners who want to turn him in to the police, "This is the first time I've ever done this"—a line that, as Alfred Hitchcock, the film's director, pointed out, "you wouldn't dream of writing into a scenario"[7]—because that's what the robber actually said to the couple who captured him. The claim often serves to prop up films whose stories, like some of Stan Mack's real-life funnies, need the support of a truth claim. The truth-is-stranger-than-fiction marketing campaigns for *I Love You to Death* (1990) and *It Could Happen to You* (1994) bolstered the films' unlikely premises—a loving wife hires hit men to kill her philandering husband, but the couple reconcile after the planned killing goes comically awry; a police officer shares the proceeds of a lottery ticket with a waitress to whom he'd offered half his possible winnings in lieu of a tip—by insisting that they were based on real-life incidents and so could not be questioned.

In *The Insider* the claim behind the truth claim is revealingly different: Now it can be told. Although tobacco spokespersons have been lying for years about their knowledge of the dangers of smoking, and although even the segment of *60 Minutes* on the subject was forced to pull its punches, this fictionalized account can give you the true story. Films register this claim whenever they purport to reveal long-held secrets, especially if those secrets have been mandated by racism (*Black like Me* [1964]), sexual prudishness (*Boys Don't Cry* [1999]), or the need to protect the innocent (*Donnie Brasco* [1997]). The broad field of such exposés includes the television films *Tonya and Nancy: The Inside Story* (1994), *Unabomber: The True Story* (1996), *Cinderella Man: The Real Jim Braddock Story* (2005), and the burlesque *The Positively True Adventures of the Alleged Texas Cheerleader–Murdering Mom* (1993). *Good Night, and Good Luck* (2005) adopts this stance (along with "Isn't this heroic?") even though its revelations about the adversarial relationship between Senator Joseph McCarthy and CBS News reporter Edward R. Murrow have been public knowledge for many years.

A related, more general claim is implied by movies that choose stories ripped from yesterday's newspapers: behind the headlines. The most influential example is the television series *Law & Order* (1990– ), which uses fictionalized versions of contemporary criminal cases to explore the legal and moral issues they raise. But many movies set forth similar premises. *I Want to Live!* (1958), *Star 80* (1983), *Dance with a Stranger* (1985), *Let Him Have It* (1991), and *Shattered Glass* (2003) all use fictionalized versions of real-life crimes to propose theories that will explain the crimes. So does each television movie based on the misdeeds of such notorious criminals as Amy Fisher (1992, 1993), Ted Bundy (1986, 1995, 2002), and Scott Peterson (2004, 2005). The more specific promise made by films like *In Cold Blood* (1967) and *Monster* (2003), which probe apparently irrational crimes or criminals, is explaining the inexplicable.

All of these claims—Don't blame us; Isn't this sad (or inspiring or heroic)? Stranger than fiction; Now it can be told; Behind the headlines; Explaining the inexplicable—not only imply a transcendental precursor master text but set that master text against an inferior alternative intertext whose competing authority is trumped by the true story. *The Insider*, in particular, sets its presumably faithful account of Brown & Williamson's knowledge about their products against two different whitewashed versions, both presented in contexts that defined themselves as nonfictional: the story the company gave to the U.S. Senate under oath on penalty of perjury and the story investigative reporter Mike Wallace presented on his original *60 Minutes* segment. In this case, at least, the fictionalized film insists that it is more accurate than the history it corrects.

Martin Scorsese's claim that *GoodFellas* is based on a true story shows this strategy can be generalized. In its attempt to show what life in a New York Mafia family is like—the indifference to family ties, the uncontrollable outbursts of irrational violence, the ruthless self-interest that leads Henry Hill (Christopher Serrone, later Ray Liotta) to betray his old friends and mentors—the film establishes itself as a point-by-point refutation of "the high style, grand opera treatment of *The Godfather*."[8] The sense of family honor so vital to the Corleones is absent from Scorsese's film. Henry has no use for his biological parents, from whom his childhood friends rescue him by introducing him to the perks available through local mob boss Paulie Cicero (Paul Sorvino). Even within Paulie's mob, family ties are matter-of-factly subordinated to the self-interest that defines them. Unlike philandering Sonny Corleone (James Caan), destroyed by his overprotective interference in his sister's marriage in *The Godfather*, Paulie's soldiers routinely cheat on their wives with no consequence. Indeed, their wives are little more than legally sanctioned prostitutes, as Karen Hill (Lorraine Bracco) shows when she goes down on her husband in exchange for some extra spending money. Tommy DeVito (Joe Pesci) reveals the gang's propensity for the sudden, unmotivated outbursts of violence that are a defining condition of life in Scorsese's mob. And when Henry is put under pressure by federal officers who have targeted Paulie's mob, his sense of loyalty is so thin that he is only too eager to sell out his former buddies before they can have him and his family killed.

Scorsese's goal, then, is not just to show what life in the Mafia is like but to show what it is *really* like, as against the way it is romanticized by Francis Coppola. It is a goal framed by a specifically generic claim—Not just another Mob movie—a claim it shares mutatis mutandis with revisionist westerns from *The Wild Bunch* (1969) to *Silverado* (1985) to *Dances with Wolves* (1990), along with the films that purport to tell, for example, the true story of Wyatt Earp (*My Darling Clementine* [1946], *Gunfight at the O.K. Corral* [1957], *Tombstone* [1993], *Wyatt Earp* [1994]). Restated in these terms, the force of the apparently intensified promise to show what the Mob or the West is really like is clearly negative. However the film may be representing historical actions and figures, it will not be representing them in the customary way.

Since the power of Coppola's mythic representation of gangster life is hardly to be refuted by giving pride of place to *GoodFellas*'s literal source, Nicholas Pileggi's *Wiseguy: Life in a Mafia Family* (1986), the film instead begins with the more ambitious, albeit more indefinite, announcement that it is based on a true story. A defender of *The Godfather* might argue that Pileggi's account, though published as an exposé, was distorted by factual error or textual bias, but no one could urge such an argument against the tag "based on a true story" because the story in question is not concretized in any particular textual actualization and so is immune from charges of error or bias.[9] It cannot be mistaken, because a true story, unlike any particular history or memoir whose authority might be challenged, is by definition true. Nor can it be biased because only actual texts can be biased, whereas an unspecified true story is a putative intertext rather than a historically specific text. Hence the tag is both a vaguer and a more powerful marker of transcendental authority than any more confirmable—that is, potentially more disconfirmable—intertext could be.

The phrase "based on a true story," then, appeals to the authority of a master text that has all the authority of a precursor novel or play or story with none of their drawbacks. Not only does "a true story" have no authors or agents to be recompensed, but its authority can never be discredited. The one distinct advantage it might seem to lack—the fact that it is not an actual text available anywhere in the world in the form of a text—is more apparent than real. For just as the 1944 *Jane Eyre* confers textual authority on its own revised opening to Charlotte Brontë's novel by inscribing it as an introductory text, "the true story" each of these films invokes is textualized precisely by being invoked. After all, a true story is both more and less than the truth: less because it is only a selection of the truth, more because it has already been constructed as a story. Labeling a film as based on a true story identifies its source as a text already concretized as a preconstituted narrative or, more accurately, imputes that its source is a narrative that is constituted only through the act of invoking it.

By declining to label or localize their intertexts, or by obscuring their specific intertexts behind the more slippery claim to be based on a true story, these films mask their internally persuasive discourse, to use Bakhtin's distinction, as authoritative discourse. Steven Spielberg's *Amistad* shows just how sweeping and how misleading these claims may be. Although the film nowhere explicitly claims to be based on a true story, the claim is everywhere implicit, from the film's precise dating in 1839 to the appearance of historical figures like Spain's Queen Isabella II (Anna Paquin); President Martin Van Buren (Nigel Hawthorne); his secretary of state, John Forsyth (David Paymer); former president John Quincy Adams (Anthony Hopkins); and a discreetly unidentified chief justice (retired justice Harry Blackmun) in its closing titles, projecting its story into the historical future. And the claim this time is clearly rhetorical: "You need to know this." If the *Amistad* rebellion and its sequel were merely fictional, a case would have to be made why audiences would care about them—specifically, what was so urgent about the claim in this day and age that slavery was immoral. As it stands, the film obscures its historical sources behind a broader claim to truth in order to imply that it is presenting the true story of Cinque and his fellow slaves. Its authority depends not on identifying the progenitor texts on which it is based but on strategically concealing them.[10]

The problems implicit in the film's truth claims are dramatized by John Quincy Adams's remark that "In the courtroom, whoever tells the best story wins. . . . What is their *story?*" Adams adds to Roger Baldwin (Matthew McConaughey), the attorney who is arguing for the slaves' freedom. His implication is that Baldwin needs to go beneath the public record—the bad story—to reveal the human truth of the slaves' identity—the good, hitherto unavailable, story, which will be authentic because, having never before been textualized, it has never been subject to the political or textual corruption that threatens all actual texts. But even though it is ultimately accepted by the courts, the story Baldwin evinces from Cinque (Djimon Hounsou), his star witness, undermines both his project and the film's, since, ignoring Cinque's early life in order to begin with the moment of his enslavement, it identifies him in legal terms only as property, not as a human being; and the visual details in the flash-back that presents it, unlike the historical facts of the case, have been invented by the film and therefore cannot serve as evidence of anything. Baldwin re-minds both the courts and the audience of what they already know—that slav-ery is deplorable—without convincingly establishing that Cinque is not legally a slave. In the same way, the film's attempt to rouse audiences' moral outrage over slavery (for example, by showing the climactic arrest of two Spanish claimants for slave trading) conveniently overlooks the fact that in 1839 slave trading was perfectly legal in much of the United States, as it had been through-out the world for much of human history, and that Cinque's status as person or property could be settled only by legal arguments, not by appeals to the au-dience's sentiment or his real story. In other words, the film, using its basis in historical actuality to insist that it is saying something its audience needs to know, ends by telling only what the audience knows already: slavery is wrong.

The true story behind each of these films, in short, is invoked as a master text, which can bolster their status as entertainment—Don't blame us; Isn't this sad/inspiring/heroic; Stranger than fiction; Now it can be told; Behind the headlines; Explaining the inexplicable; Not just another movie; You need to know this—more effectively than any specific intertext, even though the label "true story" is textualized, like Cinque's allegedly true story, by the very act of being invoked. The shifting relations between those aspects of textuality that are invoked and those that are concealed by the label are best indicated by con-sidering the work of four auteurs of such films.

The very notion of an auteur of based-on-a-true-story movies may seem contradictory. Yet it is no more contradictory than the notion of auteurs of adaptation like Hitchcock, Kubrick, and Disney. The most important differ-ence is that true-story auteurs do not restrict themselves to this single genre. The relation between their true-story films and their other films is one of the primary differences among them.

The preeminent auteur of films that are based on true stories is Oliver Stone. The tendency of each of Stone's movies, whether or not it is based on a true story, is tendentious muckraking. Whatever his ostensible subject, Stone con-sistently offers a left-liberal critique of American political culture. The central manifestation of that culture in Stone's films is the Vietnam War, in which Stone himself served from 1967 to 1968. He distilled his experiences of the war into *Platoon* (1986), then followed it with two other films examining the legacy of the war for Americans who served there (*Born on the Fourth of July* [1989]) and Vietnamese civilians who became its victims (*Heaven & Earth* [1993]). None of these films, however, is identified in its credits as being based on a true story[11] because Stone's aims are both more modest and more ambitious— more modest because the second and third films of the trilogy credit as their sources memoirs by Ron Kovic and Le Ly Hayslip, more ambitious because Stone's films pose not as based on a true story but as the simple truth American political adventurers have never admitted. Stone has no use for invitations to emotionalism (Isn't this sad? Isn't this inspiring?). Instead, his work combines two claims: Now it can be told, and You need to know this. Hence he claims that *Salvador* (1986), based on the unpublished diaries of freelance reporter Richard Boyle, shows "what's really happening in El Salvador"; that he made *Platoon* because "I felt that the truth of this war had not been shown," and that "I didn't approach *Platoon* as a genre film, but rather as real life"; and that in the aftermath of *JFK* (1991), "We believe that we have the truth on our side."[12]

Stone immediately clarifies this last remark, however, with a revealing coda: "The more we can get these facts out there, the more we can begin to debate seriously some of these issues." Elsewhere in the same interview he defends *JFK* as "a hypothesis. I've never said it was the truth. I said it was a combination of acts plus speculation. . . . I'm presenting what I call the countermyth to the myth of the Warren Commission because, honestly, I don't have all the facts."[13] Hence he is gratified not so much in that "newly released documentary evidence from the [JFK] Assassination Records Review Board provides 'a kind of defense for Oliver Stone,'" in Michael Kurtz's judgment, as in the release of "the information in those documents, which probably would never have seen the light of day, at least in our lifetime, had the film not caused the uproar it did."[14]

This apparently more modest claim puts Stone as a writer of history on a par with print and archival historians in educating his fellow citizens by marshaling available evidence as persuasively as possible in support of often tendentious propositions. Chiding Arthur Schlesinger Jr. for his criticism of *JFK* as "corrupted by ideology," he asserts that "a historian, by profession, should stay inductive; otherwise, it speaks of an agenda and is a perfect example of the deductive thinking that some critics accuse me of." He adds: "Money and power have corrupted our Republic. This conclusion is not a belief-based dramatic license corrupted by ideology, but rather one of inductive thinking."[15] Filmmaking is for Stone a supreme act of responsible citizenship, a corrective to the irresponsible citizenship displayed by the statesmen who embroiled the nation in Vietnam heedless of the consequences.

From *Salvador* to *World Trade Center* (2006) Stone's films have aimed to set the historical record straight by quibbling on the relation between fiction and history. Indeed, it would be as difficult to separate fiction from history within Stone's filmography as within his individual films. His early screenplays for *Midnight Express* (1978), *Scarface* (1983), and *Year of the Dragon* (1985) are notable for the way they weld political critique to popular genres. *Wall Street* (1987), *Talk Radio* (1988), and *Any Given Sunday* (1999) present fictional critiques of American capitalism with journalistic immediacy. *The Doors* (1991) is a fictional account of Jim Morrison and his band that takes the form of a biographical docudrama. And Stone's political conviction that the most ardent idealists may be most tempted to violence and aggression drives films as different as *Natural Born Killers* (1994) and *Alexander* (2004).

Given the intimate relation between fiction and history throughout Stone's work, it is no surprise that he is the filmmaker most often cited by editorialists who worry that schoolchildren will accept the inventions of *JFK* and *Nixon* (1995) as history because of their vivid impact and their licentious inattention to the line between truth and fiction. For example, Stone's claim that *Salvador* (1986) is "based on a true story" allows him to invoke those aspects of textuality that trade on the specific impact of the muckraking journalistic exposé while disavowing those aspects of textuality whose invocation would risk his polemics' being unmasked by contrary evidence. Stone has often protested that this charge is undeserved. Rejecting the labels of both "historian" and "entertainer," he prefers to call himself "a dramatist . . . working to achieve what he believes to be the truth."[16] After the outcry among historians watching *JFK*, he was careful to begin *Nixon* with a precise summary of his historical technique: "This film is a dramatic interpretation of events and characters based on public records and an incomplete historical record. Some scenes and events are presented as composites or have been hypothesized or condensed." Even though this summary never uses words like *invented* or *imaginary*, it warns viewers that Stone's version of history does not restrict itself to known facts.

Stone's critics have dismissed such paratextual markers as fig leaves, gestures toward accurate labeling whose marginal force is swiftly overwhelmed by the torrent of polemical images and arguments Stone's films mount as they bombard their audience "with images, sounds, cuts, and flashes, like a music video."[17] The montage of television images that opens *JFK* is a brilliant example of the way Stone can suck viewers into his tendentious view that John Kennedy was assassinated not by a lone anti-American gunman but by the all-too-American CIA by challenging viewers' ability to construct a coherent narrative from this prologue and by inviting their uncritical acceptance of his organizing principles when they succeed. A more cogent defense, however, and one less dependent on cinema's allegedly unique power to manipulate a mass audience, would stress two points. First, Stone frankly offers his historical films not as the truth but as revisions subject to further revision themselves, "as *Gone with the Wind* replaced *Uncle Tom's Cabin* and was in turn replaced by *Roots* and *The Civil War*."[18] Furthermore, even if Stone does freely mix fact, conjecture, and invention, so do putatively objective government investigations, the news media, and print historians. Stone's licentiousness in rewriting history aims to expose the scandal of the similar but disavowed licentiousness of official American history. No other contemporary filmmaker could as plausibly release a feature-length interview entitled *Oliver Stone's America* (2001), confident that a significant audience would want to know just what the filmmaker thought of America.

The case of Sidney Lumet, the second auteur of films based on a true story, offers a dramatic contrast. Like Stone's films, Lumet's offer a liberal critique of America, but both the subject and the nature of the critique are very different. Lumet's most celebrated true-story films—*Serpico* (1973), *Dog Day Afternoon*, and *Prince of the City* (1981)—all focus on some aspect of the criminal justice system, which Lumet sees as riven by temptations to greed and pathological conformity. Stone's most memorable figures—Barnes (Tom Berenger) and Elias (Willem Dafoe) in *Platoon*, Gordon Gekko (Michael Douglas) in *Wall Street*, Ron Kovic (Tom Cruise) in *Born on the Fourth of July*, New Orleans district attorney Jim Garrison (Kevin Costner) in *JFK*, Mickey (Woody Harrelson) and Mallory (Juliette Lewis) in *Natural Born Killers*, President Richard Nixon (Anthony Hopkins) in *Nixon*, Alexander the Great (Colin Farrell) in *Alexander*—rise to increasingly grandiose powers they can scarcely control. Lumet's heroes, by contrast, are well-intentioned but crippled by a gallery of weaknesses, from the rift that arises with a gay lover saving for a sex-change operation in *Dog Day Afternoon* to the wall of blue that stifles Frank Serpico (Al Pacino), the lone cop in *Serpico* who refuses to go on the take, and Daniel Ciello (Treat Williams), who internalizes all the temptations he is supposed to be investigating for Internal Affairs in *Prince of the City*.

Unlike Stone, who looks around the world for evidence of the American imperium's rottenness, Lumet has always been identified with New York, which becomes in his films not so much the quintessential American city as the capital of a fallen and deeply conflicted world. The ideological contradictions that destroy Stone's heroes become more internalized in Lumet, whose fictional films sympathetically anatomize souls tormented by moral conflicts that pit right against right (*12 Angry Men* [1957]; *Fail-Safe* [1964]; *Murder on the Orient Express* [1974]) or, more often, wrong against wrong (*The Fugitive Kind* [1959]; *Long Day's Journey into Night* [1962]; *The Pawnbroker* [1964]; *The Anderson Tapes* [1971]; *Child's Play* [1972]; *Network* [1976]; *The Verdict* [1982]; *The Morning After* [1986]; *Q & A* [1990]; *Night Falls on Manhattan* [1997]; *Find Me Guilty* [2006]). Like Stone's true-story films, Lumet's are virtually continuous with his frankly fictional oeuvre. In Lumet's case, however, the overriding concern in both kinds of films is moral rather than political. Real-life tales of criminal incompetence and police corruption offer Lumet compelling metaphors for spiritual decay and challenge. But these metaphors are no more or less compelling than the fictional situation of *The Pawnbroker*'s former concentration-camp inmate, Sol Nazerman (Rod Steiger), eternally imprisoned in a New York neighborhood that condemns him to remember the horrors he survived, or *The Verdict*'s down-at-heels Boston attorney Frank Galvin (Paul Newman), desperate for the personal redemption a courtroom victory will give him.

It is not only Lumet's material that is different but the nature of his social critique. Although his own apprenticeship in television shapes the indictment of media-fueled justice in *Network* and *Find Me Guilty,* Lumet is less interested than Stone in television's ability to mold mass opinion by manipulating images than in its ability to bring realist drama to a mass audience. It is eminently logical that Frank R. Cunningham would praise *Prince of the City* as "an original literary film from nonfictional material, one that . . . reveals its excellence centrally in literary terms."[19] Lumet's films generally eschew the possibilities of Stone's barrages of montage in favor of the aesthetics of conventionally genre-specific stagings of the his characters' external and internal conflicts. Despite his obvious liberal sympathies, Lumet reverses Stone's diagnosis by tracing systemic corruption to individual failings. The system is rotten because of selfish or greedy individuals, not the other way around. Stone sees individuals like S.Sgt. Barnes, Gordon Gekko, and Richard Nixon as embodying the flaws of the social systems they represent. They have risen to power for the same reason that they will ultimately be destroyed: they incarnate the contradictions of that system. For Lumet, by contrast, the system is the individual writ large, and the only hope for addressing the corruption endemic to the NYPD is more cops like Frank Serpico. In Lumet's films heroic individuals like Frank Galvin really can rise at least momentarily above the system that crushes them in Stone's.

Unlike Stone, who has an overriding interest in both exploiting and exposing the razor-thin divide between fiction and history, Lumet values stories based on current institutional abuses, whether or not they have already been filtered through fictional sources like the best-selling novels on which *The Pawnbroker* and *The Anderson Tapes* and *The Verdict* are based, because of the topicality that gives his moral parables their edge. The aspect of their true-story sources his films seek to deny is their perishability. Lumet follows Ezra Pound's definition of literature in seeking to make his films "news that STAYS news."[20] Whether they can remain both topical and enduring, whether they will outlast Stone's equally topical corpus, remains to be seen.

Lumet has even less interest than Stone in going back through history for stories that will provide the parables of moral temptation he favors. Contemporary headlines provide both directors virtually all the material they need. But some filmmakers value universality as much as topicality. Of all the directors who have produced a substantial body of work based on true stories, the one who best exemplifies the quest for the universal is Martin Scorsese. Scorsese began his career as the celebrated chronicler of the seamy side of New York's Little Italy in films like *Who's That Knocking at My Door* (1968) and *Mean Streets* (1973). But his portfolio soon included both documentaries like *Street Scenes* (1970) and *Italianamerican* (1974) and period films like *Boxcar Bertha* (1972) and *New York, New York* (1977). Like Stone, Scorsese produced a valentine to a rock band, *The Last Waltz* (1978); like Lumet, he has maintained his close identification with New York City in films from *Taxi Driver* (1976) to *Gangs of New York* (2002).

But if New York is the capital of Scorsese's world, that world is far more extensive than Lumet's or even Stone's. Like Lumet, whose adaptations range from the acidly observed postcollegiate portrait *The Group* (1966) to the eerie psychoanalytic thriller *Equus* (1977) to the African American *Wizard of Oz* update *The Wiz* (1978) to the hospital farce *Critical Care* (1997), as well as plays by Chekhov and Eugene O'Neill, Scorsese finds his stories in a wide range of times and places. *Alice Doesn't Live Here Anymore* (1974) is set in the contemporary American Southwest, *Cape Fear* (1991) in the Southeast, *The Departed* (2006) in south Boston. *Casino* is set during the period of Las Vegas's turbulent early growth fifty years ago. *The Age of Innocence* (1993) is a nineteenth-century costume drama. *Kundun* (1997) ranges over China and Tibet, and *The Last Temptation of Christ* (1988) provides an extrabiblical perspective on the humanity of Jesus Christ.

What is remarkable about this range of subjects, and what separates it from Lumet's equally wide range, is Scorsese's thematic consistency. Whether the setting is the seedy billiard parlors of *The Color of Money* (1986) or the Hollywood of industrialist Howard Hughes in *The Aviator* (2004), Scorsese is always telling the same story. His heroes and heroines are free spirits struggling for survival in a world determined to crush them into conformity. Although Jimmy Doyle (Robert De Niro) eventually realizes his dream of opening his own club in *New York, New York* and Howard Hughes (Leonardo DiCaprio) goes from one hugely ambitious project to the next in *The Aviator,* most of Scorsese's heroes have little hope of changing their world; they only want, like Chris Taylor (Charlie Sheen) in *Platoon,* to survive it.

Scorsese's sympathies are clearly with his embattled heroes rather than the stifling cultural norms they fight. Whether his chosen mode is the urban nightmare of *Taxi Driver* or the neo-noir gallows humor of *Bringing Out the Dead* (1999), his eye is always on the maverick or iconoclast, even when that free spirit is as weak-willed as Paul Hackett (Griffin Dunne) in *After Hours* (1985) or Newland Archer (Daniel Day Lewis) in *The Age of Innocence.* Like Lumet, Scorsese moves readily between avowedly fictional and nonfictional subjects. He has continued to make an unusual number of documentaries (*American Boy: A Profile of Steven Prince* [1978]; *Made in Milan* [1990]; *No Direction Home: Bob Dylan* [2005]) for an A-list director. Many of Scorsese's features have an ambiguous relation to earlier biographical or historical sources. Miles beneath *Gangs of New York*'s screenwriting credits for Jay Cocks, Steven Zaillian, and Kenneth Lonergan is buried the line "suggested by the [1927] book by Herbert Asbury." And *Kundun,* which uses nonprofessional actors to dramatize the early life of the fourteenth Dalai Lama, has a screenplay by Melissa Mathison, with no mention of any biographical sources apart from the listing of Lobsang Samten as religious technical adviser and an acknowledgment of "His Holiness the Dalai Lama."

Scorsese's continued interest in fact-based films and the fluidity he maintains between fact and fiction do not stem from anything like Stone's interest in blurring the boundaries, or exposing the blurred boundaries, between fiction and history. Nor do they stem from Lumet's search for topical stories that will give his abiding concerns an edge. Instead, they seem to reflect Scorsese's belief that the conflict he is dramatizing between repressive cultures and the underdogs who dare to challenge them is universal, beyond time or place or the imperatives of any particular culture. Throughout Scorsese's work, however, this assumption of universality is counterpointed by an exceptional attention to the mores of each culture he examines, from the decorous manners of Old New York in *The Age of Innocence* to the use of excerpts from the actual radio announcements that called Jake La Motta's boxing matches for *Raging Bull* (1980). Whenever Scorsese films like *GoodFellas, Casino, Kundun, Gangs of New York,* and *The Aviator* explicitly or implicitly announce themselves as based on a true story, they expose this paradox but decline to resolve it. For Scorsese, social culture is always based on self-alienating mechanisms of repression akin to Louis Althusser's ideological state apparatuses. But Scorsese has no special interest in analyzing the historical or ideological content of specific mechanisms of repression. Unlike both Althusser and Stone, his focus is more allegorical than political, and true stories simply provide more evidence that the same conflict is being played out in still another subculture.

The least ideological of all true-story auteurs, however, is Steven Spielberg. Even more than Scorsese, Spielberg casts his stories of little people who are given the opportunity for social transcendence in resolutely nonideological terms. Just as fictional heroes like Roy Neary (Richard Dreyfuss) in *Close Encounters of the Third Kind* (1977) and Elliott (Henry Thomas) in *E.T. the Extraterrestrial* (1982) are chosen by extraplanetary visitors to forge connections with them because of their nonthreatening ordinariness, the visitors and their communities are chosen by the filmmaker because of their freedom from any specific ideology. Even when Indiana Jones (Harrison Ford) battles the Nazis in *Raiders of the Lost Ark* (1981), *Indiana Jones and the Temple of Doom* (1984), and *Indiana Jones and the Last Crusade* (1989), the Nazis seem to have no ideological principles except for a generalized imperialistic greed.

When Spielberg turns to films based on true stories, as he does as early as *The Sugarland Express* (1974), he searches, like Lumet and Scorsese, for heroes who can transcend the limitations imposed by their historical circumstances. In most of his true-story films, however, Spielberg is not interested in the particular circumstances that define the conflict between individuals and their specific cultures. Even more broadly than Scorsese's, his films present themselves as allegories of innocents trapped by an oppressive system (*Empire of the*

*Sun* [1987]), or, more often, individuals triumphing over the limitations the system imposes.

In fantasies like *Dr. Strangelove* (1964), *2001: A Space Odyssey* (1968), and *The Shining* (1980), Stanley Kubrick explicitly attacks the antihumanism threatened by internalizing the technological imperatives of self-perfection. In a fundamental sense Spielberg's portraits of oppressive historical social cultures take the opposite tack, couching their critique in the science-fiction terms he made explicit in *Artificial Intelligence: AI* (2001), *Minority Report* (2002), and *War of the Worlds* (2005). In *Jaws* (1975), which another director might have turned into a referendum on the petty tyranny of self-serving civic leaders or a critique of federalist democracy, mayor Larry Vaughn (Murray Hamilton) is mainly a nuisance to be swept aside before police chief Martin Brody (Roy Scheider) can bond with oceanographer Matt Hooper (Richard Dreyfuss) and seadog Quint (Robert Shaw) to destroy the beast from twenty thousand fathoms.

Several of Spielberg's films that are based on true stories are cast in terms that similarly echo the conventions of science fiction. Who would have thought that a couple would go to such extreme lengths to recover their child, or to confound government forces so long and so successfully, as Lou Jean Poplin (Goldie Hawn) and her husband Clovis (William Atherton) do in *The Sugarland Express?* How on earth could confidence man Frank Abnagale (Leonardo DiCaprio) have gotten away with so many audacious masquerades in *Catch Me If You Can* (2002)? How could a foreign national stranded for months inside an airport, as Viktor Navorski (Tom Hanks) was in *The Terminal* (2004), not only have survived but have created a supportive community immeasurably enriched by his presence? These films inspire the free-floating wonder Spielberg taps into in *Close Encounters of the Third Kind* and *E.T.* But they are also linked to stranger-than-fiction films like *The Wrong Man* and populist fables like *Apollo 13* (1995) and *Erin Brockovich* (2000).

Feel-good films like these, darkly parodied by Roman Polanski's existentialist fable *The Pianist* (2002), celebrate the triumph of the human spirit. As much in Spielberg as in Polanski, however, it is never clear what the human spirit is triumphing over, whether it is political oppression, moral evil, bureaucratic inertia, or bad luck. Certainly Spielberg's little guys are always triumphing over their littleness, their own alleged limitations. But this self-transcendence often seems to operate in an ideological vacuum. Even when the system they are bucking is acutely oppressive, as it is in the fictional *The Color Purple* (1985) and the based-on-a-true-story *Amistad,* the oppressor's specific ideological content is submerged in what Stephen J. Dubner has called "one long argument for tolerance, a plea to accept the outsider."[21]

This ideological effacement continues even in Spielberg's most ambitious and explicitly historical films. *Schindler's List* (1993), which tells the story of Nazi industrialist Oskar Schindler, who saved more than a thousand Jews from the death camps, followed a well-worn path to the screen, from what Thomas Keneally called his "facticious" novel, whose film rights Spielberg purchased shortly after its publication in 1982, to Spielberg's based-on-a-true-story film. *Saving Private Ryan* (1998) is a fictional story whose World War II setting is strenuously invoked as real through the unprecedented ferocity of the battles that bookend it. Robert Rodat's screenplay, so pitiless in its examination of the physical and moral costs of war, empties its few German characters of any ideological impulses. The German soldier (Joerg Stadler) captured by Captain Miller (Tom Hanks) and his troops is so desperate to save his life that he blurts out a fusillade of hollow all-American phrases ("Fancy schmancy! What a cinch! . . . Fuck Hitler!"). And the ideological debates among Miller's melting-pot Americans all end by breaking down into arguments about what Miller calls "the choice between the mission and the man."

The closer look *Schindler's List* takes at Nazis is not a closer look at national socialism. The core of the film is the conflict between the insidiously self-serving Amon Goeth (Ralph Fiennes), whose racial hatred and lust for power grow until they destroy him, and the initially self-serving Schindler, whose eye for the main chance gradually dims as he seizes opportunities to save prospective workers. Celebrating the destruction of Krakow's Jewish ghetto, Goeth insists: "Today is history." But history, the film maintains, is created by individual heroes like Schindler, not rabid partisans of supposedly unstoppable historical forces like Goeth. *Schindler's List* tells the story of a heroic individual's struggle with history. In Stone, Lumet, and Scorsese history typically wins this struggle; in Spielberg it loses. Spielberg told Stephen Schiff that "I made *Schindler's List* thinking that if it did entertain, then I would have failed."[22] For better or worse, critics agreed, *Schindler's List* was entertaining—probably the most entertaining Holocaust film that will ever be made—precisely because, like *Gone with the Wind* (1939), it celebrated the power of a single determined individual to triumph over history.

*Munich* (2005) finds this same moral power triumphant even in apparent bewilderment and disengagement. Tony Kushner's revision of Eric Roth's screenplay, based in turn on George Jonas's *Vengeance: The True Story of an Is-raeli Counter-Terrorist Team* (1984), begins with the kidnapping of Israeli ath-letes competing in the 1972 Munich Olympics by militant Palestinians and the deaths of the athletes in a shootout with German authorities. When Spielberg's hero, Avner (Eric Bana), a former bodyguard to Premier Golda Meir (Lynn Co-hen), and his four colleagues are recruited to avenge the attack by identifying and assassinating the terrorists, he deeply believes in the justice of his cause. As Meir tells him, "Every civilization needs to negotiate compromises with its own values." The story of his squad's success in killing nine of the eleven terrorists, however, is interwoven with the story of his gradual disillusionment with his charge. He spirals down into paranoia, moves his family from Israel to Brook-lyn, and ultimately concludes, "Jews don't do wrong because our enemies do wrong." This determinedly centrist conclusion won Spielberg both strong praise and furious recriminations from Jewish critics and fans. But in fact it has little to do with the specific historical circumstances of Israel and even less, de-spite a tensely comic scene in which Avner converses with a PLO operative whose team has been booked into the same safe house in Greece, with those of the Palestinians. Its real focus, as both Meir's and Avner's speeches indicate, is a universal moral riddle—is it ever right to do what you believe to be wrong?—rather than any historical or ideological realities.

What Spielberg finds in the true stories on which so many of his films are based is history and ideology as worthy antagonists for little-man heroes who are studiously nonaligned apart from a humanism that is assumed to be foun-dational rather than ideological. In Spielberg's world, as in Frank Capra's, every historical conflict or obstacle becomes an opportunity for self-actualization and a radical renewal of the social contract among the characters in the movie and between the movie and its audience. The films scrupulously recreate their historical settings while insisting on their heroes' essential freedom from his-torical imperatives, their status as agents in history who are not agents of his-tory. No wonder Spielberg told John H. Richardson: "It's magic, no matter what the movie's about. Whether you watch eight hours of *Shoah* or whether it's *Ghostbusters,* when the lights go down in the theater and the movie fades in, it's magic."[23]

Even if they are not magic in the way Spielberg means, films that announce themselves as based on a true story are magical in at least two other important ways. First, they define themselves by announcing their fidelity to a text to which they can never be compared, one which just happens to be congruent with the truth. Their alleged source is not the truth equally elusive to novelists, philosophers, historians, evangelists, and Pontius Pilate but a story extracted from reality yet already formed into a story. Although historiographers from Hayden White to Simon Schama have argued that extracting stories from the flux of reality already constitutes a foundational act of fictionalizing,[24] the credit "based on a true story" assumes that stories, like history itself, are found, fully formed as such, rather than made and that these found stories are true. Films based on true stories authenticate themselves by appealing to precursor texts that are nonexistent.

Moreover, this appeal to nonexistent precursor texts has the effect of creating these texts through the very act of invoking them. The true story behind *Dog Day Afternoon, Salvador, GoodFellas,* or *Schindler's List* may be buried in newspaper accounts or fictionalized exposés or the historical record, but once these stories have been invoked, they have the same textual status as the books by Nicholas Pileggi or Thomas Keneally. *The Texas Chain Saw Massacre* and *Fargo* show that a source can even be textualized as a true story without being either preexistent or true. If *Fargo* creates its own textual source by creating an original story and then framing it as if it were true, it would seem that anything can be made to assume textual authority, even if it is not a source, not a text, not true, and nonexistent outside the imagination of the filmmakers. Given these films' challenge to the distinction between films that are adaptations and films that are not, the slippery slope away from adaptation studies to intertextual studies seems dangerous indeed.

Yet the future of adaptation studies, and of textual studies generally, depends on our ability to negotiate this slope. The lesson of films that identify themselves as based on a true story is only a more urgent version of the lesson of all the adaptations I have been considering in this book. Adaptation studies will rest on a firmer foundation when its practitioners direct their attention away from films that present themselves as based on a single identifiable literary source—preferably a canonical work of fiction like *Pride and Prejudice* or *A Christmas Carol*—and toward the process of adaptation. Instead of distinguishing sharply between original texts and intertexts, future students of adaptation will need to focus less on texts and more on textualizing (the processes by which some intertexts become sanctified as texts while others do not) and textuality (the institutional characteristics that mark some texts, but not others, as texts). The study of adaptations offers a matchless opportunity to treat every text, whether or not it is canonical, true, or even physically extant, as the work-in-progress of institutional practices of rewriting. Instead of viewing literature from afar and from below as a collection of canonized works, it offers a foundational invitation to scholars in textual studies to place at the center of their investigations the theory and practice in allegedly original texts, in their rereading through adaptation, in our own work, and the work of our students, of still further rereading and rewriting—of literacy.

# Notes

CHAPTER 1: Literature versus Literary

1. See Bluestone, *Novels into Film*. The two most frequently cited early essays on literature and film are Eisenstein, "Dickens, Griffith, and the Film Today"; and Bazin, "In Defense of Mixed Cinema." For two good brief surveys of other early writing on adaptation see Jenkins, *Stanley Kubrick and the Art of Adaptation*, 3–23; and Aragay, "Introduction: Reflection to Refraction."

2. Wilmington, "For Mira Nair, 'Vanity Fair' Was a World of Its Own."

3. All quotes in this paragraph are from Indiana University's VICTORIA listserv, Sep. 13 and 14, 2004, and are archived at https://listserv.indiana.edu/cgi-bin/wa-iub.exe?A1=ind0409b&L=victoria&D=0&H=0&I=-3&O=T&T=1#56 (all accessed Oct. 24, 2006).

4. Elliott, *Rethinking the Novel/Film Debate*, 13.

5. Bluestone, *Novels into Film*, 5–6.

6. See Cardwell, *Adaptation Revisited*; and Cartmell and Whelehan, *Adaptation*.

7. Naremore, "Introduction," 2.

8. Arnold, *The Works of Matthew Arnold*, 4:2.

9. Compare Charles Barr's complaint, in *English Hitchcock*, that "a film criticism centred on directors . . . has not been concerned to follow up Hitchcock's statements . . . of indebtedness to English literary figures" (8). Barr has been virtually alone among Hitchcock commentators in tracking elements often considered quintessentially Hitchcockian to the films' literary originals.

10. Michael A. Anderegg, for example, notes that "a Conrad enthusiast might be excused for feeling that *Sabotage* betrays its source on a rather fundamental level" (Anderegg, "Conrad and Hitchcock," 217).

11. Andrew, *Concepts in Film Theory*, 100.

12. Selznick, *Memo from David O. Selznick*, 266.

13. Truffaut, *Hitchcock*, 71.

14. *Compact Edition of the Oxford English Dictionary*, s.v. "literacy"; Hirsch, *Cultural Literacy*, 2.

15. Hirsch, *Cultural Literacy*, 14.

16. Ibid., 23.

17. Ibid., xiv.

18. Hirsch, *Validity in Interpretation*, 8.

19. Ibid.; Hirsch, *The Philosophy of Composition*, 78.

20. Hirsch, *The Philosophy of Composition*, 74.

21. Hirsch, *Cultural Literacy*, 142.

22. Barthes, "From Work to Text," 156, 159, 157, 163.
23. Barthes, *S/Z*, 4, 5.
24. Bakhtin, *The Dialogic Imagination*, 342, 346, 345.
25. Forster, *Aspects of the Novel*, 101.
26. Barthes, "From Work to Text," 162.
27. The problematic opposition between reading and writing is a founding trope of the fields of literacy studies, composition theory, and institutional histories of English. See, among many others, Moran, "Reading like a Writer"; Friend, "The Excluded Conflict"; Elbow, "The War between Reading and Writing"; Barton, *Literacy*; Scholes, *The Rise and Fall of English*; and Seitz, *Motives for Metaphor*.
28. Elbow, "The Cultures of Literature and Composition," 533.
29. Arnold, *The Works of Matthew Arnold*, 3:42, 20.
30. Hirsch, *Cultural Literacy*, 133.
31. Zingrone, *The Media Symplex*, 237.
32. Bakhtin, *The Dialogic Imagination*, 418.
33. Elbow, "The War between Reading and Writing," 13.
34. Hoder-Salmon, *Kate Chopin's "The Awakening,"* 7.
35. Iser, *The Act of Reading*, 169.
36. Schreiner, *The Story of an African Farm*, 169.
37. Dovey, "Towards an Art of Adaptation," 52, 60.
38. Ross, *Film as Literature, Literature as Film*, 56.

CHAPTER 2: One-Reel Epics

1. Tibbetts, *The American Theatrical Film*, 10.
2. See Barthes, "Introduction to the Structural Analysis of Narratives," 93–94.
3. See Bazin, "The Ontology of the Photographic Image."
4. Initially reluctant to embrace the demotic medium, Bernhardt wrote of her filmed performance in *Queen Elizabeth* (1912): "I rely for my immortality on these records." See Gold and Fizdale, *The Divine Sarah*, 309.
5. Robinson, *From Peep Show to Palace*, 70.
6. See Gunning, "An Aesthetic of Astonishment," 864–65.
7. For more on the popularity of tableaux vivants in the late nineteenth century see McCullough, *Living Pictures on the New York Stage*.
8. Truffaut, *Hitchcock*, 71.
9. Simmon, Program notes to *More Treasures from American Film Archives*, 105.
10. Gunning, "An Aesthetic of Astonishment," 869.
11. In *High-Class Moving Pictures* Charles Musser and Carol Nelson establish the importance of the travel lecture presented by a live narrator and illustrated by film clips as a central mode of presentation between 1896 and 1904. L. Frank Baum, author of *The Wonderful Wizard of Oz*, adapted this form to fictional narrative in his 1908 *Fairylogue and Radio-Plays*, which Mark Evan Swartz calls "a travelogue of some of the fairy lands . . . that he had created in his books," with Baum himself as onstage narrator (Swartz, *Oz before the Rainbow*, 161–62).
12. The weight of these films depended on their extant footage and the uses to which they were put. *King John*, which served to advertise a contemporary stage production, evidently included other scenes that have been lost. Judith Buchanan notes that in

1907 the duel scene, retitled "A Scottish Combat," was incorporated into Biograph's anthology film *Fights of Nations.* See Buchanan, *Shakespeare on Film,* 36.

13. Tibbetts, *The American Theatrical Film,* 15.

14. Musser, *Before the Nickelodeon,* 372, 393.

15. Jacobs, *The Rise of the American Film,* 76.

16. Sklar, *Movie-Made America,* 42.

17. In *D. W. Griffith: An American Life* Richard Schickel notes that *Pippa Passes* was the first film the *New York Times* saw fit to review, and Schickel reproduces the entire review, including its revealing conclusion: "The adventurous producers who inaugurated these departures from cheap melodrama are being overwhelmed by offers from renting agents. Not only the nickelodeons of New York but those of many less pretentious cities and towns are demanding Browning and the other 'high-brow' effects" (142).

18. Loughney, "In the Beginning Was the Word," 211.

19. Bowser, *History of the American Cinema,* 56.

20. Ibid., 256.

21. Buchanan, *Shakespeare on Film,* 41.

22. Interestingly, brief excerpts from Shakespeare's dialogue appear appended to the expository intertitles that introduce each scene in the two-reel British version of *Richard III* (1911).

23. Musser, *History of the American Cinema,* 380, 453, 460.

24. Tom Gunning quotes the *Biograph Bulletin*'s publicizing of *Resurrection*—"Restricted as we were as to length, we have successfully portrayed a story which comprises the most stirring incidents with an absolute continuity that is wonderful in motion pictures"—as evidence of the studio's unusual acknowledgment of the film's brevity and the film's unusual attempt to balance "the cachet of literary adaptation . . . with narrative coherence and comprehensibility" (Gunning, *D. W. Griffith,* 173–74).

25. Quoted in Bowser, *History of the American Cinema,* 210.

26. Hansen, *Babel and Babylon,* 52.

27. On the unfinished *Epic of the Wheat* trilogy see Norris, *Novels and Essays,* 577.

28. For a more detailed account of Griffith's adaptation see Pratt, *Spellbound in Darkness,* 67–80.

29. Gunning, *D. W. Griffith,* 244.

30. Quoted in ibid., 241.

31. Ibid., 244.

32. Ibid., 251.

33. It is a peculiarity of these films, in fact, that although Griffith's soldiers are always country boys who live amid the solitude of picturesque scenery, a parade is invariably passing their front door as they leave.

34. Jesionowski, *Thinking in Pictures,* 33.

35. In his program notes to the film's DVD release on *More Treasures from American Film Archives, 1894–1931,* Scott Simmon observes: "That one can begin to make these sorts of ethical judgment about a fictional character—to weigh the doctor's psychological flaws against his selfless heroism—is one mark of how far this 1909 film has already moved beyond 'primitive' filmmaking to something modern" (12).

36. Quoted in Jacobs, *The Rise of the American Film,* 119.

37. Griffith's interest in metafiction seems to have been limited to the foursquare playfulness of *Those Awful Hats* (1909), whose clever fable of the dark fate of well-bred

ladies whose headgear obstructed the view of audience members behind them, designed as a monitory introduction to a picture show, confirmed rather than challenged the line between fiction and reality.

38. In *Eloquent Gestures* Roberta E. Pearson, presumably thinking of the costumes of Henry B. Walthall's court musician and the workers who wall the lovers in the dovecote, refers to the film's "medieval" setting (105). But the costumes of the king, the queen, and their courtiers—long coats, wigs, and ruffs for the men, lace-trimmed robes for the women—are unmistakably eighteenth-century, and both of the musician's lutes look suspiciously like modern guitars. The point of the film's ambiguous historical setting, as in its allusion to two quite different literary sources, is that consistency and fidelity are less important values than the impressiveness the institutions of literature and history can lend his project.

39. The other Griffith films based more or less loosely on this story, all starring Griffith's wife, Linda Arvidson, in the role of the bereft wife, are *After Many Years* (1908), *Lines of White on a Sullen Sea* (1909), and *Enoch Arden* (1911).

CHAPTER 3: The Word Made Film

1. Boyer, "The Jesus War," 69.
2. Ibid., 61.
3. Waldman, "Passion Misplay."
4. Boyer, "The Jesus War," 64.
5. Quoted in Dubin, "Passionate Controversy."
6. In "Passions and the Passion Play" Charles Musser suggests that this list could be extended back to the dawn of cinema as a medium that traded on magic-lantern shows' ability to present the Passion story without fear of the censorship awaiting theatrical narratives stigmatized by the "curse of presence" (65).
7. Frei, *The Eclipse of Biblical Narrative*, 311.
8. Auerbach, *Mimesis*, 14–15.
9. Bakhtin, *The Dialogic Imagination*, 342, 345.
10. Zeffirelli, *Zeffirelli*, 274.
11. Ibid., 277.
12. Reinhartz, "Jesus of Hollywood," 173.
13. Noerdlinger, *Moses and Egypt*, 1.
14. Ibid., 17.
15. Wright, *Moses in America*, 126.
16. DeMille, *The Autobiography of Cecil B. DeMille*, 275.
17. Ibid., 282.
18. Frei, *The Eclipse of Biblical Narrative*, 310.
19. Gibson quoted in Boyer, "The Jesus War," 60.
20. Eisenschitz, *Nicholas Ray*, 368.
21. Sawyer, "Transcript: The Passion."
22. Fredriksen, "Gospel Truths," 31–32. Compare Amy-Jill Levine's summary in "First Take the Log Out of Your Own Eye," 207.
23. Prothero, "Jesus Nation, Catholic Christ," 275.
24. Frizzell, "The Death of Jesus and the Death of the Temple," 75.

25. Wallis, "*The Passion* and the Message," 117; Wieseltier, "The Worship of Blood," 256.

26. Martin, "The Last Station," 109. See also Witherington, "Numb Struck," 88; Fredriksen, "Gospel Truths," 33.

27. Thistlethwaite, "Mel Makes a War Movie," 137, 134.

28. Ibid., 132.

29. Prothero, "Jesus Nation, Catholic Christ," 273; Wieseltier, "The Worship of Blood," 255–56.

30. "Report of the Ad Hoc Scholars Group," 232–33.

31. Wallis, "*The Passion* and the Message," 123.

32. Boys, "Seeing Different Movies, Talking Past Each Other," 154–55.

33. Thistlethwaite, "Mel Makes a War Movie," 136.

34. Sawyer, "Transcript: The Passion."

35. Fredriksen, "Gospel Truths," 33.

36. Cunningham, "Much Will Be Required," 56. Other contributors to *Perspectives* are in strong agreement. See especially Fredriksen, "Gospel Truths," 33; Martin, "The Last Station," 97–98; and Levine, "First Take the Log," 202–7.

37. See Witherington, "Numb Struck," 82–88.

38. Martin, "The Last Station," 103.

39. Quoted by Reinhartz, "Jesus of Hollywood," 175.

40. Boys, "Seeing Different Movies, Talking Past Each Other," 150.

41. Cunningham, "Much Will Be Required," 49.

42. Reinhartz, "Jesus of Hollywood," 175.

43. Quoted by Levine, "First Take the Log," 207.

44. Quoted in appendix 5, "Report of the Ad Hoc Scholars Group," 253.

45. Wieseltier, "The Worship of Blood," 262. Compare Frizzell: "Artists are free, but they are also responsible for the works they create" ("The Death of Jesus," 77).

46. Abbott, *The Documents of Vatican II*, 666.

47. Quoted in Tolson and Kulman, "The Other Jesus," 20.

48. Boys, "Seeing Different Movies, Talking Past Each Other," 161.

49. Caldwell, "Selling *Passion*," 222.

50. Burnham, foreword to *Perspectives*, xii.

51. Martin, "Studio Script Notes on 'The Passion,'" 283.

52. Fredriksen, "Gospel Truths," 46. Compare Reinhartz, "Jesus of Hollywood," 179.

53. See Meacham, "Who Really Killed Jesus?" 11.

54. Cunningham, "Much Will Be Required," 62.

55. Boys, "Seeing Different Movies, Talking Past Each Other," 163.

56. Shohat, "Sacred Word, Profane Image," 24.

CHAPTER 4: Entry-Level Dickens

1. DeBona, "Dickens, the Depression, and MGM's *David Copperfield*," 109–10.

2. Guida, *"A Christmas Carol" and Its Adaptations*, 209, 212, 223, 217, 221.

3. Bazin, "In Defense of Mixed Cinema," 65.

4. Guida, *"A Christmas Carol" and Its Adaptations*, 133, 224.

5. Jaffe, "Spectacular Sympathy," 255.

6. Davis, *The Lives and Times of Ebenezer Scrooge*, 107, 93.

7. Here and subsequently, parenthetical pagination refers to Dickens, *Christmas Books*.

8. This is true even in the farcical inversion *Blackadder's Christmas Carol* (1988), in which Ebenezer Blackadder (Rowan Atkinson), originally "the kindest and loveliest man in London," awakens determined to act greedy and self-serving after seeing visions of his grasping, successful relatives past and future.

9. Fawcett, *Dickens the Dramatist*, 207.

10. Wilson, *The Wound and the Bow*, 53.

11. Davis notes that Dickens himself freely cut his story for his own public reading version, which first ran some three hours but was successively shortened to ninety minutes. See Davis, *The Lives and Times of Ebenezer Scrooge*, 56.

12. Wilson quoted in ibid., 53. Davis suggests (163) that Wilson is remembering this scene from the 1938 MGM version of the film, one of many in which it appears.

13. Ibid., 83, 85. The image is based on Dickens's description of Bob returning home from church on Christmas with "Tiny Tim upon his shoulder" (Dickens, *Christmas Books*, 44).

14. Guida, *"A Christmas Carol" and Its Adaptations*, 169.

15. Although all adaptations faithfully reproduce the snow outside Scrooge's old school, virtually none of them reproduces the fog outside his office. The two versions that most closely approach the weather Dickens describes are the 1984 version with George C. Scott and, surprisingly, *The Muppet Christmas Carol* (1993).

16. Even *An All Dogs Christmas Carol*, which begins with Charlie Barkin saying, "I can't promise you real snow," in San Francisco, features a dramatic climax in which the angel Annabelle buries Belladonna and her henchmen under a miraculous snowstorm with the words: "Nobody messes with heaven."

17. Examples of this pattern are legion, from the softening of the ending of *Suspicion* (1941) on behalf of audiences who might refuse to accept Cary Grant as a wife killer to the extensive rewriting of *Sister Act* (1992), after Whoopi Goldberg replaced Bette Midler as the heroine.

18. The apparent exception is the 1938 MGM adaptation, which features character actor Reginald Owen in the only starring role of his film career only because an injury prevented Lionel Barrymore, for whom the film had been planned, from playing Scrooge. See Guida, *"A Christmas Carol" and Its Adaptations*, 95–97.

19. See ibid., 74.

20. Davis, *The Lives and Times of Ebenezer Scrooge*, 62–63, 61. The quotation is from Whipple, *Charles Dickens*, 2:276–77.

21. In *Making "Christmas Carol: The Movie"* (2003), Kate Winslet—who voices Belle and sings "What If?"—comments laughingly on the recording of the song she released after producing the film: "This is not me trying to launch my pop career." Her self-deprecating promise comes midway through a producing-the-song segment with exactly the look and feel of a pop music video.

22. Guida, *"A Christmas Carol" and Its Adaptations*, 75.

23. Murray Baumgarten suggests that Bill Murray's depiction of his character's conversion to full humanity is more convincingly handled in *Groundhog Day* (1993), which, "less true to the original narrative, is perhaps truer to the central themes of Dickens's tale" (Baumgarten, "Bill Murray's Christmas Carols," 61).

24. Pointer, *Charles Dickens on the Screen,* 99.

25. A characteristically ironic example of one such analogue is in *The Smothers Brothers Comedy Hour*'s 1967 parody of *A Christmas Carol,* whose Bob Cratchit is played by Jack Benny, a legendary radio and television miser who at one point turns to address the audience: "I bet you thought I was gonna play Scrooge" (Guida, *"A Christmas Carol" and Its Adaptations,* 195).

26. Davis, *The Lives and Times of Ebenezer Scrooge,* 76.

27. Schickel, *The Disney Version,* 225.

28. In a later featurette, "Mickey's Cartoon Comeback" (2004), film critic Leonard Maltin introduces an interview with Mark Henn and Andreas Deja by a brief tour of the Walt Disney Feature Animation Library, where white-gloved technicians sort through files as reverently as the excavators of Tutankhamen's tomb.

29. Screenwriter Jerry Juhl and Brian Henson exclude from the cast Muppets like Ernie, Bert, Big Bird, Cookie Monster, and Oscar the Grouch, whose mode of existence on *Sesame Street* is considerably less subject to self-reflexive humor.

CHAPTER 5: Between Adaptation and Allusion

1. Wagner, *The Novel and the Cinema,* 222, 223, 227.

2. Andrew, *Concepts in Film Theory,* 98, 99, 101.

3. See Elliott, *Rethinking the Novel/Film Debate,* 133–83.

4. Genette, *Palimpsests,* 1–5.

5. Andrew, *Concepts in Film Theory,* 100.

6. Elliott, *Rethinking the Novel/Film Debate,* 135.

7. Ibid., 174.

8. Vincendeau, introduction to *Film/Literature/Heritage,* xviii.

9. Braudy, *The World in a Frame,* 185.

10. Griffin's footprints, in fact, involve a well-known continuity error. Although Griffin is invisible only when he is naked, the prints are clearly those of a man wearing shoes.

11. Elliott, *Rethinking the Novel/Film Debate,* 161.

12. Ibid., 150.

13. See Chatman, *Story and Discourse,* 19–20; and McFarlane, *Novel to Film,* 19–20.

14. See, e.g., McFarlane, *Novel to Film,* 109–10.

15. See Harrison, *Adaptations.* Mary Orr had dramatized her own short story "The Wisdom of Eve" into a stage play that served in turn as the basis for Joseph L. Mankiewicz's screenplay for *All about Eve.*

16. See Doran, introduction, 12–14.

17. Elliott, *Rethinking the Novel/Film Debate,* 157.

18. Pope, "An Essay on Criticism," 148.

19. For a contrary view of *Clueless* as a neoclassical imitation see Harris, "'Such a Transformation!'" 51–66.

20. A demonstration that the illumination can cut both ways is the breathless reaction a friend of my daughter's had to seeing Gwyneth Paltrow in *Emma:* "It's the same story as *Clueless!*"

21. Mosier, "Clues for the Clueless," 242.

22. Ibid., 243.

23. Mosier (ibid., 247) sees this deflation as a poke at "the Austen cognoscenti"; David Monaghan, in "*Emma* and the Art of Adaptation," sees it as directed at "an audience reared on Hollywood comedies" (219). For a more detailed look at the film's antecedents in Hollywood screwball comedy see Turim, "Popular Culture and the Comedy of Manners," 39–41.

24. Griffith, *Adaptations as Imitations,* 36, 39.

25. Compare the Toho monster franchise that began with *Gojira* (1954; recut and released in America as *Godzilla, King of the Monsters* [1956]), in which the monster, arriving from outside the community, is a sign of sociopolitical rather than psychological or spiritual problems.

26. Elliott, *Rethinking the Novel/Film Debate,* 138.

27. See Johnson, "*Mansfield Park.*"

28. Rozema, director's commentary track, *Mansfield Park.*

29. Internet Movie Database, www.imdb.com/title/tt0178737/ (accessed Sep. 8, 2006).

30. Mireia Aragay has perceptively noted that although many reviewers professed outrage at the liberties Rozema took with Austen, Emma Thompson's extensive revisions to *Sense and Sensibility* passed virtually without notice. See Aragay, "Possessing Jane Austen," 180.

31. In *Jane Austen on Film and Television* Sue Parrill notes (85) that scholars do not all agree in dating the events of *Mansfield Park.* Ellen Moody's timeline, which records many of these disagreements, is available online at www.jimandellen.org/austen/mp.calendar.html (accessed Sep. 8, 2006).

32. Quoted in Moussa, "*Mansfield Park* and Film," 256.

33. Coppola and Hart, "Bram Stoker's 'Dracula,'" 3.

34. Montalbano, "From Bram Stoker's *Dracula* to Bram Stoker's '*Dracula,*'" 386. The passage quoted is from Saberhagen and Hart, "Bram Stoker's 'Dracula,'" 1.

35. Elliott, *Rethinking the Novel/Film Debate,* 143, 144.

36. Thompson, *The "Sense and Sensibility" Screenplay and Diaries,* 220.

37. Stam, *Literature through Film,* 22. See also Alter, *Partial Magic,* xi.

38. Bevington, Welsh, and Greenwald, *Shakespeare,* 46.

39. The scenes focusing on Scott and Bob constitute less than a quarter of the film and correspond roughly to *1 Henry IV* 1.2, 2.2, 2.4, 3.2; *2 Henry IV* 5.5; and *Henry V* 2.3.

40. Davis, "*My Own Private Idaho* and Shakespeare in the Streets," 119.

41. Jameson, program notes to *My Own Private Idaho.*

42. The subject index of the Library of Congress lists 351 works on parody but none on pastiche. Harry Shaw, who does a perfectly serviceable job of defining parody as "any humorous, satirical, or burlesque imitation of a person, event, or serious work of literature" (*Concise Dictionary of Literary Terms,* 202), includes no entry on pastiche.

43. Jameson, "Postmodernism, or The Cultural Logic of Late Capitalism (1984)," 202.

44. It is hard to imagine the opening paragraph of Caroline Campbell's *Love Masque,* a typical Regency romance, without Austen's model, despite the post-Regency emphasis on work: "My dear, it is entirely out of the question." Austin Larch laid down his pen to stare reprovingly at his wife. "We can't possibly entertain another visitor just now, when I have so much work to do and I'm behindhand as it is. You ought to know that; I can't think how you can ask such a thing of me!" (3).

45. Bakhtin's major work on the topic is "Discourse in the Novel," in *The Dialogic Imagination* (259–422). See also Bakhtin, *Problems of Dostoevsky's Poetics*.

46. Griffith, *Adaptations as Imitations*, 72.

47. In an earlier ending, included on the DVD release of *Fatal Attraction* (Paramount, 2002), Alex stabs herself to death, though she attempts, unlike Cio-Cio-San, to fix the blame for her death on Dan Gallagher (Michael Douglas), the lover who abandoned her. According to Adrian Lyne's commentary, preview audiences rejected the ending because they felt it did not punish Alex harshly enough.

48. Davis, "*My Own Private Idaho* and Shakespeare in the Streets," 116.

49. See Gottlieb, "*Persuasion* and Cinematic Approaches to Jane Austen," 108–9.

50. Belton, "Reimagining Jane Austen," 175.

51. Carroll, "A Consideration of Times and Seasons," 171, 170.

CHAPTER 6: Exceptional Fidelity

1. This ability was confirmed in the publishing world in 1991, when Alexandra Ripley's *Scarlett*, a sequel to *Gone with the Wind* authorized by Margaret Mitchell's estate, sold five and a half million copies in two months, surpassing even the torrid pace of Mitchell's own sales.

2. Selznick, *Memo from David O. Selznick*, 149, 183.

3. Harmetz, *On the Road to Tara*, 62.

4. Mitchell, *Margaret Mitchell's "Gone with the Wind" Letters*, 72.

5. Duncan, "Ring Masters," 66.

6. "From Book to Script."

7. When Thomas Dixon, author of *The Clansman*, the novel on which *The Birth of a Nation* was based, wrote Mitchell to congratulate her on having written "the great American novel," she replied, "I was practically raised on your books and love them very much." See Wood, "From *The Clansman* and *Birth of a Nation* to *Gone with the Wind*," 123.

8. Selznick, *Memo from David O. Selznick*, 151.

9. Ibid., 143.

10. Ibid., 148–49.

11. In a 1955 letter to Houghton Mifflin, Tolkien emphasized that "the book is *not* of course a 'trilogy.' That and the title of the volumes was a fudge thought necessary for publication, owing to length and cost. There is no real division into 3, nor is any one part intelligible alone. The story was conceived and written as a whole" (Tolkien, *The Letters of J. R. R. Tolkien*, 221).

12. Harwell, introduction to *"Gone with the Wind" as Book and Film*, xv.

13. For a brief account of the myriad textual problems in *Lord of the Rings* see Anderson, "Note on the Text," xi–xiv.

14. For a detailed discussion of these revisions see Christensen, "Gollum's Character Transformation in *The Hobbit*."

15. See Porter, *Unsung Heroes of "The Lord of the Rings*," 135, 136–37.

16. "From Book to Script."

17. See Shippey, *J. R. R. Tolkien*.

18. Harwell, introduction to *GWTW: The Screenplay*, 33.

19. For a review of this misunderstanding see Vertrees, *Selznick's Vision*, 33–34.
20. Selznick, *Memo from David O. Selznick*, 148.
21. Ibid., 153.
22. Quoted in Harmetz, *On the Road to Tara*, 39.
23. Selznick, *Memo from David O. Selznick*, 155.
24. Harmetz, *On the Road to Tara*, 39.
25. Selznick, *Memo from David O. Selznick*, 169.
26. Berg, *Max Perkins*, 369.
27. Quoted in Harwell, introduction to *GWTW: The Screenplay*, 17.
28. Selznick, *Memo from David O. Selznick*, 191–92.
29. Fordham, "Q & A: Peter Jackson," 57.
30. "From Book to Script: Finding the Story."
31. In *GWTW: The Making of "Gone with the Wind"* Gavin Lambert notes that "because of the figure of Scarlett O'Hara, the overwhelming effect of *Gone with the Wind* in 1936 was on women" (26).
32. Shippey, "Another Road to Middle-earth," 245–48.
33. West, "The Interlace Structure of *The Lord of the Rings*," 76.
34. Shippey, "Another Road to Middle-earth," 253.
35. See TheOneRing.net.
36. "From Book to Script."
37. Porter, *Unsung Heroes of "The Lord of the Rings*," 21.
38. Shippey, "Another Road to Middle-earth," 236.
39. Chance, "Is There a Text in This Hobbit?" 84.
40. Harvey, *Romantic Comedy in Hollywood*, 282–83.
41. Harmetz, *On the Road to Tara*, 145.
42. Ibid., 147.
43. Moss, "An Open Letter to Mr. Selznick," 157.
44. Harmetz, *On the Road to Tara*, 62.
45. Myrick, *White Columns in Hollywood*, 166.
46. Fordham, "Journey's End," 71.
47. Lambert, *GWTW*, 35.
48. Rudy Behlmer speculates that once Selznick began a serious pursuit of the relatively unknown Leigh, his correspondence concerning her "was probably marked [as] the equivalent of 'highly confidential' for fear of a premature leak to the press and members of the industry" (Selznick, *Memo from David O. Selznick*, 186).
49. Ibid., 157.
50. Lambert, *GWTW*, 51.
51. Ibid., 84–85.
52. See Bridges, "*Frankly, My Dear . . . ,*" 181.
53. See ibid., plate VI.
54. Finkle, "Tara! Tara! Tara!"
55. Bridges, "*Frankly, My Dear . . . ,*" 133.
56. Porter, *Unsung Heroes of "The Lord of the Rings*," 176.
57. Slipcase for *Gone with the Wind*, four-disc collector's edition DVD (Warner Bros., 2004).

CHAPTER 7: Traditions of Quality

1. Truffaut, "A Certain Tendency of the French Cinema," 229, 234.
2. Ibid., 235.
3. Macdonald, "Masscult and Midcult," 37.
4. Selznick, *Memo from David O. Selznick*, 266–67.
5. Ibid., 86–87.
6. See Forster, *Aspects of the Novel*, 67.
7. Elliott, *Rethinking the Novel/Film Debate*, 89–90.
8. See Ross, *Picture*, 167, 172.
9. Brontë, *Jane Eyre*, 19.
10. Sconce, "Narrative Authority and Social Narrativity," 53.
11. Selznick, *Memo from David O. Selznick*, 488–89.
12. Truffaut, "A Certain Tendency of the French Cinema," 230.
13. Truffaut goes on to argue that Aurenche and Bost choose only "subjects that favor the misunderstandings on which the whole system rests" so that "under the guise of literature—and, of course, of quality—they give the public its habitual dose of smut, non-conformity and facile audacity" (ibid., 230). Surely no one would apply this latter claim to Merchant Ivory. Their fetish is thematic consistency, not smut, nonconformity, or facile audacity.
14. It is tempting to add that the ultimate Merchant Ivory film is *A Passage to India* (1983), even though it was written and directed by David Lean without the participation of Merchant, Ivory, or Jhabvala. Ivory gives several reasons why he and his collaborators avoided Forster's most ambitious novel: It was so well-known that it set an impossibly high standard, Forster had forbidden even Satyajit Ray from filming it during his lifetime, and when it became available on Forster's death and Ray withdrew his expressions of interest, Ivory felt too awkward to enter negotiations. See Long, *The Films of Merchant Ivory*, 139–41.
15. For a dissenting view that reads this climactic scene as "elegiac, perhaps even dismissive," and the film's sexual politics as "reactionary," see Person, "Still Me(n)," 121.
16. Long, *The Films of Merchant Ivory*, 117.
17. Macnab, *"The Remains of the Day,"* 160.
18. Ivory, foreword, 12.
19. Craig, "Rooms without a View," 4, 6.
20. Long, *The Films of Merchant Ivory*, 206.
21. Mitchell, "'Based on the Novel by Henry James,'" 288.
22. Vincendeau, introduction to *Film/Literature/Heritage*, xviii, xvii.
23. Jarvik, *"Masterpiece Theatre" and the Politics of Quality*, 41.
24. Truffaut, "A Certain Tendency of the French Cinema," 233.
25. The avoidance of cultural conflict that cannot be reduced to psychological conflict is one of the marks that distinguishes the 1995 *Pride and Prejudice*, for example, from Patricia Rozema's tendentious adaptation of *Mansfield Park* (1999), which insisted, as Sue Parrill observes, on "pointing out social and political realities which [Rozema claimed] would have been obvious to contemporary readers" in order to provide historical contexts for its characters' more decorous psychological conflicts. See Parrill, *Jane Austen on Film and Television*, 85.

26. See Cardwell, *Adaptation Revisited*, 133–35.

27. Sturridge, "The Making of *Brideshead*," 6.

28. Cooke, *Masterpieces*, 181.

29. Cardwell, *Adaptation Revisited*, 108, 109.

30. Ibid., 134. For a close study of the domesticating implications of these opening shots see Pucci, "The Return Home."

31. Ellington, "'A Correct Taste in Landscape,'" 91.

32. Birtwistle and Conklin, *The Making of Pride and Prejudice*, 37.

33. Austen, *The Novels of Jane Austen*, 2:3.

34. Cartmell, "Introduction," 24.

35. Birtwistle and Conklin, *The Making of Pride and Prejudice*, vi. As Sue Parrill points out, it was left to Patricia Rozema's *Mansfield Park* to leave "most Janeites . . . horrified at the very thought of this most moral of novels being made into a film which exhibited nudity" (Parrill, *Jane Austen on Film and Television*, 84).

36. Aragay and López, "Inf(l)ecting *Pride and Prejudice*," 211.

37. Austen, *The Novels of Jane Austen*, 2:94.

38. Ibid., 2:5, 70.

CHAPTER 8: Streaming Pictures

1. Bluestone, *Novels into Film*, 1.

2. Cohen, *Film and Fiction*, 4.

3. Andrew, *Concepts in Film Theory*, 103, 101.

4. Mitchell, *Picture Theory*, 5.

5. Elliott, *Rethinking the Novel/Film Debate*, 16–17.

6. McFarlane, *Novel to Film*, 29.

7. Kooistra, *The Artist as Critic*, 5.

8. Elliott, *Rethinking the Novel/Film Debate*, 42.

9. In addition to Kooistra see Miller, *Illustration;* and Curtis, *Visual Words*. For studies that range beyond the Victorian era see Katz, *A History of Book Illustration*.

10. Parenthetical references to Tenniel's illustrations are to Carroll, *The Complete Works of Lewis Carroll*. Parenthetical references to Carroll's illustrations are to Carroll, *Alice's Adventures Under Ground*.

11. The screen Alice who most closely resembles Tenniel's drawings is Kate Burton, outfitted with a blonde wig, in Kirk Browning's 1983 WNET television adaptation. The stars who least resemble Tenniel's Alice are Kate Beckinsale, in John Henderson's *Alice through the Looking Glass* (1998), and dark-haired, plump-faced Tina Majorino in Nick Willing's 1999 adaptation for NBC television.

12. Nodelman, *Words about Pictures*, 70.

13. See Elliott, *Rethinking the Novel/Film Debate*, 184–233.

14. The literature on Carroll's intricate web of cross-references and conundrums is vast. A good starting place is Carroll, *The Annotated Alice*, which includes an extensive bibliography as well as running commentary.

15. Elliott remarks that this parable of acculturation through performance is paralleled with surprising exactness in *Alice's Adventures in Wonderland: The World's Favorite Bedtime Story*, the 1976 adaptation Bud Townsend directed for Playboy Films, in which

"Wonderland [also] serves as a training ground in which Alice learns to perform in more socially acceptable ways" (Elliott, *Rethinking the Novel/Film Debate*, 194).

16. Thurber, "The Lady on the Bookcase," 660, 662–63.

17. Nodelman, *Words about Pictures*, 185–86.

18. The Jones film adds eight spoken couplets to Seuss's story but omits two of Seuss's original couplets:

> The Grinch had been caught by this tiny *Who* daughter
> Who'd got out of bed for a cup of cold water. (35)

and:

> He stared down at *Who*-ville! The Grinch popped his eyes!
> Then he shook! What she saw was a shocking surprise! (48)

The first couplet is omitted because Cindy Lou is awakened by a ball that rolls into her bedroom after falling from the Christmas tree that the Grinch is stealing, the second in order to proceed more quickly to the Whos' climactic song, which takes considerably more time in the film than in the book.

19. Seuss's biographer, Charles D. Cohen, notes that the author had originally regarded the Whos in his work-in-progress as "bugs" until his wife Helen disagreed: "They are not bugs. . . . Those Whos are just small people" (Cohen, *The Seuss, the Whole Seuss, and Nothing but the Seuss*, 329).

20. Ironically, Schulz had begun his *Peanuts* strip in 1950 with a far more simple and stylized use of outlines. By the time his work first came to be adapted for television in *A Charlie Brown Christmas* (1965), his trademark line had become more textured and less firm, and the adaptations took as their model this equally recognizable but more difficult line.

21. Beginning with *Happy Birthday to You!* (1959), Seuss used seven colors roughly corresponding to the colors Messecar's adaptation uses.

22. Seuss, *How the Grinch Stole Christmas!* not paginated [50–51].

23. Nodelman, *Words about Pictures*, 183.

24. McCloud, *Understanding Comics*, 7–8.

25. Baudry, "Ideological Effects of the Basic Cinematographic Apparatus," 536.

26. Metz, *The Imaginary Signifier*, 76.

27. McCloud, *Understanding Comics*, 69.

28. Iser, *The Act of Reading*, 169.

29. Ebert, review of *Batman*.

30. Brooker, "Batman," 191.

31. Ebert, review of *Dick Tracy*.

32. Duncan, "Cool Cars," 16–17.

33. Ibid., 17.

34. See Srebnick, "Working with Hitch," 25.

35. Duncan, "Cool Cars," 19.

36. Hall, review of *Girl with a Pearl Earring*. See also Mitchell, "Painting Interiors of the Heart"; Rea, "Tale of Painter Lacks Color"; Alexander, review of *Girl with a Pearl Earring*; Klass, review of *Girl with a Pearl Earring*; and Anon., review of *Girl with a Pearl Earring*.

37. Raymond Chandler, who cowrote the screenplay for *Double Indemnity* (1944), the most successful Cain adaptation, suggested that Cain's famously realistic dialogue was unfilmable for the paradoxical reason that it was too visual. "Nothing could be more natural and easy and to the point on paper, and yet it doesn't quite play," he wrote the novelist, adding, "The effect of your written dialogue is only partly sound and sense. The rest of the effect is the appearance on the page. These unevenly shaped hunks of quick-moving speech hit the eye with a sort of explosive effect. You read the stuff in batches, not in individual speech and counterspeech. On the screen this is all lost, and the essential mildness of the phrasing shows up as lacking in sharpness" (Chandler, *Later Novels and Other Writings*, 1071).

38. In addition to the painting for which she poses, Griet describes *Woman with a Pearl Necklace* (36), *The Milkmaid* (38), *Woman with a Water Jug* (90), *Lady Writing a Letter* (129), *The Guitar Player* (129), *The Music Lesson* (154), *The Concert* (163), *The Procuress*—the only painting Griet names (169, 182)—and *Head of a Girl* (224). Parenthetical page references are to Chevalier, *Girl with a Pearl Earring*.

39. Blankert, *Vermeer of Delft*, 46.

40. Antani, "Sizzling Girls & Middle-Age Maidens."

41. Christopher, review of *Girl with a Pearl Earring*.

42. Miller, *Illustration*, 150.

CHAPTER 9: The Hero with a Hundred Faces

1. To take the most obvious example of this disproportion: Basil Rathbone, one of the screen's most durable and well-regarded Holmeses, appeared in a mere fourteen feature films between 1939 and 1946. Over the same period he played Holmes in 219 radio episodes. See Haydock, *Deerstalker!* 122–24.

2. Bazin, "In Defense of Mixed Cinema," 53.

3. See Peake, "Presumption; or, The Fate of Frankenstein"; and Milner, "Frankenstein; or, The Man and the Monster."

4. Page references to Conan Doyle's four Holmes novels—*A Study in Scarlet* (1887), *The Sign of the Four* (1890), *The Hound of the Baskervilles* (1902), and *The Valley of Fear* (1915)—and fifty-six short stories are to Doyle, *The New Annotated Sherlock Holmes*.

5. See Kooistra, *The Artist as Critic*, 62–63. The quoted description of Holmes is from Doyle, *Memories and Adventures*, 101.

6. Quoted in Pohle and Hart, *Sherlock Holmes on the Screen*, 67. The line "Elementary, my dear Watson," though it never appears in Conan Doyle, becomes the single most durable identifier of Holmes throughout his film career.

7. Bunson, *Encyclopedia Sherlockiana*, 90.

8. In "Sherlock Modernized for Films" Frederick C. Othman complained while *Sherlock Holmes and the Secret Weapon* (1943) was still in production that updating Holmes's milieu left the hero "without his two-way cap, or his calabash pipe, or his magnifying glass. . . . He has a pipe, but it is a briar." See *Hollywood Citizen News*, May 20, 1942, quoted in Haydock, *Deerstalker!* 130. For Othman at least, Gillette's calabash has clearly replaced Doyle's briar as canonical.

9. Doyle mentions a pageboy in "A Case of Identity" (1891) and several other adventures that predate Gillette's play but does not name him as Billy until afterward. So Gillette's influence may extend only to the name, not the character.

10. See Williams, *Dr. Mortimer and the Barking Man Mystery;* and Williams, *Dr. Mortimer and the Aldgate Mystery.*

11. See Davies, *Mrs. Hudson and Spirits' Curse;* and Davies, *Mrs. Hudson and the Malabar Rose.*

12. Wiggins stars in Norman Schreiber's "Call Me Wiggins" and Billy in Gerard Dole's "The Witch of Greenwich." Both stories first appeared in Kurland, *My Sherlock Holmes,* which also includes stories featuring Chevalier Auguste Dupin, James Phillimore, Colonel Sebastian Moran, Reginald Musgrave, and both the first and second Mrs. Watson.

13. See Kaye, *The Resurrected Holmes.*

14. Holmz and Moratorium share the spotlight in Fred and Joe Evans's *A Study in Skarlit* (1915). See Haydock, *Deerstalker!* 36.

15. The complete text of Doyle's remarks in this film is transcribed in Nollen, *Sir Arthur Conan Doyle at the Cinema,* 96–99.

16. Klinger, preface, xii. Klinger's success at maintaining this pose without sounding delusional is impressive. See, for example, his introductory comment on *The Case-Book of Sherlock Holmes:* "Curiously, it contains a preface by Arthur Conan Doyle, and doubt has been raised as to whether Dr. Watson wrote all of the stories credited to him in the volume. There are suggestions that some of the stories may have been written by Watson's wife or cousin; some may even have been written by Sir Arthur Conan Doyle!" (2:1451). See also Baring-Gould, *Sherlock Holmes of Baker Street;* and Baring-Gould, *The Annotated Sherlock Holmes.*

17. In "The Five Orange Pips," set in 1887, Watson indicates that he is married ("my wife was on a visit to her mother's" [1:135]), but he is clearly single when he proposes the following year to Mary Morstan, who tells Holmes in *The Sign of the Four* that "my mother was dead" (1:230) by the time her father disappeared in 1878. Mary Watson evidently dies during the Great Hiatus, since Watson alludes in "The Adventure of the Empty House," set in 1894, to "my own sad bereavement" (2:794; see Klinger's note on 2:798–99). But Watson seems to have married at least once more, since Holmes himself notes in "The Adventure of the Blanched Soldier," set in 1903, that "the good Watson had at that time deserted me for a wife" (2:1487; see Klinger's note on 2:1488).

18. David Grann has noted an equally unusual instance of the reverse process demonstrating the porous boundaries between Sherlockian history and commentary in his article on the violent death of eminent Sherlockian Richard Lancelyn Green, who had edited *The Adventures of Sherlock Holmes* and *The Return of Sherlock Holmes* for *The Oxford Sherlock Holmes:* "Within hours of Green's death [on March 26, 2004], Sherlockians seized on the mystery, as if it were another case in the canon" (Grann, "Mysterious Circumstances," 61).

19. For a particularly good recent example of how closely these different kinds of writing blend into one another see Kaye, *The Game Is Afoot.*

20. Haydock, *Deerstalker!* 28. The precise terms of this contract are a subject of some debate. Nollen maintains that "for a yearly fee of $36,000, Universal purchased the rights to Conan Doyle's short stories, stipulating that the studio could film up to three adaptations plus one original screenplay annually. (None of the novels were included in the deal.)" (Nollen, *Sir Arthur Conan Doyle at the Cinema,* 135). Pohle and Hart contend that "Universal . . . bought the rights to use the stories and characters from the Doyle estate for 300,000 dollars" (Pohle and Hart, *Sherlock Holmes on the Screen,* 169–

70). All commentators agree with Nollen that "Conan Doyle's works have been adapted much more faithfully on both radio and television than on the cinema screen" (Nollen, *Sir Arthur Conan Doyle at the Cinema,* 224).

21. Although Moriarty has been a staple figure of Holmes adaptations ever since Gillette, Doyle introduces him in only one story, "The Final Problem," though he mentions him in "The Adventure of the Empty House" and indicates that he is working behind the scenes in *The Valley of Fear.*

22. Interestingly, *Murder at the Baskervilles,* retaining Wontner but replacing Hunter with Ian Fleming, shows Mrs. Hudson announcing Watson on his first entrance, broadly implying that he is no longer sharing rooms with Holmes.

23. Miller, "Zelig on Baker Street."

24. Robson, introduction to *The Hound of the Baskervilles,* xvi.

25. Like many another tale of Holmes, *The Hound* is impossible to date with consistency, although the most explicit evidence, Holmes's reference to Dr. Mortimer's departure "five years ago" (3:392) from Charing Cross Hospital in 1884 (3:387), seems unmistakably to indicate 1889. For a succinct summary of the textual problems see Robson, introduction, xix–xx; and Doyle, *The New Annotated Sherlock Homes,* 3:626–27.

26. Rosenberg, *Naked Is the Best Disguise,* 188.

27. Campbell, *The Hero with a Thousand Faces,* 391.

28. Rathbone describes his well-known frustration at his inability to separate either his screen career or his private life from the character of Holmes in his autobiography, *In and Out of Character,* 178. But the confusion between actor and character, echoing the earlier confusion the franchise had created between fiction and real life, was well-established as early as 1921, when, according to Pohle and Hart, "fans wrote Eille [Norwood] hundreds of letters, some of them asking him how to solve their problems; telling him how to outwit Moriarty; what disguises he should wear; and sometimes writing their letters in invisible ink" (Pohle and Hart, *Sherlock Holmes on the Screen,* 75).

29. Doyle, *Memories and Adventures,* 97.

30. Nollen, *Sir Arthur Conan Doyle at the Cinema,* 135.

31. Valley, program notes. Bill Treadway suggests a different explanation for the franchise's move from 20th Century–Fox to Universal: "Studio head Darryl Zanuck decided to drop the Holmes series" because of his "misguided belief that a Victorian-era mystery would have no box office potential while a world war was raging." See Treadway, "The Sherlock Holmes DVD Collection." However misguided this explanation may make Zanuck's judgment seem, it is supported by the studio's decision to discontinue two of its other B-movie franchises, those featuring the Japanese detective Mr. Moto and the teenage detective Nancy Drew, in 1939 as well.

32. Doyle, *The New Annotated Sherlock Holmes,* 2:1426n1.

33. Ibid., 3:34.

34. Starrett, *The Private Life of Sherlock Holmes,* 58.

35. Apart from Dennis Hoey, who played Lestrade, and Mary Gordon, who played Mrs. Hudson, a bevy of contract players returned to play multiple roles in the Universal Holmes films: Evelyn Ankers, Holmes Herbert, Hillary Brooke, Paul Cavanagh, Olaf Hytton, Gavin Muir, Frederic Worlock, Gerald Hamer, Ian Wolfe, Miles Mander, Vernon Downing, Arthur Hohl, and Billy Bevan. The Reynolds series, produced in France, recycled performers even more thriftily over a much shorter period, with Yves Brain-

ville, Margaret Russell, Eugene Decker, Colin Drake, Roland Bartrop, Alvys Mahen, Duncan Elliott, and Maurice Teynac all returning in different roles. Even Archie Duncan, the series' regular Lestrade, turned up to play Lestrade's Scottish cousin Inspector Macdougal in "The Case of the Jolly Hangman."

36. See Richard Valley's unpaged program notes to MPI's DVD release of the film in *The Sherlock Holmes Feature Collection* [5].

37. Basil Rathbone wears this signature outfit sparingly in *The Hound of the Baskervilles* and *The Adventures of Sherlock Holmes* and not at all in the modern-dress Universal films (though in the first of them, *Sherlock Holmes and the Voice of Terror,* he does begin to don the deerstalker on his way out the door when Watson entreats him, "Holmes, you promised," and he exchanges it for a more nondescript slouch hat). In the Sheldon Reynolds series, however, Ronald Howard wears the distinctive cap and cape nearly every time he goes outdoors. In *The Case of the Whitechapel Vampire* (2002), Matt Frewer wears it to Brother John's funeral. Generally speaking, the strongest performers who have assayed Holmes depend least on his iconic clothing.

38. For Klinger's discussion of possible candidates for the snake, none of which fills all the criteria Doyle's story lays down, see Klinger, "'It Is a Swamp Adder! . . . The Deadliest Snake in India.'"

39. Valley, program notes for *The Return of Sherlock Holmes,* not paginated [9].

40. For Mrs. Watson's much-noted error see Doyle, *The New Annotated Sherlock Homes,* 1:161; for a summary of Sherlockian commentary see Klinger, "'A Rose by Any Other Name . . .'"

41. See Doyle, *The New Annotated Sherlock Homes,* 2:860n18.

42. For the reasons why October 9 is impossible see ibid., 1:54n36.

43. See ibid., 1:541n30.

44. See ibid., 1:415; and Klinger, "'I Stand to Win a Little on This Next Race . . .'"

45. See Doyle, *The New Annotated Sherlock Homes,* 2:1318n25.

46. See www.imdb.com/title/tt0096454/ (accessed Oct. 22, 2004).

47. Elliott, *Rethinking the Novel/Film Debate,* 157.

48. Rathbone, *In and Out of Character,* 180. Disney did not accept the implied invitation until *The Great Mouse Detective* (1986), in which Basil of Baker Street takes on the evil Professor Ratigan.

CHAPTER 10: The Adapter as Auteur

1. A recent DVD collection of ten films, including two directed by Tourneur—*Cat People* (1942) and *I Walked with a Zombie* (1943)—was labeled "The Val Lewton Collection," suggesting that Tourneur's name is a less potent selling point than that of his RKO producer. Nor has there yet been a boxed set of films directed by Lewis, Ophüls, or Sirk.

2. Selznick, *Memo from David O. Selznick,* 266, 272, 266.

3. Truffaut, *Hitchcock,* 71.

4. As Charles Barr has noted, Hitchcock's commentators have picked up their cue from the director in largely ignoring the literary antecedents of his films. See Barr, *English Hitchcock,* 8–12.

5. LoBrutto, *Stanley Kubrick,* 178.

6. Ustinov, *Dear Me,* 296–97.

7. Douglas, *The Ragman's Son*, 323.

8. LoBrutto, *Stanley Kubrick*, 184, 193; Gelmis, *The Film Director as Superstar*, 294.

9. Kagan, *The Cinema of Stanley Kubrick*, 3rd ed., 104.

10. Douglas, *The Ragman's Son*, 275.

11. Sikov, *Mr. Strangelove*, 159.

12. Nabokov, *Lolita: A Screenplay*, 675, 676.

13. See ibid., 769–70.

14. Kubrick, "Words and Movies," 14.

15. Quoted in LoBrutto, *Stanley Kubrick*, 225.

16. Kubrick, "Words and Movies," 14.

17. Walker, *Stanley Kubrick, Director*, 114.

18. Gelmis, *The Film Director as Superstar*, 309.

19. Jenkins, *Stanley Kubrick and the Art of Adaptation*, 150, 160.

20. Kagan, *The Cinema of Stanley Kubrick*, xiii.

21. Sarris, *The American Cinema*, 196.

22. Sarris, *The Primal Screen*, 202.

23. Sarris, *Confessions of a Cultist*, 144.

24. Mosley, *The Real Walt Disney*, 93–94.

25. Quoted in Solomon, *The Disney That Never Was*, 126, 121.

26. See, e.g., Anon., "Adriana Caselotti"; Anon. "Adriana Caselotti"; and Michaels, "Adriana Caselotti."

27. For more information about the dramatic rise in Dr. Seuss's sales during 1957 and 1958 see Cohen, *The Seuss, the Whole Seuss, and Nothing but the Seuss*, 332–33.

28. Schickel, *The Disney Version*, 191.

29. Mosley, *The Real Walt Disney*, 191.

30. Thomas, *Walt Disney*, 164.

31. Ibid., 178.

32. At the same time, Theodor Seuss Geisel, shedding his alter ego Dr. Seuss, went to work directly for the War Department to develop a series of short animated films about Private Snafu, an example of what not to do in support of the war effort. See Cohen, *The Seuss, the Whole Seuss, and Nothing but the Seuss*, 247–60.

33. Schickel, *The Disney Version*, 313.

34. Maltin, introduction to "The Disneyland Story."

35. The premiere ends with a preview of the program's second episode: the television screening of Disney's 1951 *Alice in Wonderland*.

36. Quoted in Thomas, *Walt Disney*, 232.

37. See Schickel, *The Disney Version*, 314.

38. Quoted in ibid., 113.

CHAPTER 11: Postliterary Adaptation

1. In a typical summary in "Literary Hollywood"—see the *Hollywood Reporter*, May 10, 2004, 12, 14—novels account for six out of thirty-nine sales.

2. Kline, "Learners, Spectators, or Gamers?"

3. Dee, "Playing Mogul," 38.

4. Wilmington, "With a Wink, 'Pirates' Rides a Slick Wave."

5. Adaptation theorists regularly deplore the principle of using fidelity to a putative original as a measure of a given adaptation's success even as many of them do exactly that themselves. For a cogent recent summary of the limits of fidelity criticism see Cardwell, *Adaptation Revisited*, 20–25.

6. The film was marketed with the tagline, "It's not just a game anymore."

7. In choosing a 1950s American setting, the film passed over the original of the Parker Brothers game, the British game Cluedo, first marketed in 1948. But two British television series (1990, 1992) were subsequently produced under the title *Cluedo*.

8. As of this writing the Internet Movie Database lists 118 films based on video games, many of them released in Japan or made directly for American television.

9. Apparent exceptions to this pattern—the Mario Brothers and Jean-Claude Van Damme's Colonel Bison—are instructive. The physically unimposing Mario Brothers implicitly pose as both brothers and blustering father and naively romantic son, and the older Colonel Bison, a hero in the mold of GI Joe, is a projection of aggressive male fantasy into the more distant future defined by military discipline and access to military materiel.

10. This pattern is evidently continued by the two-disk special edition of *Pirates of the Caribbean: Dead Man's Chest*, scheduled as this volume was going to press to be released on the same date as the single-disk edition (December 6, 2006).

11. According to Jonathan Dee, "Enter the Matrix," the video-game version of *The Matrix* trilogy, released the same day as *The Matrix Reloaded*, was based on "a 244-page script written by [writer-directors Andy and Larry Wachowski] themselves, and included scenes shot on the movie's sets and with the movie's actors, but exclusive to the game" (Dee, "Playing Mogul," 39).

12. Taub, "For This Animated Movie."

CHAPTER 12: Based on a True Story

1. Coen and Coen, *Fargo*, 8.

2. An exception must be made for those few historical novels whose mode of presentation (e.g., the avoidance of sentences beginning "He thought" or "She thought," which would be improper to written history) mimics that of narrative history so closely that they could be mistaken for histories themselves.

3. Mack, *Stan Mack's Real Life Funnies*, not paginated [vi]. All four examples quoted below are reproduced on the volume's paperback cover.

4. Bakhtin, *The Dialogic Imagination*, 342.

5. Andrew, *Concepts in Film Theory*, 96.

6. Andrew, "Adapting Cinema to History," 191. For another provocative treatment of the relations between historical and fictional adaptations see Mazumdar, "Memory and History in the Politics of Adaptation."

7. Truffaut, *Hitchcock*, 238–39.

8. Nyce, *Scorsese Up Close*, 115.

9. Scorsese follows a similar strategy in his equally unsentimental look at the Las Vegas mob in *Casino* (1995), credited to Pileggi's *Casino: Love and Honor in Las Vegas* (1995) but, according to its opening titles, was "inspired by a true story."

10. Although the end credits prominently identify David Franzoni as the screen-

writer, it is not until much later that they identify a particular intertext, William A. Owens's 1953 *Black Mutiny: The Revolt on the Schooner "Amistad,"* as "a major source of reference material."

11. Although *Heaven & Earth* was marketed with the tagline "An amazing true story of survival," no such claim appears in the film's credits.

12. Stone, "On Seven Films," 219; Ciment, "Interview with Oliver Stone," 39, 40; Gary Crowdus, "Clarifying the Conspiracy," 104.

13. Crowdus, "Clarifying the Conspiracy," 98, 99.

14. Stone, "On *Nixon* and *JFK*," 259, 260. See Kurtz, "Oliver Stone, *JFK*, and History," 175–77.

15. Stone, "On *Nixon* and *JFK*," 291, 292.

16. Stone, "Stone on Stone's Image," 46, 47.

17. Schlesinger, "On *JFK* and *Nixon*," 212. Kurtz briefly summarizes such responses to *JFK* in "Oliver Stone, *JFK*, and History," 169–70. A more detailed comparison of books and movies as history can be found in Rosenstone, "*JFK:* Historical Fact/Historical Film"; Rosenstone, "Oliver Stone as Historian"; and Toplin's introduction to *Oliver Stone's USA.* The conflict between Stone and academic historians continues apace.

18. Stone, "Oliver Stone Talks Back," 68.

19. Cunningham, *Sidney Lumet,* 225.

20. See Pound, *ABC of Reading,* 15.

21. Dubner, "Steven the Good," 235.

22. Schiff, "Seriously Spielberg," 176.

23. Richardson, "Steven's Choice,"169.

24. See White, *Tropics of History;* and Schama, *Dead Certainties.*

# Bibliography

Abbott, Walter M., ed. *The Documents of Vatican II*. Translation ed. Joseph Gallagher. New York: Guild Press, 1966.

Alexander, Victoria. Review of *Girl with a Pearl Earring*. www.rottentomatoes.com/click/movie-1128236/reviews.php?critic=columns&sortby=default&page=1&rid=1246313 (accessed Sep. 13, 2006).

Alter, Robert. *Partial Magic: The Novel as a Self-Conscious Genre*. Berkeley: Univ. of California Press, 1975.

Anderegg, Michael A. "Conrad and Hitchcock: *The Secret Agent* Inspires *Sabotage*." *Literature/Film Quarterly* 3, no. 3 (1975): 215–25.

Anderson, Douglas A. "Note on the Text." In Tolkien, *The Lord of the Rings*, xi–xiv.

Andrew, Dudley. "Adapting Cinema to History: A Revolution in the Making." In Stam and Raengo, *Companion to Literature and Film*, 189–204.

———. *Concepts in Film Theory*. New York: Oxford Univ. Press, 1984.

Anon. "Adriana Caselotti." *Am I Annoying?* www.amiannoying.com/2002/view.aspx?ID=6331 (accessed Sep. 18, 2006).

———. "Adriana Caselotti." *Ladies First*. http://web.ukonline.co.uk/m.gratton/Ladies%201st%20-%20A.htm (accessed Oct. 17, 2006).

———. Review of *Girl with a Pearl Earring*. *E! Online*, Dec. 12, 2003. www.eonline.com/Reviews/Facts/Movies/Reviews/0,1052,88314,00.html (accessed Sep. 13, 2006).

Antani, Jay. "Sizzling Girls & Middle-Age Maidens." *LA Alternative Press*, Dec. 10–22, 2003. www.laalternativepress.com/v02n18/film/reviews.php (accessed Sep. 13, 2006).

Aragay, Mireia, ed. *Books in Motion: Adaptation, Intertextuality, Authorship*. Amsterdam: Rodopi, 2005.

———. "Introduction: Reflection to Refraction: Adaptation Studies Then and Now." In Aragay, *Books in Motion*, 11–34.

———. "Possessing Jane Austen: Fidelity, Authorship, and Patricia Rozema's *Mansfield Park*." *Literature/Film Quarterly* 31, no. 3 (2003): 177–85.

Aragay, Mireia, and Gemma López. "Inf(l)ecting *Pride and Prejudice*: Dialogism, Intertextuality, and Adaptation." In Aragay, *Books in Motion*, 201–19.

"Are You Game?" *Lara Croft: Tomb Raider*. Special Collector's Edition DVD. Hollywood: Paramount Home Video, 2001.

Arnold, Matthew. *The Works of Matthew Arnold*. 15 vols. London: Macmillan, 1903–4.

Auerbach, Erich. *Mimesis: The Representation of Reality in Western Literature*. Trans. Willard R. Trask. Princeton, NJ: Princeton Univ. Press, 1953.

Austen, Jane. *The Novels of Jane Austen*. Ed. R. W. Chapman. 3rd ed. 6 vols. Oxford: Oxford Univ. Press, 1966–69.

Bakhtin, M. M. *The Dialogic Imagination: Four Essays.* Trans. Caryl Emerson and Michael Holquist. Austin: Univ. of Texas Press, 1981.

———. *Problems of Dostoevsky's Poetics.* Ed. and trans. Caryl Emerson. Minneapolis: Univ. of Minnesota Press, 1984.

Baring-Gould, William S., ed. *The Annotated Sherlock Holmes.* 2 vols. New York: Clarkson N. Potter, 1967.

———. *Sherlock Holmes of Baker Street: A Life of the World's First Consulting Detective.* New York: Clarkson N. Potter, 1962.

Barr, Charles. *English Hitchcock.* Moffat: Cameron and Hollis, 1999.

Barthes, Roland. "From Work to Text." In *Image-Music-Text.* Trans. Stephen Heath, 155–64. New York: Hill and Wang, 1977.

———. "Introduction to the Structural Analysis of Narratives." In *Image-Music-Text.* Trans. Stephen Heath, 79–124. New York: Hill and Wang, 1977.

———. *S/Z.* Trans. Richard Miller. New York: Hill and Wang, 1974.

Barton, David. *Literacy: An Introduction to the Ecology of Written Language.* Oxford: Blackwell, 1994.

Baudry, Jean-Louis. "Ideological Effects of the Basic Cinematographic Apparatus." Trans. Alan Williams. In Nichols, *Movies and Methods,* 2:531–42.

Baumgarten, Murray. "Bill Murray's Christmas Carols." In *Dickens on Screen,* ed. John Glavin, 61–71. Cambridge, MA: Cambridge Univ. Press, 2003.

Bazin, André. "In Defense of Mixed Cinema." In Bazin, *What Is Cinema?* 1:53–75.

———. "The Ontology of the Photographic Image." In Bazin, *What Is Cinema?* 1:9–16.

———. *What Is Cinema?* Selected and trans. Hugh Gray. 2 vols. Berkeley: Univ. of California Press, 1967.

Belton, Ellen. "Reimagining Jane Austen: The 1940 and 1995 Film Versions of *Pride and Prejudice.*" In Macdonald and Macdonald, *Jane Austen on Screen,* 175–96.

Berg, A. Scott. *Max Perkins: Editor of Genius.* New York: Dutton, 1978.

Bevington, David, Anne Marie Welsh, and Michael L. Greenwald. *Shakespeare: Script, Stage, Screen.* New York: Pearson, 2005.

Birtwistle, Sue, and Susie Conklin. *The Making of "Pride and Prejudice."* London: Penguin/BBC, 1995.

Blankert, Albert. *Vermeer of Delft: Complete Edition of the Paintings.* Oxford: Phaidon, 1978.

Bluestone, George. *Novels into Film.* Baltimore: Johns Hopkins Press, 1957.

Bowser, Eileen. *History of the American Cinema.* Vol. 2, *The Transformation of Cinema, 1907–1915.* New York: Scribner, 1990.

Boyer, Peter J. "The Jesus War." *New Yorker,* Sep. 15, 2003, 58–71.

Boys, Mary C. "Seeing Different Movies, Talking Past Each Other." In *Perspectives on "The Passion of the Christ,"* 147–64.

Braudy, Leo. *The World in a Frame: What We See in Films.* Garden City, NY: Anchor/Doubleday, 1976.

Bridges, Herb. *"Frankly, My Dear . . .": "Gone with the Wind" Memorabilia.* 2nd ed. Macon, GA: Mercer Univ. Press, 1995.

Brontë, Charlotte. *Jane Eyre.* Ed. Beth Newman. Boston: Bedford/St. Martin's, 1996.

Brooker, Will. "Batman: One Life, Many Faces." In Cartmell and Whelehan, *Adaptations,* 185–98.

Buchanan, Judith. *Shakespeare on Film.* Harlow, UK: Longman, 2005.

Bunson, Matthew E. *Encyclopedia Sherlockiana: An A-to-Z Guide to the World of the Great Detective.* New York: Macmillan, 1994.

Burnham, Jonathan. Foreword to *Perspectives on "The Passion of the Christ,"* xi–xii.

Caldwell, Deborah. "Selling *Passion.*" In *Perspectives on "The Passion of the Christ,"* 211–24.

Campbell, Caroline. *Love Masque.* New York: Walker, 1982.

Campbell, Joseph. *The Hero with a Thousand Faces.* 2nd ed. Princeton, NJ: Princeton Univ. Press, 1968.

Cardwell, Sarah. *Adaptation Revisited: Television and the Classic Novel.* Manchester, UK: Manchester Univ. Press, 2002.

Carroll, Laura. "A Consideration of Times and Seasons: Two Jane Austen Adaptations." *Literature/Film Quarterly* 31, no. 3 (2003): 169–76.

Carroll, Lewis. *Alice's Adventures Under Ground: A Facsimile of the Original Lewis Carroll Manuscript.* Ann Arbor, MI: Univ. Microfilms, 1964.

———. *The Annotated Alice: The Definitive Edition: "Alice's Adventures in Wonderland" & "Through the Looking-Glass."* Ed. Martin Gardner. New York: Norton, 2000.

———. *The Complete Works of Lewis Carroll.* New York: Modern Library, n.d.

Cartmell, Deborah. "Introduction." In Cartmell and Whelehan, *Adaptations,* 23–28.

Cartmell, Deborah, and Imelda Whelehan, eds. *Adaptations: From Text to Screen, Screen to Text.* London: Routledge, 1999.

Chance, Jane. "Is There a Text in This Hobbit? Peter Jackson's *Fellowship of the Ring.*" *Literature/Film Quarterly* 30, no. 2 (2002): 79–85.

Chandler, Raymond. *Later Novels and Other Writings.* New York: Library of America, 1995.

Chatman, Seymour. *Story and Discourse: Narrative Structure in Fiction and Film.* Ithaca, NY: Cornell Univ. Press, 1978.

Chevalier, Tracy. *Girl with a Pearl Earring.* New York: Plume, 2001.

Christensen, Bonniejean. "Gollum's Character Transformation in *The Hobbit.*" In Lobdell, *A Tolkien Compass,* 7–26.

Christopher, James. Review of *Girl with a Pearl Earring. Times* (London), Jan. 15, 2004. www.timesonline.co.uk/article/0,,7943-963705,00.html (accessed Sep. 13, 2006).

Ciment, Michel. "Interview with Oliver Stone." In Silet, *Oliver Stone Interviews,* 39–49.

Coen, Ethan, and Joel Coen. *Fargo.* London: Faber and Faber, 1996.

Cohen, Charles D. *The Seuss, the Whole Seuss, and Nothing but the Seuss: A Visual Biography of Theodor Seuss Geisel.* New York: Random House, 2004.

Cohen, Keith. *Film and Fiction: The Dynamics of Exchange.* New Haven, CT: Yale Univ. Press, 1979.

*The Compact Edition of the Oxford English Dictionary.* 2 vols. New York: Oxford Univ. Press, 1971.

Cooke, Alistair. *Masterpieces: A Decade of "Masterpiece Theatre."* New York: VNU/Knopf, 1981.

Coppola, Francis, and James V. Hart. *"Bram Stoker's 'Dracula'": The Film and the Legend.* New York: New Market Press, 1992.

Craig, Cairns. "Rooms without a View." In Vincendeau, *Film/Literature/Heritage,* 3–6.

Crowdus, Gary. "Clarifying the Conspiracy: An Interview with Oliver Stone." In Silet, *Oliver Stone Interviews,* 96–104.

Cunningham, Frank R. *Sidney Lumet: Film and Literary Vision*. 2nd ed. Lexington: Univ. Press of Kentucky, 2001.

Cunningham, Philip. "Much Will Be Required of the Person Entrusted with Much: Assembling a Passion Drama from the Four Gospels." In *Perspectives on "The Passion of the Christ*," 49–64.

Curtis, Gerard. *Visual Words: Art and the Material Book in Victorian England*. Aldershot, UK: Ashgate, 2002.

Davies, Martin. *Mrs. Hudson and the Malabar Rose*. New York: Berkley, 2005.

———. *Mrs. Hudson and the Spirits' Curse*. New York: Berkley, 2004.

Davis, Hugh H. "*My Own Private Idaho* and Shakespeare in the Streets." *Literature/Film Quarterly* 29, no. 2 (2001): 116–21.

Davis, Paul. *The Lives and Times of Ebenezer Scrooge*. New Haven, CT: Yale Univ. Press, 1990.

DeBona, Guerric. "Dickens, the Depression, and MGM's *David Copperfield*." In Naremore, *Film Adaptation*, 106–28.

Dee, Jonathan. "Playing Mogul." *New York Times Magazine*, Dec. 21, 2003, 36–41, 52–53, 66–68.

DeMille, Cecil B. *The Autobiography of Cecil B. DeMille*. Ed. Donald Hayne. Englewood Cliffs, NJ: Prentice-Hall, 1959.

Dickens, Charles. *Christmas Books*. Oxford: Oxford Univ. Press, 1954.

"Digging into *Tomb Raider*." *Lara Croft: Tomb Raider*. Special Collector's Edition DVD. Hollywood: Paramount Home Video, 2001.

Dole, Gerard. "The Witch of Greenwich." In Kurland, *My Sherlock Holmes*, 133–59.

Doran, Lindsay. Introduction to Thompson, *The "Sense and Sensibility" Screenplay and Diaries*, 7–16.

Douglas, Carole Nelson. *Good Night, Mr. Holmes*. New York: Forge, 1990.

———. *Spider Dance*. New York: Forge, 2004.

Douglas, Kirk. *The Ragman's Son: An Autobiography*. New York: Simon and Schuster, 1988.

Dovey, Lindiwe. "Towards an Art of Adaptation: Film and the New Criticism-as-Creation." *Iowa Journal of Cultural Studies*, no. 2 (2002): 51–61. www.uiowa.edu/~ijcs/mediation/dovey.htm (accessed Sep. 18, 2006).

Doyle, Sir Arthur Conan. *Memories and Adventures*. Boston: Little, Brown, 1924.

———. *The New Annotated Sherlock Holmes*. Ed. Leslie S. Klinger. 3 vols. New York: Norton, 2004–5.

———. *The Oxford Sherlock Holmes*. General ed. Owen Dudley Edwards. Oxford: Oxford Univ. Press, 1993.

Dubin, Murray. "Passionate Controversy." *Philadelphia Inquirer*, Aug. 13, 2003.

Dubner, Stephen J. "Steven the Good." In Friedman and Notbohm, *Steven Spielberg Interviews*, 223–41.

Duncan, Jody. "Cool Cars, Hot Women and Hard Bastard Men." *Cinefex*, no. 102 (July 2005): 15–30.

———. "Ring Masters." *Cinefex*, no. 89 (April 2002): 64–131.

Ebert, Roger. Review of *Batman*. *Chicago Sun-Times*. June 23, 1989. http://rogerebert.suntimes.com/apps/pbcs.dll/article?AID=/19890623/REVIEWS/906230301/1023 (accessed Oct. 13, 2006).

———. Review of *Dick Tracy. Chicago Sun-Times.* June 15, 1990. http://rogerebert.
suntimes.com/apps/pbcs.dll/article?AID=/19900615/REVIEWS/6150301/1023 (accessed Oct. 13, 2006).

Eisenschitz, Bernard. *Nicholas Ray: An American Journey.* Trans. Tom Milne. London:
Faber and Faber, 1993.

Eisenstein, Sergei. "Dickens, Griffith, and the Film Today." In *Film Form: Essays on Film
Theory.* Trans. and ed. Jay Leyda, 195–255. New York: Harcourt, Brace, 1949.

Elbow, Peter. "The Cultures of Literature and Composition: What Could Each Learn
from the Other?" *College English* 64 (May 2002): 533–46.

———. "The War between Reading and Writing—And How to End It." *Rhetoric Review* 12 (fall 1993): 5–24.

Ellington, H. Elisabeth. "'A Correct Taste in Landscape': Pemberley as Fetish and Commodity." In *Jane Austen in Hollywood,* ed. Linda Troost and Sayre Greenfield, 90–110. Lexington: Univ. Press of Kentucky, 1998.

Elliott, Kamilla. *Rethinking the Novel/Film Debate.* Cambridge, UK: Cambridge Univ.
Press, 2003.

Fawcett, F. Dubrez. *Dickens the Dramatist: On Stage, Screen, and Radio.* London: W. H.
Allen, 1952.

Finkle, David. "Tara! Tara! Tara!" *New York Times Book Review,* Dec. 10, 1989.

Fordham, Joe. "Journey's End." *Cinefex,* no. 96 (January 2004): 66–142.

———. "Q & A: Peter Jackson." *Cinefex,* no. 96 (January 2004): 55–61.

Forry, Steven Earl. *Hideous Progenies: Dramatizations of "Frankenstein" from Mary Shelley to the Present.* Philadelphia: Univ. of Pennsylvania Press, 1990.

Forster, E. M. *Aspects of the Novel.* New York: Harcourt, 1927.

Fredriksen, Paula. "Gospel Truths: Hollywood, History, and Christianity." In *Perspectives on "The Passion of the Christ,"* 31–48.

Frei, Hans W. *The Eclipse of Biblical Narrative: A Study in Eighteenth and Nineteenth
Century Hermeneutics.* New Haven, CT: Yale Univ. Press, 1974.

Friedman, Lester D., and Brent Notbohm, eds. *Steven Spielberg Interviews.* Jackson:
Univ. Press of Mississippi, 2000.

Friend, Christie. "The Excluded Conflict: The Marginalization of Composition and
Rhetoric Studies in Graff's *Professing Literature.*" *College English* 54 (1992): 276–86.

Frizzell, Lawrence. "The Death of Jesus and the Death of the Temple." In *Perspectives on
"The Passion of the Christ,"* 65–80.

"From Book to Script." *The Fellowship of the Ring.* Extended DVD ed. *The Appendices,*
Part One. New Line Home Entertainment, 2002.

"From Book to Script: Finding the Story." *The Two Towers.* Extended DVD ed. *The Appendices,* Part Three. New Line Home Entertainment, 2003.

Gelmis, Joseph. *The Film Director as Superstar.* Garden City: Doubleday, 1970.

Genette, Gérard. *Palimpsests: Literature in the Second Degree.* Trans. Channa Newman
and Claude Doubinsky. Lincoln: Univ. of Nebraska Press, 1997.

Gold, Arthur, and Robert Fizdale. *The Divine Sarah: A Life of Sarah Bernhardt.* New
York: Knopf, 1991.

Gottlieb, Sidney. "*Persuasion* and Cinematic Approaches to Jane Austen." *Literature/
Film Quarterly* 30, no. 2 (2002): 104–10.

Grann, David. "Mysterious Circumstances." *New Yorker,* Dec. 13, 2004, 58–73.

Griffin, Susan, ed. *Henry James Goes to the Movies.* Lexington: Univ. Press of Kentucky, 2002.

Griffith, James. *Adaptations as Imitations: Films from Novels.* Newark: Univ. of Delaware Press, 1997.

Guida, Fred. *"A Christmas Carol" and Its Adaptations: A Critical Examination of Dickens's Story and Its Productions on Screen and Television.* Jefferson, NC: McFarland, 2000.

Gunning, Tom. "An Aesthetic of Astonishment: Early Film and the (In)Credulous Spectator." In *Film Theory and Criticism: Introductory Readings,* ed. Leo Braudy and Marshall Cohen, 862–76. 6th ed. New York: Oxford Univ. Press, 2004.

———. *D. W. Griffith and the Origins of American Narrative Film.* Urbana: Univ. of Illinois Press, 1991.

Hall, Phil. Review of *Girl with a Pearl Earring. Film Threat,* Dec. 12, 2003. www.filmthreat .com/index.php?section=reviews&Id=5243 (accessed Oct. 24, 2006).

Hansen, Miriam. *Babel and Babylon: Spectatorship in American Silent Film.* Cambridge, MA: Harvard Univ. Press, 1991.

Harmetz, Aljean. *On the Road to Tara: The Making of "Gone with the Wind."* New York: Abrams, 1996.

Harris, Jocelyn. "'Such a Transformation!': Translation, Imitation, and Intertextuality in Jane Austen on Screen." In Macdonald and Macdonald, *Jane Austen on Screen,* 44–68.

Harrison, Stephanie, ed. *Adaptations: From Short Story to Big Screen: 35 Great Stories That Have Inspired Great Films.* New York: Three Rivers, 2005.

Harvey, James. *Romantic Comedy in Hollywood, from Lubitsch to Sturges.* New York: Knopf, 1987.

Harwell, Richard, ed. *"Gone with the Wind" as Book and Film.* Columbia: Univ. of South Carolina Press, 1983.

———. Introduction to *"Gone with the Wind" as Book and Film.* Columbia: Univ. of South Carolina Press, 1983.

———. Introduction to *GWTW: The Screenplay,* by Sidney Howard, 7–44. New York: Macmillan, 1980.

Haydock, Ron. *Deerstalker! Holmes and Watson on Screen.* Metuchen, NJ: Scarecrow, 1978.

Hirsch, E. D., Jr. *Cultural Literacy: What Every American Needs to Know.* Boston: Houghton Mifflin, 1987.

———. *The Philosophy of Composition.* Univ. of Chicago Press, 1977.

———. *Validity in Interpretation.* New Haven, CT: Yale Univ. Press, 1967.

Hoder-Salmon, Marilyn. *Kate Chopin's "The Awakening": Screenplay as Interpretation.* Gainesville: Univ. Press of Florida, 1992.

Internet Movie Database. "*Mansfield Park.*" www.imdb.com/title/tt0178737 (accessed Oct. 13, 2006).

Iser, Wolfgang. *The Act of Reading: A Theory of Aesthetic Response.* Baltimore: Johns Hopkins Univ. Press, 1974.

Ivory, James. Foreword to *Merchant Ivory's English Landscape: Rooms, Views, and Anglo-Saxon Attitudes,* by John Pym, 9–12. New York: Abrams, 1995.

Jacobs, Lewis. *The Rise of the American Film: A Critical History.* New York: Harcourt Brace, 1939.

Jaffe, Audrey. "Spectacular Sympathy: Visuality and Ideology in Dickens's *A Christmas Carol*." *PMLA* 109 (March 1994): 254–65.

Jameson, Fredric. "Postmodernism, or The Cultural Logic of Late Capitalism" (1984). In *The Jameson Reader*, ed. Michael Hardt and Kathi Weeks, 188–232. Oxford: Blackwell, 2000.

Jameson, Richard. Program notes for *My Own Private Idaho*. Laser disc. Chatsworth, CA: Image Entertainment, 1993.

Jarvik, Laurence A. *"Masterpiece Theatre" and the Politics of Quality*. Lanham, MD: Scarecrow, 1999.

Jenkins, Greg. *Stanley Kubrick and the Art of Adaptation: Three Novels, Three Films*. Jefferson, NC: McFarland, 1997.

Jesionowski, Joyce E. *Thinking in Pictures: Dramatic Structure in D. W. Griffith's Biograph Films*. Berkeley: Univ. of California Press, 1987.

Johnson, Claudia L. "*Mansfield Park*." *Times Literary Supplement*, Dec. 31, 1999, 16.

Kagan, Norman. *The Cinema of Stanley Kubrick*. New York: Holt, Rinehart and Winston, 1972.

———. *The Cinema of Stanley Kubrick*. 3rd ed. New York: Continuum, 2000.

Katz, Bill, ed. *A History of Book Illustration: 29 Points of View*. Metuchen, NJ: Scarecrow, 1994.

Kaye, Marvin, ed. *The Game Is Afoot: Parodies, Pastiches, and Ponderings of Sherlock Holmes*. New York: St. Martin's, 1995.

———, ed. *The Resurrected Holmes: New Cases from the Notes of John H. Watson, M.D.* New York: St. Martin's, 1997.

Klass, Shirley. Review of *Girl with a Pearl Earring*. *Fantastica Daily*. www.fantasticadaily.com/movie_review.php?aID=891 (accessed Aug. 22, 2005).

Kline, Stephen. "Learners, Spectators, or Gamers? An Investigation of the Impact of Digital Media on the Media Saturated Household." www2.sfu.ca/media-lab/risk/docs/media-lab/Learnerfin11pt-2.doc (accessed Sep. 18, 2006).

Klinger, Leslie S. "'I Stand to Win a Little on This Next Race . . .'" In Doyle, *The New Annotated Sherlock Holmes*, 1:420–21.

———. "'It Is a Swamp Adder! . . . The Deadliest Snake in India.'" In Doyle, *The New Annotated Sherlock Holmes*, 1:259–61.

———. Preface to Doyle, *The New Annotated Sherlock Holmes*, 1:xi–xii.

———. "'A Rose by Any Other Name . . .'" In Doyle, *The New Annotated Sherlock Holmes*, 1:194–96.

Kooistra, Lorraine Janzen. *The Artist as Critic: Bitextuality in Fin-de-siècle Illustrated Books*. Aldershot, UK: Scolar, 1995.

Kubrick, Stanley. "Words and Movies." *Sight and Sound* 30, no. 1 (winter 1960–61): 14.

Kurland, Michael, ed. *My Sherlock Holmes: Untold Stories of the Great Detective*. New York: St. Martin's, 2003.

Kurtz, Michael L. "Oliver Stone, *JFK*, and History." In Toplin, *Oliver Stone's USA*, 166–77.

Lambert, Gavin. *GWTW: The Making of "Gone with the Wind."* Boston: Atlantic Monthly/Little, Brown, 1973.

Levine, Amy-Jill. "First Take the Log Out of Your Own Eye: Different Viewpoints, Different Movies." In *Perspectives on "The Passion of the Christ,"* 197–210.

Lobdell, Jared, ed. *A Tolkien Compass*. 2nd ed. Chicago: Open Court, 2003.

LoBrutto, Vincent. *Stanley Kubrick: A Biography.* New York: Donald I. Fine, 1997.

Long, Robert Emmet. *The Films of Merchant Ivory.* Newly updated ed. New York: Abrams, 1997.

Loughney, Patrick G. "In the Beginning Was the Word: Six Pre-Griffith Motion Picture Scenarios." In *Early Cinema: Space, Frame, Narrative,* ed. Thomas Elsaesser with Adam Barker, 211–19. London: British Film Institute, 1990.

Macdonald, Dwight. "Masscult and Midcult." In *Against the American Grain,* 3–75. New York: Vintage, 1962.

Macdonald, Gina, and Andrew F. Macdonald, eds. *Jane Austen on Screen.* Cambridge, UK: Cambridge Univ. Press, 2003.

Mack, Stan. *Stan Mack's Real Life Funnies.* New York: Putnam, 1979.

Macnab, Geoffrey. "*The Remains of the Day.*" In Vincendeau, *Film/Literature/Heritage,* 159–61.

*Making "Christmas Carol: The Movie."* DVD. MGM Home Entertainment, 2003.

"The Making of *Mickey's Christmas Carol.*" *Mickey Mouse in Living Color. Volume 2: 1939–Today.* Walt Disney Treasures DVD. Disk 2. Burbank, CA: Buena Vista Home Entertainment, 2004.

Maltin, Leonard. Introduction to "The Disneyland Story." *Walt Disney Treasures—Disneyland USA.* DVD. Disk 1. Burbank, CA: Walt Disney Studios, 2001.

Martin, James. "The Last Station: A Catholic Reflection on *The Passion.*" In *Perspectives on "The Passion of the Christ,"* 95–110.

Martin, Steve. "Studio Script Notes on 'The Passion.'" In *Perspectives on "The Passion of the Christ,"* 283–85.

Mazumdar, Ranjani. "Memory and History in the Politics of Adaptation: Revisiting the Partition of India in *Tamas.*" In Stam and Raengo, *Literature and Film,* 313–30.

McCloud, Scott. *Understanding Comics.* New York: HarperPerennial, 1994.

McCullough, Jack W. *Living Pictures on the New York Stage.* Ann Arbor, MI: UMI Research Press, 1983.

McFarlane, Brian. *Novel to Film: An Introduction to the Theory of Adaptation.* Oxford: Clarendon, 1996.

Meacham, Jon. "Who Really Killed Jesus?" In *Perspectives on "The Passion of the Christ,"* 1–15.

Metz, Christian. *The Imaginary Signifier: Psychoanalysis and the Cinema.* Trans. Celia Britton, Annwyl Williams, Ben Brewster, and Alfred Guzzetti. Bloomington: Indiana Univ. Press, 1982.

Michaels, Scott. "Adriana Caselotti." Findadeath.com. www.findadeath.com/Decesed/c/Adriana%20Caselotti/adriana_caselotti.htm (accessed Sep. 18, 2006).

"Mickey's Cartoon Comeback." *Mickey Mouse in Living Color. Volume 2: 1939–Today.* Walt Disney Treasures DVD. Disk 2. Burbank, CA: Buena Vista Home Entertainment, 2004.

Miller, J. Hillis. *Illustration.* Cambridge, MA: Harvard Univ. Press, 1992.

Miller, Laura. "Zelig on Baker Street." *New York Times Book Review,* Oct. 10, 2004.

Milner, Henry M. "Frankenstein; or, The Man and the Monster." 1826. Repr. in Forry, *Hideous Progenies,* 187–204.

Mitchell, Elvis. "Painting Interiors of the Heart, with Eros in Restrained Hues." *New York Times,* Dec. 12, 2003. http://query.nytimes.com/gst/fullpage.html?res=9B06E3D8173 CF931A25751C1A9659C8B63 (accessed Sep. 13, 2006).

Mitchell, Lee Clark. "'Based on the Novel by Henry James': *The Golden Bowl* 2000." In Griffin, *Henry James Goes to the Movies*, 281–304.

Mitchell, Margaret. *Gone with the Wind*. New York: Macmillan, 1936.

———. *Margaret Mitchell's "Gone with the Wind" Letters, 1936–1949*. Ed. Richard Harwell. New York: Macmillan, 1976.

Mitchell, W. J. T. *Picture Theory: Essays on Verbal and Visual Representation*. Chicago: Univ. of Chicago Press, 1994.

Monaghan, David. "*Emma* and the Art of Adaptation." In Macdonald and Macdonald, *Jane Austen on Screen*, 197–227.

Montalbano, Margaret. "From Bram Stoker's *Dracula* to Bram Stoker's '*Dracula*.'" Stam and Raengo, *A Companion to Literature and Film*, 385–98.

Moran, Charles. "Reading like a Writer." In *Vital Signs*, ed. James L. Collins, 60–71. Portsmouth, NH: Boynton/Cook, 1990.

Mosier, John. "Clues for the Clueless." In Macdonald and Macdonald, *Jane Austen on Screen*, 228–53.

Mosley, Leonard. *The Real Walt Disney: A Biography*. London: Grafton, 1985.

Moss, Carlton. "An Open Letter to Mr. Selznick." In Harwell, *"Gone with the Wind" as Book and Film*, 156–59.

Moussa, Hiba. "*Mansfield Park* and Film: An Interview with Patricia Rozema." *Literature/Film Quarterly* 32, no. 4 (2004): 255–60.

Musser, Charles. *Before the Nickelodeon: Edwin S. Porter and the Edison Manufacturing Company*. Berkeley: Univ. of California Press, 1991.

———. *History of the American Cinema*. Vol. 1, *The Emergence of Cinema: The American Screen to 1907*. New York: Scribner, 1990.

———. "Passions and the Passion Play." In *Movie Censorship and American Culture*, ed. Francis G. Couvares, 43–72. Washington: Smithsonian Institution Press, 1996.

Musser, Charles, and Carol Nelson. *High-Class Moving Pictures: Lyman H. Howe and the Forgotten Era of Traveling Exhibition*. Princeton, NJ: Princeton Univ. Press, 1990.

Myrick, Susan. *White Columns in Hollywood*. Ed. Richard Harwell. Macon, GA: Mercer Univ. Press, 1982.

Nabokov, Vladimir. *Lolita: A Screenplay*. In *Nabokov: Novels 1955–1962*. New York: Library of America, 1996.

Naremore, James, ed. *Film Adaptation*. New Brunswick, NJ: Rutgers Univ. Press, 2000.

———. "Introduction: Film and the Reign of Adaptation." In Naremore, *Film Adaptation*, 1–16.

Nichols, Bill, ed. *Movies and Methods*. 2 vols. Berkeley: Univ. of California Press, 1976–85.

Nodelman, Perry. *Words about Pictures: The Narrative Art of Children's Picture Books*. Athens: Univ. of Georgia Press, 1988.

Noerdlinger, Henry S. *Moses and Egypt: The Documentation to the Motion Picture "The Ten Commandments."* Los Angeles: Univ. of Southern California Press, 1956.

Nollen, Scott Allen. *Sir Arthur Conan Doyle at the Cinema*. Jefferson, NC: McFarland, 1996.

Norris, Frank. *Novels and Essays*. New York: Library of America, 1986.

Nyce, Ben. *Scorsese Up Close: A Study of the Films*. Lanham, MD: Scarecrow, 2004.

Parrill, Sue. *Jane Austen on Film and Television: A Critical Study of the Adaptations*. Jefferson, NC: McFarland, 2002.

Peake, Richard Brinsley. "Presumption; or, The Fate of Frankenstein." 1823. Repr. in Forry, *Hideous Progenies*, 135–60.

Pearson, Roberta E. *Eloquent Gestures: The Transformation of Performance Style in the Griffith Biograph Films*. Berkeley: Univ. of California Press, 1992.

Person, Leland S. "Still Me(n): Superman Meets *The Bostonians*." In Griffin, *Henry James Goes to the Movies*, 99–124.

*Perspectives on "The Passion of the Christ": Religious Thinkers and Writers Explore the Issues Raised by the Controversial Movie*. New York: Miramax/Hyperion, 2004.

Pohle, Robert W., Jr., and Douglas C. Hart. *Sherlock Holmes on the Screen: The Motion Picture Adventures of the World's Most Popular Detective*. South Brunswick, NJ: Barnes, 1977.

Pointer, Michael. *Charles Dickens on the Screen: The Film, Television, and Video Adaptations*. Lanham, MD: Scarecrow, 1996.

Pope, Alexander. "An Essay on Criticism." In *The Poems of Alexander Pope*. Ed. John Butt, 143–68. New Haven, CT: Yale Univ. Press, 1963.

Porter, Lynette R. *Unsung Heroes of "The Lord of the Rings": From the Page to the Screen*. Westport, CT: Praeger, 2005.

Pound, Ezra. *ABC of Reading*. New Haven, CT: Yale Univ. Press, 1934.

Pratt, George C. *Spellbound in Darkness: A History of the Silent Film*. Rev. ed. Greenwich, CT: New York Graphic Society, 1973.

Prothero, Stephen. "Jesus Nation, Catholic Christ." In *Perspectives on "The Passion of the Christ,"* 267–82.

Pucci, Suzanne R. "The Return Home." In Pucci and Thompson, *Jane Austen and Co.*, 133–56.

Pucci, Suzanne R., and James Thompson, eds. *Jane Austen and Co.: Remaking the Past in Contemporary Culture*. Albany: SUNY Press, 2003.

Rathbone, Basil. *In and Out of Character*. 1962. Repr. New York: Limelight, 1997.

Rea, Steven. "Tale of Painter Lacks Color." *Philadelphia Inquirer*, Jan. 23, 2004. http://ae.philly.com/entertainment/ui/philly/movie.html?id=118531 (accessed Sep. 13, 2006).

Reinhartz, Adele. "Jesus of Hollywood." In *Perspectives on "The Passion of the Christ,"* 165–80.

"Report of the Ad Hoc Scholars Group: Reviewing the Script of *The Passion*." In *Perspectives on "The Passion of the Christ,"* 225–54.

Richardson, John H. "Steven's Choice." In Friedman and Notbohm, *Steven Spielberg Interviews*, 157–69.

Robinson, David. *From Peep Show to Palace: The Birth of American Film*. New York: Columbia Univ. Press, 1996.

Robson, W. W. Introduction to *The Hound of the Baskervilles: Another Adventure of Sherlock Holmes*, xi–xxix. The Oxford Sherlock Holmes. Oxford: Oxford Univ. Press, 1993.

Rosenberg, Samuel. *Naked Is the Best Disguise: The Death and Resurrection of Sherlock Holmes*. Indianapolis: Bobbs-Merrill, 1974.

Rosenstone, Robert A. "*JFK*: Historical Fact/Historical Film." *American Historical Review* 97 (1992): 496–511.

———. "Oliver Stone as Historian." In Toplin, *Oliver Stone's USA*, 26–39.

Ross, Harris. *Film as Literature, Literature as Film: An Introduction to and Bibliography of Film's Relation to Literature.* New York: Greenwood, 1987.

Ross, Lillian. *Picture.* 1952. Repr. New York: Garland, 1985.

Rozema, Patricia. Commentary track on *Mansfield Park.* DVD. Miramax, 2000.

Saberhagen, Fred, and James V. Hart. *"Bram Stoker's 'Dracula'": A Francis Ford Coppola Film.* New York: Signet, 1992.

Sarris, Andrew. *The American Cinema: Directors and Directions, 1929–1968.* New York: Dutton, 1978.

———. *Confessions of a Cultist: On the Cinema, 1955–1969.* New York: Simon and Schuster, 1970.

———. *The Primal Screen: Essays on Film and Related Subjects.* New York: Simon and Schuster, 1973.

Sawyer, Diane. "Transcript: The Passion." *60 Minutes.* Feb. 22, 2004. http://sixtyminutes .ninemsn.com.au/sixtyminutes/stories/2004_02_22/story_1034.asp (accessed Sep. 18, 2006).

Schama, Simon. *Dead Certainties: Unwarranted Speculations.* New York: Knopf, 1991.

Schickel, Richard. *D. W. Griffith: An American Life.* New York: Simon and Schuster, 1984.

———. *The Disney Version: The Life, Times, Art, and Commerce of Walt Disney.* 3rd ed. Chicago: Ivan R. Dee, 1997.

Schiff, Stephen. "Seriously Spielberg." In Friedman and Notbohm, *Steven Spielberg Interviews,* 170–92.

Schlesinger, Arthur, Jr., "On *JFK* and *Nixon.*" In Toplin, *Oliver Stone's USA,* 212–16.

Scholes, Robert. *The Rise and Fall of English: Reconstructing English as a Discipline.* New Haven, CT: Yale Univ. Press, 1998.

Schreiber, Norman. "Call Me Wiggins." In Kurland, *My Sherlock Holmes,* 67–99.

Schreiner, Olive. *The Story of an African Farm.* Middlesex: Penguin, 1939.

Sconce, Jeffrey. "Narrative Authority and Social Narrativity: The Cinematic Reconstitution of Brontë's *Jane Eyre.*" *Wide Angle* 10, no. 1 (1988): 46–61.

Seitz, James E. *Motives for Metaphor: Literacy, Curriculum Reform, and the Teaching of English.* Pittsburgh: Univ. of Pittsburgh Press, 1999.

Selznick, David O. *Memo from David O. Selznick.* Ed. Rudy Behlmer. New York: Viking, 1972.

Seuss, Dr. *How the Grinch Stole Christmas!* New York: Random House, 1957.

Shaw, Harry. *Concise Dictionary of Literary Terms.* New York: McGraw-Hill, 1972.

Shippey, Tom. "Another Road to Middle-earth: Jackson's Movie Trilogy." In *Understanding "The Lord of the Rings": The Best of Tolkien Criticism,* ed. Rose A. Zimbardo and Neil D. Isaacs, 233–56. Boston: Houghton Mifflin, 2004.

———. *J. R. R. Tolkien: Author of the Century.* Boston: Houghton Mifflin, 2000.

Shohat, Ella. "Sacred Word, Profane Image: Theologies of Adaptation." In Stam and Raengo, *A Companion to Literature and Film,* 23–45.

Sikov, Ed. *Mr. Strangelove: A Biography of Peter Sellers.* New York: Hyperion, 2002.

Silet, Charles L. P., ed. *Oliver Stone Interviews.* Jackson: Univ. Press of Mississippi, 2001.

Simmon, Scott. Program notes to *More Treasures from American Film Archives, 1894–1931.* DVD. San Francisco: National Film Preservation Foundation, 2004.

Sklar, Robert. *Movie-Made America: A Cultural History of American Movies.* Revised and updated. New York: Vintage, 1994.

Solomon, Charles. *The Disney That Never Was: The Stories and Art from Five Decades of Unproduced Animation.* New York: Hyperion, 1995.

Spleen. Comment at "IMDb User Comments for *Without a Clue* (1988)." Internet Movie Database. www.imdb.com/title/tt0096454/usercomments (accessed Oct. 13, 2006).

Srebnick, Walter, ed. "Working with Hitch: A Screenwriter's Forum with Evan Hunter, Arthur Laurents, and Joseph Stefano." *Hitchcock Annual* 10 (2001–2): 1–37.

Stam, Robert. *Literature through Film: Realism, Magic, and the Art of Adaptation.* London: Blackwell, 2005.

Stam, Robert, and Alessandra Raengo, eds. *A Companion to Literature and Film.* London: Blackwell, 2004.

———, eds. *Literature and Film: A Guide to the Theory and Practice of Film Adaptation.* London: Blackwell, 2005.

Starrett, Vincent. *The Private Life of Sherlock Holmes.* Rev. ed. New York: Pinnacle, 1975.

Stone, Oliver. "Oliver Stone Talks Back." *Premiere* 5, no. 5 (Jan. 1992): 66–72.

———. "On *Nixon* and *JFK.*" In Toplin, *Oliver Stone's USA,* 249–98.

———. "On Seven Films." In Toplin, *Oliver Stone's USA,* 219–48.

———. "Stone on Stone's Image (As Presented by Some Historians)." In Toplin, *Oliver Stone's USA,* 40–65.

Sturridge, Charles. "The Making of *Brideshead.*" Companion guide to *Brideshead Revisited,* 4–9. DVD. Silver Spring, MD: Acorn Media, 2002.

Swartz, Mark Evan. *Oz before the Rainbow: L. Frank Baum's "The Wonderful Wizard of Oz" on Stage and Screen to 1939.* Baltimore: Johns Hopkins Univ. Press, 2000.

Taub, Eric A. "For This Animated Movie, a Cast of Household Names." *New York Times,* May 17, 2004.

TheOneRing.net. www.theonering.net/movie/rotkreviews/review.php?id=2201 (accessed Oct. 13, 2006).

Thistlethwaite, Susan. "Mel Makes a War Movie." In *Perspectives on "The Passion of the Christ,"* 127–46.

Thomas, Bob. *Walt Disney: An American Original.* 2nd ed. New York: Hyperion, 1994.

Thompson, Emma. *The "Sense and Sensibility" Screenplay and Diaries: Bringing Jane Austen's Novel to Film.* New York: Newmarket, 1995.

Thurber, James. "The Lady on the Bookcase." 1948. Repr. in *Writings and Drawings.* New York: Library of America, 1996.

Tibbetts, John C. *The American Theatrical Film: Stages in Development.* Bowling Green, OH: Bowling Green State Univ. Popular Press, 1985.

Tolkien, J. R. R. *The Letters of J. R. R. Tolkien.* Selected and ed. Humphrey Carpenter, with the assistance of Christopher Tolkien. Boston: Houghton Mifflin, 1981.

———. *The Lord of the Rings.* Boston: Houghton Mifflin, 1994.

Tolson, Jay, and Linda Kulman. "The Other Jesus: How a Jewish Reformer Lost His Jewish Identity." In *Perspectives on "The Passion of the Christ,"* 17–30.

Toplin, Robert Brent. Introduction to Toplin, *Oliver Stone's USA,* 3–25.

———, ed. *Oliver Stone's USA: Film, History, and Controversy.* Lawrence: Univ. Press of Kansas, 2000.

Treadway, Bill. "The Sherlock Holmes DVD Collection, Volume 1." *DVD Verdict.* March 19, 2004. www.dvdverdict.com/reviews/holmescoll1 (accessed Sep. 14, 2006).

Truffaut, François. "A Certain Tendency of the French Cinema." In Nichols, *Movies and Methods,* 1:224–37.

————. *Hitchcock*. Rev. ed. New York: Simon and Schuster, 1983.

Turim, Maureen. "Popular Culture and the Comedy of Manners: *Clueless* and Fashion Clues." In Pucci and Thompson, *Jane Austen and Co.*, 33–52.

Ustinov, Peter. *Dear Me*. 1977. Repr. London: Mandarin, 1992.

Valley, Richard. Program notes for *The Return of Sherlock Holmes*. DVD. Orland Park, IL: MPI, 2003.

————. Program notes for *The Sherlock Holmes Feature Collection*. DVD. Orland Park, IL: MPI, 2003.

Vertrees, Alan David. *Selznick's Vision: "Gone with the Wind" and Hollywood Filmmaking*. Austin: Univ. of Texas Press, 1997.

VICTORIA listserv. https://listserv.indiana.edu/cgi-bin/wa-iub.exe?A1=ind0409b&L=victoria&D=0&H=0&I=-3&O=T&T=1#56 (accessed Oct. 24, 2006).

Vincendeau, Ginette, ed. *Film/Literature/Heritage: A Sight and Sound Reader*. London: British Film Institute, 2001.

————. Introduction to Vincendeau, *Film/Literature/Heritage*, xi–xxv.

Wagner, Geoffrey. *The Novel and the Cinema*. Rutherford, NJ: Fairleigh Dickinson Univ. Press, 1975.

Waldman, Steven. "Passion Misplay." Sep. 17, 2003. http://slate.msn.com/id/2088417 (accessed Sep. 18, 2006).

Walker, Alexander, with Sybil Taylor and Ulrich Ruchti. *Stanley Kubrick, Director: A Visual Analysis*. New York: Norton, 1999.

Wallis, Jim. "*The Passion* and the Message." In *Perspectives on "The Passion of the Christ*," 111–26.

West, Richard C. "The Interlace Structure of *The Lord of the Rings*." In Lobdell, *A Tolkien Compass*, 75–92.

Whipple, Edwin. *Charles Dickens: The Man and His Work*. 2 vols. Boston: Houghton Mifflin, 1912.

White, Hayden. *Tropics of History: Essays in Cultural Criticism*. Baltimore: Johns Hopkins Univ. Press, 1978.

Wieseltier, Leon. "The Worship of Blood." In *Perspectives on "The Passion of the Christ*," 255–66.

Williams, Gerard. *Dr. Mortimer and the Aldgate Mystery*. New York: St. Martin's, 2001.

————. *Dr. Mortimer and the Barking Man Mystery*. New York: St. Martin's, 2001.

Wilmington, Michael. "For Mira Nair, 'Vanity Fair' Was a World of Its Own." *Chicago Tribune*, Sep. 10, 2004, Tempo section.

————. "With a Wink, 'Pirates' Rides a Slick Wave." *Chicago Tribune*, July 9, 2003, Tempo sec.

Wilson, Edmund. *The Wound and the Bow: Seven Studies in Literature*. 1941. Repr. New York: Farrar Straus Giroux, 1978.

Witherington, Ben, III. "Numb Struck: An Evangelical Reflects on Mel Gibson's *Passion*." In *Perspectives on "The Passion of the Christ*," 81–94.

Wood, Gerald. "From *The Clansman* and *Birth of a Nation* to *Gone with the Wind:* The Loss of American Innocence." *Recasting: "Gone with the Wind" in American Culture*, ed. Darden Asbury Pyron, 123–36. Miami: Florida International Univ./Univ. Presses of Florida, 1983.

Wright, Melanie J. *Moses in America: The Cultural Uses of Biblical Narrative.* Oxford: AAR/Oxford Univ. Press, 2003.

Zeffirelli, Franco. *Zeffirelli: The Autobiography of Franco Zeffirelli.* London: Weidenfeld & Nicolson, 1986.

Zingrone, Frank. *The Media Symplex: At the Edge of Meaning in the Age of Chaos.* Toronto: Stoddart, 2001.

# Index

Books, plays, stories, essays, and poems are indexed under their authors' names. Radio and television programs and films are indexed under their titles, with the production company or station (for radio and television programs or series) or the director (for films) and year within parentheses. When different film adaptations share the same title, they are listed chronologically, not alphabetically.

*Jefferson in Paris* (Ivory, 1995), 170

Jenkins, Greg, 244, 305n1

Jesionowski, Joyce E., 307n34

Jesus, 47–66, 105, 122, 124; as intertext, 66; as problem text, 58–59

*Jesus Christ Superstar* (Jewison, 1973), 49, 51, 53, 58

*Jesus of Nazareth* (Zeffirelli, 1977), 49, 53, 57

*Jetsons Christmas Carol* (Hanna-Barbera, 1985), 76

*JFK* (Stone, 1991), 292, 293, 294

Jhabvala, Ruth Prawer, 163–67, 170–71, 315n14

Johnson, Claudia L., 107

Jones, Chuck, 69, 191–92, 193

Joyce, James: *Ulysses*, 17, 132

Kagan, Norman, 241, 244

Kasanoff, Larry, 279

Kaufman, Charlie, 112

Kaye, Marvin, 319n13, 319n19

Keller, Lillian, 146–47

Keneally, Thomas: *Schindler's List*, 282, 300, 302

*Kentucky Feud* (Mutoscope, 1905), 31

*Killers* (Siodmak, 1946), 99

*King John* (Dando and Dickson, 1899), 26, 260

*King Lear* (Kozintsev, 1969), 110

*King of Kings* (DeMille, 1927), 49, 54–56, 58

*King of Kings* (Ray, 1961), 49, 50, 51, 57

King, Stephen, 61, 98

Kline, Stephen, 258

Klinger, Leslie S., 212, 319n17, 321n38, 321n40, 321n44

Kooistra, Lorraine Janzen, 180, 318n5

Koszarski, Richard, 35

Kubrick, Stanley, 237, 240–45, 247, 256, 291, 299

*Kundun* (Scorsese, 1996), 280, 297, 298

Kurtz, Michael L., 292, 324n14, 324n17

Kurtz, Wilbur, 142, 143

Lambert, Gavin, 314n31, 314n47, 314n50–51

*Land beyond the Sunset* (1912), 35

Langton, Jane, 181

lantern slides, 24, 50

Lapotaire, Jane, 170

*Lara Croft: Tomb Raider* (West, 2001), 265–73 passim

*Last Action Hero* (McTiernan, 1993), 117

*Last Temptation of Christ* (Scorsese, 1988), 48, 49–50, 58, 297

*Last Vampyre* (Granada, 1992), 226, 228

*Law & Order* (NBC, 1990-), 287

*Le Divorce* (Ivory, 2003), 164, 165, 170

Lee, Ang, 109

Leech, John, 78–79, 181–82

Lessing, Gotthold Ephraim, 5

*Letter* (Wyler, 1940), 155, 161

Levine, Amy-Jill, 308n22, 309n36

liberation, 98

*Life of an American Fireman* (Porter, 1903), 27

*Limejuice Mystery* (Harrison, 1930), 213

Lindsay, Cynthia, 255

*Lines of White on a Sullen Sea* (Griffith, 1909), 308n39

Lipscomb, W. P., 156

literacy, 10–12, 18–20, 303; genre, 272–73; vs. counterliteracy, 15–16. vs. illiteracy, 7; vs. preliteracy, 16

literalization, 98

literary cachet, 32, 46, 158, 239, 242, 246, 258

literary classics, 69, 72, 82, 84, 108–9, 169, 172; vs. cartoon classics, 89; vs. film classics, 106

literary studies, 19

literature vs. literacy, 12–20

LoBrutto, Vincent, 321n5, 322n8

*Lolita* (Kubrick, 1962), 240–42

*Lonely Villa* (Griffith, 1909), 36, 40

*Lonesome Ghosts* (Gillett, 1937), 253

Long, Robert Emmet, 167, 315n14

*Long Day's Journey into Night* (Lumet, 1962), 295

*Looking for Richard* (Pacino, 1996), 111

López, Gemma, 316n36

*Lord of the Rings* (Bakshi, 1978), 130

*Lord of the Rings* (Jackson, 2001–3), 20, 23, 127–50 passim, 151, 285

*Lorna Doone* (BBC, 2000), 177

*Lost in La Mancha* (Fulton and Pepe, 2002), 111

Loughney, Patrick G., 27–28

*Love* (Goulding, 1927), 100

*Love Potion No. 9* (Launer, 1992), 99

Lucas, George, 130, 148–49

Lumet, Sidney, 294–96, 298, 300

Lyons, Alexander, 55, 64

Printed in the United States
150670LV00001B/204/P

9 780801 892714